*To our parents Amata, Jack, Connie, George,
and our children Jeremiah, Hannah, and Zachariah,*

for your faith, hope, and unending love.

works and projects 2004–2014

neri & hu design and research office

如 恩 设 计 研 究 室

works and projects 2004–2014

contributions by alejandro zaera-polo and david chipperfield

PARK BOOKS

CONTENTS

Introduction	5
Building with Presence	11
Diachronic Matters	15
Buildings and Interiors	**17**
The Reverse Courtyard. Design Republic Flagship Store	18
The Vertical Lane House. Waterhouse at South Bund	34
The Black Box. Neri&Hu + Design Republic Offices	68
The Recontextualization of History. Design Commune and Commune Social	86
The Split House. Private Residence In Tianzifang	126
The Marketplace. Mercato Restaurant by Jean-Georges Vongerichten	144
The Recycled Lane House. Camper China Showroom in Shanghai	162
The Overlapping Land/House. Private Residence in Singapore	182
Ongoing Projects	**193**
The Shunting House. Indian River Private House	194
The Magistrates Court. Bow Street Boutique Hotel	200
The Garden Units. Kuala Lumpur Residential Tower	212
The Heritage Journey. Sentul Contemporary Art Museum	218
Products	**225**
Zisha Tea Project	226
Extend Mirror	228
Solo Chair	230
Sedan Chair	232
Ming Chair	234
Utility Chair	236
Wild Feast Picnic Basket	238
Appendix	**241**
Project Details	242
Biographies	246
Collaborators	252

Introduction

In recent decades, living and traveling extensively throughout Asia, we have observed the alarming trend of Asia's major metropolises becoming more and more alike. From Shenzhen or Seoul to Kuala Lumpur or Bangkok, the army of glassy high-rise towers marching through each of their CBDs nearly obliterates any perceivable differences between these cities which are otherwise culturally unique and highly distinguishable. As the race towards urbanization and densification continues with no end in sight, we cannot help but want to stop and lament—wax nostalgic perhaps—on what is being sacrificed in this process.

> *Thus the union between the past and the future exists in the very idea of the city that it flows through in the same way that memory flows through the life of a person; and always, in order to be realized, this idea must not only shape but be shaped by reality. This shaping is a permanent aspect of a city's unique artifacts, monuments, and the idea we have of it.*[1]

In China this phenomenon is exacerbated by the sheer scale at which its process of urbanization and modernization has occurred; it is the fastest growing economy in history, and the result is a vast landscape of anonymous cities. The character of what defines Chinese architecture is in crisis, and for a nation that takes such pride in its history and culture, there is little to show for it, at least with regard to recent architectural output. There are certainly iconic monuments that have been preserved, those that feature on tourist destination lists, but the commercialization of these relics renders them incompetent to represent the depth of Chinese culture, both modern and historic. Any remaining sections of historic urban fabric are constantly under threat—from the *hutong* of Beijing to the *lilong* of Shanghai—we believe these are sites full of potential for more engaged architectural design.

The notion of critical regionalism certainly resonates with us, the fundamental strategy "to mediate the impact of universal civilization with elements derived *indirectly* from the peculiarities of a particular place."[2] So the question is not *if*, but how? In our practice we often examine vernacular typologies such as the

---

1 Aldo Rossi, *The Architecture of the City* (New York: Opposition Books, 1982), 131.
2 Kenneth Frampton, "Towards a Critical Regionalism: Six Points for an Architecture of Resistance," *Anti-Aesthetic. Essays on Postmodern Culture* (Seattle: Bay Press, 1983), 21.

hutong and *lilong* that have persisted for centuries and generations. Our research and investigations into these typologies has been a fertile means of critically understanding how to tie our projects into a broader historical context and lineage. The *hutong* courtyard house originating in the Northern regions of China, for example, reveals the inseparable relationship between humans and nature, the integration of public and private space, as well as the familial hierarchy which shapes every aspect of Chinese living. And the *lilong* alley row house that first appeared in Shanghai in the 1850s, still very much alive today, is a fascinating case study for the blurred boundaries of domesticity and notions of "home," as well as communal living conditions instigated by the permeability and overlapping of spaces.

With this research, what becomes productive for us is to understand each typology as a complex entity that has evolved continually over space and time, accumulating layers of collective experiences and memories; its material nature, or form, cannot be reduced to an image. So, even as we pay homage to history and the vernacular, we have no desire to reconstruct the past, to mimic its physicality as a cartoon or diagram. In articulating our attitude towards the issue of preservation versus adaptation, we still find Aldo Rossi's seminal *The Architecture of the City* particularly relevant: "It is hardly surprising that this concept of context is espoused and applied by those who pretend to preserve the historical cities by retaining their ancient facades or reconstructing them in such a way as to maintain their silhouettes and colors and other such things; but what do we find after these operations when they are actually realized? An empty, often repugnant stage."[3] What we are looking for is an alternative reading of these historical typologies, which is not empty, but full—full of stories, life, and memories, those idiosyncratic fragments that make up our humanity.

> *The fantasies of the past, determined by the needs of the present, have a direct impact on the realities of the future. The consideration of the future makes us take responsibility for our nostalgic tales.*[4]

---

3 Rossi, 123.
4 Svetlana Boym, *The Future of Nostalgia* (New York: Basic Books, 2001), xvi.

Practicing in China, at this critical moment, we find ourselves caught between "the optimization of advanced technology and the ever-present tendency to regress into nostalgic historicism."[5] Nostalgia can be a problematic notion for some; it tends to be taken dismissively, as Charles Maier remarks: "Nostalgia is to longing as kitsch is to art."[6] But we feel strongly that there is a potential to be constructive with nostalgia, rather than merely reductive. As we formulate a strategy for how to operate within a historic context or lineage, we find productivity in the concepts of Restorative Nostalgia and Reflective Nostalgia, terms coined by scholar Svetlana Boym.

According to Boym, restorative nostalgia is more literal and direct by comparison; it attempts a "transhistorical reconstruction of the lost home," and does not think itself as nostalgia, "rather as truth and tradition." A bit harder to pinpoint, "reflective nostalgia thrives on *algia* (the longing itself) and delays the homecoming—wistfully, ironically, desperately. Reflective nostalgia does not follow a single plot but explores ways of inhabiting many places at once and imagining different time zones. It loves details, not symbols."[7] In short, reflective nostalgia offers a critical distance that is less regressive than the former restorative nostalgia, and for that reason reflective nostalgia is the concept that struck a chord with our own thinking. "While restorative nostalgia returns and rebuilds one's homeland with paranoic determination, reflective nostalgia fears return with the same passion. Instead of recreation of the lost home, reflective nostalgia can foster a creative self."[8] That it thrives on contradiction, ambivalence, irony, discomfort, details, fragments, and the present fleeting moment—while denying absolutes, linear plots, and symbols—is immensely appealing as we try ourselves (often without clear resolution) to make sense of the complexities of the context in which we work.

> *If we have retained an element of dream in our memories, if we have gone beyond merely assembling exact recollections, bit by bit the house that was lost in the mists of time will appear from out of the shadow. We do nothing to reorganize it; with intimacy it recovers its entity, in the mellowness and*

5 Frampton, 20.
6 Maier xxx.
7 Boym, *The Future of Nostalgia,* xviii.
8 Boym, *The Future of Nostalgia*, 354.

*imprecision of inner life. It is as though something fluid had collected our memories and we ourselves were dissolved in this fluid of the past.*⁹

Many of our well-known projects have dealt with historic sites and existing buildings, and some have "accused" us of being nostalgic when we intentionally leave untouched portions of the near-ruinous buildings, bringing into question the value of such attachments to a decaying past. But what is unquestionable is that the ruinous condition has the power to move people in an inexplicable way. On some level, we think nostalgia is simply intrinsic to human experience, a universal ailment and collective sentiment. Due to the fast pace of change we encounter in our environments, with the future uncertain and the present precarious, we predictably look towards the past as a stable time, often imploring it to inject some meaningful content into the present. "Ruins make us think of the past that could have been and the future that never took place, tantalizing us with utopian dreams of escaping the irreversibility of time. At the same time, the fascination for ruins is not merely intellectual, but also sensual. Ruins give us a shock of vanishing materiality."¹⁰

In our projects, when we celebrate a "ruin," there is certainly the power of the visceral experience that we are putting forth, the beauty of a decaying surface whose history is written into every crack and crevice. But that alone puts it in danger of mere sentimental manipulation, or even less critically, a matter of "style." The key for us is actually in the relationship between old and new, not simply to put relics on a pedestal for worship. When we choose to keep a section of crumbling wall for example, we often frame and encase it behind glass in an archival fashion, or juxtapose it directly against a section of smooth white wall. This is a way to distance oneself from the actual material reality of the wall, instead of focusing on the thing itself, the intention is to highlight our desire or longing for it and what it represents. "There is a historic distinctiveness to the 'ruin gaze' that can be understood as the particular optics that frames our relationship to ruins. Contemporary ruinophilia relates to the prospective dimension of nostalgia,

---

9 Gaston Bachelard, *The Poetics of Space,* trans. Maria Jolas (Boston: Beacon Press, 1994), 57.
10 Svetlana Boym, *"Ruinophilia," Atlas of Transformation,* http://monumenttotransformation.org/atlas-of-transformation/html/r/ruinophilia/ruinophilia-appreciation-of-ruins-svetlana-boym.html

the type of nostalgia that is reflective rather than restorative and dreams of the potential futures rather than imaginary pasts."[11]

The other crucial aspect of nostalgia, we believe, is the very human attachment to objects. So often, it is an object that triggers a wave of nostalgic sentiment, where the object is a tangible stand-in for some other distant time, place, or person. Objects certainly have individual value on some level, but it is their accumulation and relationship to each other upon which we build our dreams and memories, for what is the notion of "home," if not a collection of objects? This is where the interdisciplinary nature of our practice becomes crucial. We consider every object—from window, wall, or door to pendant light, stool, candle holder, or mirror—a reason to call upon not only personal obsessions and memories, but collective traditions and histories.

On all scales of design, we embrace nostalgia as a productive lens through which we can consider an alternative reading of historical contexts as well as a different process of design within that context. It is a methodology that urges us to look closely at the details of the mundane in hopes of achieving a deeper understanding of the heritage of those places that we want to not only participate in presently, but to extend to the future. In understanding the richness of life in the old alleyways of Shanghai or courtyard houses of Beijing, we hope to preserve their cultural heritage through the stories they contain within their threadbare walls and among the hodgepodge of its residents' belongings. As the spaces shape their narratives, we consider whether narrative can, in turn, shape spaces, deriving a constructive and meaningful process of space-making in our practice.

11 Svetlana Boym, *"Ruinophilia"*

BUILDING WITH PRESENCE
DAVID CHIPPERFIELD

The cultural dialogue between China and what is loosely referred to as "the West" over the last fifteen years has been variable in quality. There is no doubt that in areas such as dance, film, and fine arts this dialogue has been both energetic and sophisticated, with artists, ideas, and experience traveling in both directions. In architecture and design the picture is less clear.

The traffic has been predominantly one way, with the West exploiting the opportunities of an open market hungry for ideas and images. The enormous program of construction and development, new buildings, new cities, and redevelopment has on the whole been disappointing. In an enthusiasm to "catch up" there has been a general lack of interest in history and in historic areas of the city. Innovation, or at least the appearance of innovation, has dominated, and there has been little consideration for existing structures or traditions.

Clearly the Cultural Revolution is partly to blame, but it also seems unfortunate that China should look to the West and imitate it at a time when we are apparently devoid of ideas ourselves. How should we design cities? How to mediate the tendencies of investment with societal ideas about the city? How to protect and integrate architecture and the organic qualities we so admire yet which seem so contradictory to the forces of the market? How to give voice to autonomous idea and spirit in a society obsessed with growth and the leveraging of value? These are questions to which the West seems unable to give compelling answers.

We cannot reflect on what has happened in China over recent years in the fields of architecture and urbanism with any sense of satisfaction, despite the respect we might have for the scale of what has been achieved. It is a well-known aphorism that design and architecture have more chance of success at the small scale, that in general terms power and money are not the friends of creativity and investigation. In our globalized world this concept is both difficult to sustain and increasingly unhelpful, as even the smallest achievement seems only to be validated by large-scale approval. However, creatively it remains the case that resistance of idea and independence of thought, so fundamental to any autonomous process, are more difficult to hold on to as the scale of investment gets bigger, as the commercial stakes get larger, and as the process of patronage and decision-making becomes more diffuse and detached.

It is within this context that we must consider and admire the work of Neri&Hu, architects and designers who have managed to speak quietly but with integrity and authority. Given their sophisticated backgrounds it is no surprise that they have been able to create small projects of exquisite quality. Their understanding that power can reside in modesty has given their voice a particular resonance over the cacophony of twenty-first-century China.

While their success may seem natural to those who know them, it is interesting to consider why they have been able to carve out a distinct identity and approach when so many others have failed to do more than be professionally successful. There are three factors that I would highlight as being critical to their development over the past ten years and to the respect that they have earned.

Firstly, while all around them were wrestling with the issues of larger projects, they developed through small-scale works. While other architects were building cities, Neri&Hu honed their architectural and intellectual ideas on shops, restaurants, hotels, and townhouses. Such beginnings have lent their work coherence and intensity.

Secondly, they embraced the potential of expanding consumerism and accepted the commercial sector as a valid territory within which to work. Neri&Hu became advocates for good design by selling it themselves at their Design Republic store. Here it was possible to collect objects and with intelligent selection and curating to suggest a more sophisticated and developed view of China's design culture, bringing together East and West in a way that architecture and planning seemed incapable of doing.

Finally, Neri&Hu have incorporated texture, history, and context into their strategy, using scenographically existing structures to impressive effect, but also finding more deeply shared aesthetic issues from East and West. They have found an approach that gives form to ideas of "Chinese-ness" but within a distinctly Western view of design, finding a bridge between tradition and modernity, between East and West. The potency of this position seems particularly interesting and important within a culture that has destroyed so much of its history and is now intent on finding an identity out of its confusion.

DIACHRONIC MATTERS
ALEJANDRO ZAERA-POLO

There are probably several remarkable traits in the work of Neri&Hu that we could foreground, but there is one which is particularly interesting to me and, I believe, worth mentioning as a line of research that will become increasingly important to architects: the consistent engagement they have maintained, for some time now, with the processes of urban recycling. From their now well-known Waterhouse at South Bund, where they addressed the redevelopment of an existing three-story Japanese Army headquarters building from the 1930s by making the preservation of decayed material textures a crucial expressive traits of the new building. This rather courageous approach—particularly poignant when working in the world of contemporary East Asian architecture, which is generally driven by newness and tabula rasa—has been continued in a few more recent projects, such as The Magistrate's House in Covent Garden, London, The Split House in Tianzifang, Shanghai, and the Design Republic Jiangning Road, Shanghai, where a similar approach has been applied.

In this approach the buildings are composed through an accretion of building matter from different times, where both the figural and the material traits are deliberately preserved and contrasted with the new construction. The resulting effect is particularly interesting as it projects an image of the city in which older building matter is incorporated as another building material which contains the material traits of former cultures, but also expresses the diachronic nature of buildings, exploiting decay as a generator of irregular textures and contingent forms. Buildings do not become the instantaneous embodiment of a well thought-out and brand new whole, but rather a literal accretion of materialities which retain their different states of decay or newness as an expressive trait. This is an architecture located in the antipodes of the glitzy image of the contemporary that prevails today, particularly in the Asian metropolis.

By preserving the traits of decay not only do the architects manage to retain cultural images through their figural and material traits; they also explicitate the process of decay that buildings are inevitably drawn into, which has been carefully eliminated from the precepts of the discipline. It seems to me that using material decay as an expressive device is a particularly interesting approach in a process which I believe will become increasingly common for architects in the near future, since we now know that buildings contain embedded energy and that the constant cycle of building and demolishing is not a viable option for the future.

buildings and interiors

THE REVERSE COURTYARD
Design Republic Flagship Store, Shanghai

The location for Design Republic's first flagship store in Shanghai was on the Bund, and although we were in love with the neighborhood, we knew from the beginning that it would be a challenge to create a successful retail space in a building type that was never intended to house such a program. Bund No. 5, like many other buildings along the historic waterfront, is a stoic relic from the turn of the century, a formidable presence in heavy granite and wrought iron. As such, it was completely lacking the openness that a retail function thrives on, and furthermore, our space was elevated from the street level and cut off from pedestrian foot traffic. So these unique obstacles became themselves the source of our design inspiration.

The concept takes the notion of window shopping—something which could not be achieved in a traditional sense "around" our site—and internalizes this experience "within" the space. The framed glass panels that encircle the room act as display windows for the objects of desire, encouraging shoppers to stroll along the edges of the enclosure. Bringing this exterior experience to the interior essentially inverts the spatial condition and creates what we call a "reverse courtyard." The courtyard, a housing typology rooted in Northern China, has been an endless source of inspiration for us—it is the physical manifestation of certain cultural values, as well as a model for the kind of blurred interior-exterior living that so fascinates us. In this case, we created an interiorized courtyard, but beyond that, there was also the idea of inverting the solid-void relationship of a courtyard.

Like the work of sculptor Rachel Whiteread, which inverts everyday objects and turns them into solid negatives of themselves, we thought it would be interesting to treat the heart of the courtyard as an object, not a void, a positive rather than a negative. The wooden element inserted into the center of the space is a sculptural piece with a raised platform. It ties into our notion of Design Republic as more

Rachel Whiteread. *House*, 1993
Perhaps her best-known work, House *is a concrete cast of the inside of an entire Victorian terraced house in East London. The themes of absence and memory are embodied in her interpretations of everyday, domestic objects and their overlooked "negative" spaces—the interior of a closet, a section of a floor, or the hollow of a chair. The artist's innovative use of the unseen areas that compliment an object's identity suggests to us the deconstruction of comfort, home, and memory.*

site map 0 200m

than just a shop, but a multi-purpose retail platform—part gallery, part classroom, part event space. Whiteread's notion of objects retaining the imprint of history and culture within them was something that resonated strongly with us as we envisioned this adaptable platform-object at the center of the space.

The material palette and details of the project, one might say, was full of early experimentation for us, experimentation which we still carry on. For us, the use of COR-TEN and raw steel is a way to bring another dimension, the fourth dimension, into a design, so that the changing patina of materials can indicate the passage of time. In that sense, we are a bit nostalgic, we don't ask for things to always be new and perfect, rather we want them to carry a certain meaning. An interesting and little-known fact is that when we moved our flagship store to the Design Commune in 2012, we actually reused a few of the steel doors from this project, a little tribute to DR's first home in Shanghai.

demolition plan

0　　15m

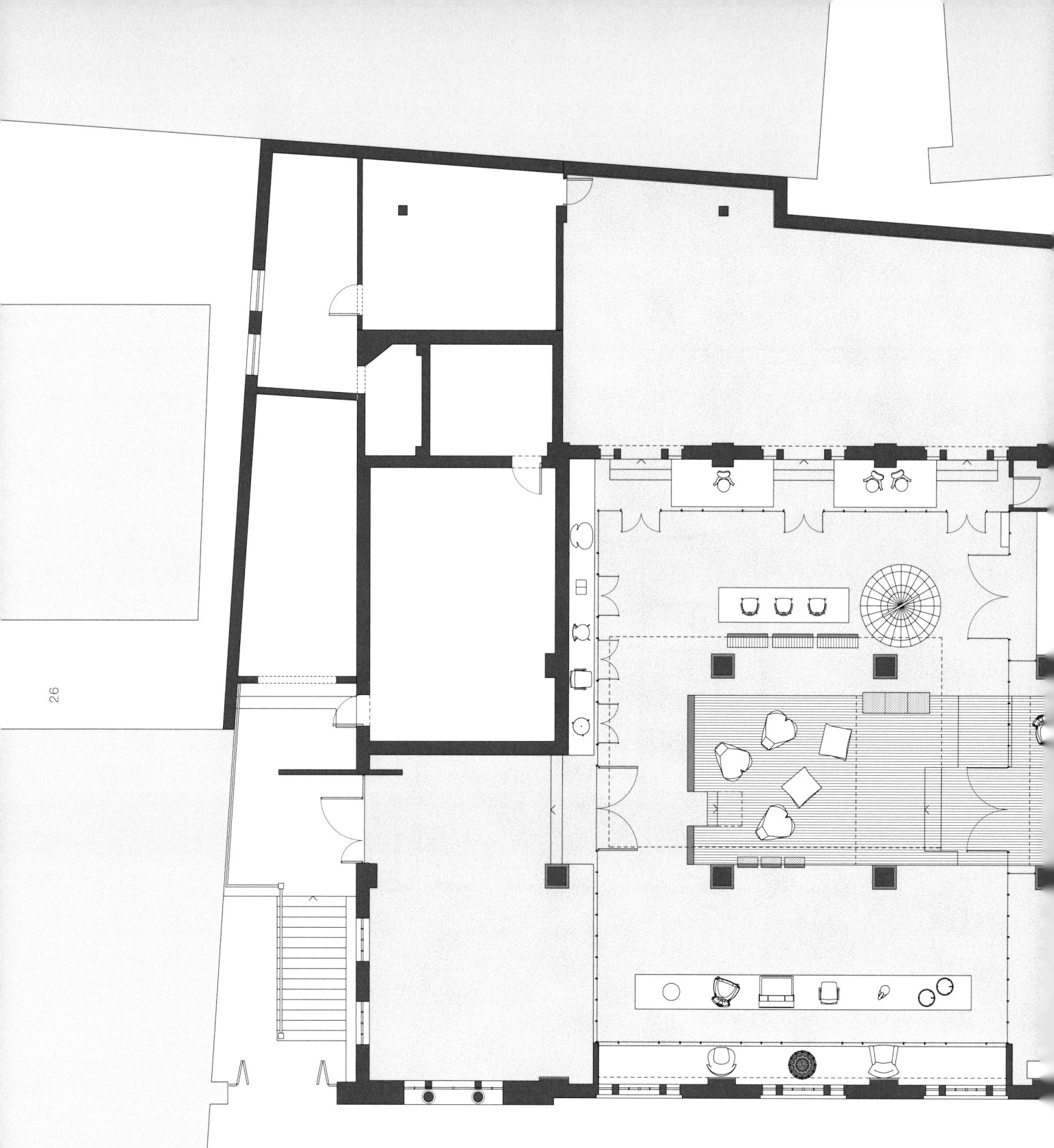

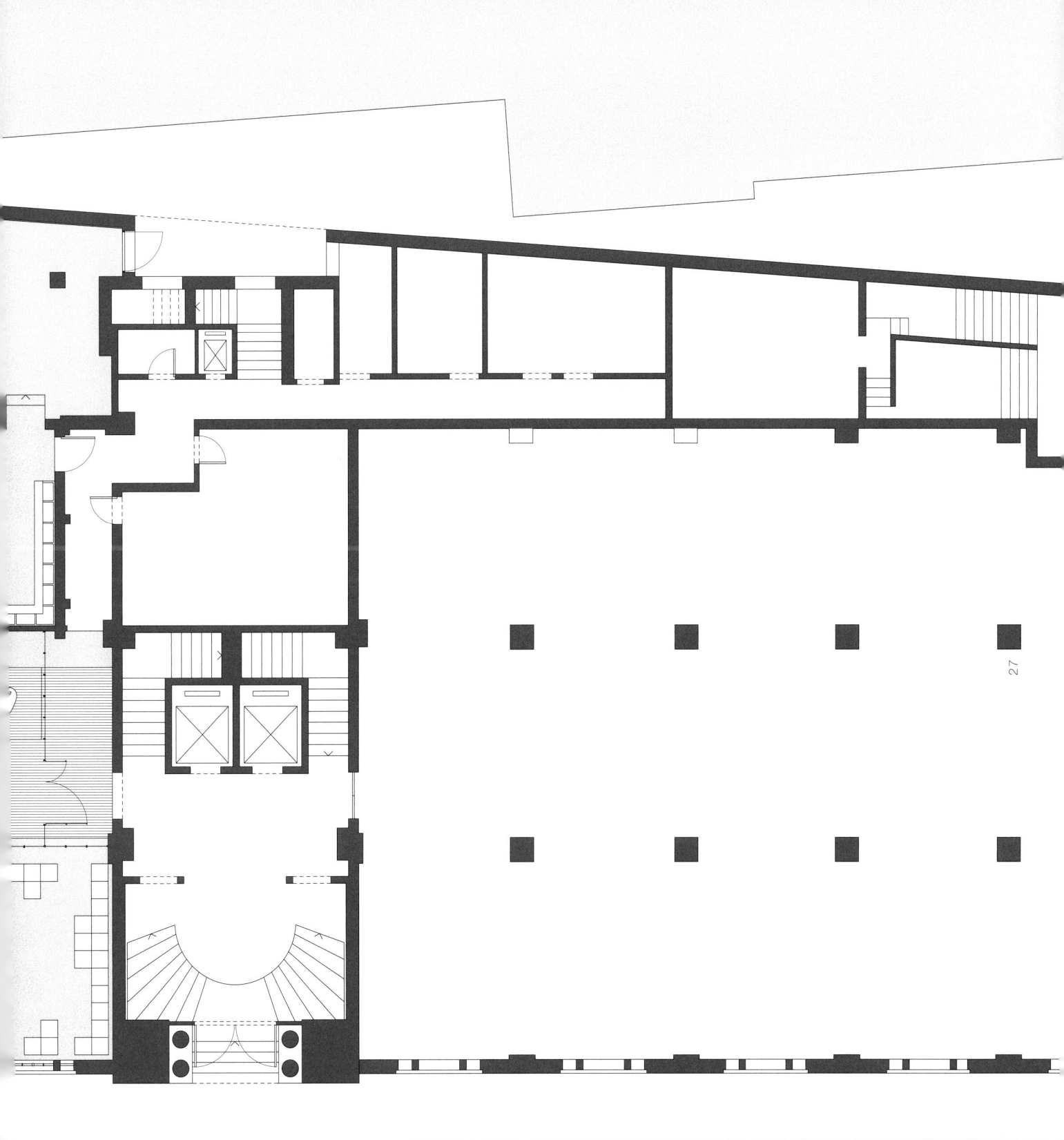

ground-floor plan

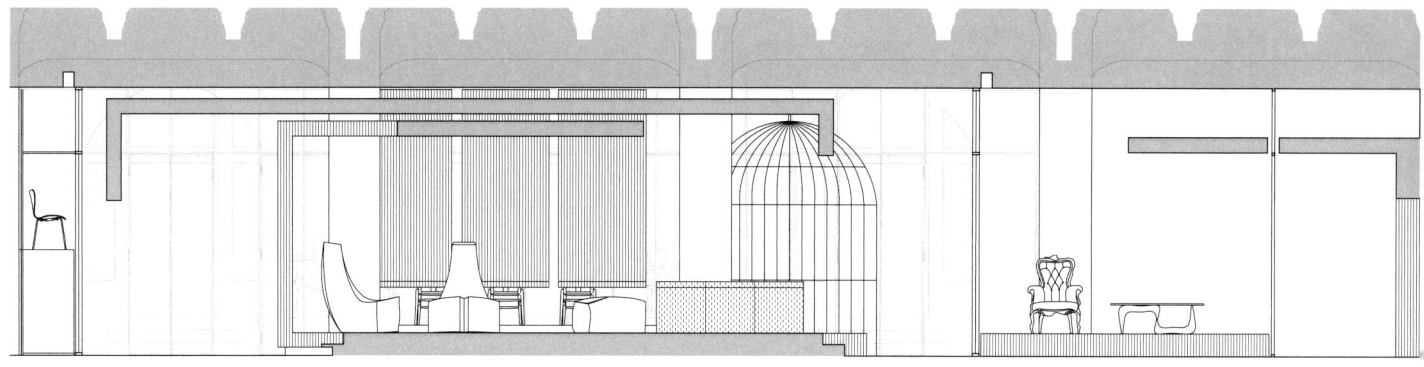
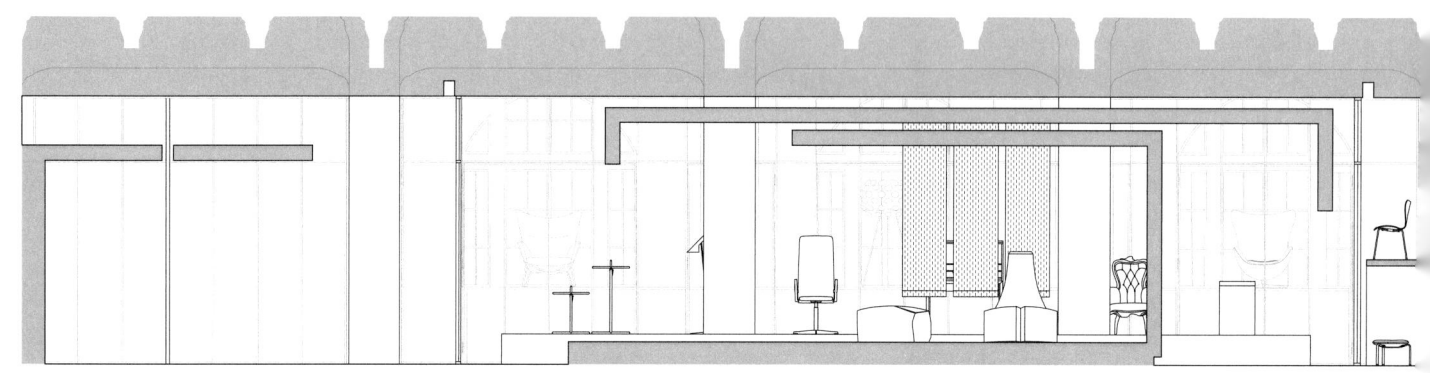

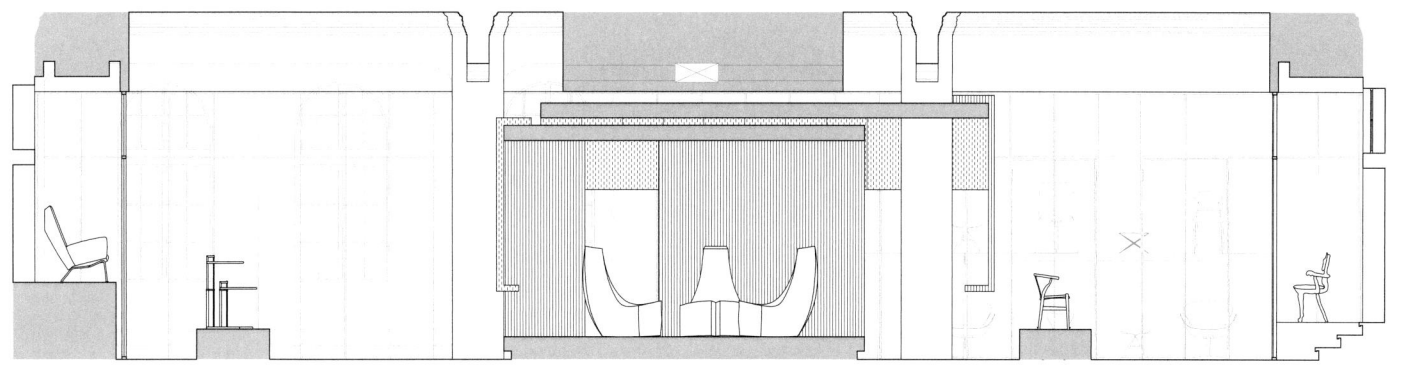
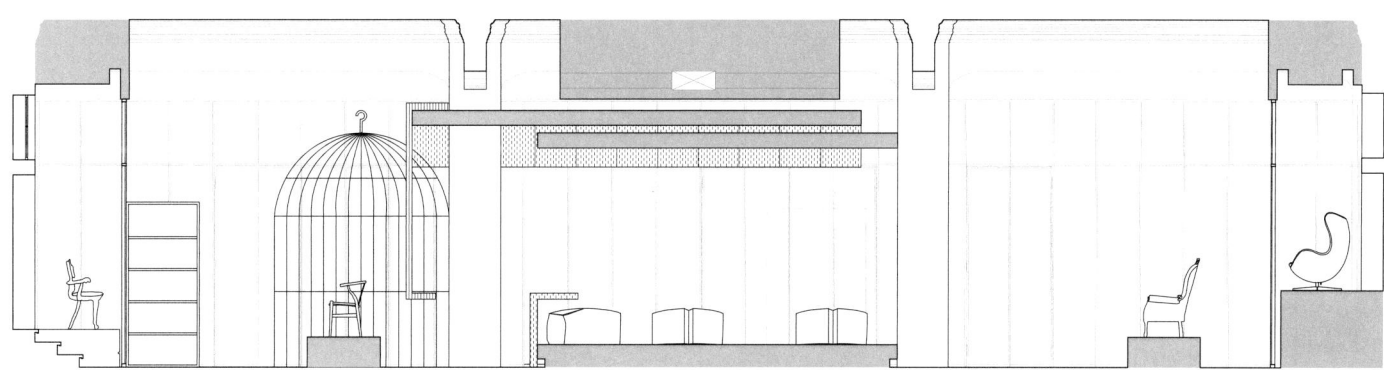

interior elevation
0 4m

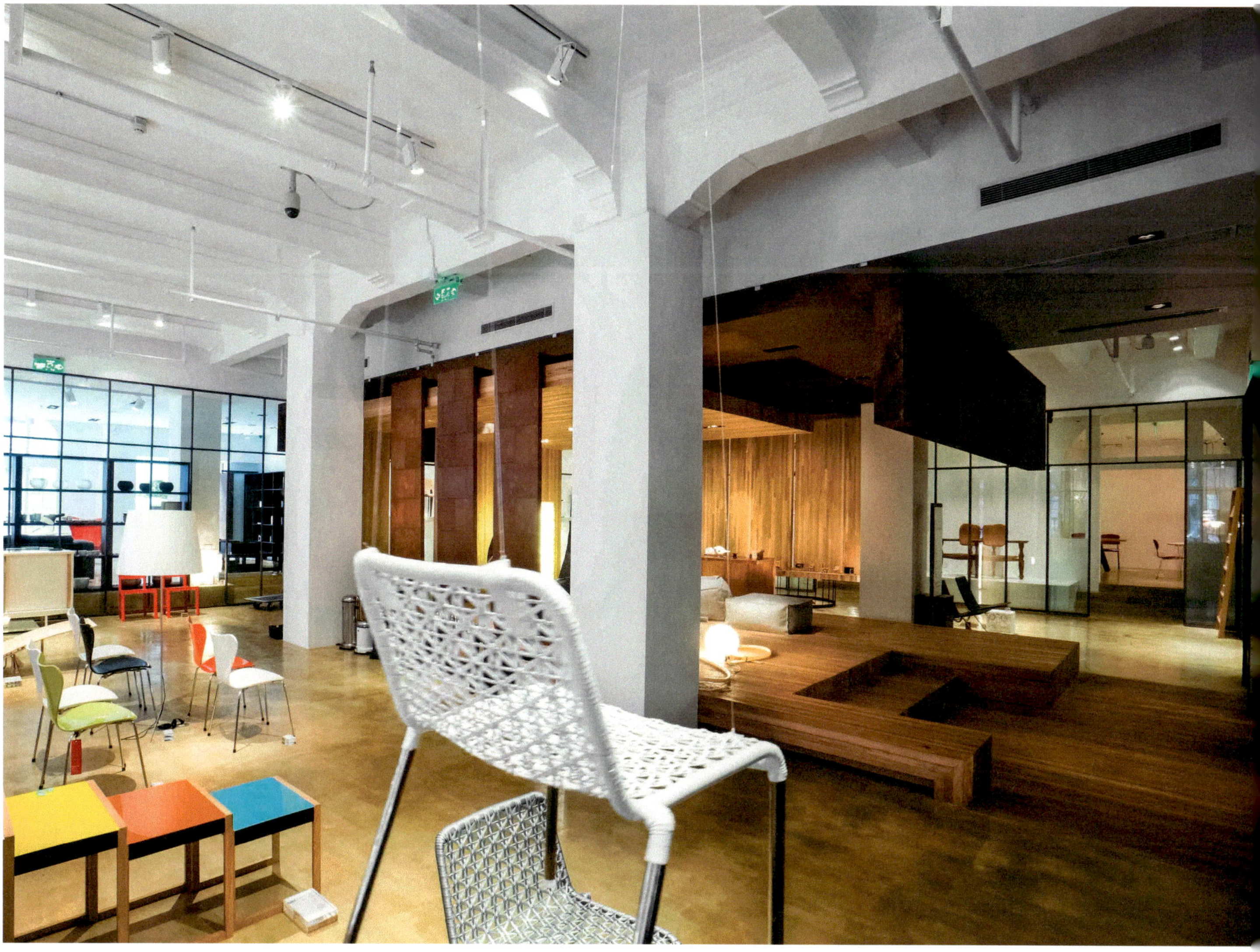

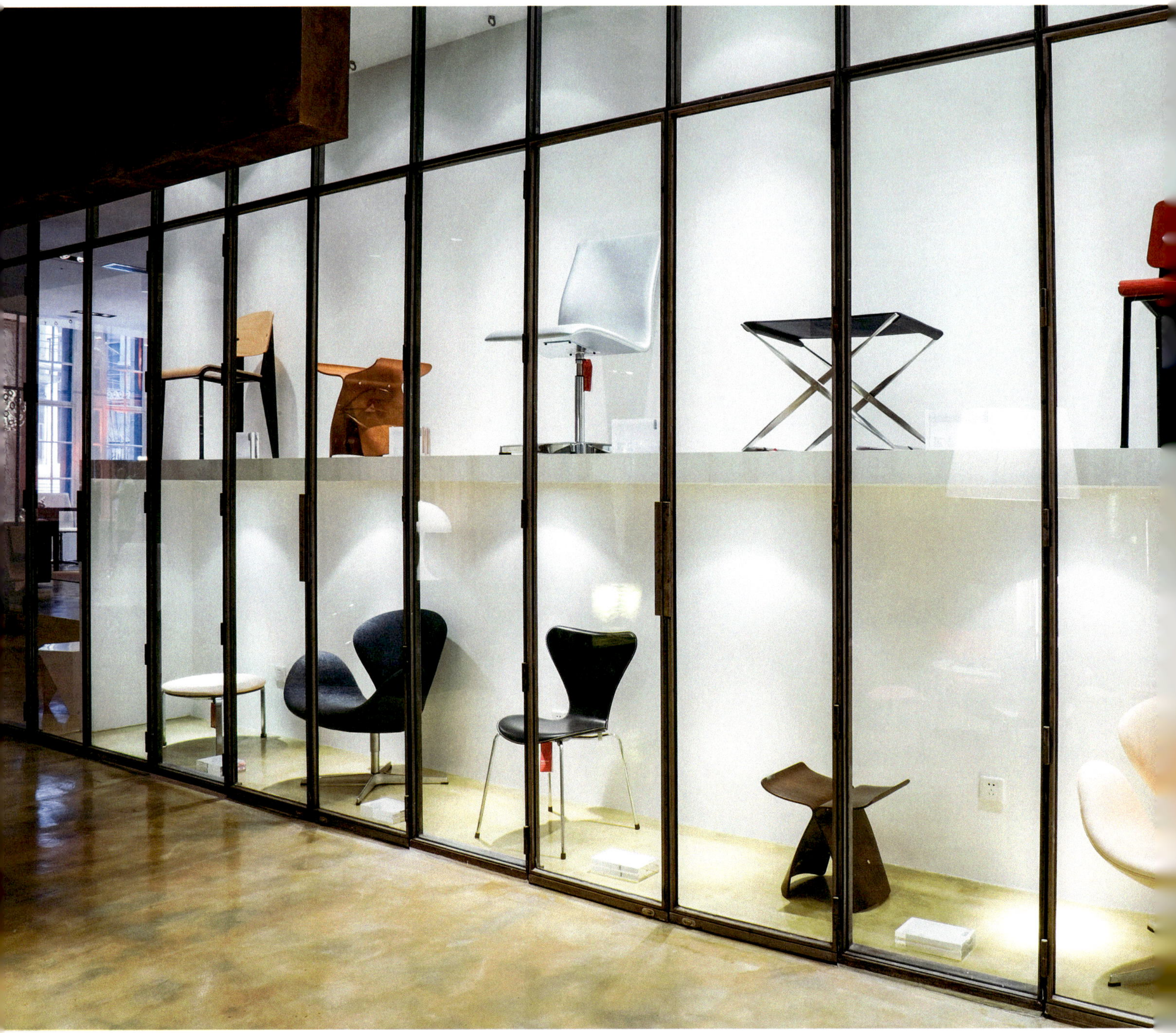

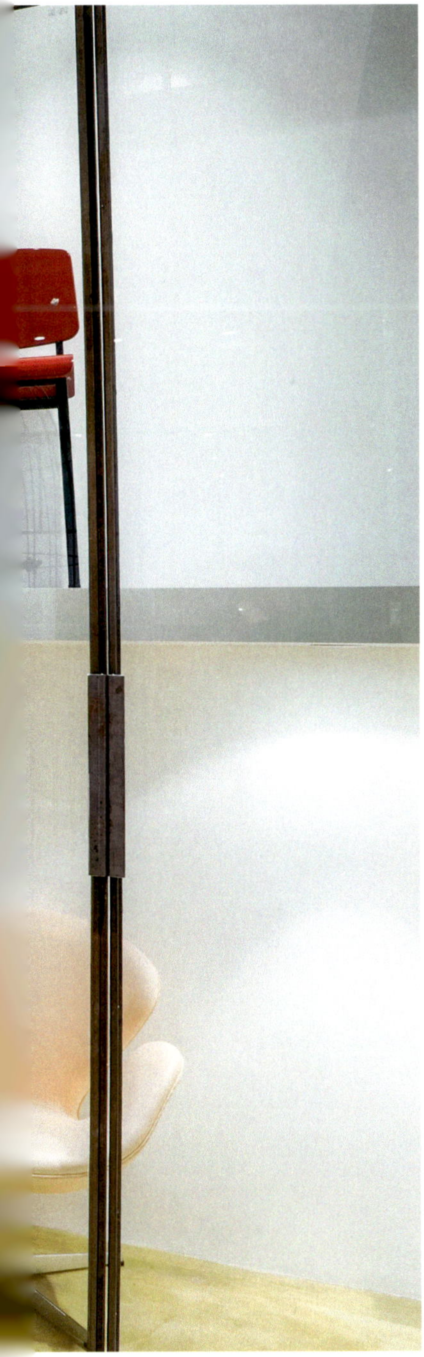

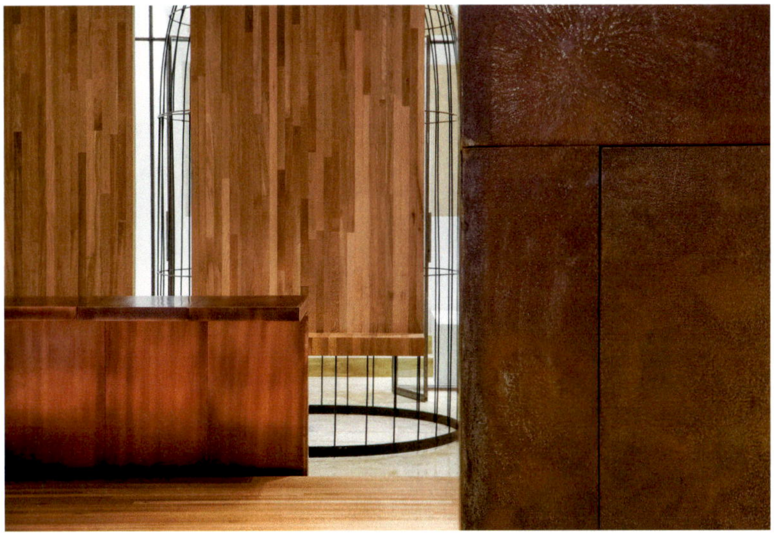

THE VERTICAL LANE HOUSE
Waterhouse at South Bund, Shanghai

Approaching the site, a Japanese army building from the 1930s, with its history written all over its surfaces, the real task at hand was to show restraint in the restoration process and resist the natural urge to fix every flaw. We were very careful to delineate where new elements were inserted and where the old remained untouched. While some of the spaces have been refinished and smoothed over, portions of wall are left crude, exposing crumbling bricks or delicate lathwork behind deteriorating plaster. Encased in a glass shield, these raw wall sections evoke the archival quality of a museum display, and suddenly the overlooked mundane is elevated to the precious. Peeling back the layers of finishes was akin to performing an autopsy—uncovering the lives and narratives hidden within each imperfection, an excavation of memories that brings the most intimate moments of inhabitation to public light.

Equally purposeful as the demarcation between old and new is, conversely, the lack of boundary between the public and the private. We are interested in breaking down, on various levels, the visual, aural, and physical limitations of personal space. The concept behind the hotel's signature restaurant, Table No. 1, is to create an extension of the street through the entire depth of the restaurant, continuing into an inner courtyard, such that the public realm invades deeply into the core of the private sphere. A cut in the ceiling of the restaurant even allows guests staying in the rooms above to participate peripherally in the lively activities of the diners below. The seemingly misplaced windows throughout, like the one above the main reception in the lobby—cleverly situated reflective surfaces and unexpected circulation paths—offer the constant thrill of a stolen view or a wayward glimpse.

In its very conception, the Waterhouse also seeks to question the typology of a hotel itself, how to translate notions of "home" and domesticity into a foreign environment, how to give meaning to the experience of a traveler. To do so, we drew

site map

0   400m

from the rich experience of residing in a typical Shanghai *nong tang* alley, where everyday living is full of discovery and surprises, and there is no such thing as true privacy. By challenging even those basic rituals of daily life, such as bathing, and transforming that familiarity into something wholly unpredictable—a glass box—there is a constant play on ideas of comfort and discomfort. These unexpected moments are meant to heighten the emotional journey of the guest. The graphic wall markings throughout the spaces evoke and suggest the complexities of the traveler's psychological state—the longing and exhilaration, the uncertainty and desire, the discomfort and relief—while the distinct rawness of the material palette establishes an intense sense of time, place, and being.

夕阳洗染房

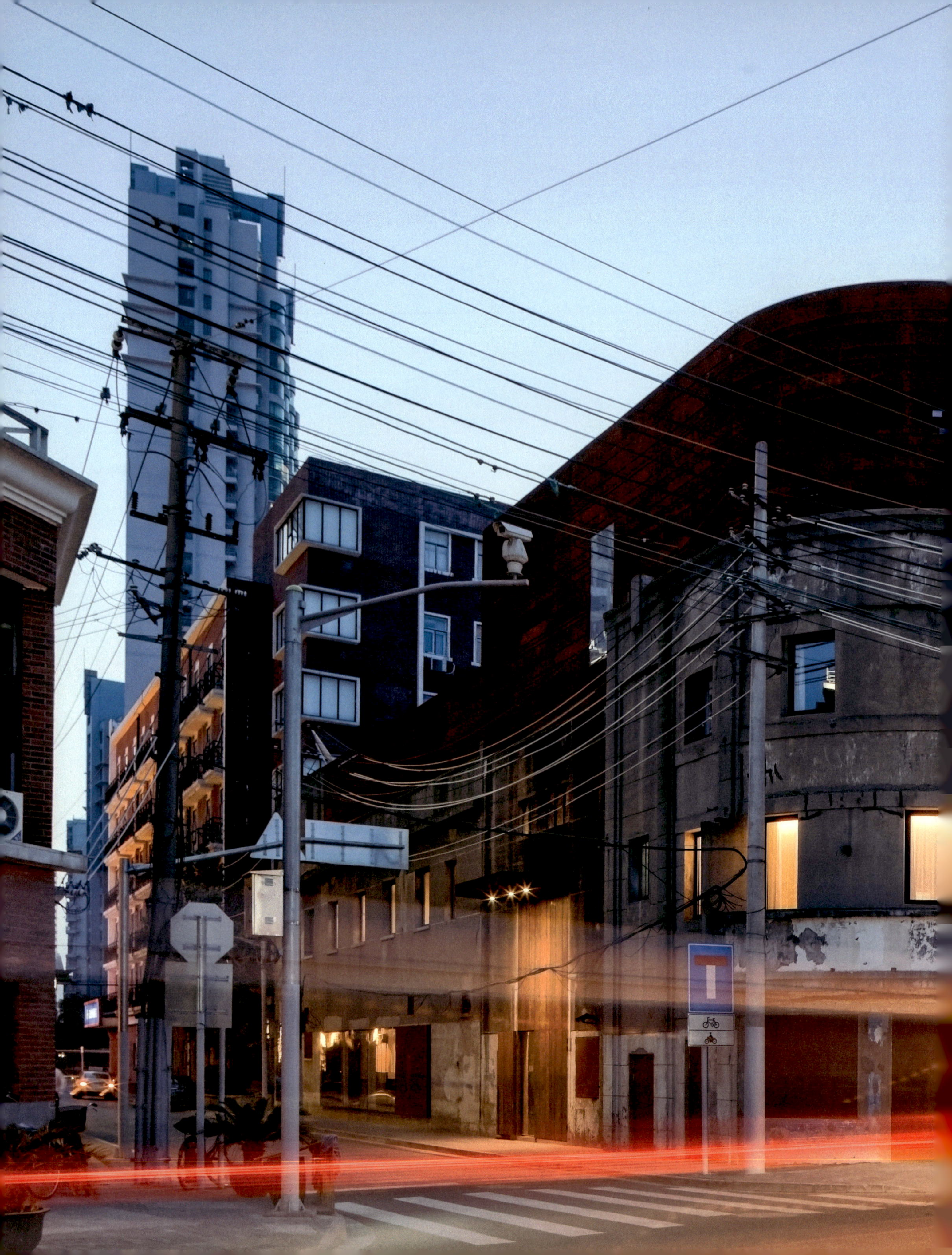

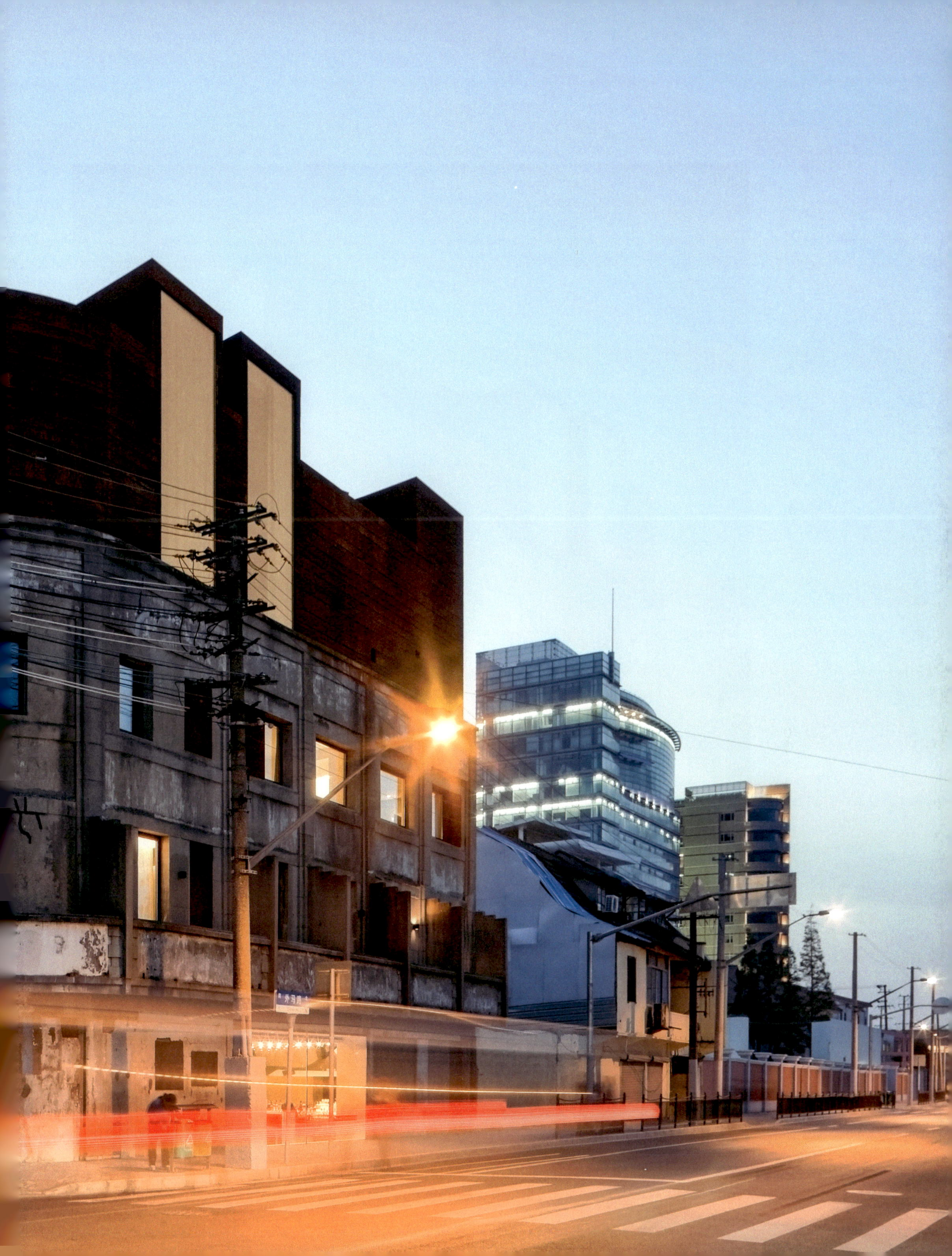

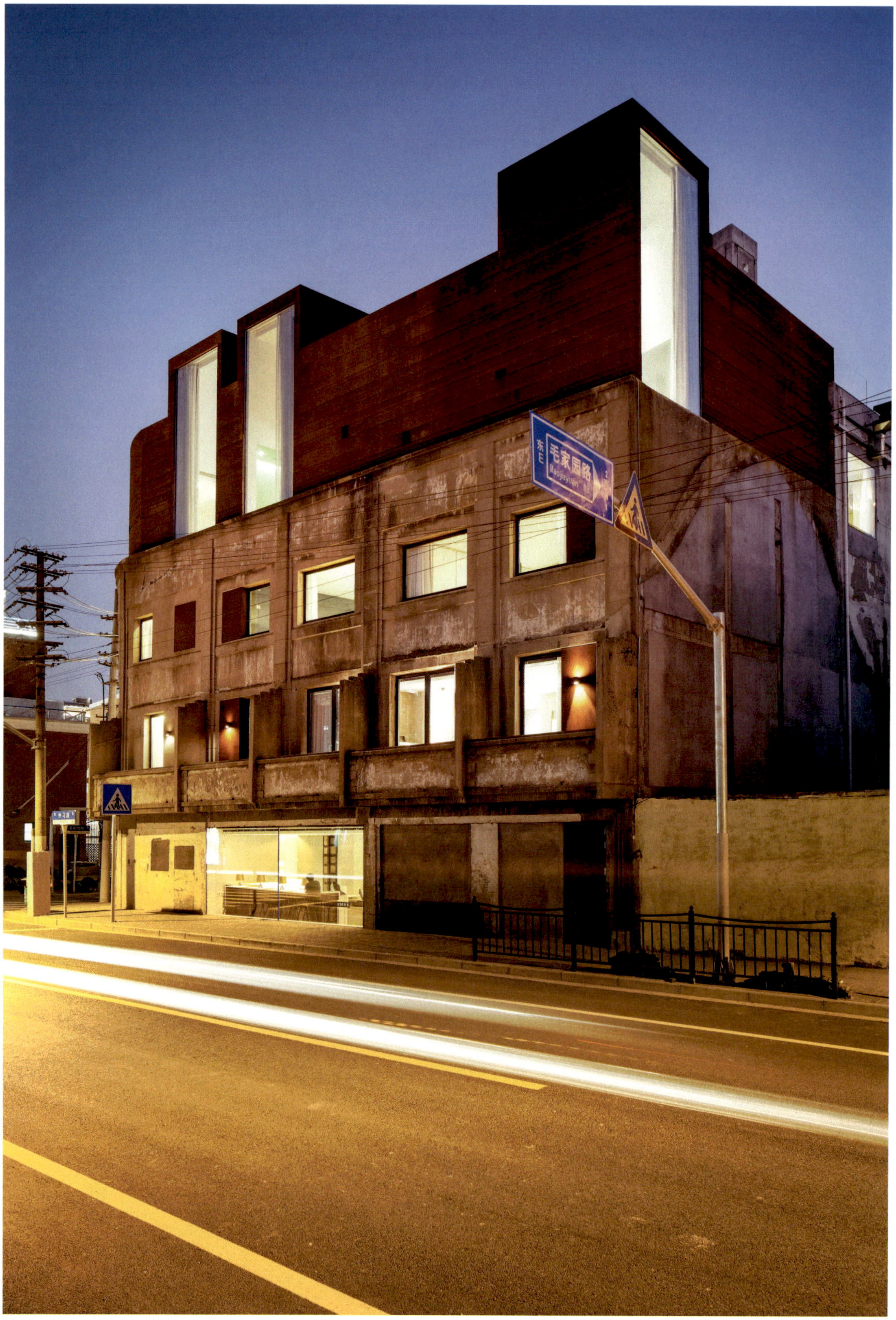
东
E
毛家园路
Maojiayuan Rd.
2

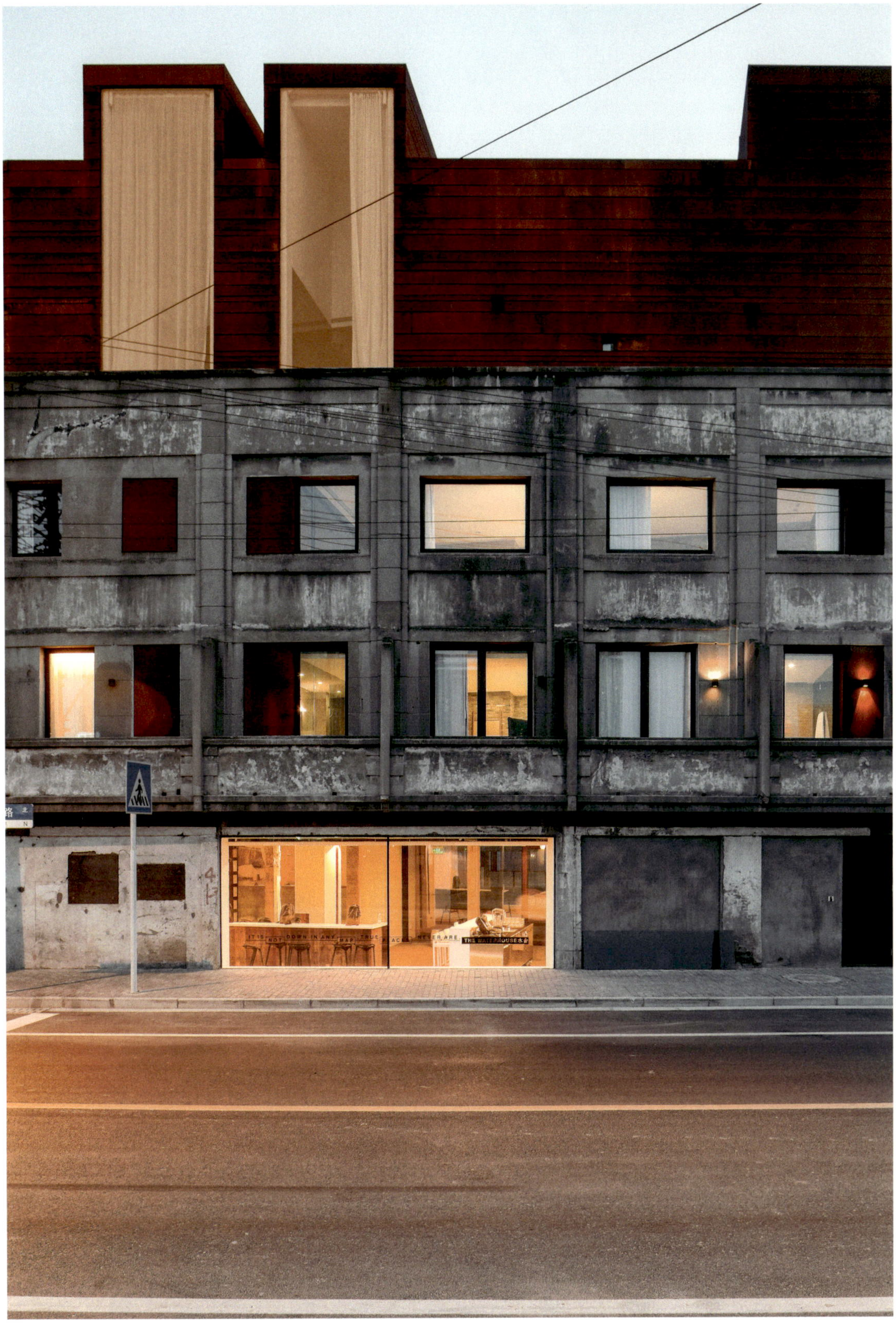

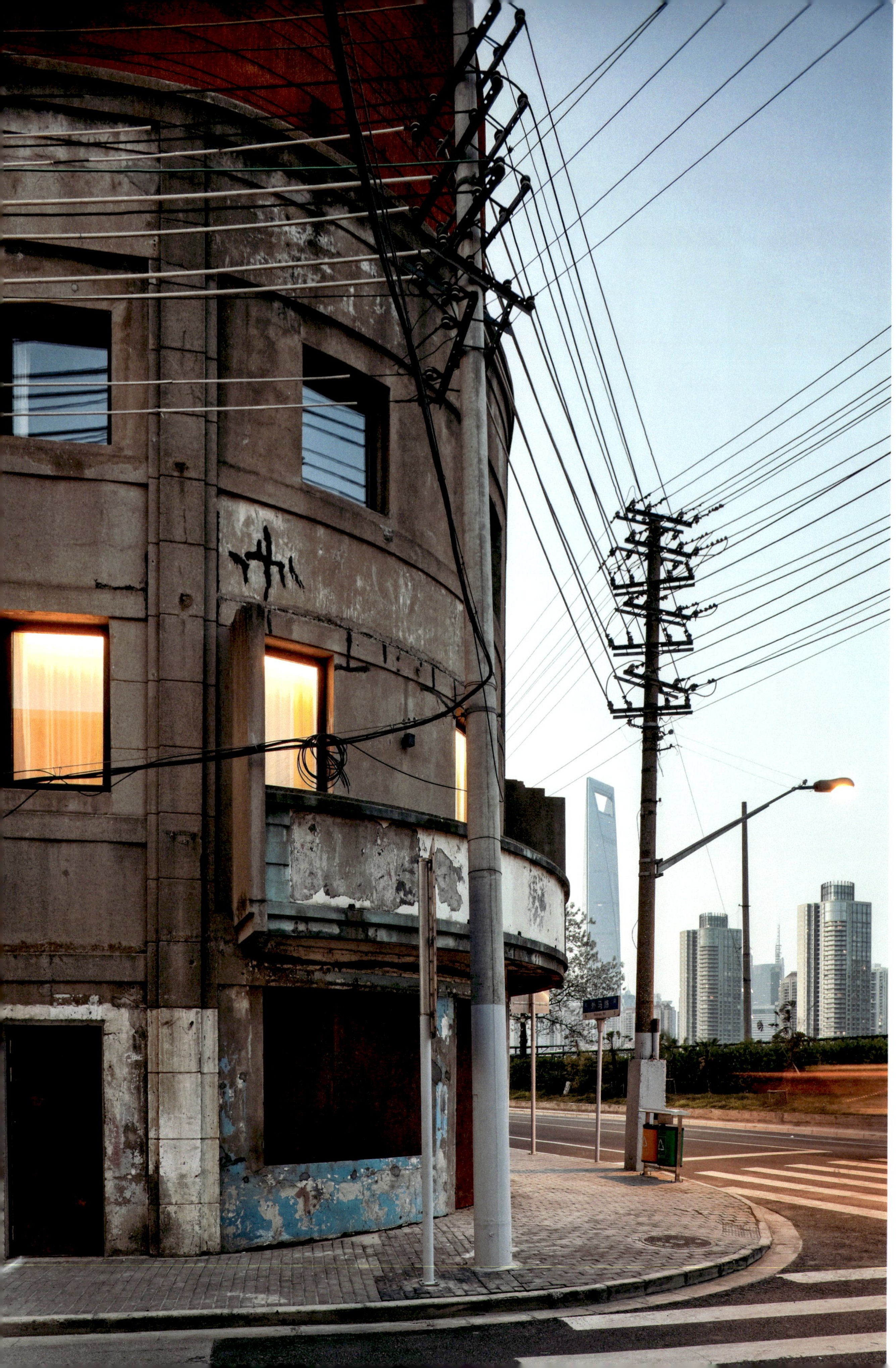

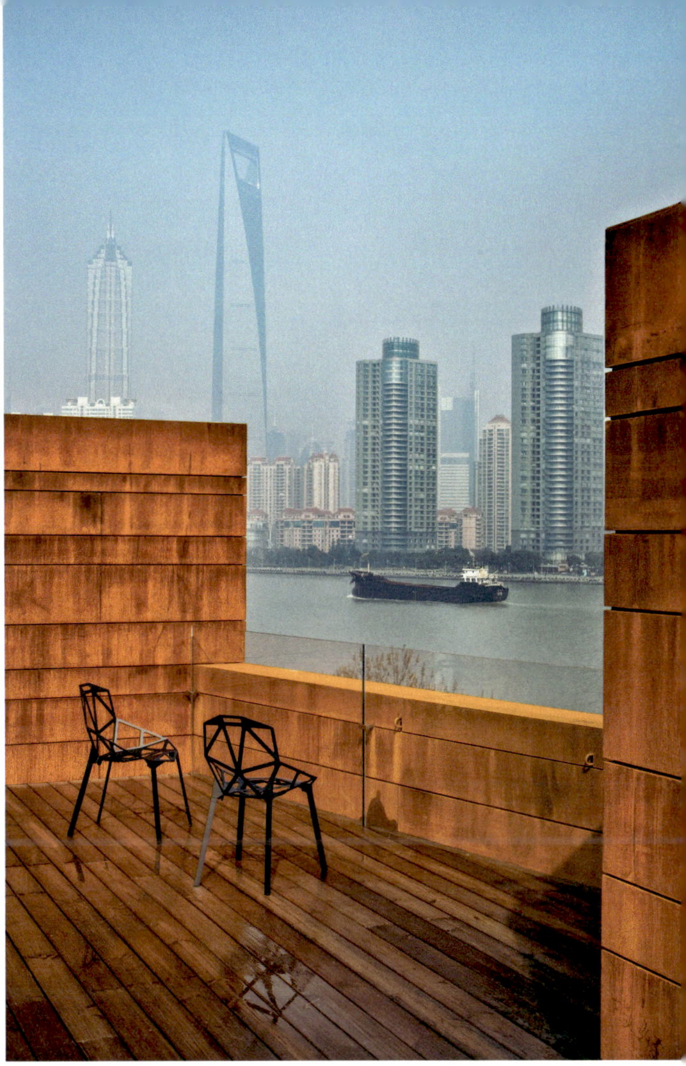

44

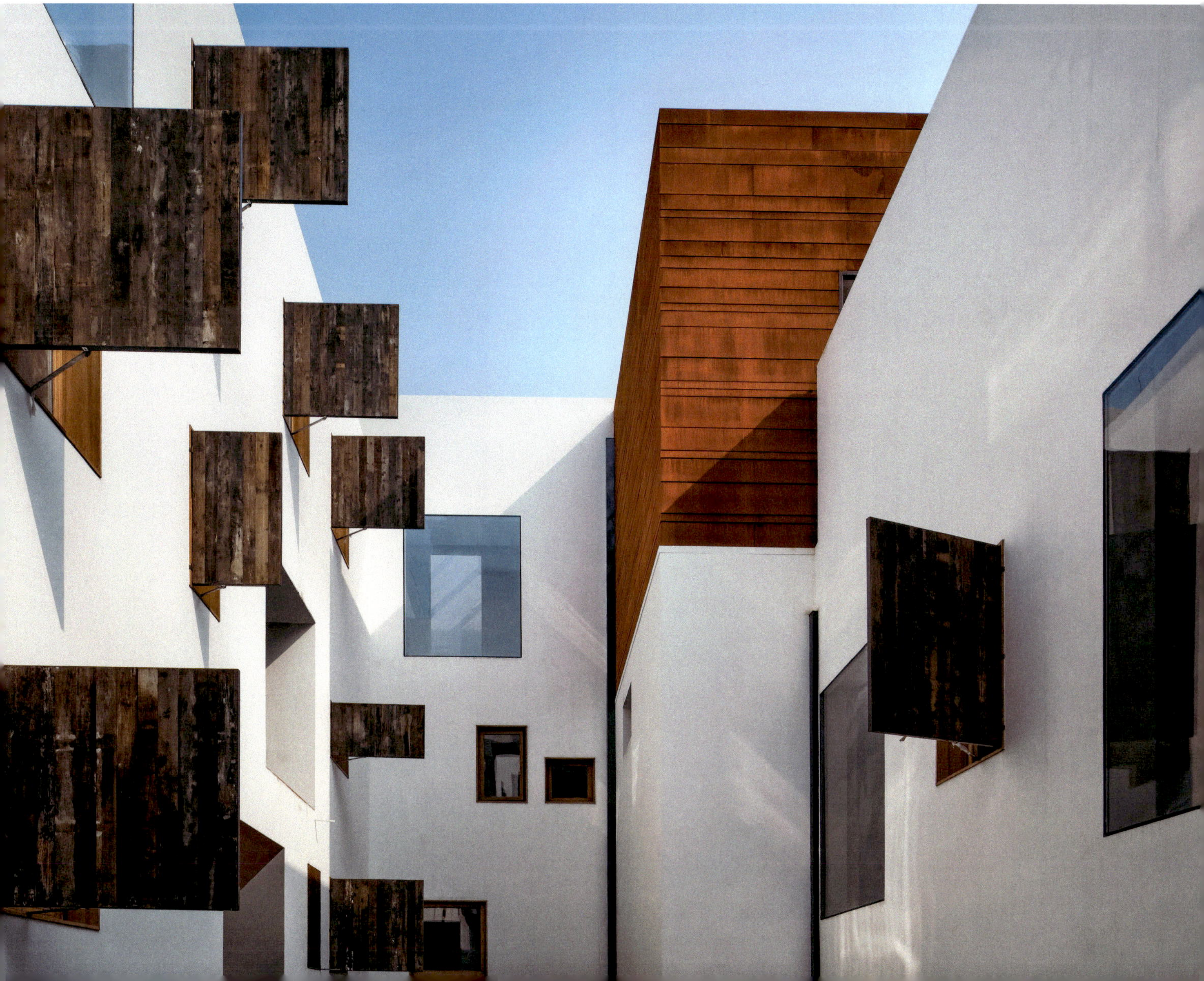

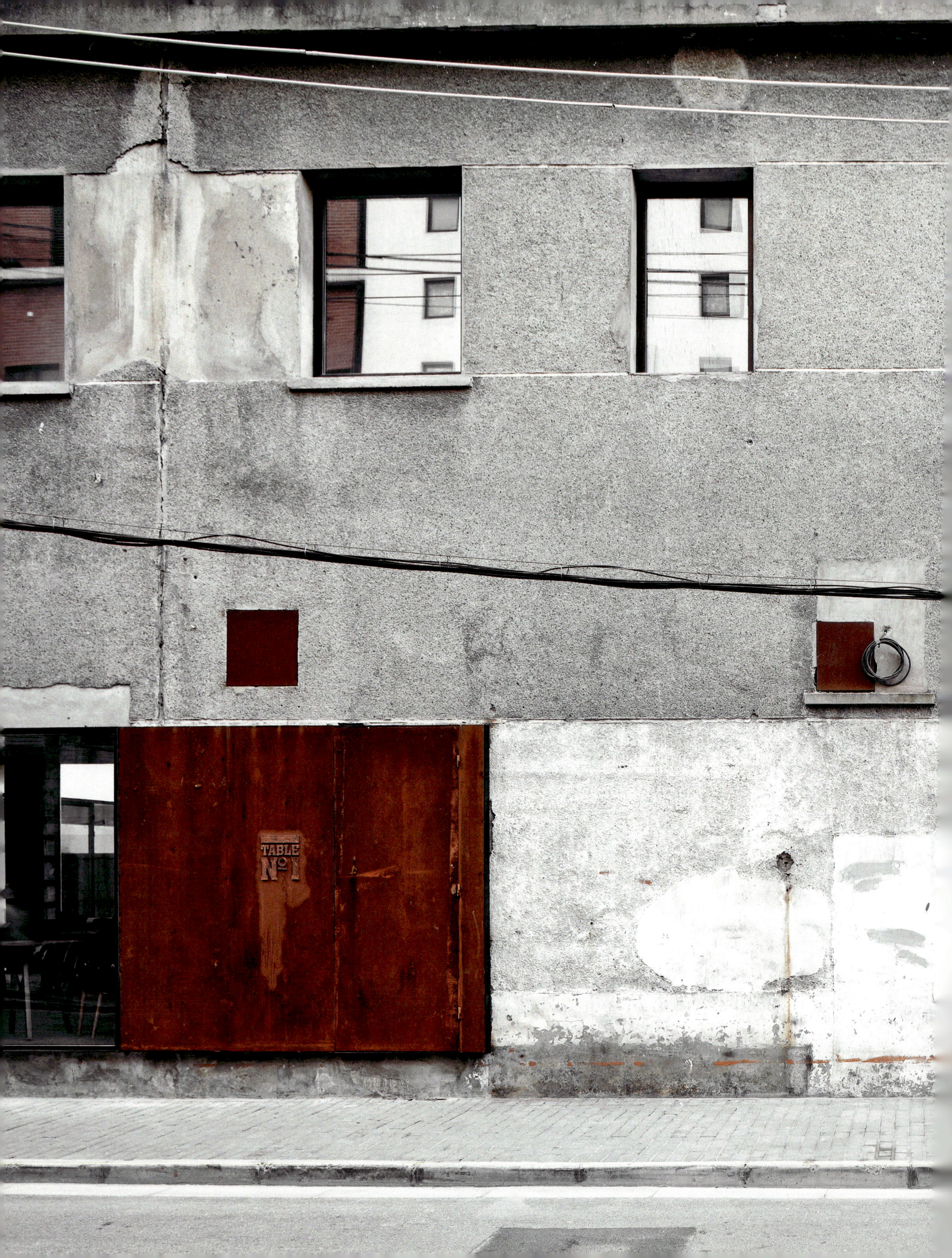
TABLE
Nº 1

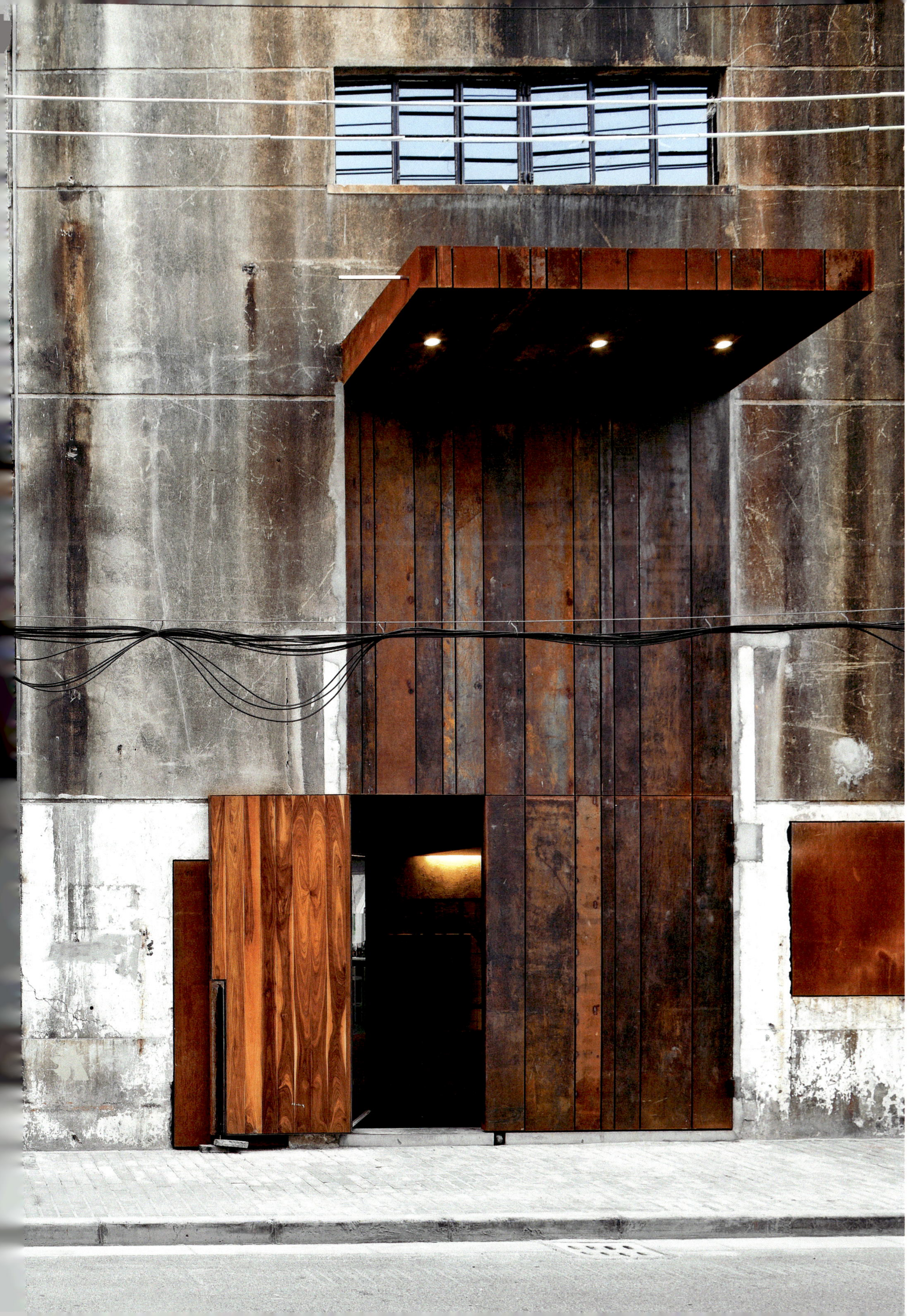

COURTYARD
3/2009

OPTION 1

OPTION 2

demolition plan | section

0 15m

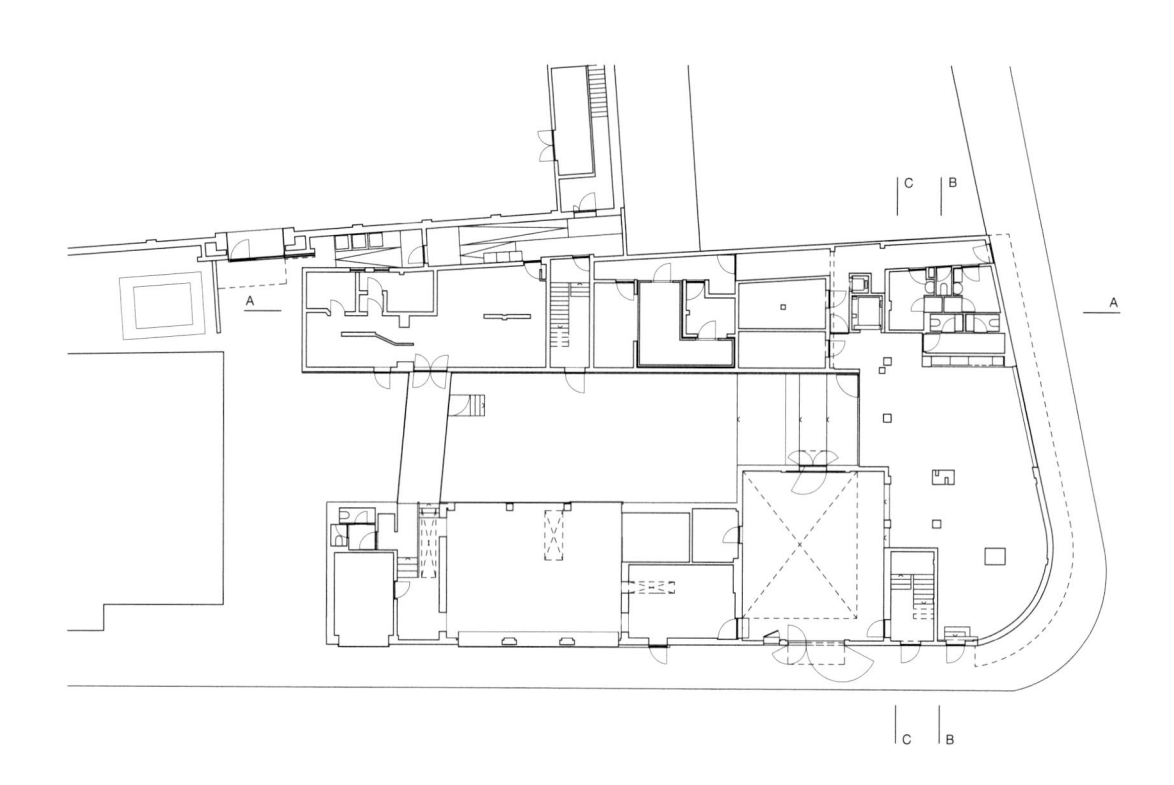

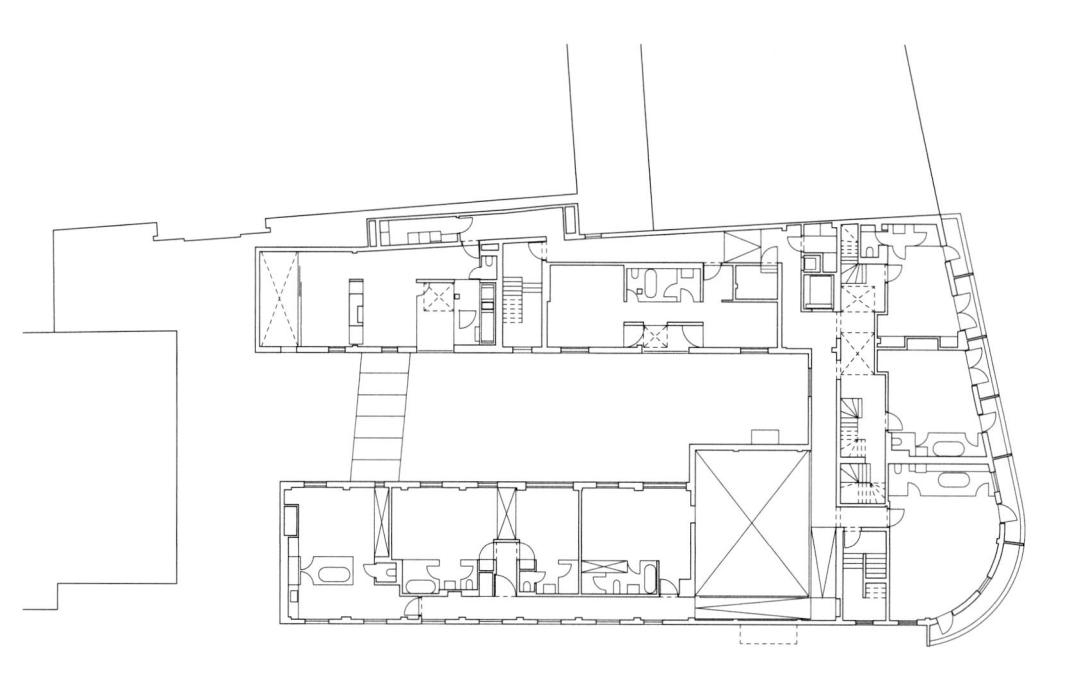

RIVERFRONT FACADE

1 Roof structure
Gravel
50-mm XPS rigid insulation
5-mm polythene membrane
Screed laid to falls
100-mm new concrete floor slab
30-mm XPS insulation
50-mm V-channel
15-mm paper-faced gypsum board

2 Corten steel elevation structure
4-mm corten steel cladding
30-mm steel stud
55-mm battens
12-mm waterproof cement
175-mm Ytong light concrete with reinforcement
50-mm XPS rigid insulation
5-mm polythene membrane
15-mm paper-faced gypsum board

3 Periscope window
8+15+8mm double glazing

4 Room floor structure
20-mm wood floorboard
30-mm battens
35-mm lightweight concrete topping
40-mm profiled steel sheet
300-mm sub-structure
100-mm new concrete floor slab
40-mm XPS insulation
3-mm polythene membrane
300-mm Cavity
50-mm V-channel
15-mm paper-faced gypsum board

5 Room window
6+12+6mm double glazing

6 3rd floor construction
20-mm wood floorboard
20-mm plywood
40-mm battens
5-mm sound insulation
100-mm new reinforced concrete slab
40-mm XPS insulation
3-mm polythene membrane
Cavity
50-mm V-channel
15-mm paper-faced gypsum board

7 Wall structure
240-mm existing brick wall
3-mm polythene vapor barrier
35-mm XPS board
3-mm polythene membrane
15-mm wood board

8 Ground floor structure
40-mm recycled grey brick
5-mm mortar bed
30-mm reinforced screed leveling
3-mm polythene membrane
40-mm XPS insulation board
5-mm polythene membrane
100-mm reinforced concrete slab
Rammed earth

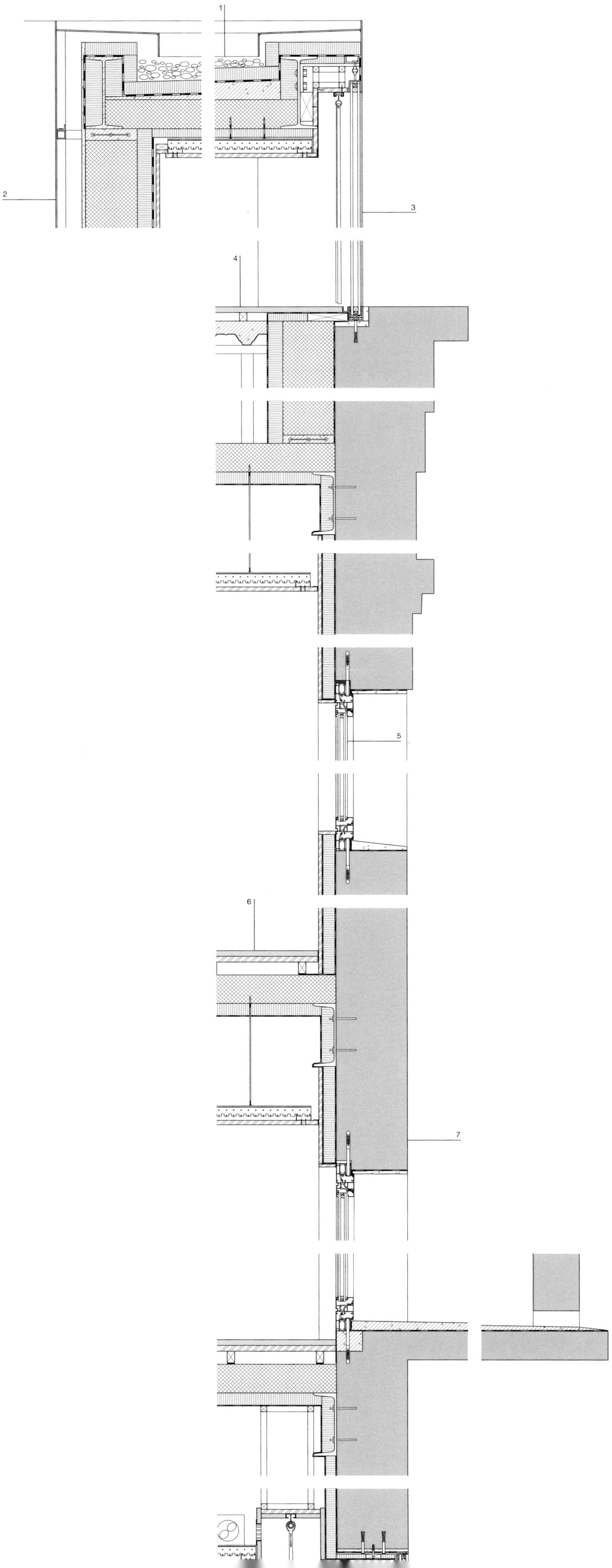

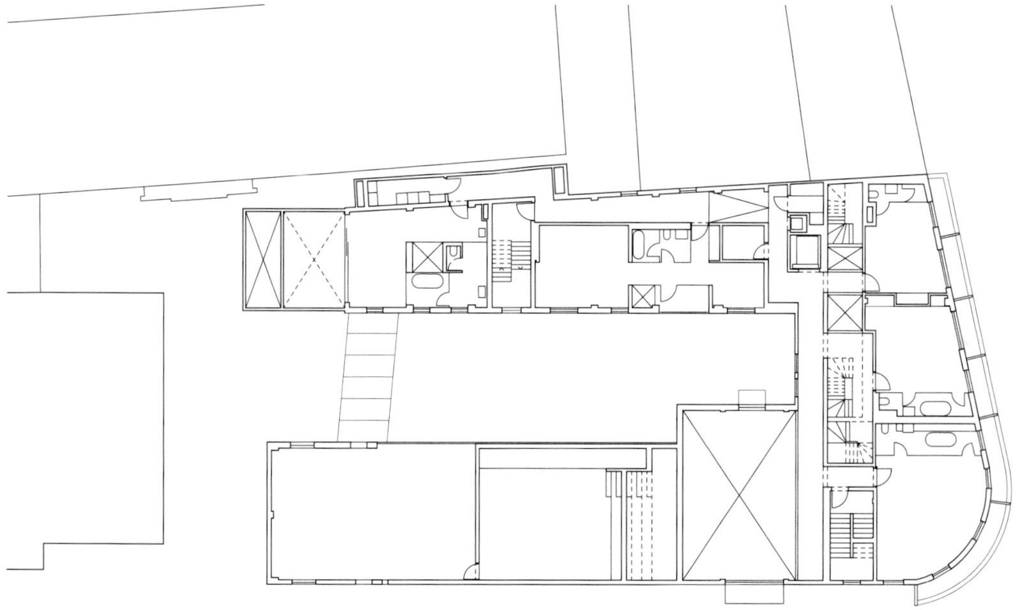

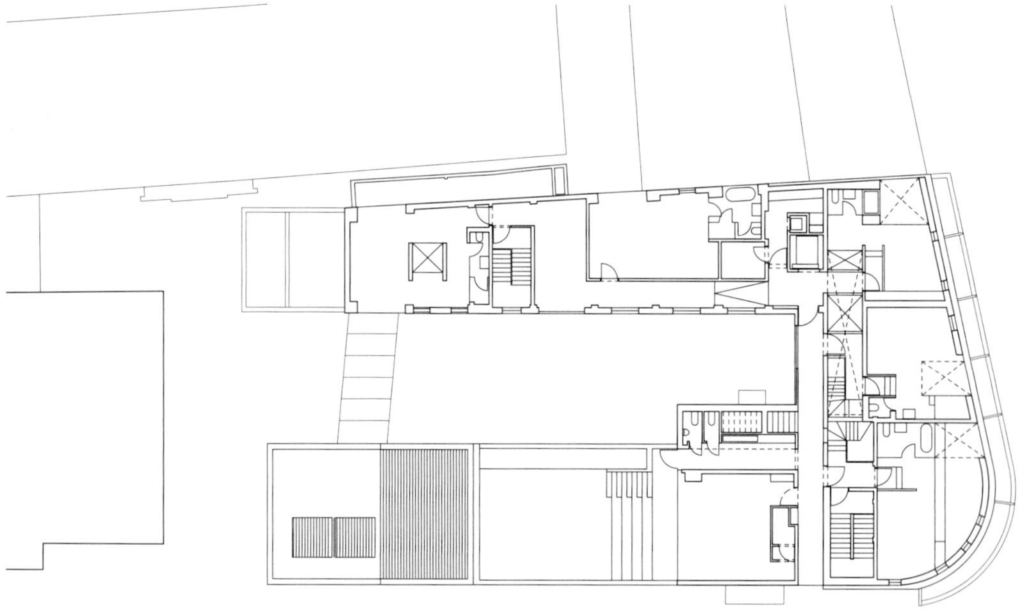

first-floor plan | second-floor plan | third-floor plan | fourth-floor plan   0   15m

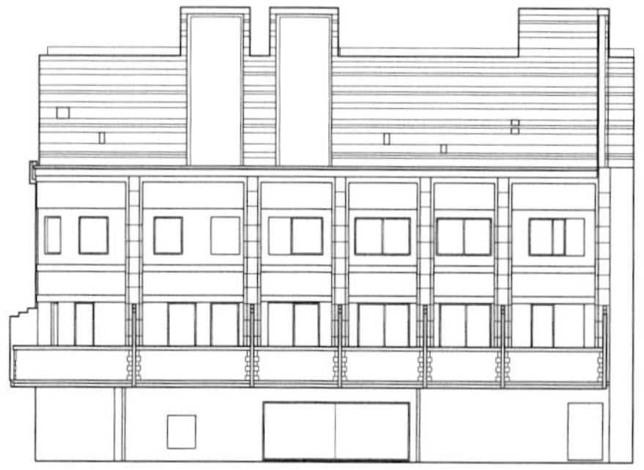

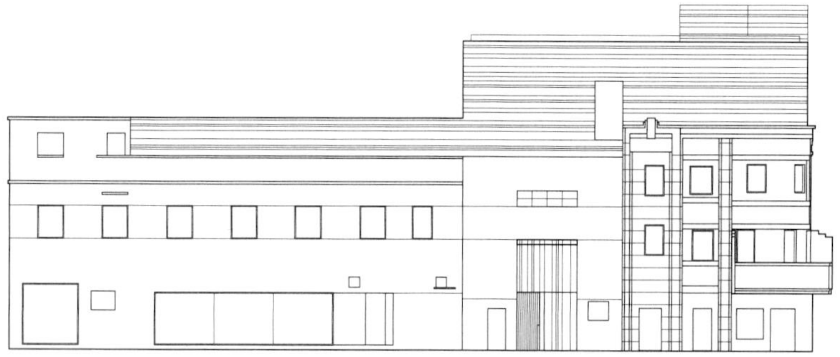

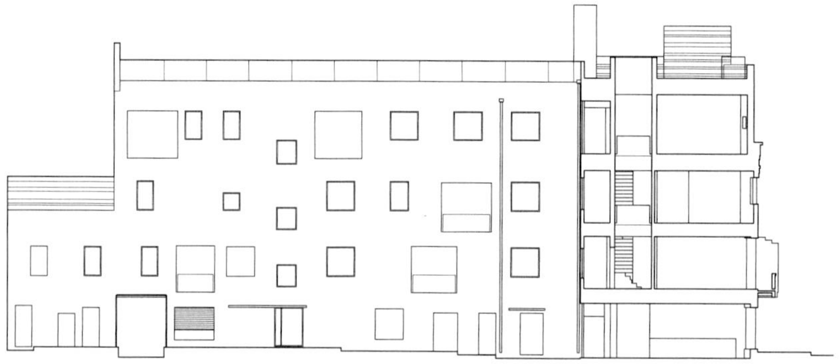

east elevation | south elevation | courtyard elevation   0   15m

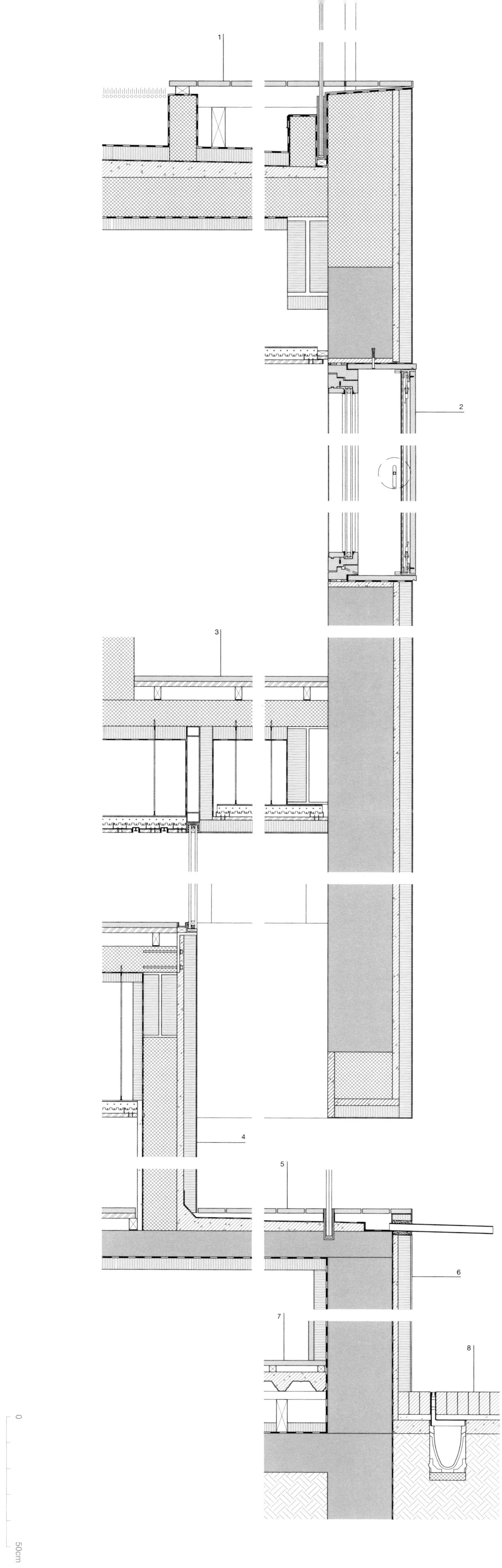

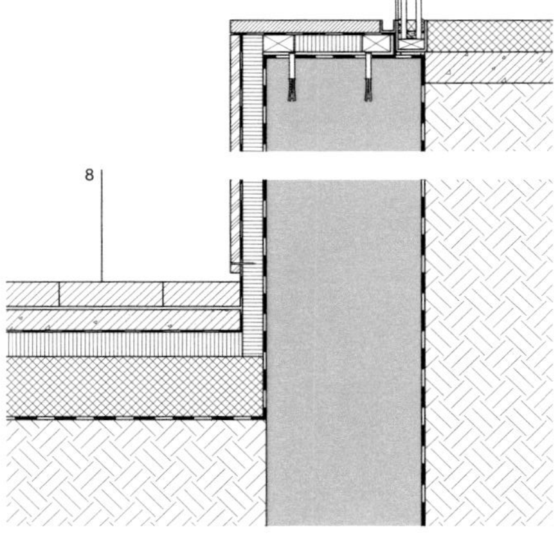

COURTYARD FACADE

1 Terrace floor structure
20-mm wood floorboard
Pressure treated sub-structure
5-mm polythene membrane
50-mm XPS rigid insulation
3-mm vapor barrier
Screed laid to falls
150-mm new concrete slab
5-mm polythene membrane
45-mm XPS rigid insulation

2 Wood window
20-mm wood board
Tensile steel cable cross bracing
6-mm fiber cement board
2-mm stainless steel, chrome mirror finish
160-mm cavity
6+15+6-mm double glazing

3 Room floor structure
20-mm wood floorboard
20-mm plywood
40-mm battens
5-mm sound insulation
100-mm existing concrete slab
50-mm XPS insulation
3-mm polythene membrane
250-mm Cavity
50-mm V-channel
15-mm gypsum board
45-mm XPS insulation
3-mm white render

4 Wall structure
White render
Mesh glued to insulation
45-mm XPS rigid board
25-mm cement leveling
100-mm new concrete block wall
3-mm polythene membrane
20-mm cement leveling

5 Balcony floor structure
18-mm Wood floorboard
70-mm battens with cavity
3-mm polythene membrane
Screed laid to falls, 5%
Existing reinforced concrete slab

6 Wall structure
5-mm white render
45-mm XPS board
20-mm screed
240-mm existing brick wall
5-mm polythene membrane
45-mm XPS board
20-mm wood baseboard

7 Floor structure
20-mm Wood floorboard
25-mm battens
35-mm lightweight concrete topping
40-mm profiled steel sheet
150-mm sub-structure with XPS rigid insulation
5-mm polythene membrane
Existing concrete base

8 Courtyard ground structure
86-mm recycled grey brick
20-mm mortar bed
55-mm screed leveling
ACO brickslot
Rammed earth

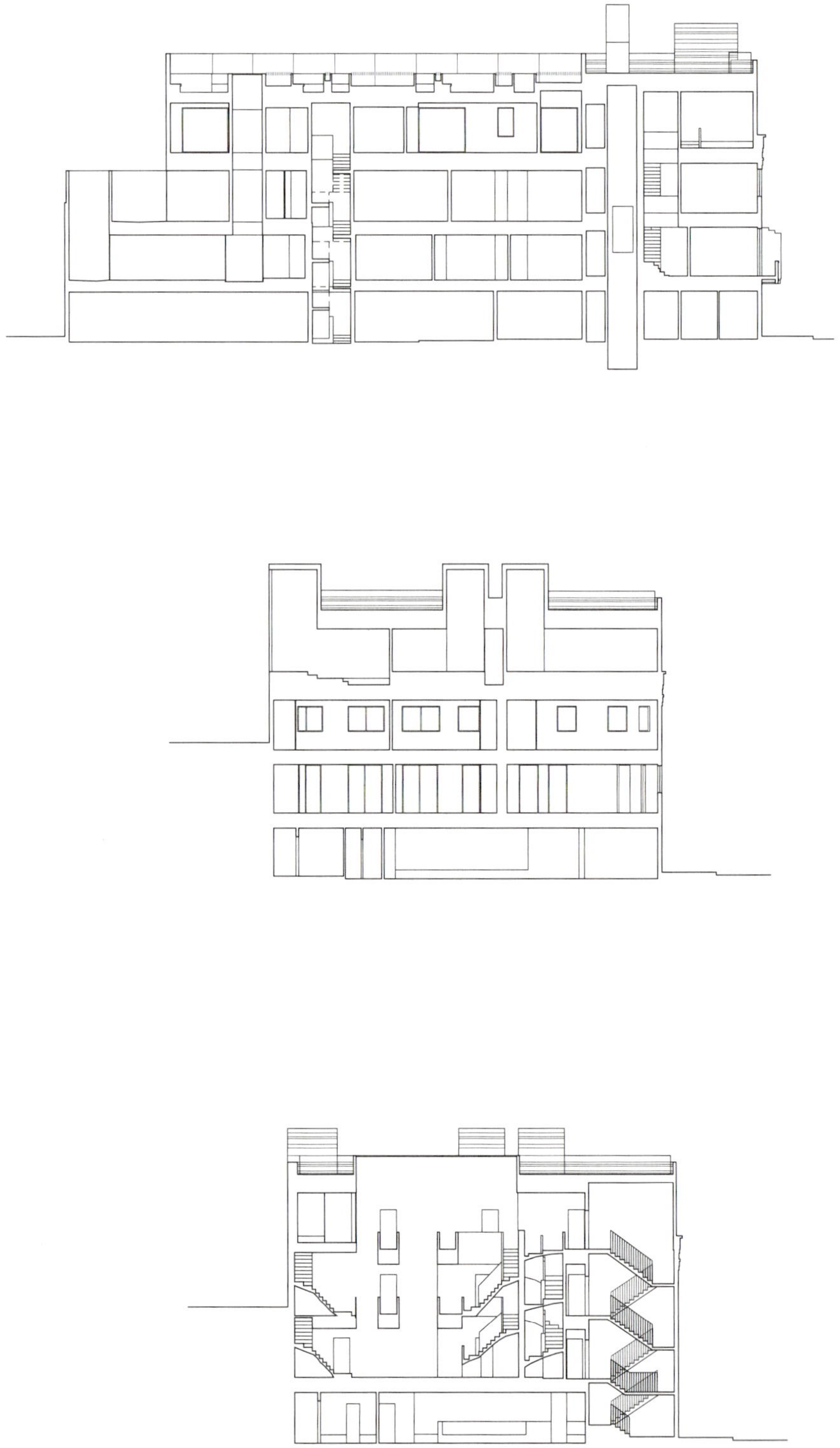

section A | section B | section C

0   15m

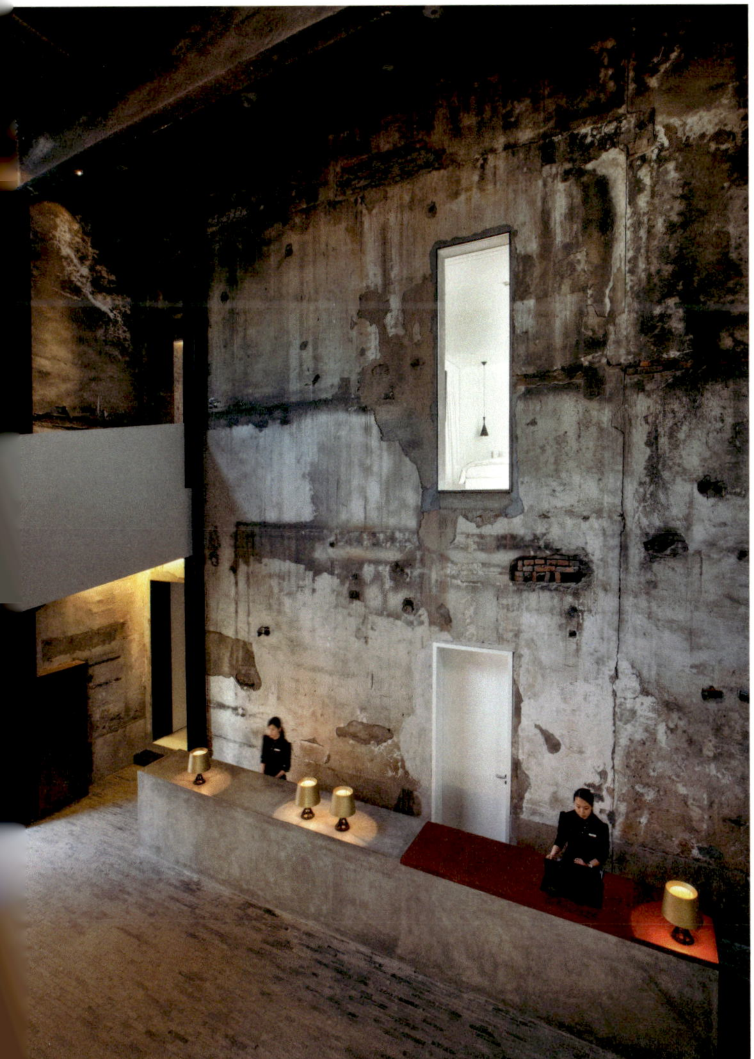

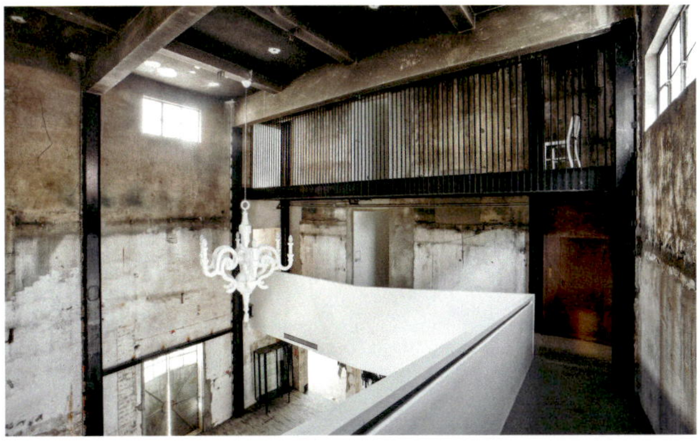

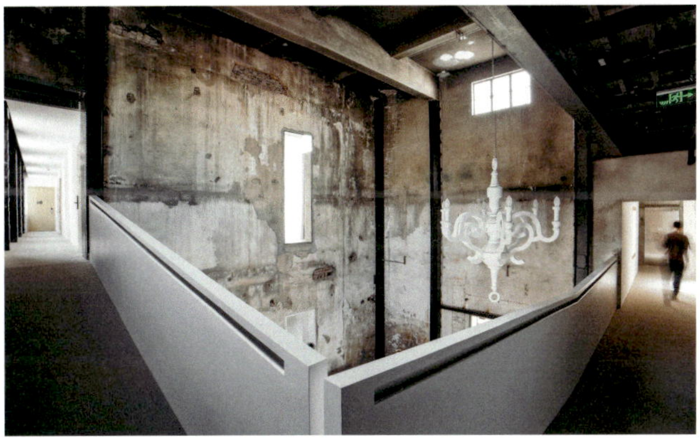

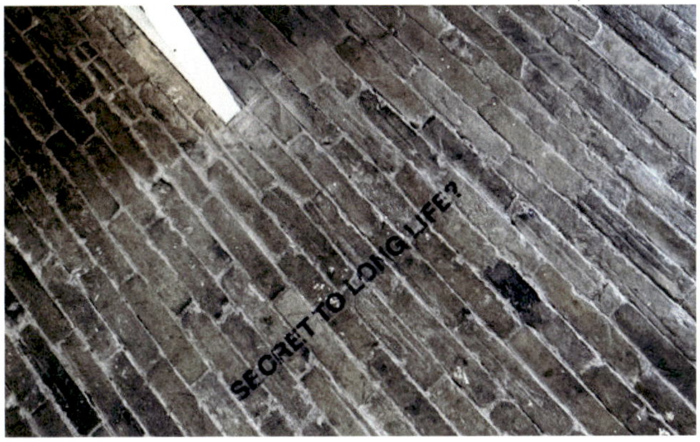
SECRET TO LONG LIFE?

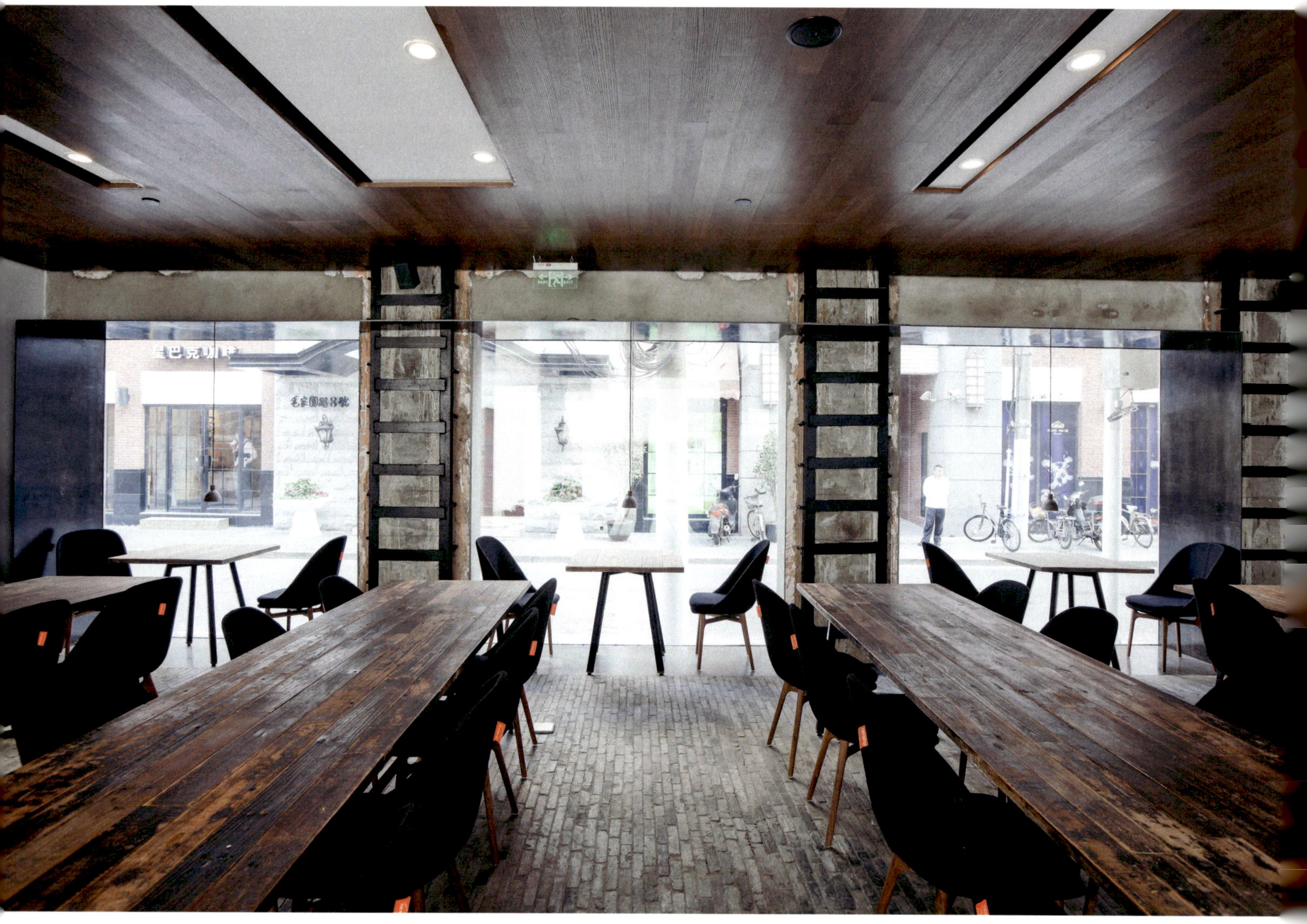

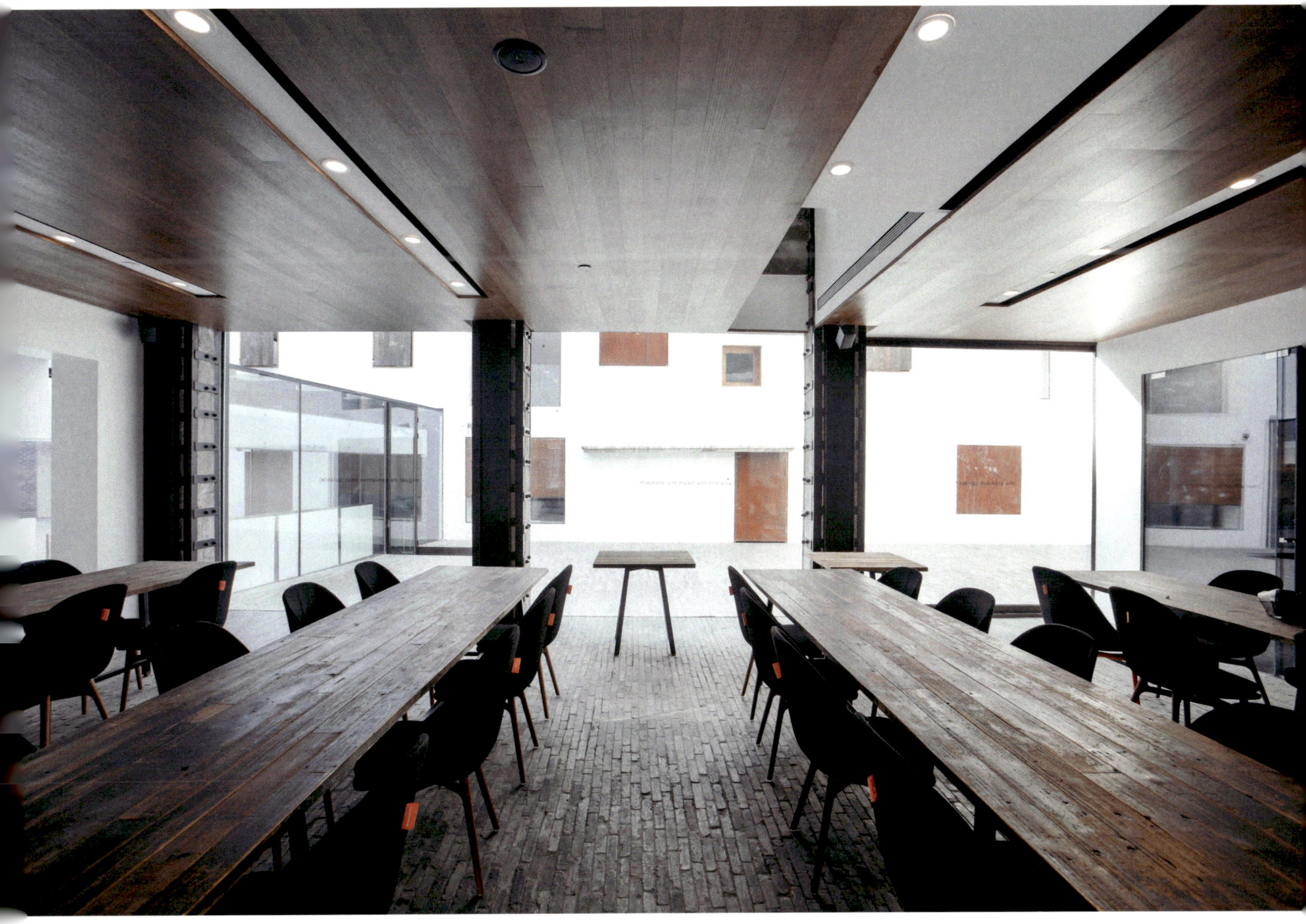

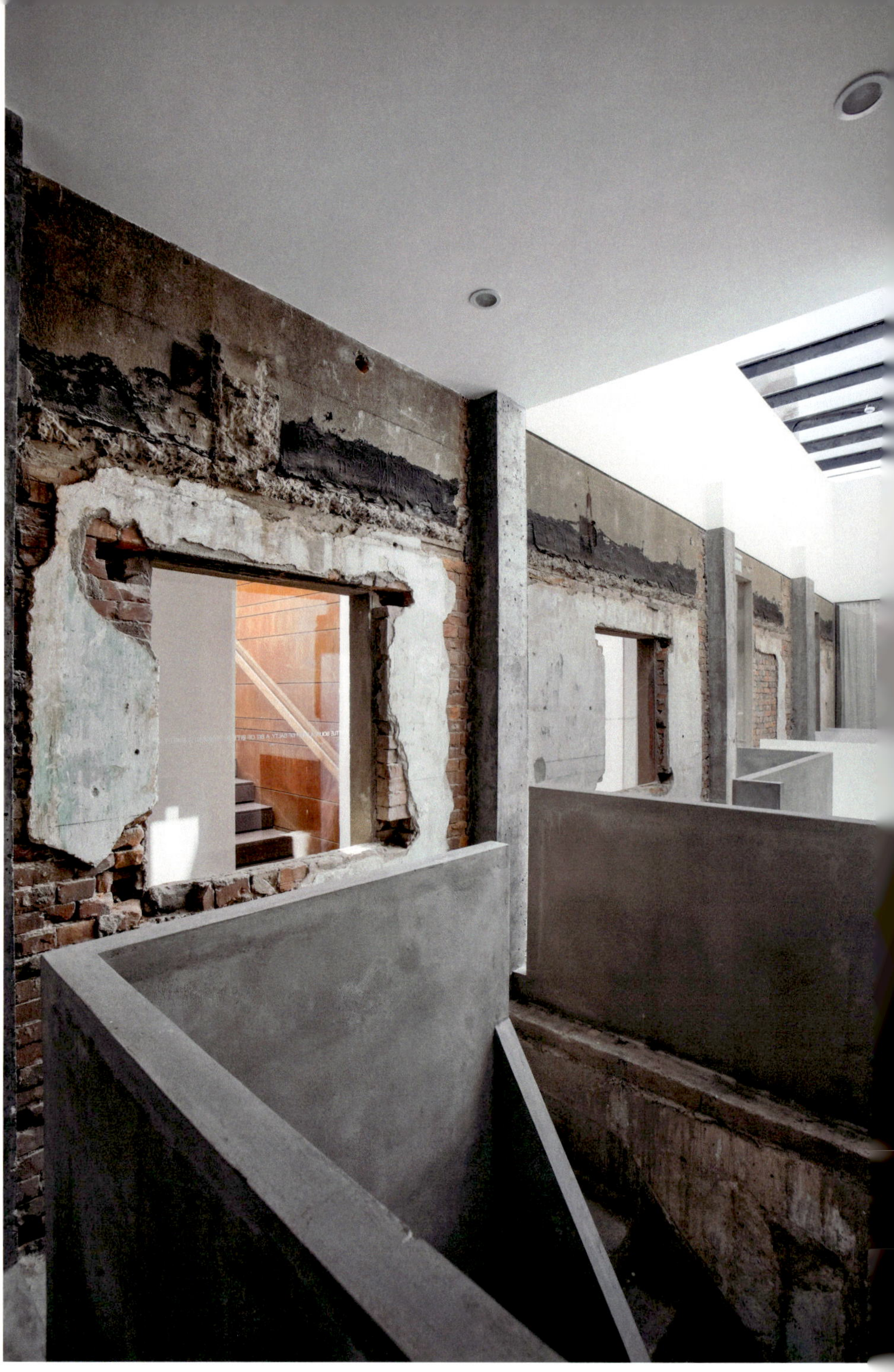

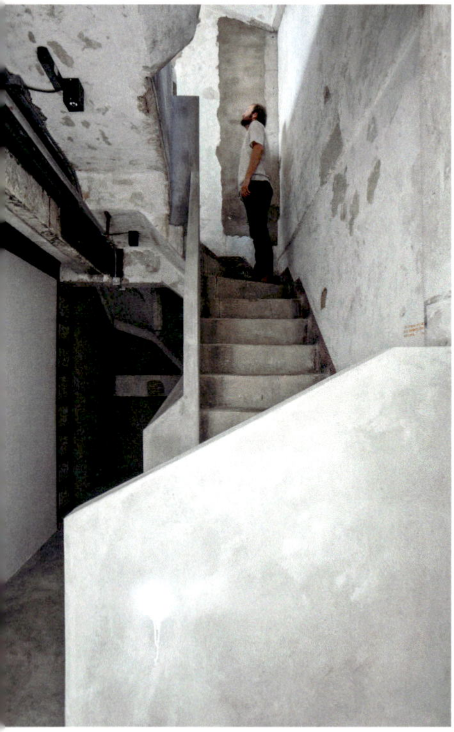

"As long as you don't stop climbing, the stairs won't end…"   - Franz Kafka

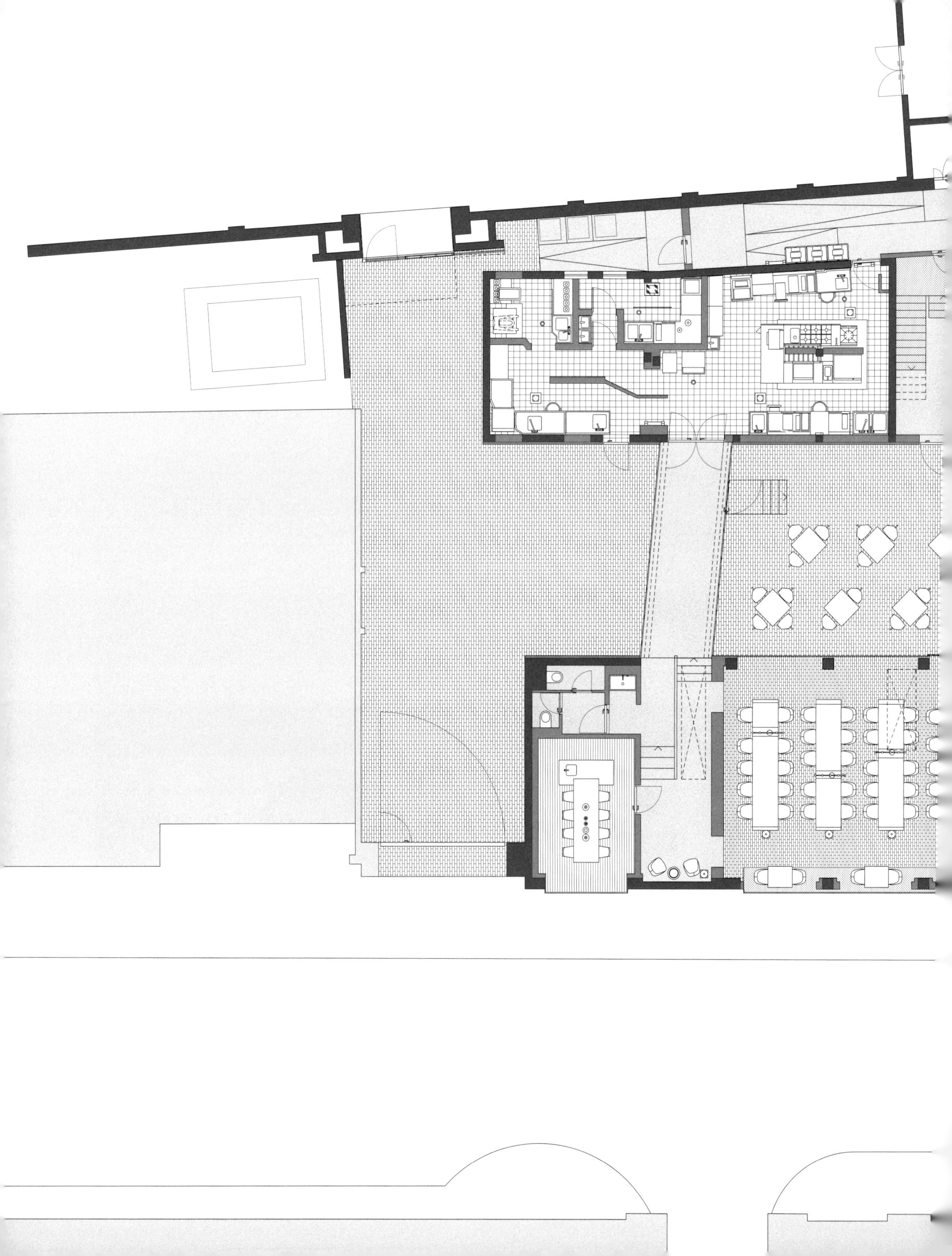

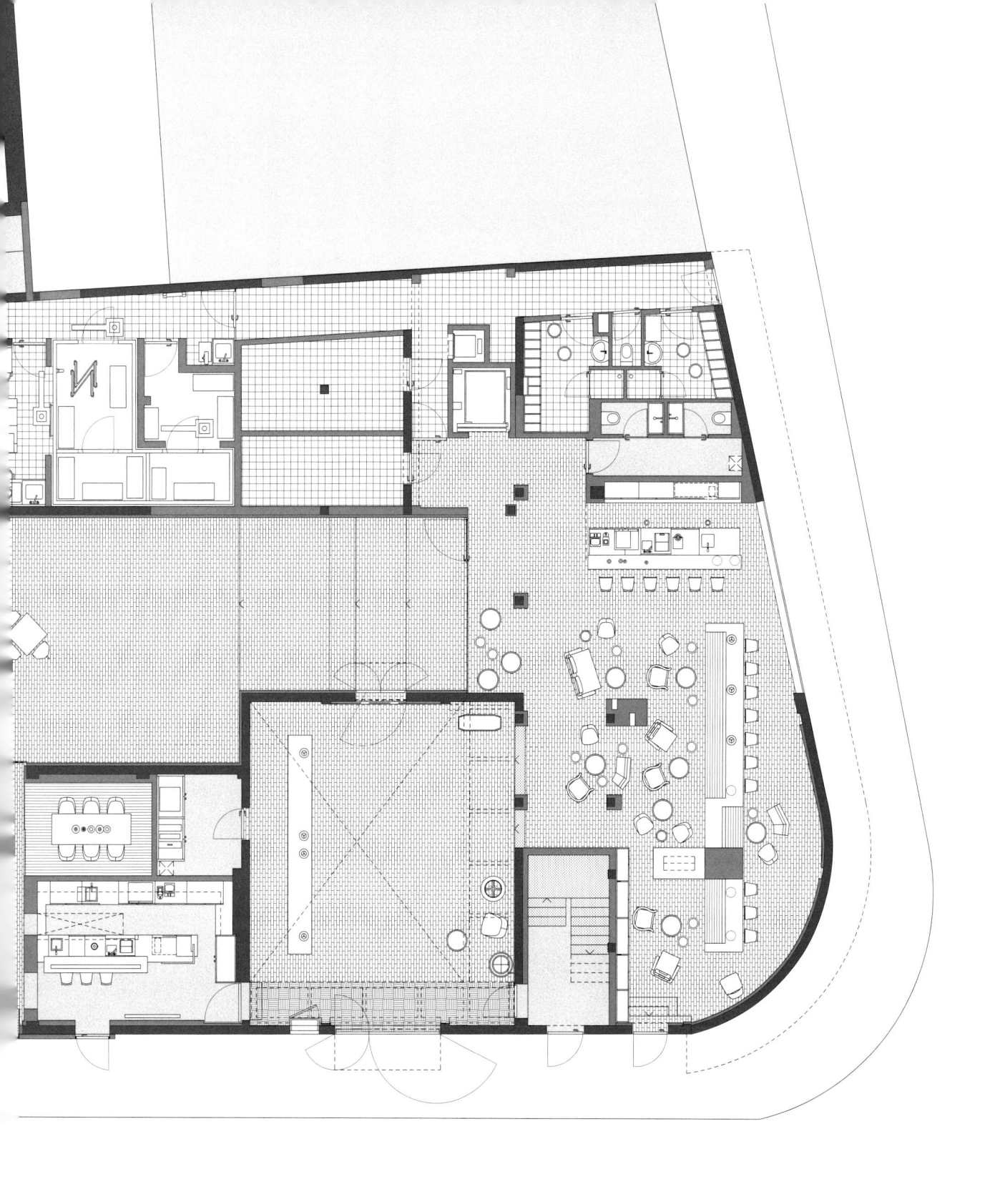

ground-floor plan

62

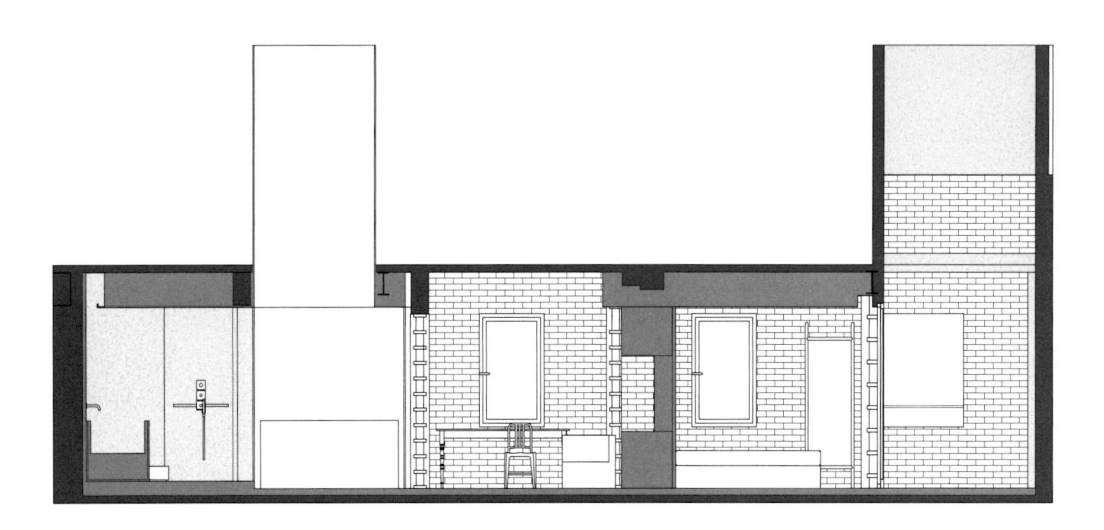

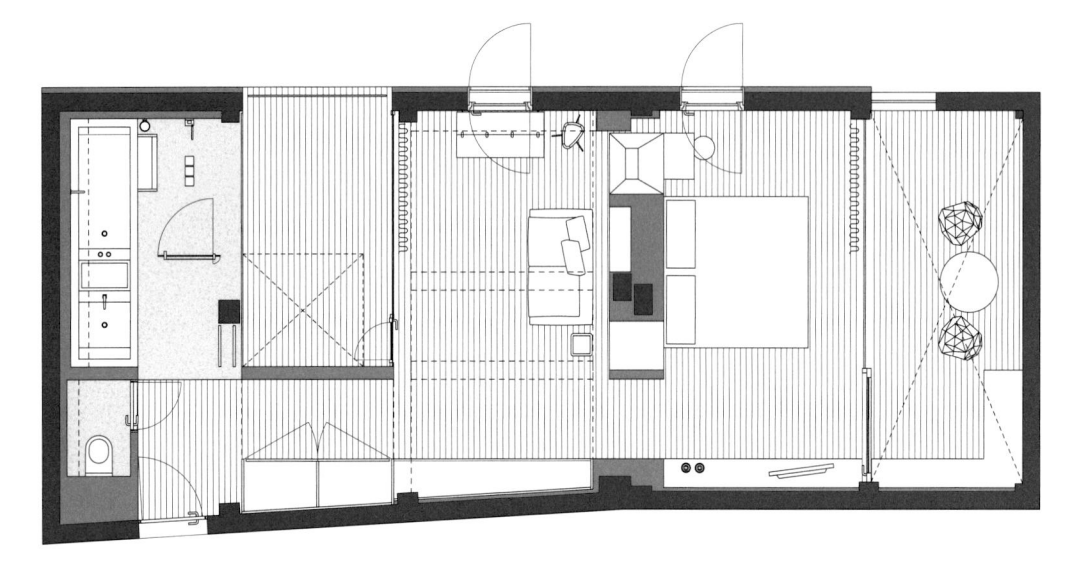

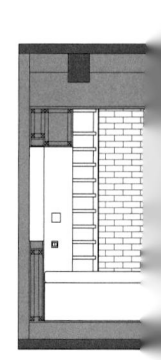

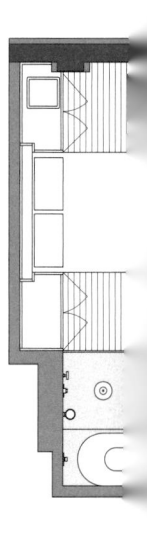

room 11 | room 18 | room 33 | plan and elevation

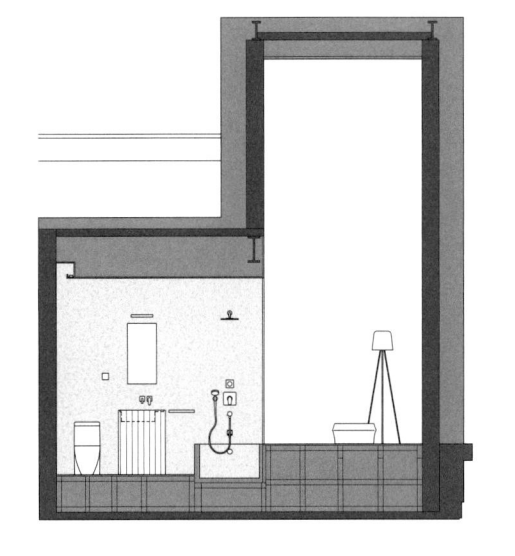

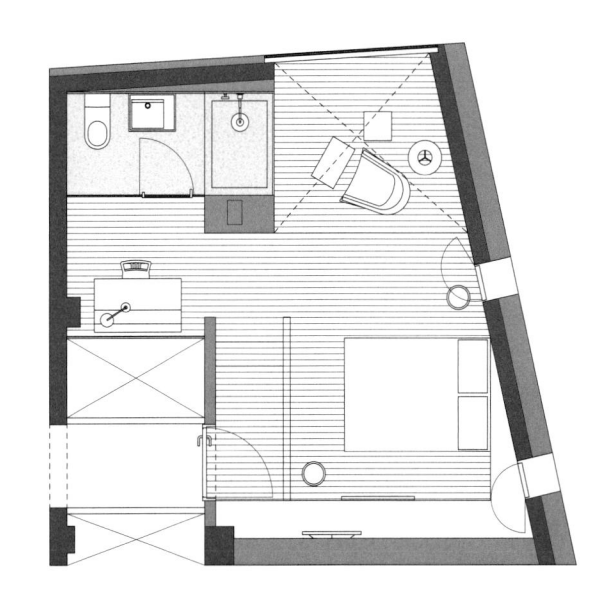

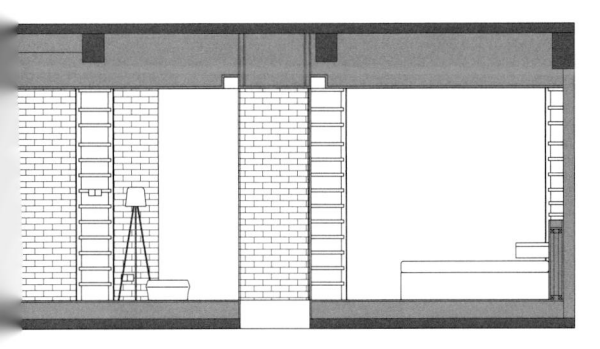

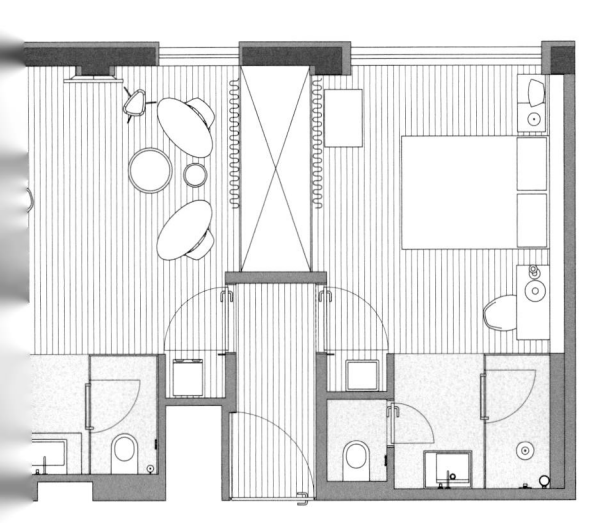

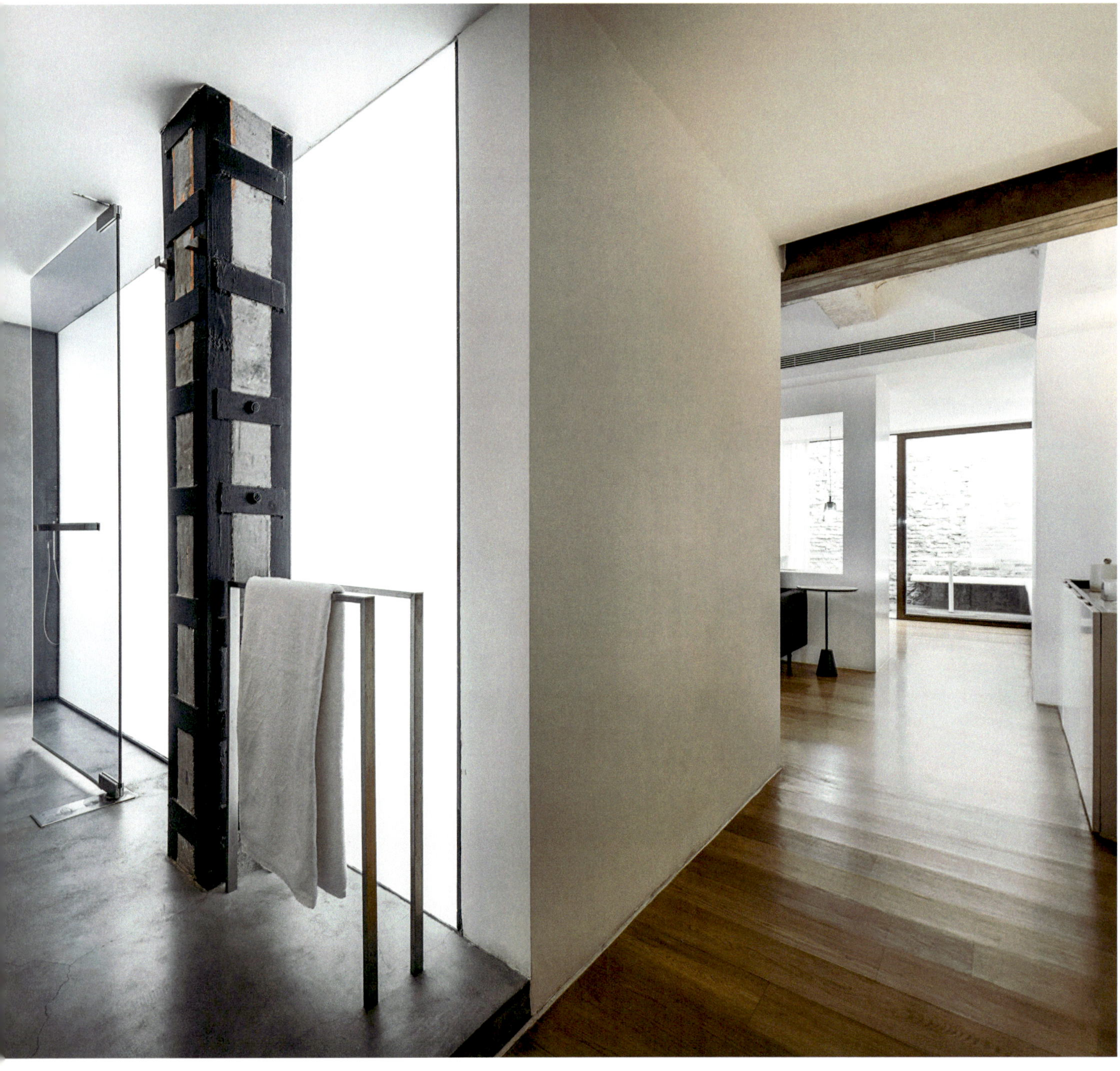

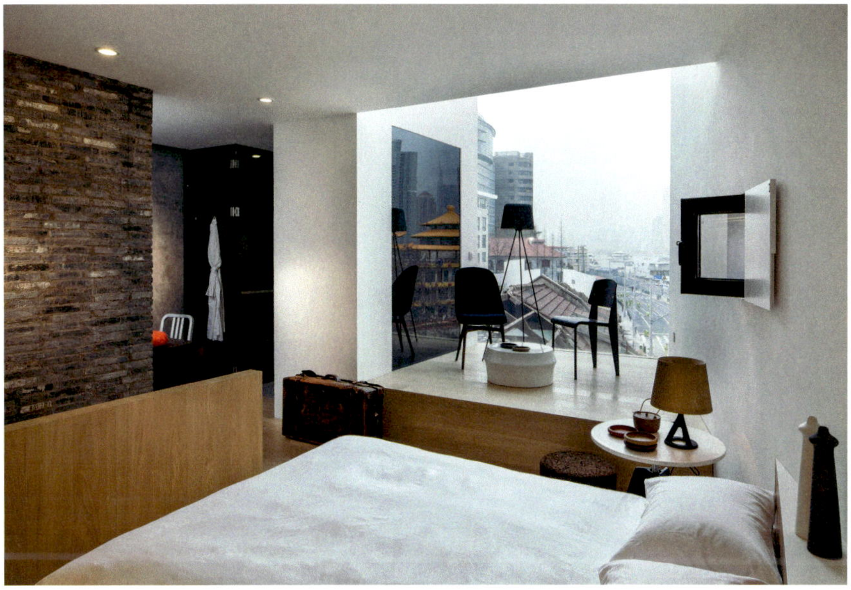

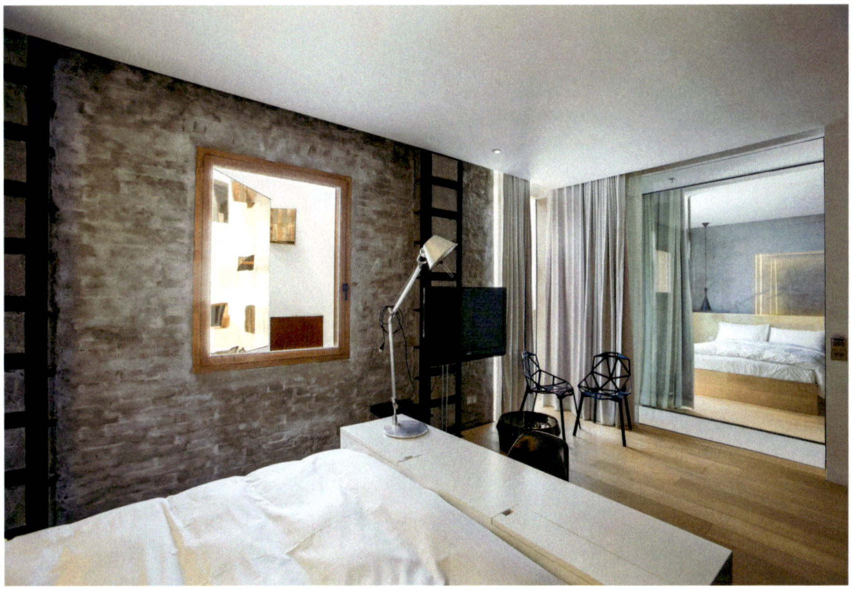

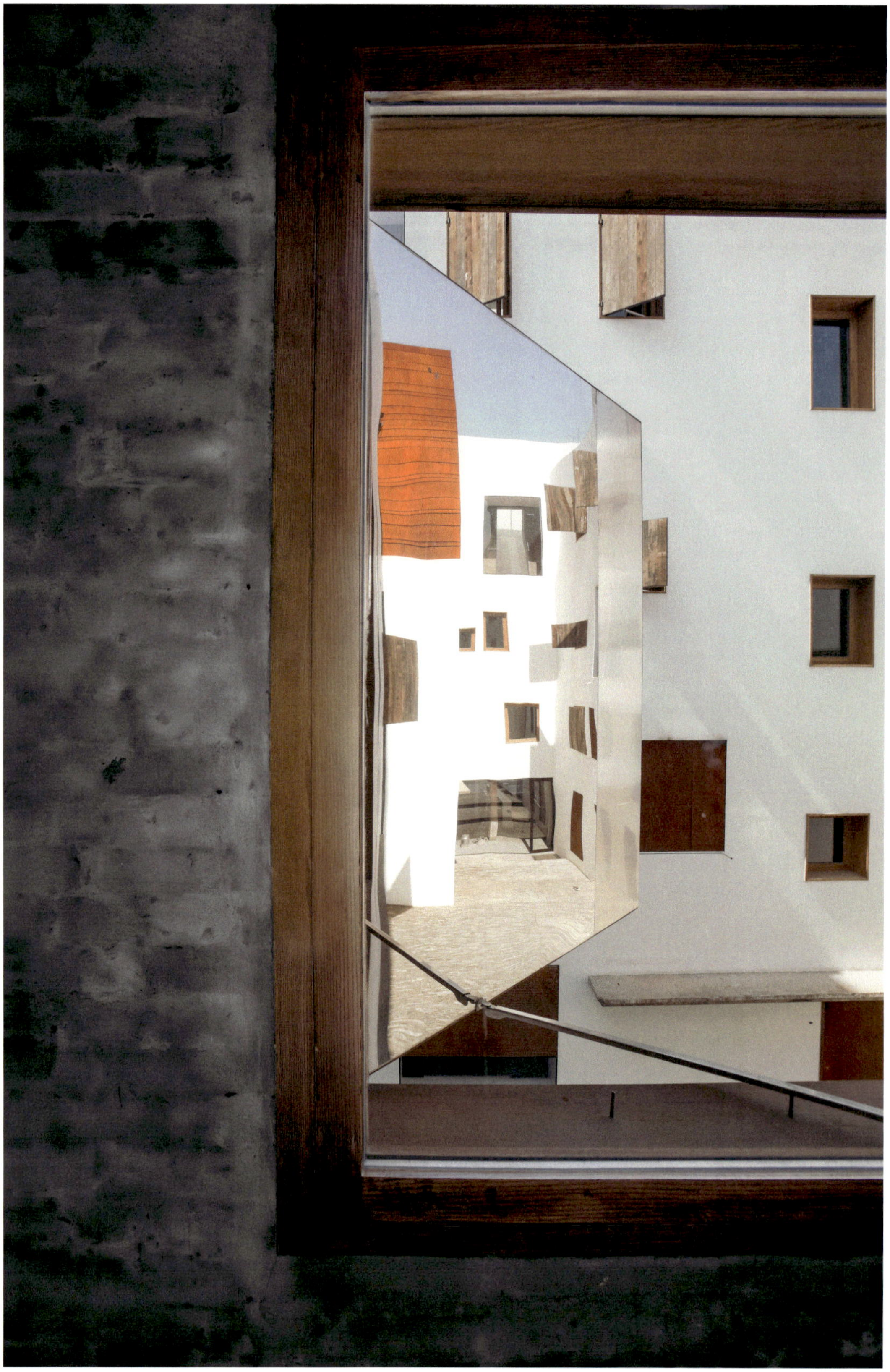

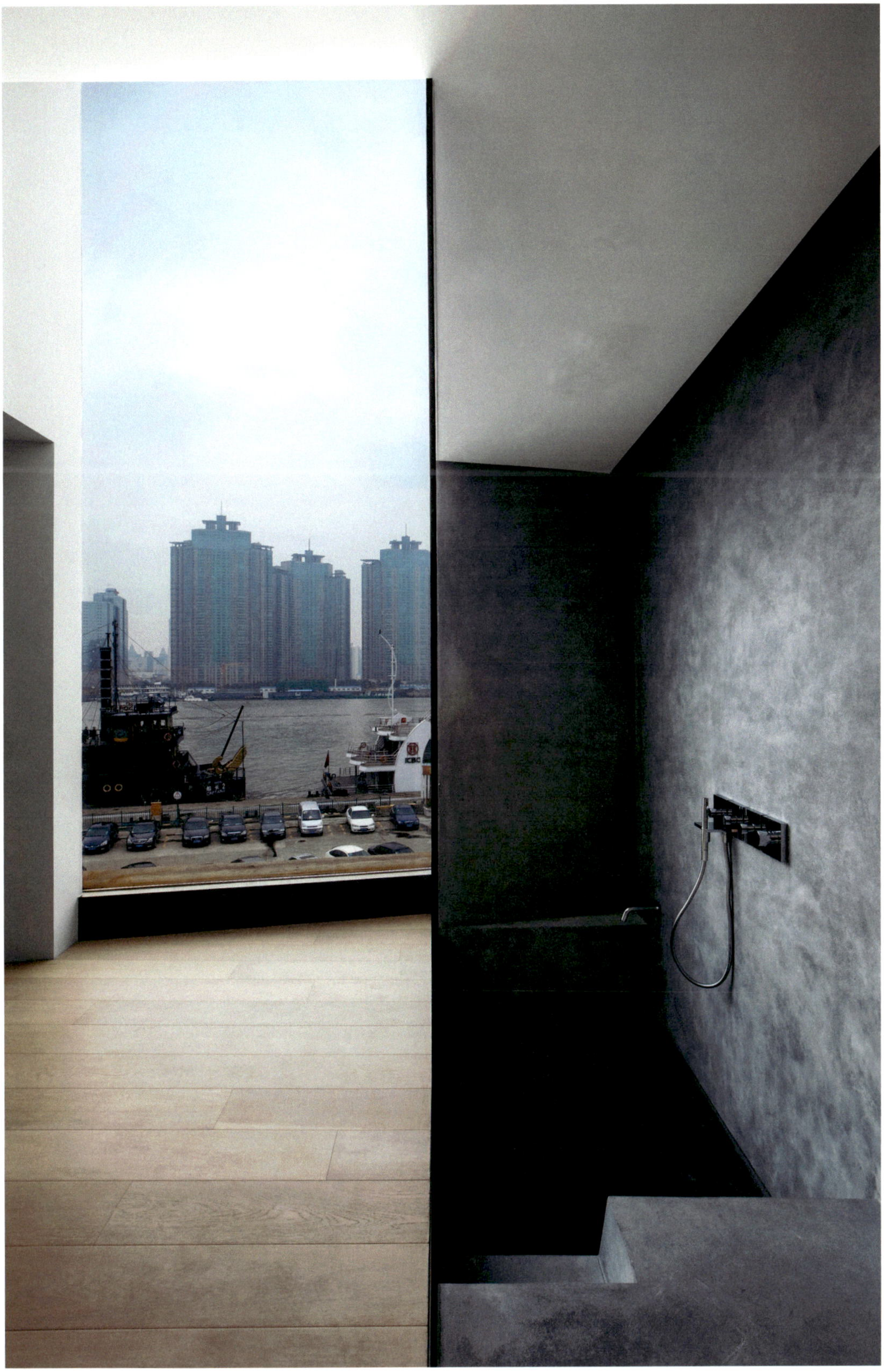

THE BLACK BOX
Neri&Hu + Design Republic Offices, Shanghai

We started out in a box, a concrete box. We found our first office by chance in a small lane; it had a raw concrete shell that used to be a small printing factory. Through the blurred seasons of Shanghai we suddenly grew from a firm of ten people to over 100. So we moved to another box, a black box this time. We affectionately named the project the "black box," liking the implied metaphor of the practice as a crucial recording device of all our design ideas, but the choice of the color was more intentional than that, a decision based on context, or rather anti-context. On our very quiet residential street in the former French Concession, the color palette is predominantly beige and white, a remnant of mid-century colonial-style houses, many of which are protected and quite well preserved in this area. Though we appreciate and take pleasure in the low density and charming streetscape that is a result of Shanghai's colonial past, we are constantly searching for new ways to represent a modern Chinese culture, so we were intent on breaking away from the immediate context.

The project contains not only the offices of Neri&Hu, the design practice, but an outlet of our retail platform Design Republic and their offices, too. We wanted to outwardly express all the components that make up our company, so each element could be visually distinguished. The wood represents Design Republic, expressed as a band across the ground floor, with a gap that delineates our main entrance and is a way to extend the street into the building. The interior of the third floor, which houses Design Republic's office space is also clad in seamless oak panels to maintain material consistency. Along the side of the building the opaque part of the black volume contains all the vertical circulation, stairs and elevator. And the main portion of the black box, of course, is the work space of Neri&Hu. Dealing with an existing building, there were certain limitations and one of those was that we could not alter the window openings. So, to give a fresh look to the rather mundane facade, we built out window frame boxes in thin metal, and the simple action of painting the inner surface in white gives the feeling of a skin peeling from inside. At night the windows glow quite brightly due to the white lining, and the whole building becomes a beacon in the neighborhood.

site map

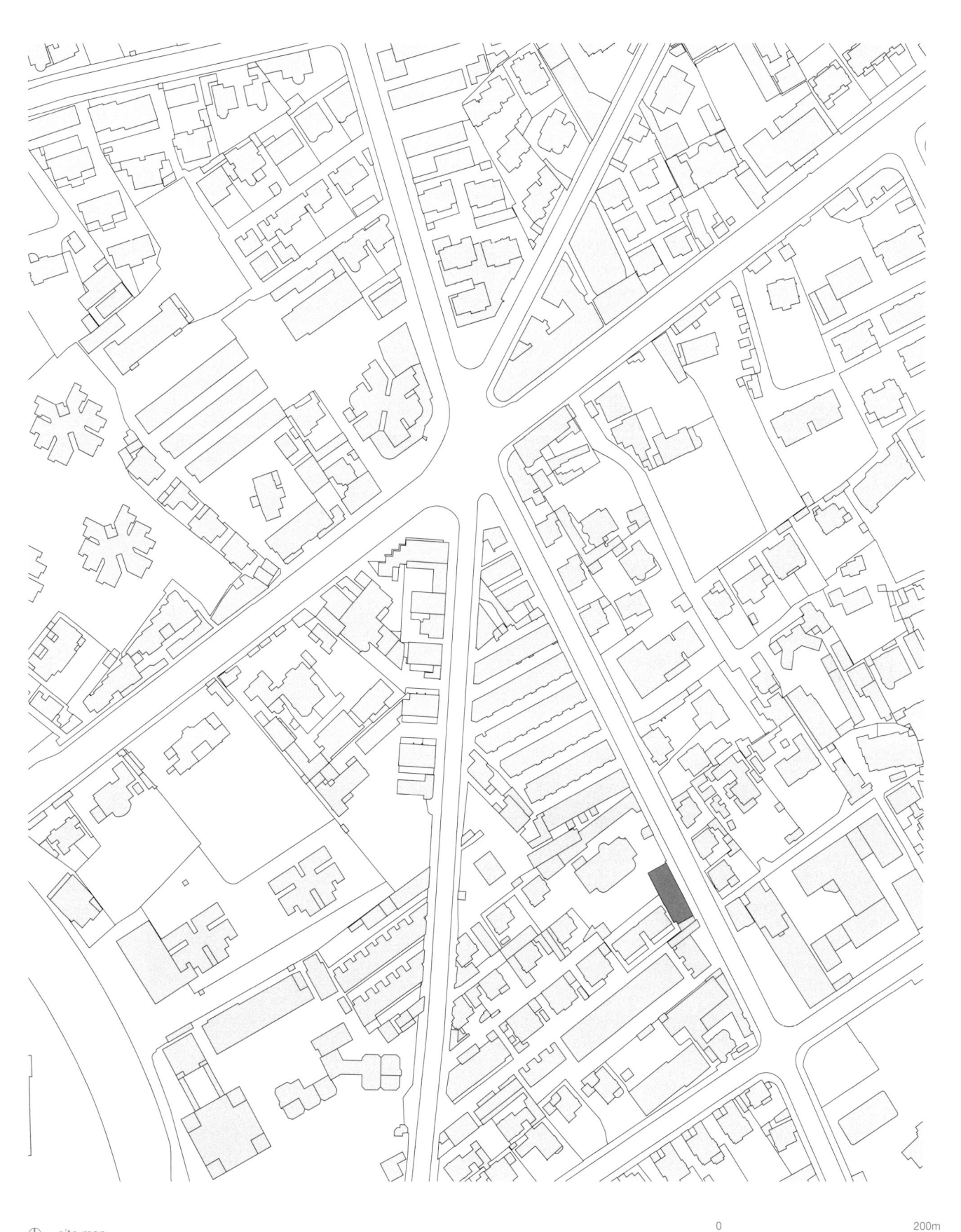

0 200m

In the interior, while maintaining the structural integrity of the existing building, we made a few cuts into the slab in key areas—the main conference room and the fourth-floor reception—which brings a lot of visual and social dynamism to our working environment. We separated out support functions like toilets and pantries to the back side of the building and left the rest as an open office, so that our designers can interact and exchange ideas freely. Enclosed in glass, our meeting rooms where we receive guests are very much visually connected to the workspace, so that clients can get a real sense of how we work and who we are. For graphics, we kept things quite simple and minimal, but with a twist—like labeling each room with its dimensions, rather than a name, so that people can use it as a reference or visual cue when discussing design.

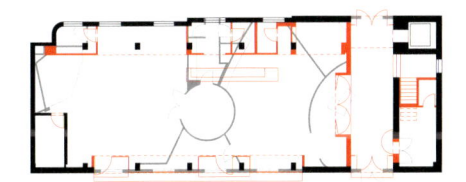

demolition plan | section

0 15m

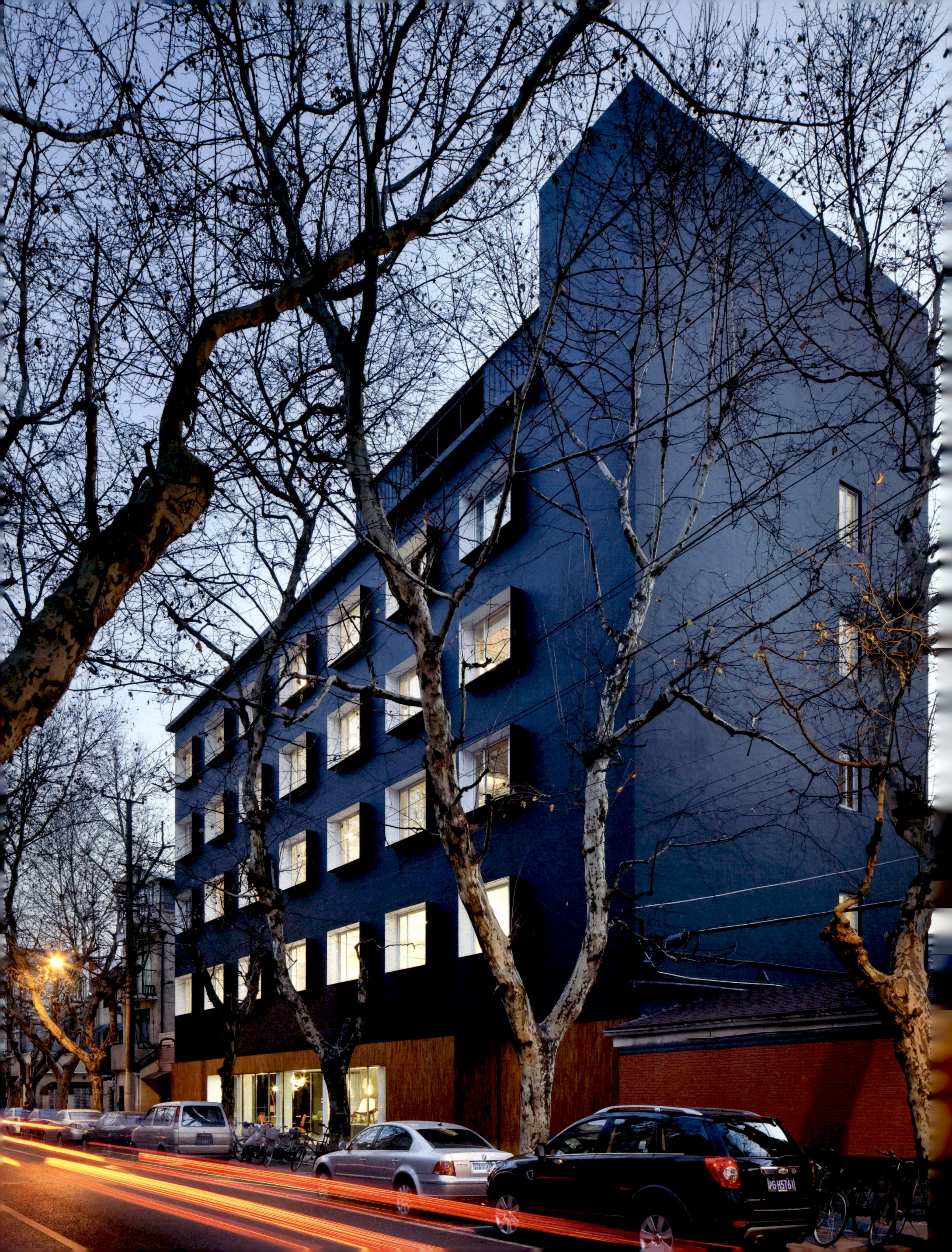

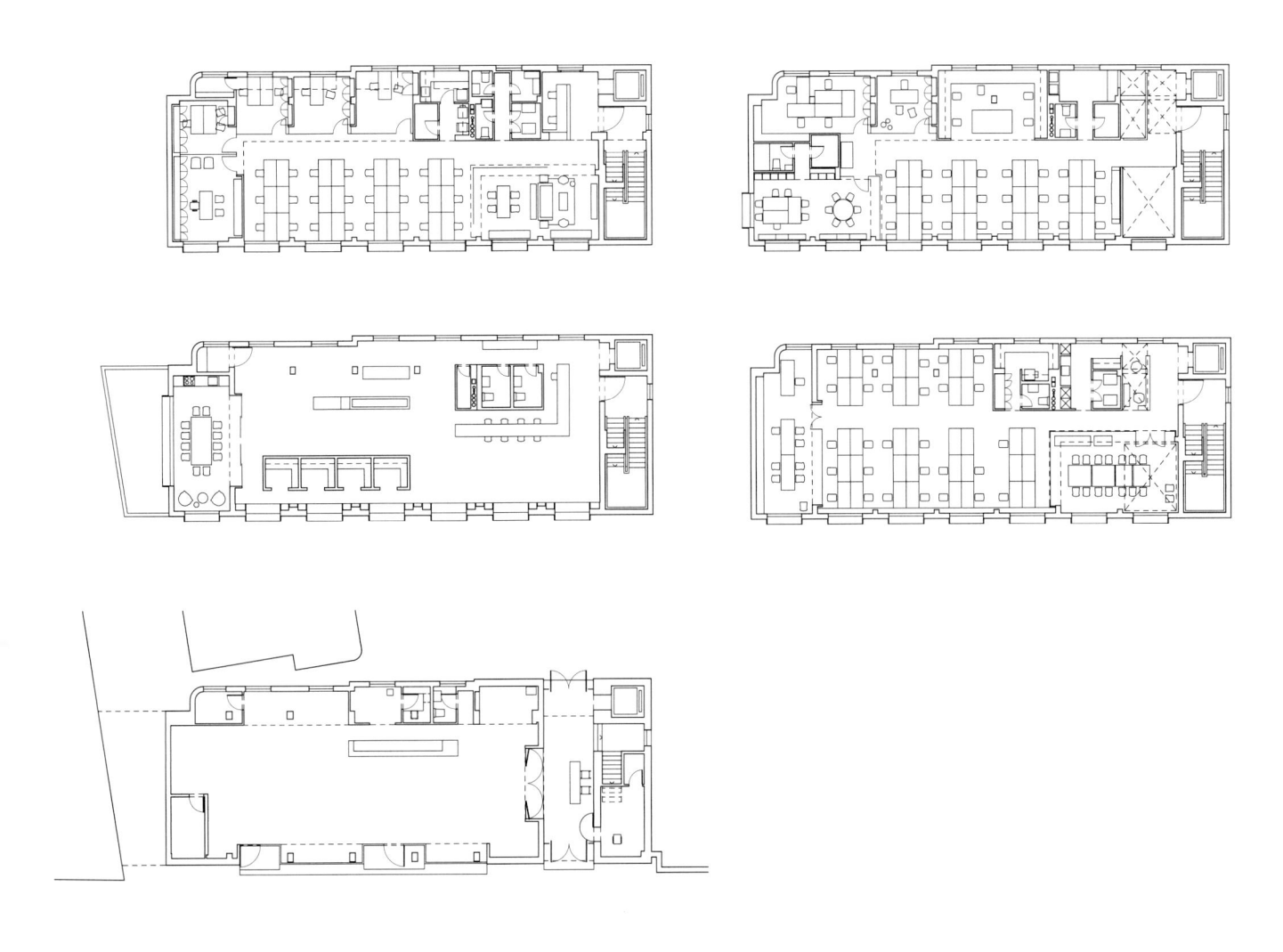

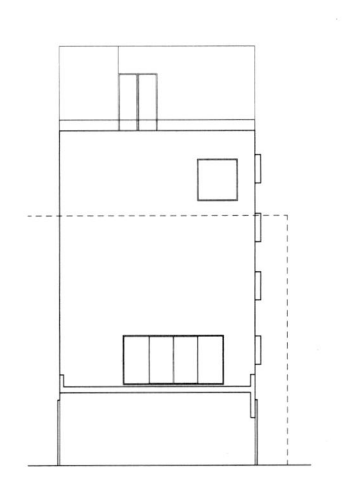

ground- to third-floor plan | east and south elevation

74

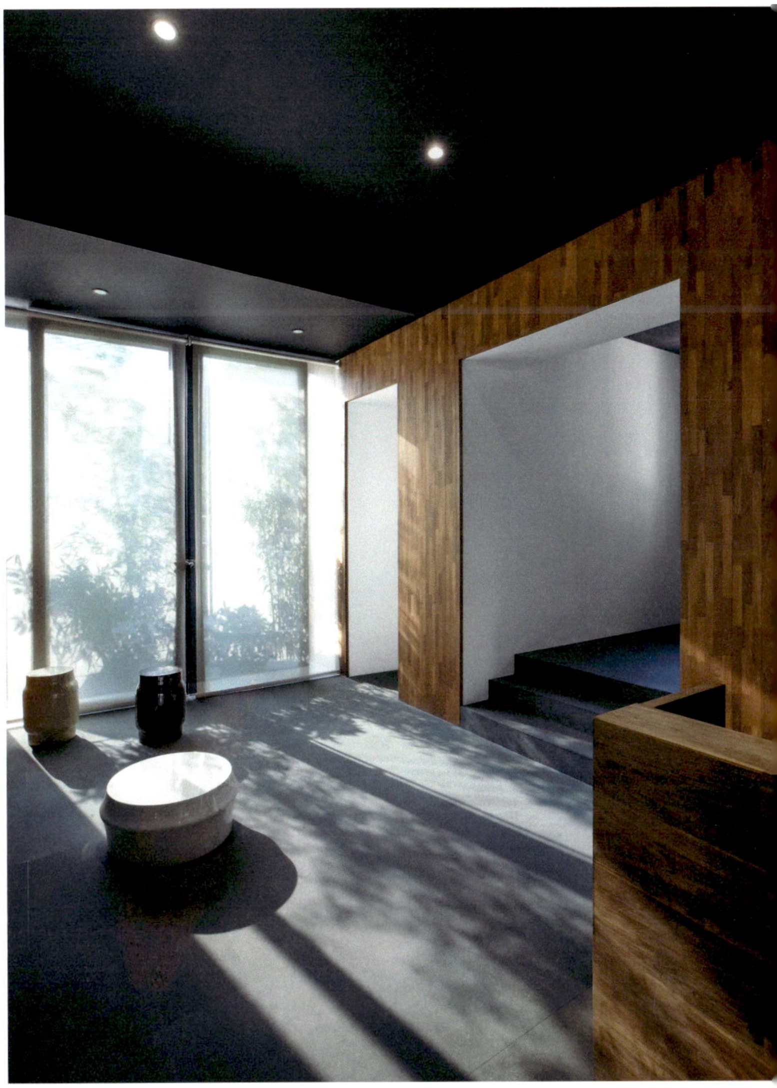
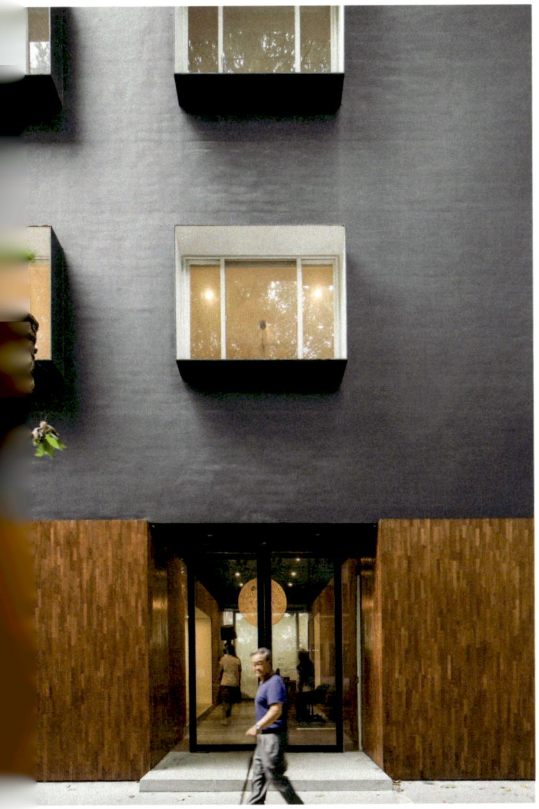

ground-floor plan

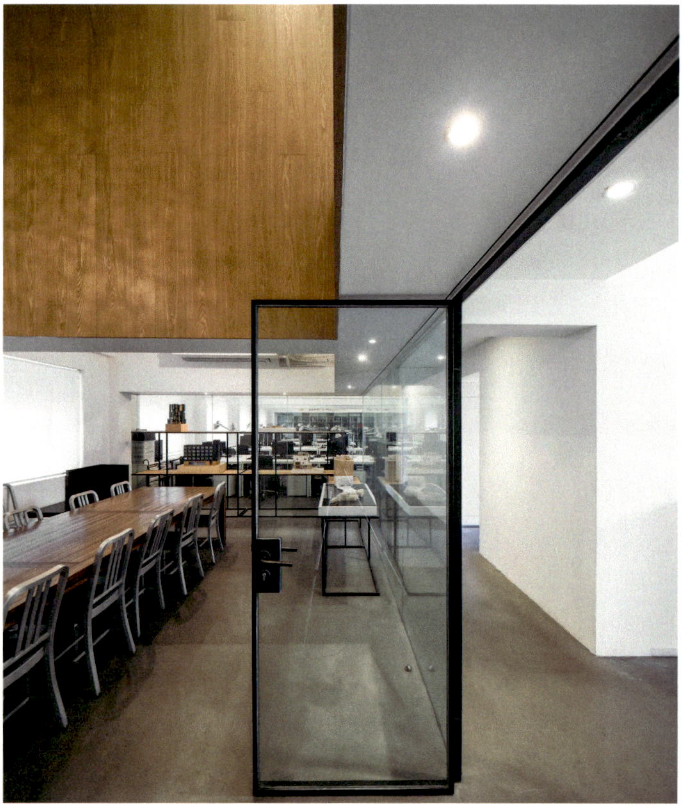

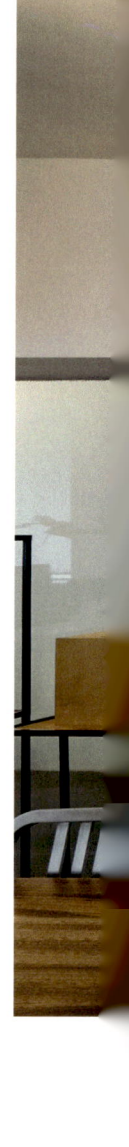

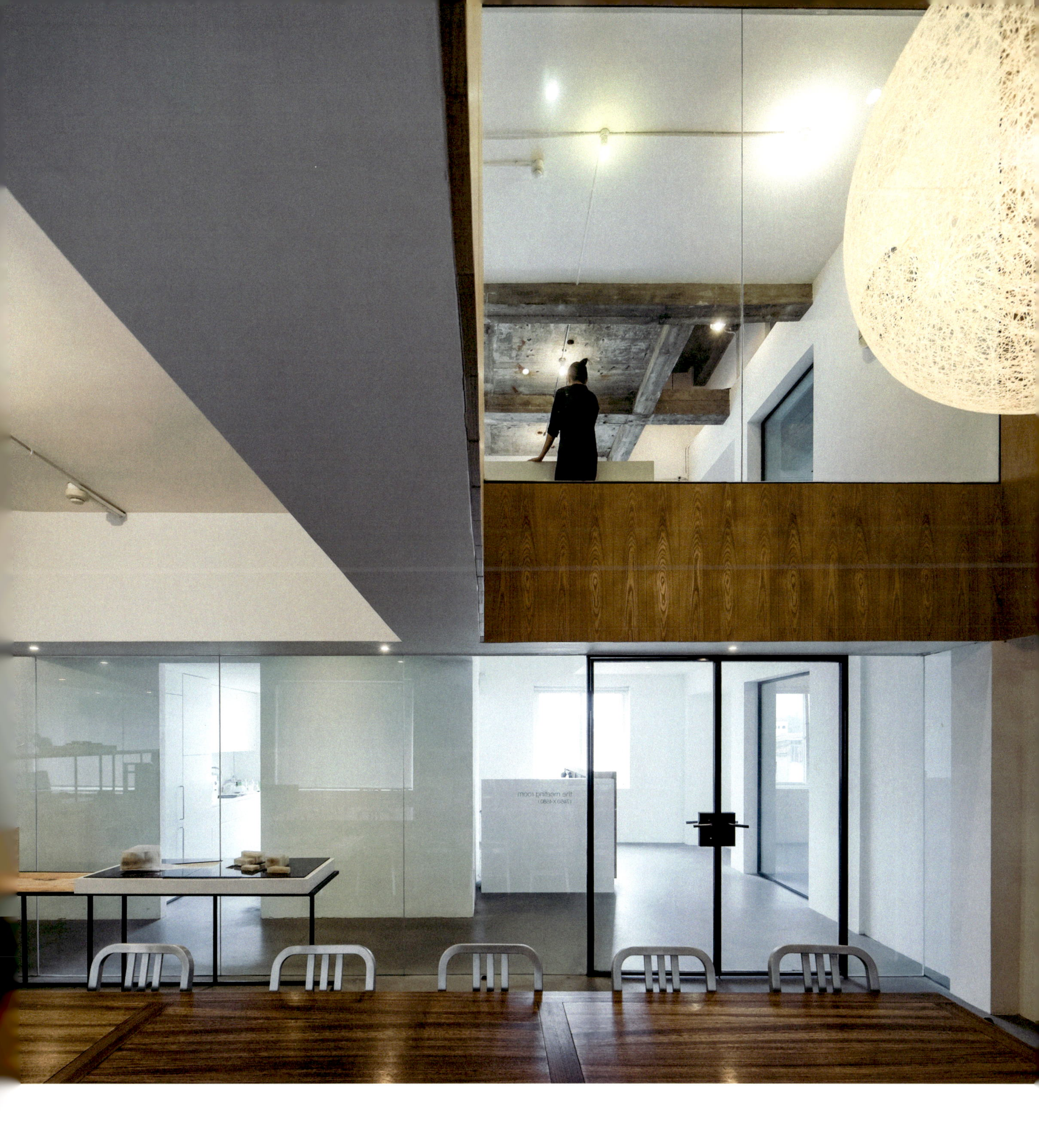

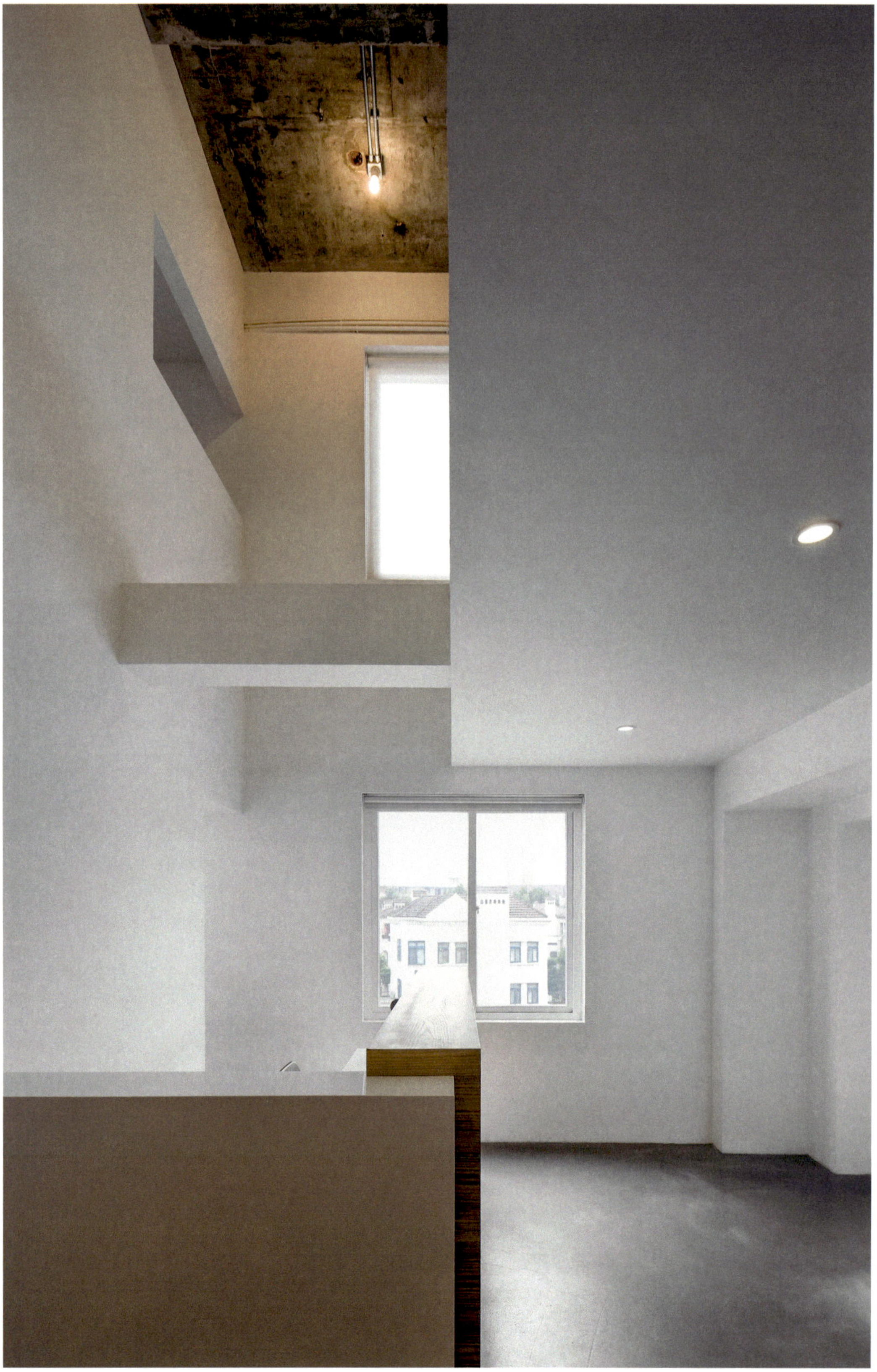

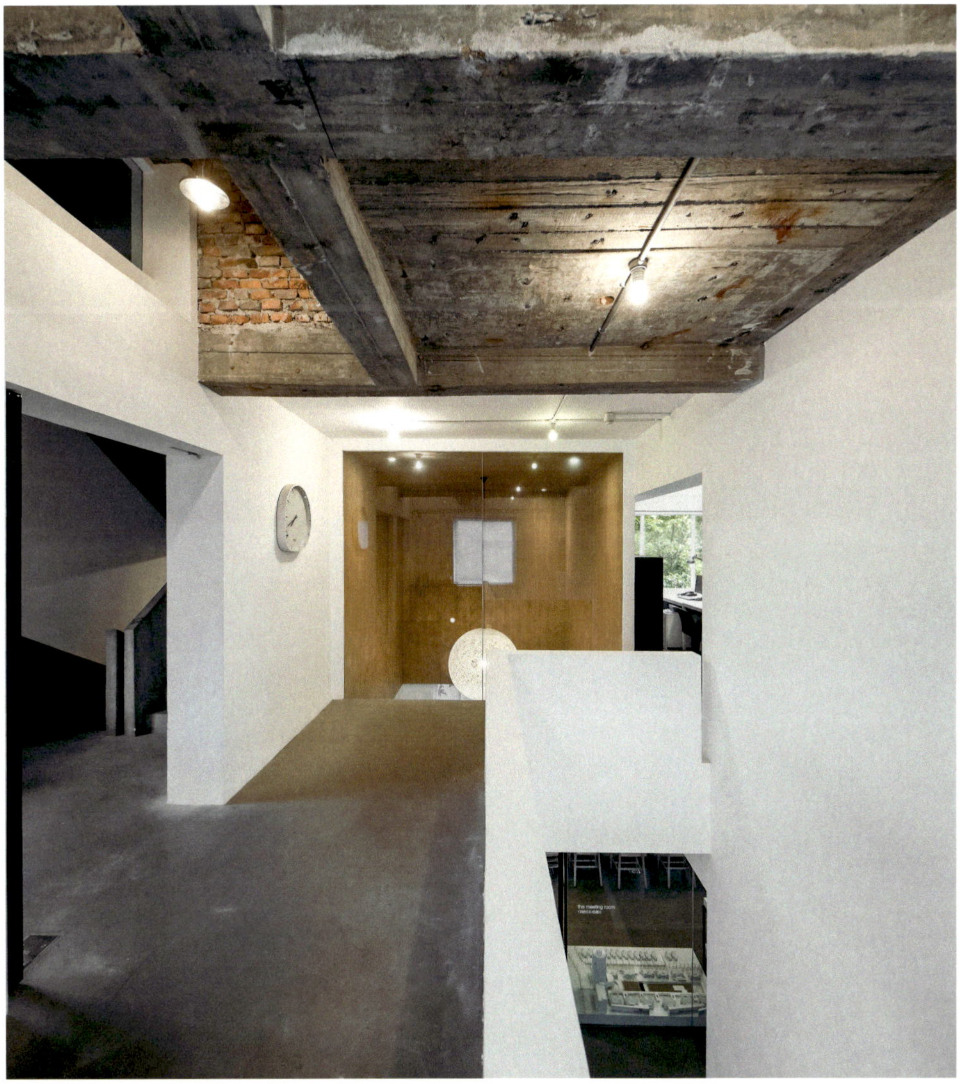

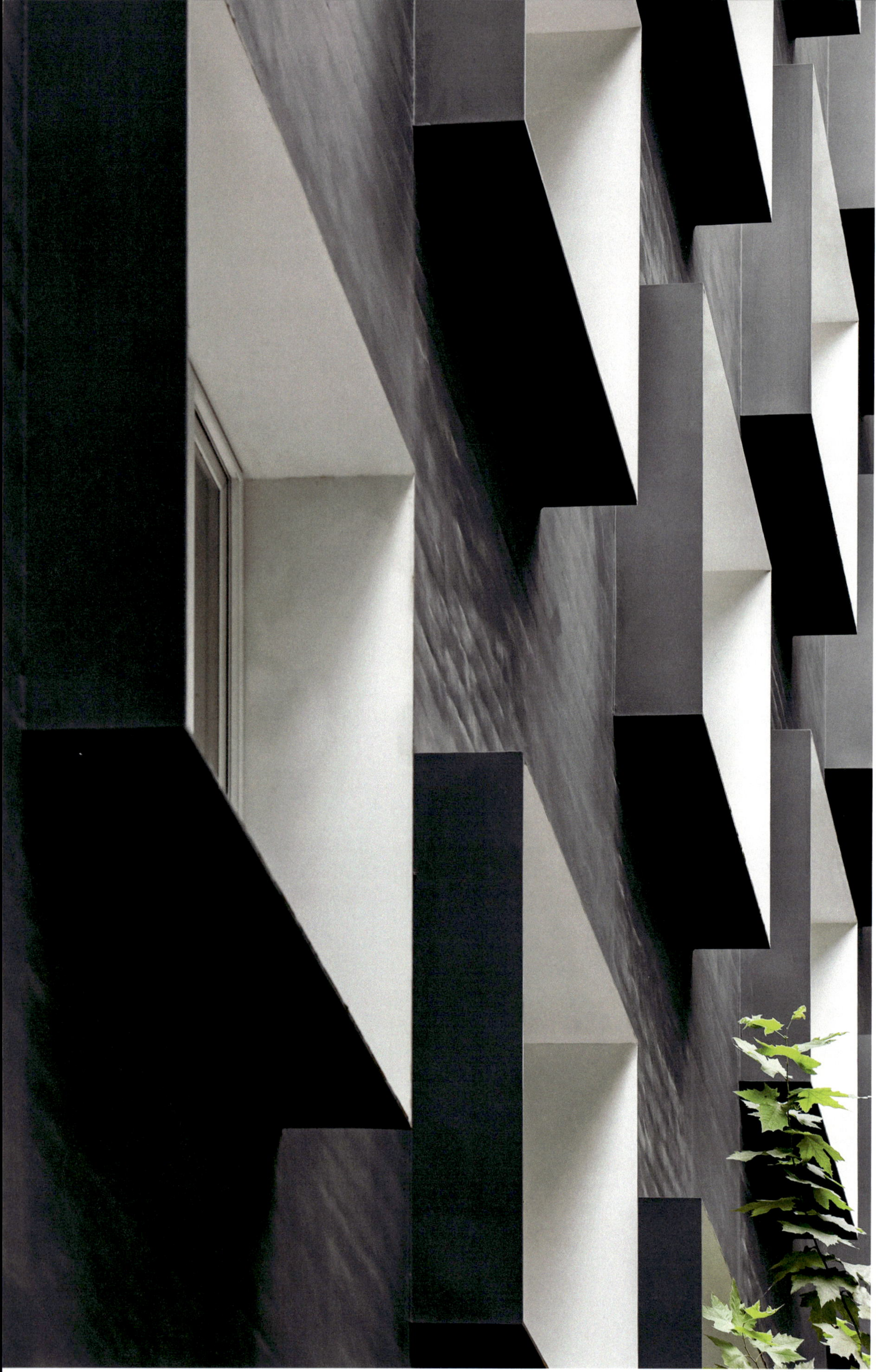

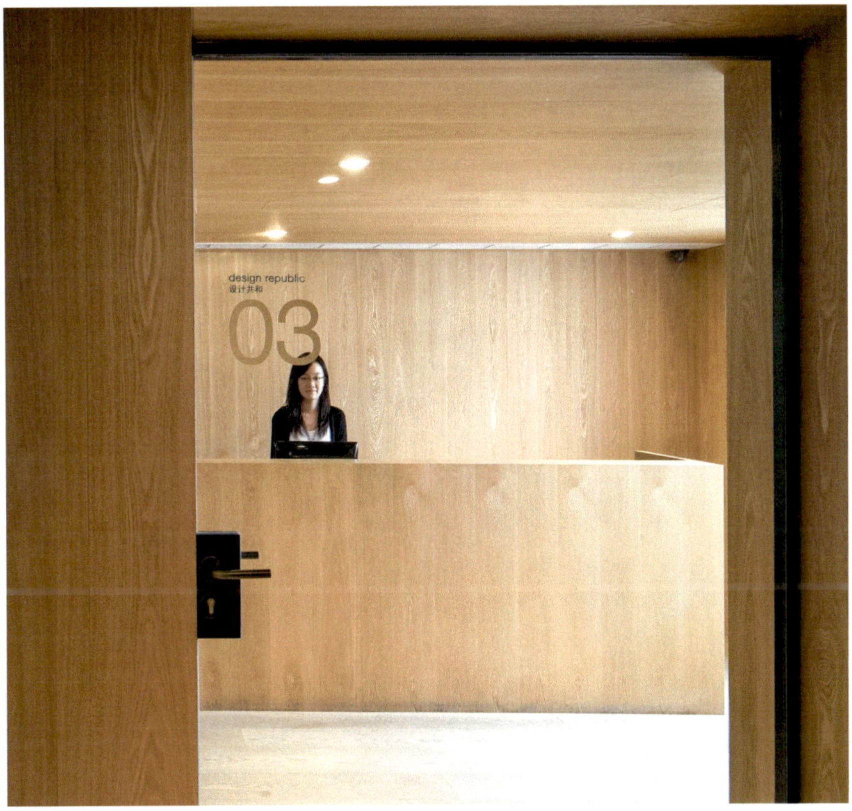
design republic
设计共和
03

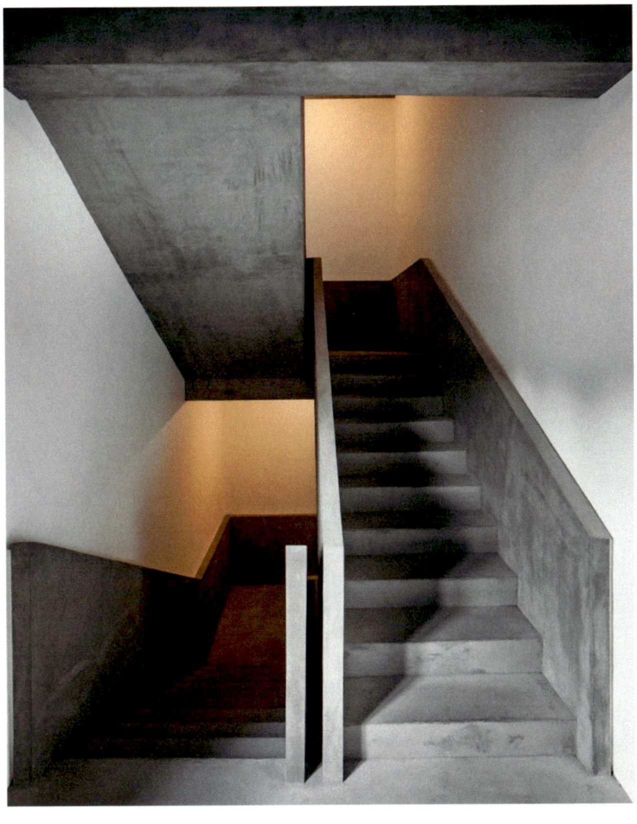

88
YUQING ROAD 余庆路

roof top
楼顶

neri&hu
如恩制作

nhdro (neri&hu design and research office)
如恩设计研究室

design republic
设计共和

design republic sales
设计共和 销售

design republic yuqing showroom
设计共和 余庆展示厅

the kitchen
(7680 X 3300)

THE RECONTEXTUALIZATION OF HISTORY
Design Commune and Commune Social, Shanghai

Built in 1909 during the British Concession, the Gordon Road Police Station served as the headquarters for the Shanghai municipal police force until 1943. In the following decades, attempts were made to adapt the building for various uses, yet none of the tenants were long-lasting, unable to find affinity with the building's colonial features. By the time it was added to a list of protected heritage buildings in 2005, it had been abandoned and fallen into disrepair. But its moment came when we sensed its vast potential, and it became an obsession of ours to take this building, transform it, and make it into our new "home" in Shanghai—not only the new flagship location for Design Republic, but an active hub for the design community at large in Shanghai, which we are deeply rooted in and committed to.

Working with a protected building, we envisioned the series of operations on the building akin to surgery: First gently removing the decaying wood and plaster, carefully restoring portions of the still-vibrant red brickwork, then grafting on skins (surfaces/partitions), joints (details/connectors), and organs (technical functions) as needed. And finally, with the attachment of a brand new appendage—the glazed retail storefront on the ground floor—like a prosthetic, it enabled a nearly abandoned building to begin performing again in a wholly new capacity.

Contrasting with the exterior which has mostly been left intact due to historic preservation guidelines, the interior has been completely transformed. In many ways these transformations are counterintuitive for the architect whose primary role is to "build"; this is a project that should be discussed in terms of its deletions rather than additions. Working within the mandate of preserving all existing structures, Neri&Hu was still able to identify opportunities for alterations. The straightforward plan and section of the existing building, with three stacked floors and a centralized spine of circulation, is disrupted as strategic cuts are made in the entry lobby and the main corridor.

Andreas Gefeller, *Supervisions*, 2004
The hyperrealistic detail in Gefeller's photographs recalls the precision of an excavation. The way he meticulously combs surfaces and reveals minute traces of human intervention, a cigarette butt or a footprint, are similar to the way we approach an old building site. Also, the concept of stitching—Gefeller stitches together thousands of photos to create the final image—resonates with our idea of these smaller parts, details, building upon each other to form a whole new building.

site map

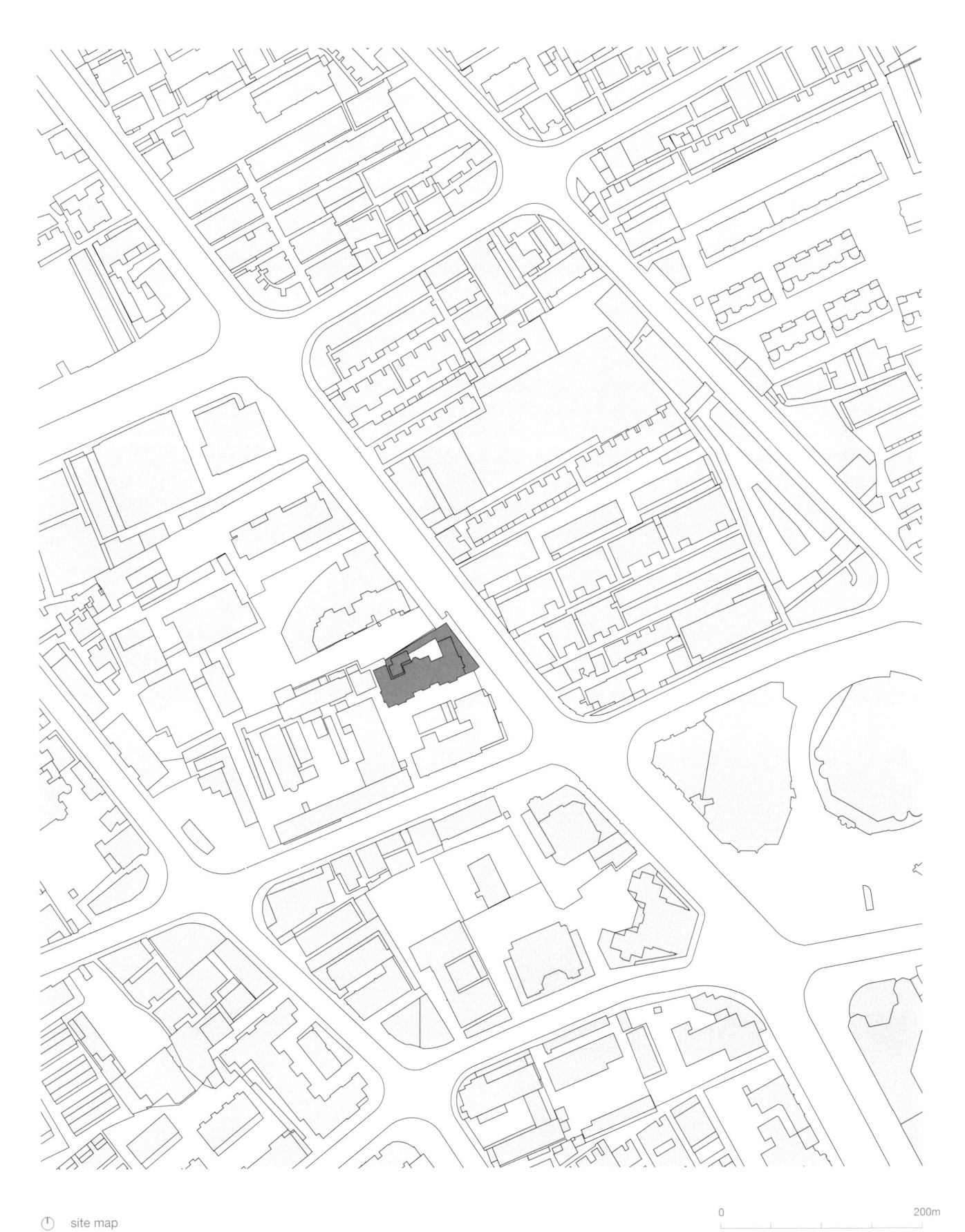

0   200m

Seemingly minute, these maneuvers convert a series of existing linear spaces into an interlocking puzzle of volumetric ones. Lined with multiple glazed openings, each featuring a vignette of the rooms beyond, the new double-height voids activate visual connections and create spatial intrigue. Circulation patterns are forced to shift around these cutouts, encouraging a visceral exploration rather than a journey guided by logic. These deceptively insignificant acts of destruction effectively alter the spatial experience and become a catalyst for the evolution of this historic building, setting the stage for new possibilities of use and occupation.

At the same time there is an unspoken understanding that some things should remain pure and untouched. Picture this ethereal scene found during an early site visit: a small platform, hovering among the wood rafters, a ladder propped up in the center, a solitary chair beside it, glowing as light streams through a hole in the collapsing roof. Captivated by this incidental staging of ordinary objects caught in a suspended moment in time, we decided to recreate this hidden room in the attic, a space with no purpose or intent, a quiet tribute to the many past and future lives of the building.

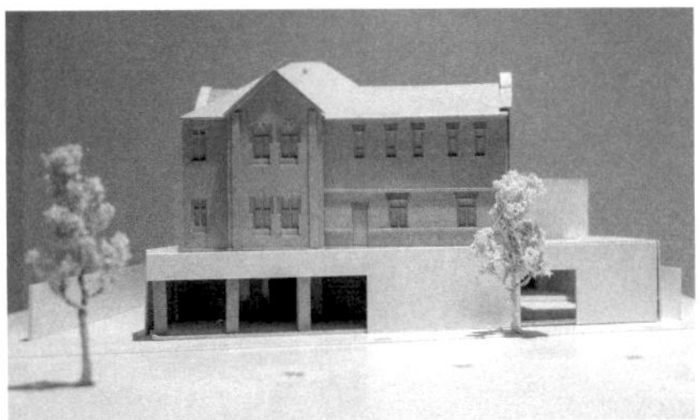

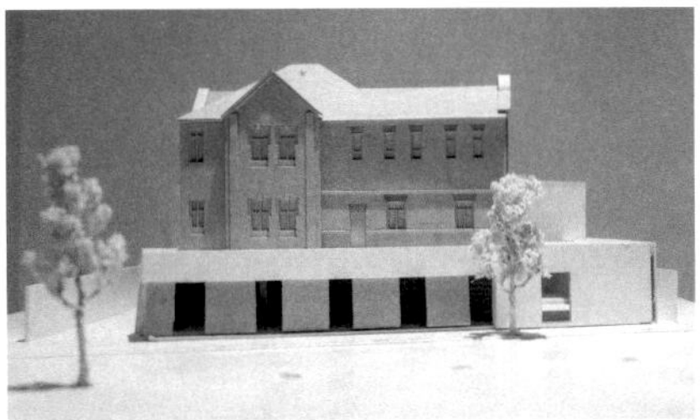

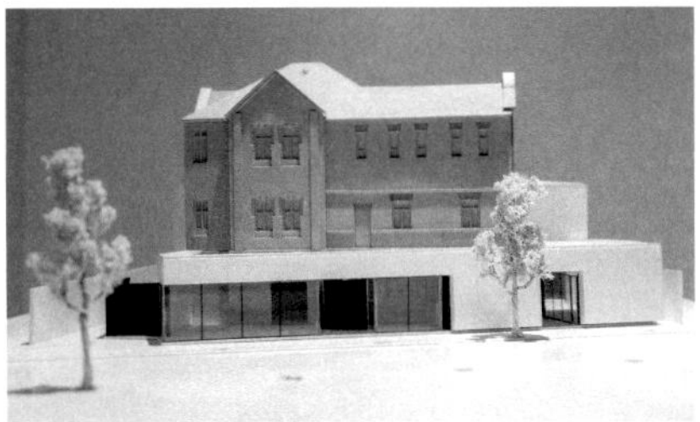

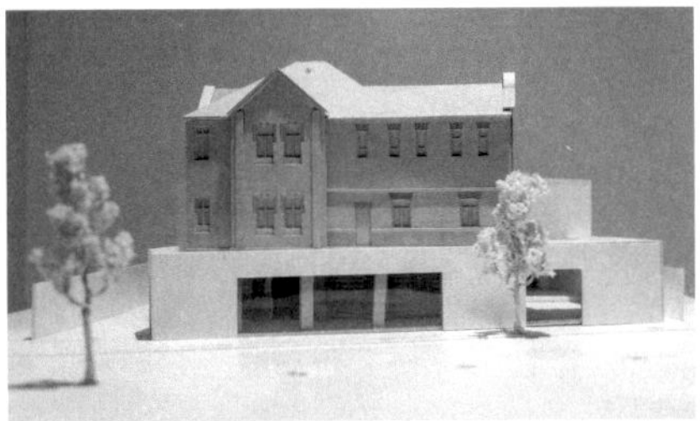

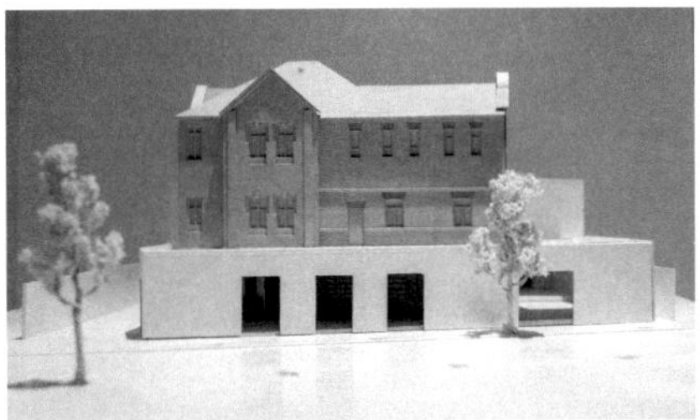

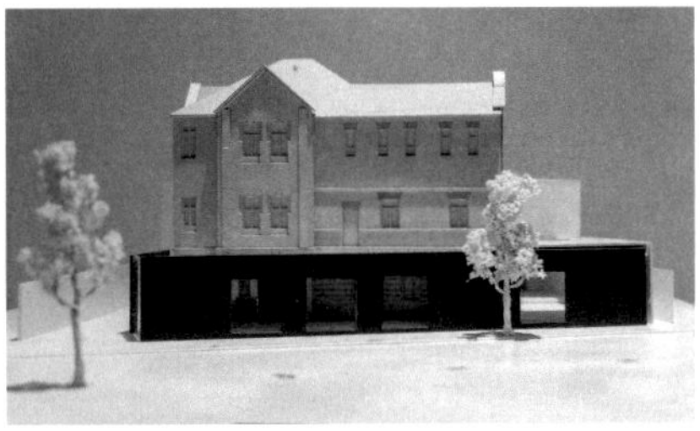

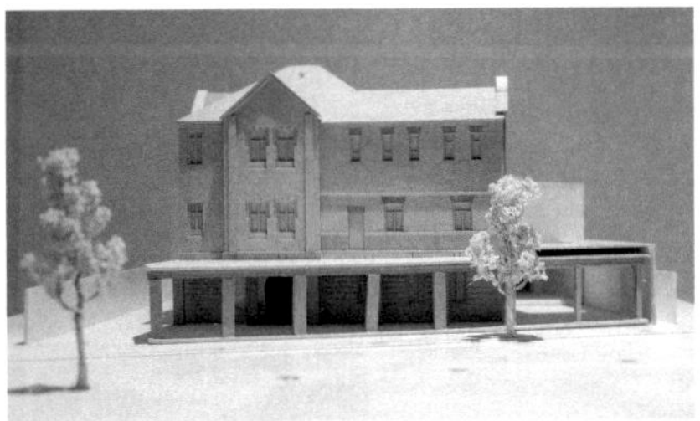

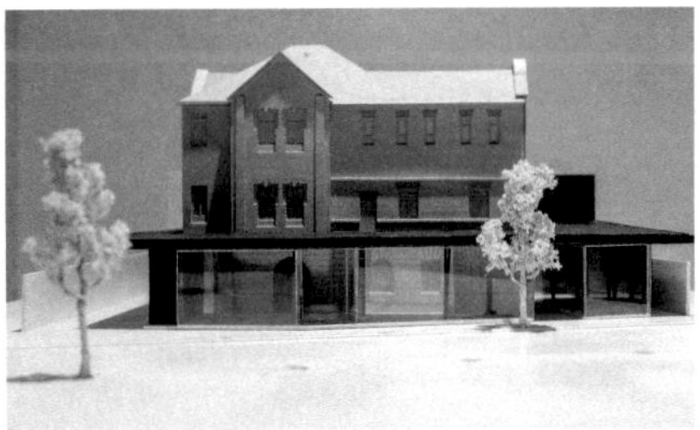

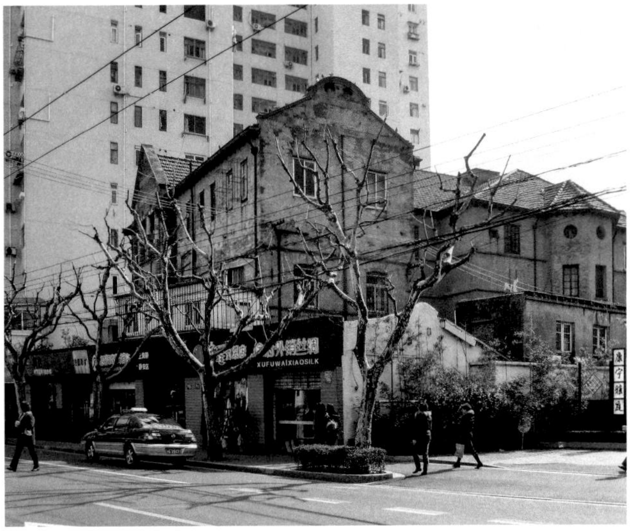
KUFUWAIXIAOSILK

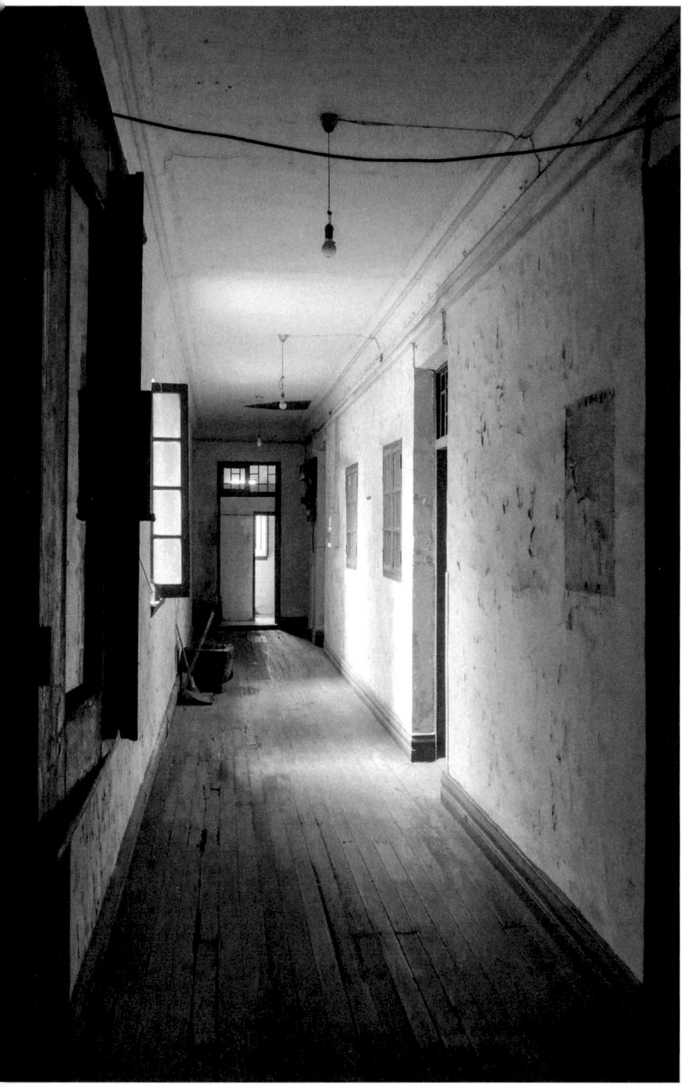

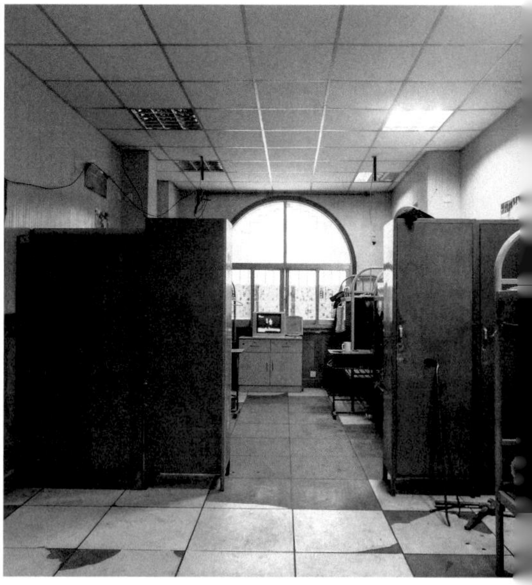

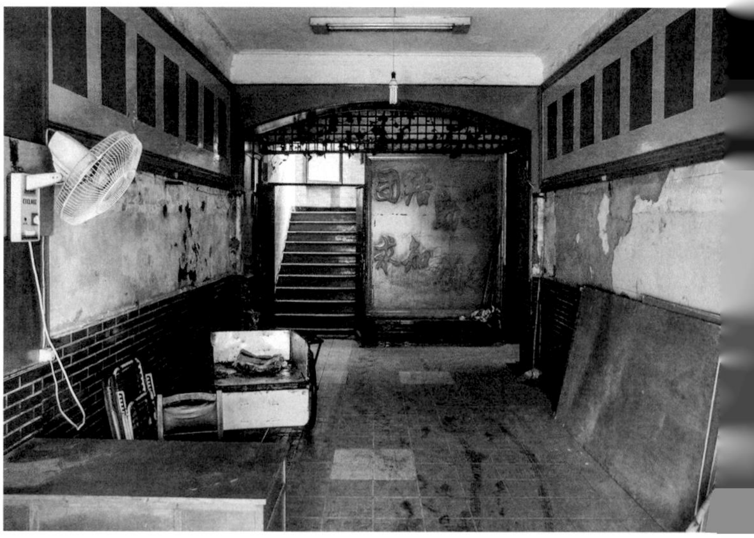

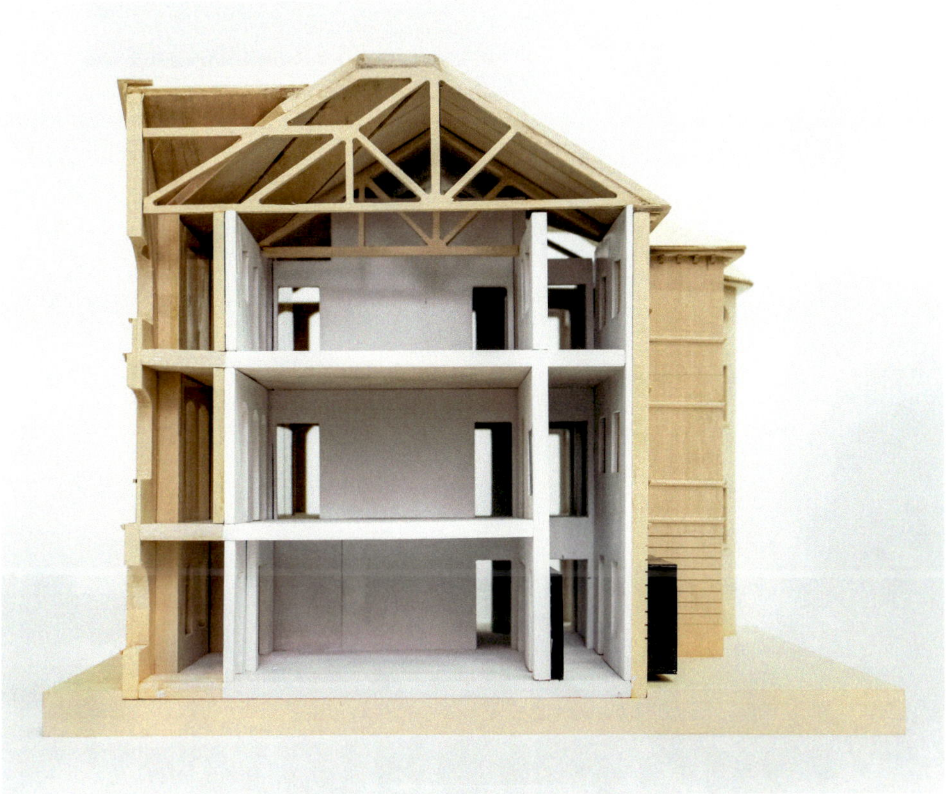

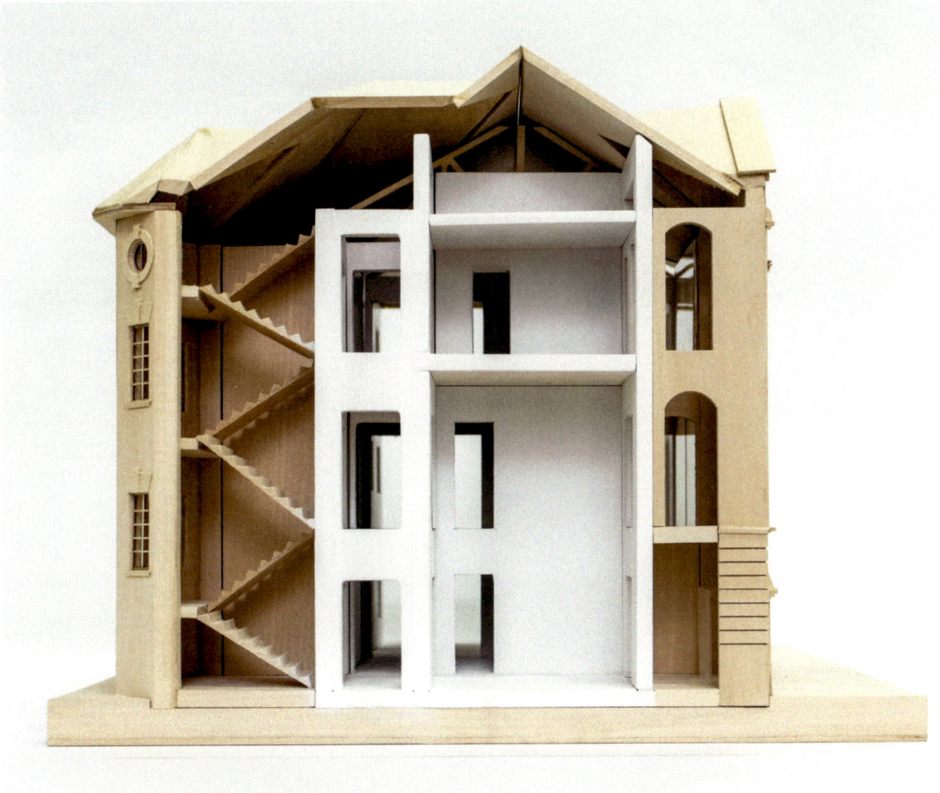

2ND FLOOR
CUT.

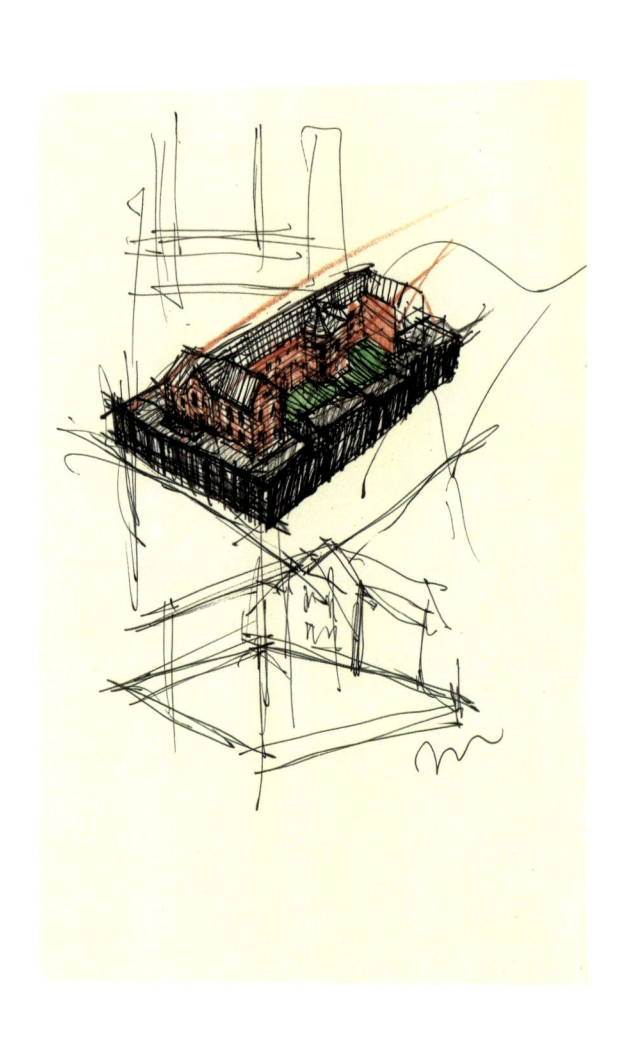

WAFFLE
ROOF

demolition plan | section

0   15m

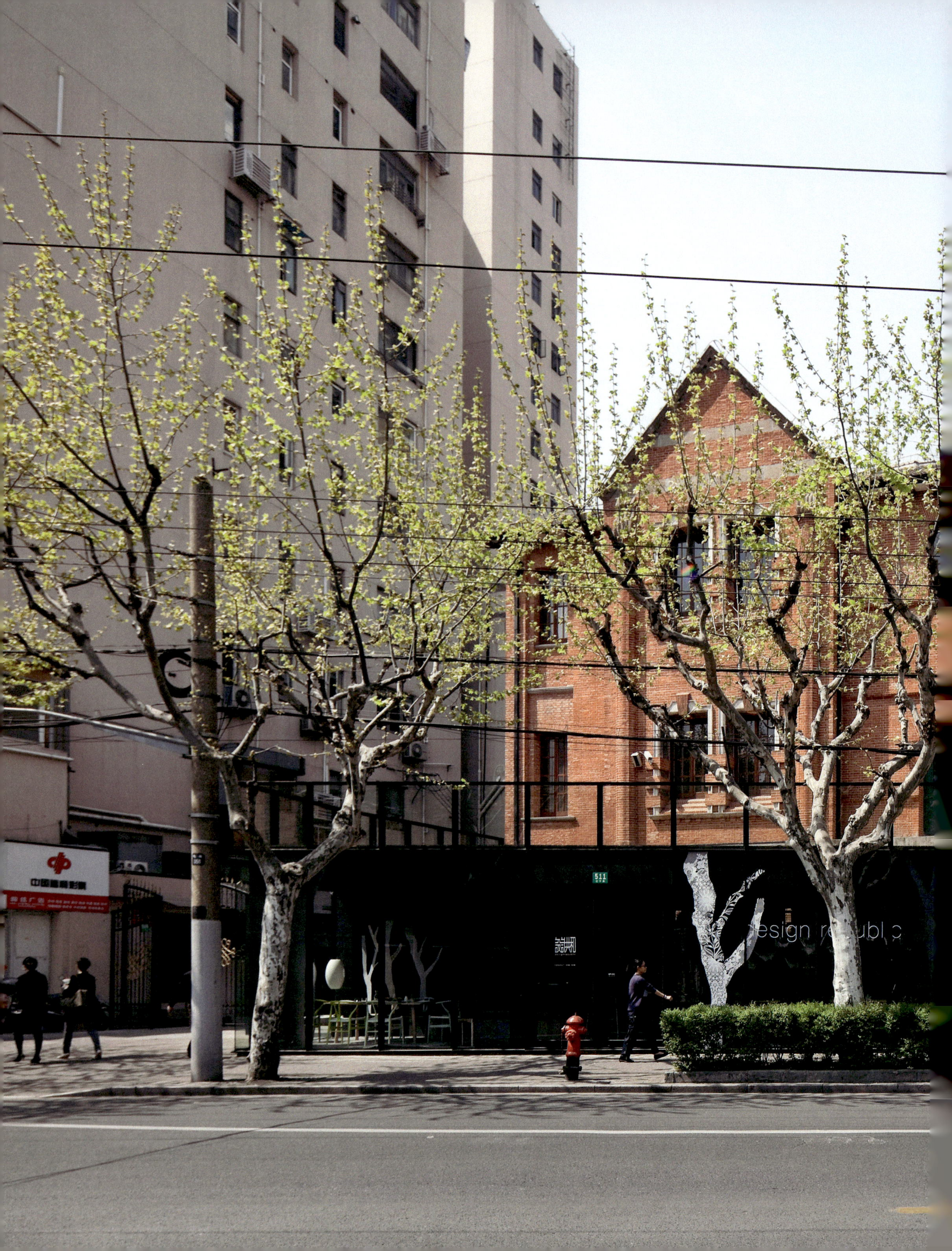
511
esign re ubl c

设计共和

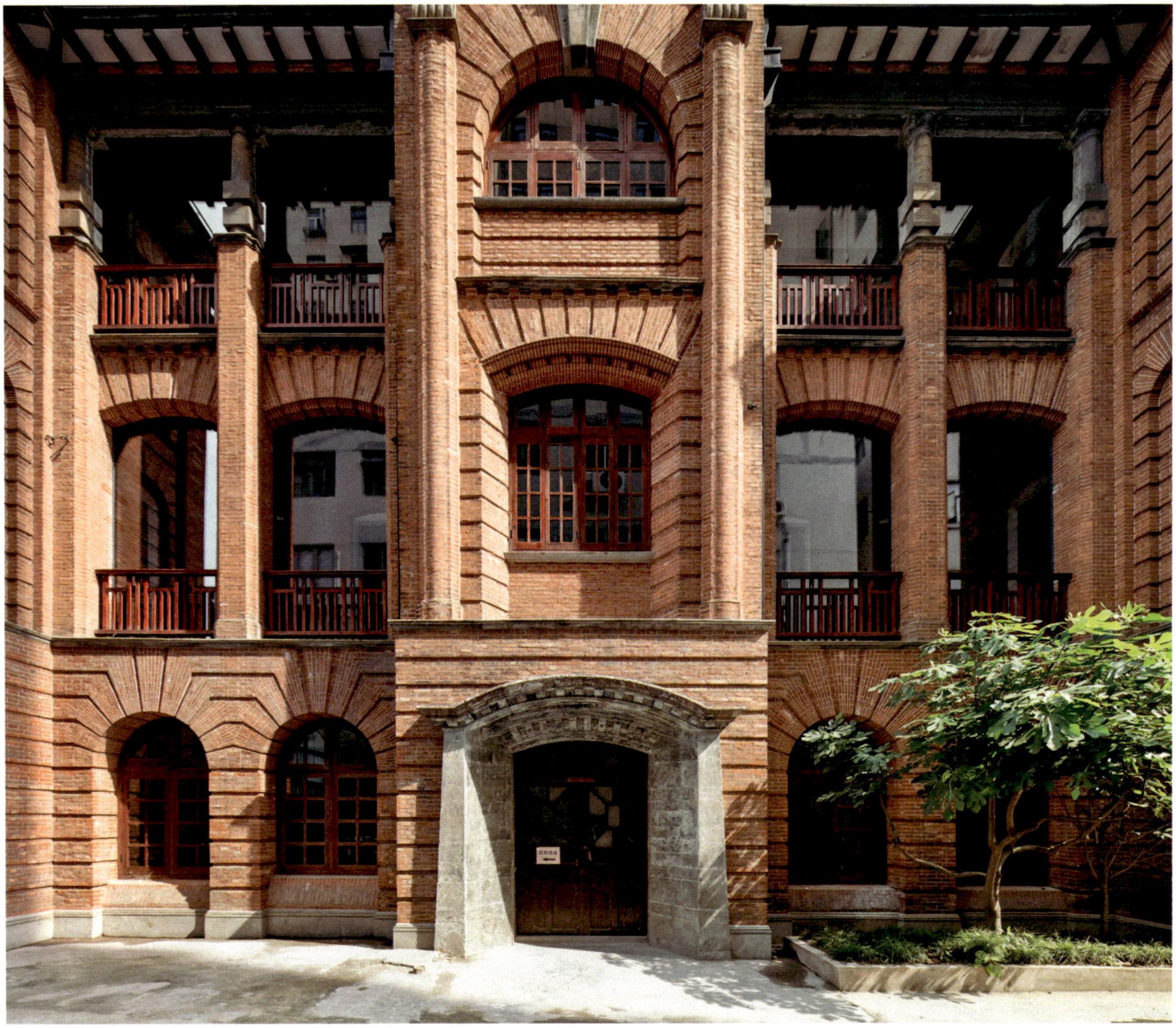

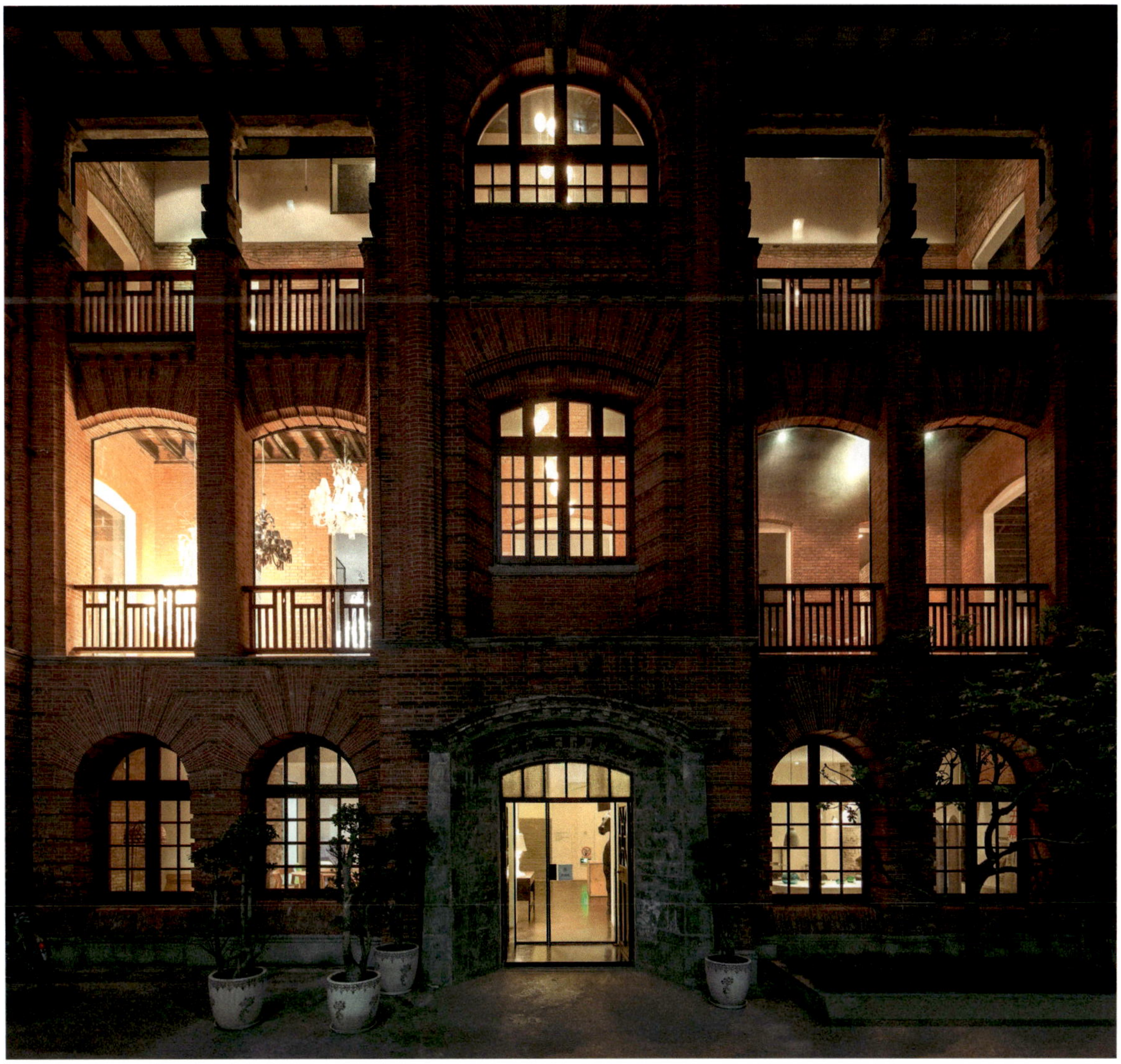

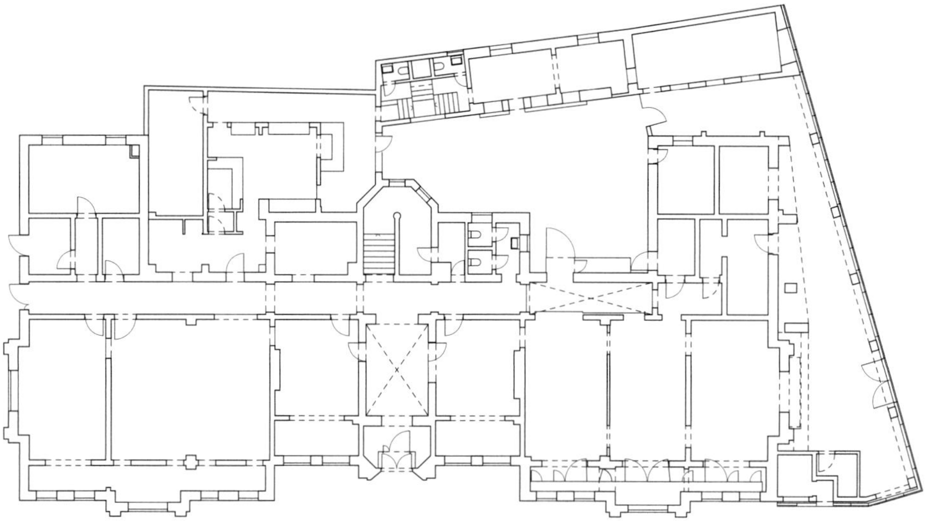

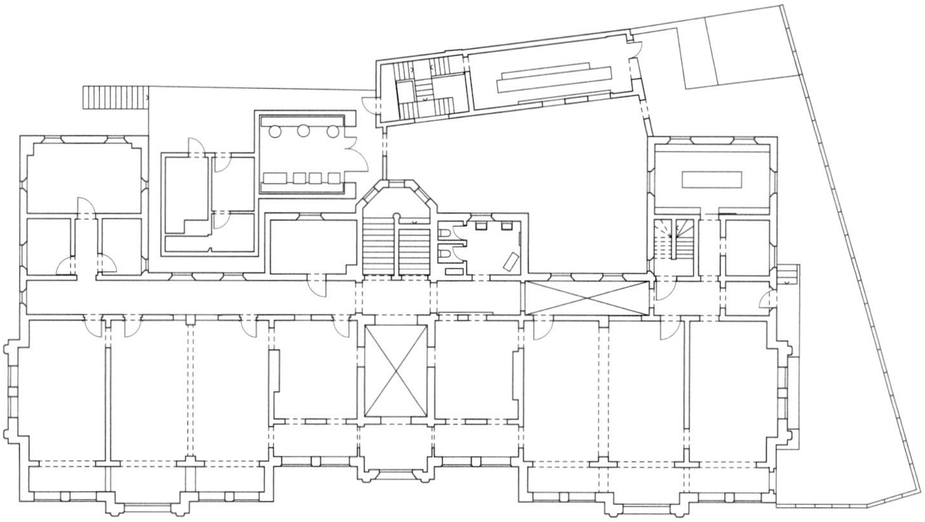

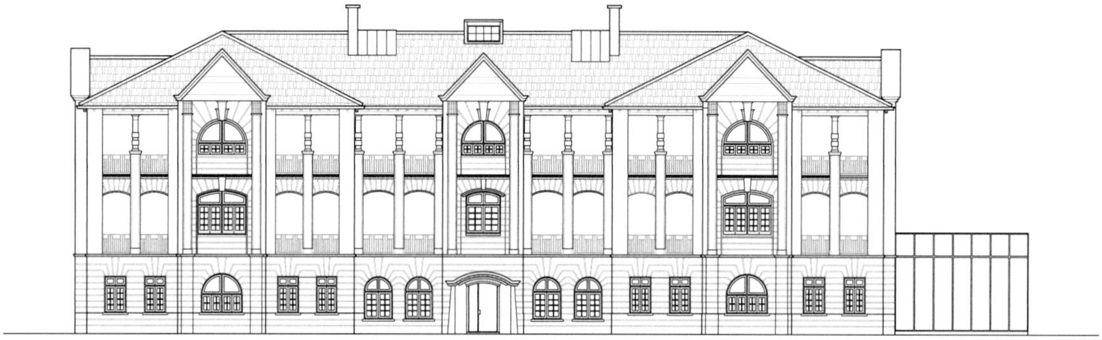

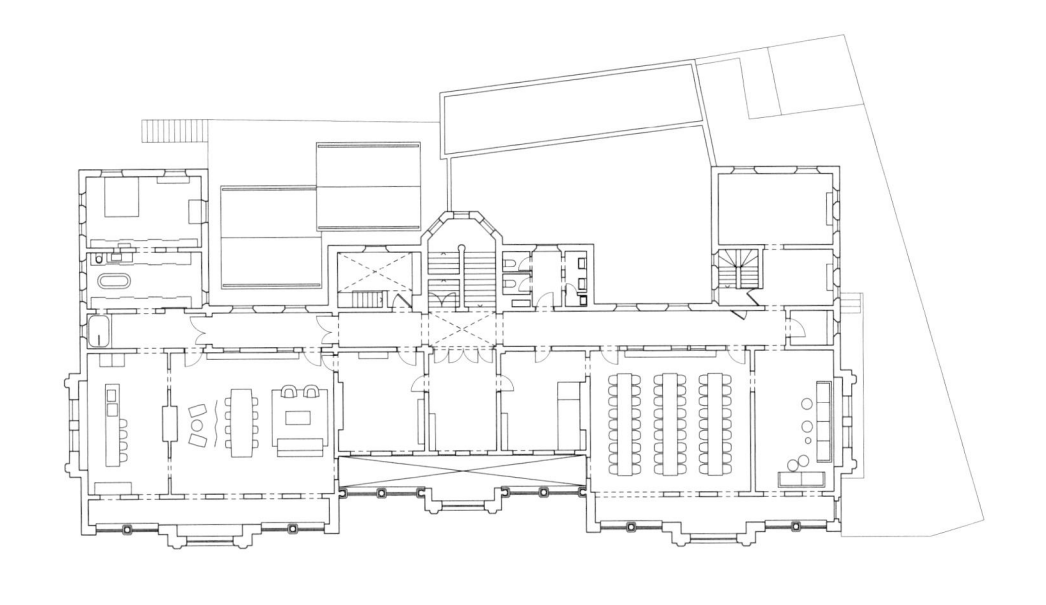

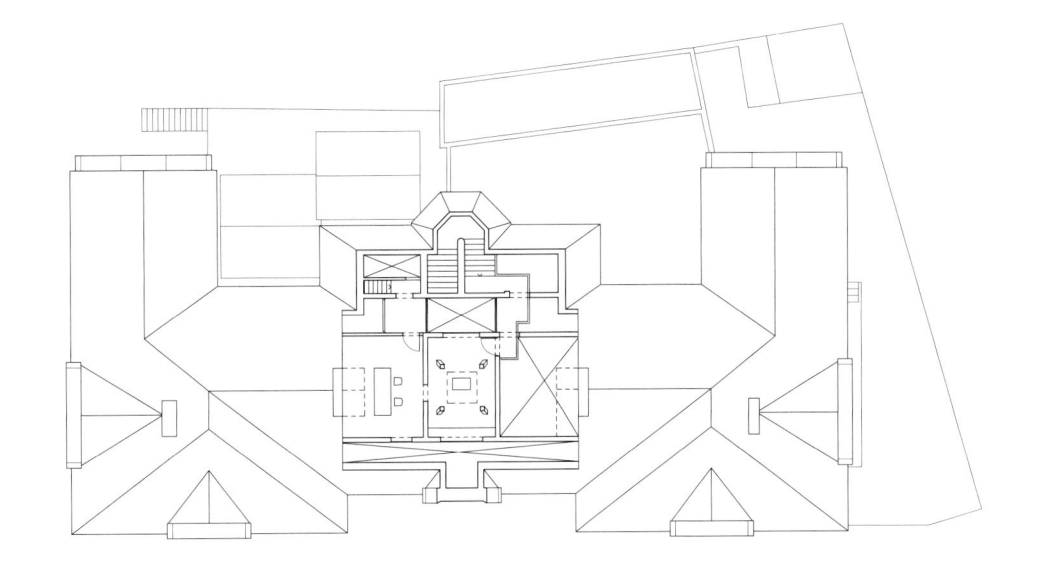

first- to third-floor plan | south elevation | section | attic and roof plan

0　　15m

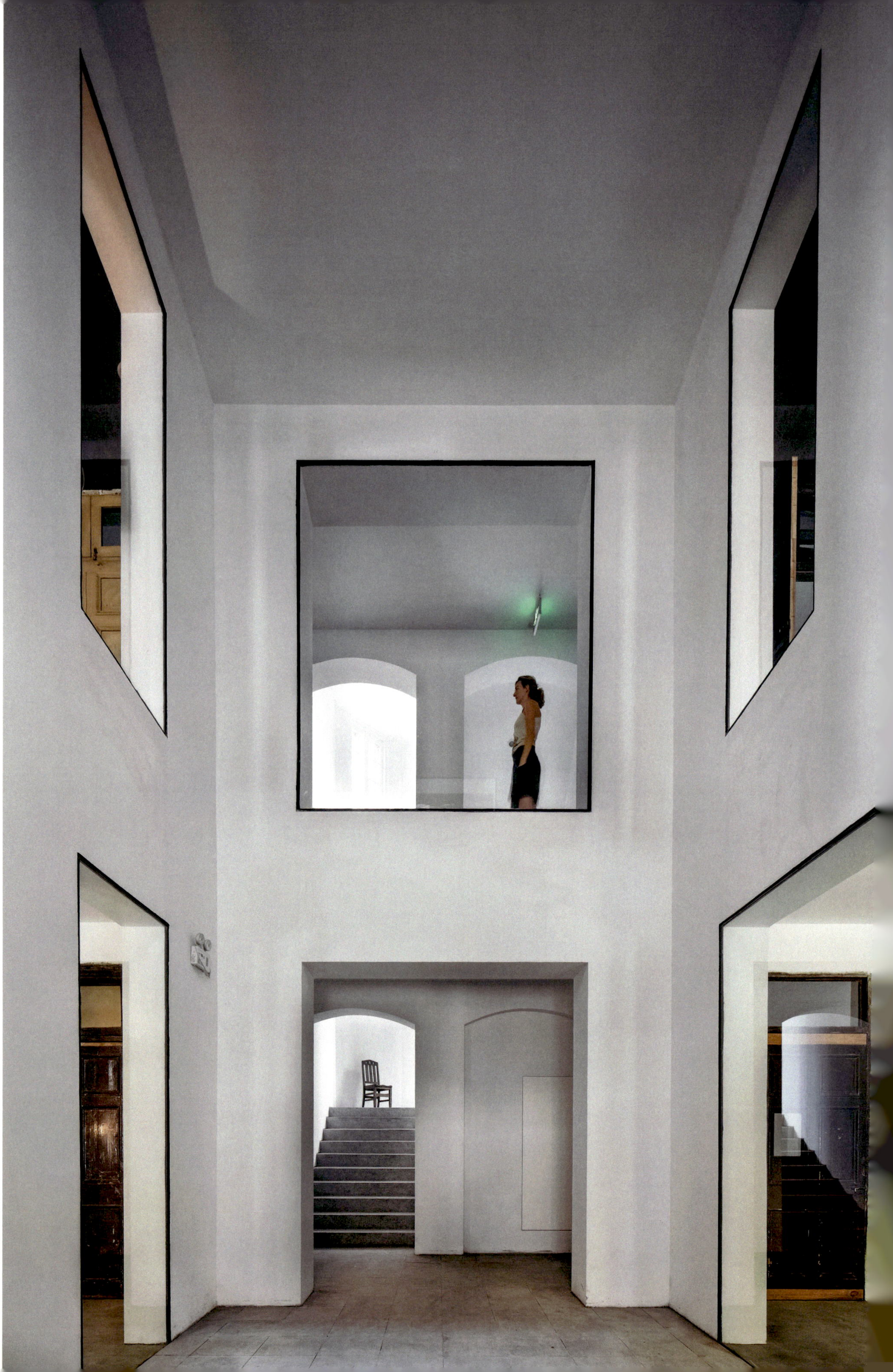

101

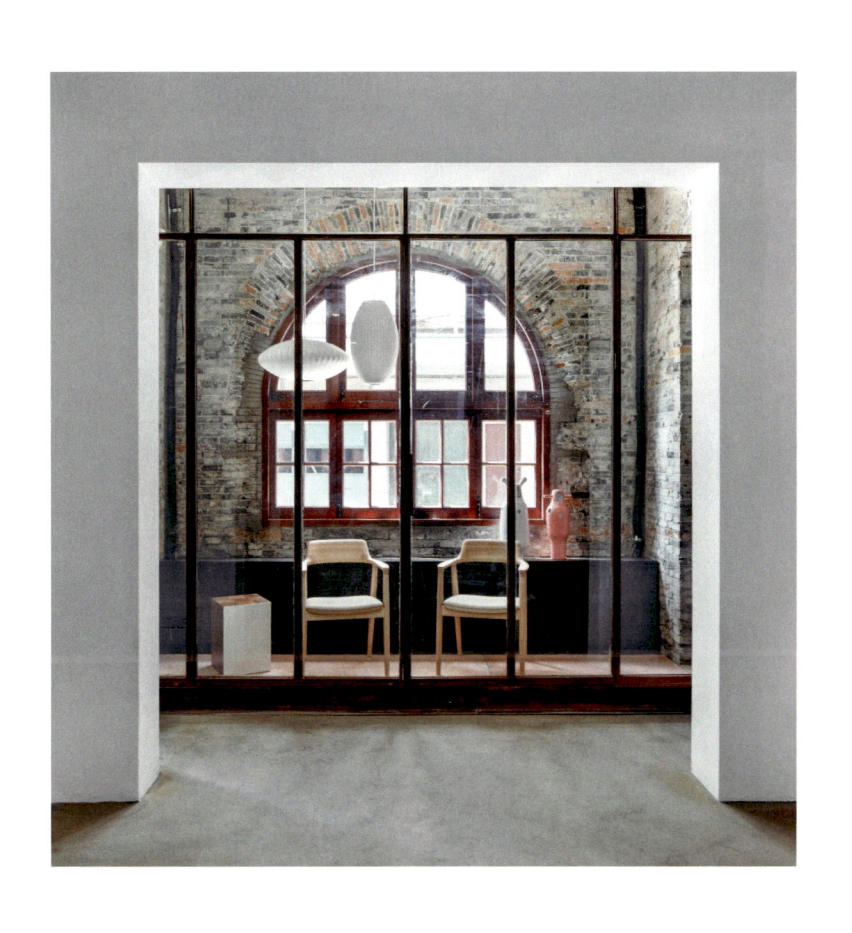

设计师知道自己的作品何时达到完美：不是当没有更多的部分可以增加时，而是当没有更多的部分可以删减时。

——圣-埃克苏佩里

103

104

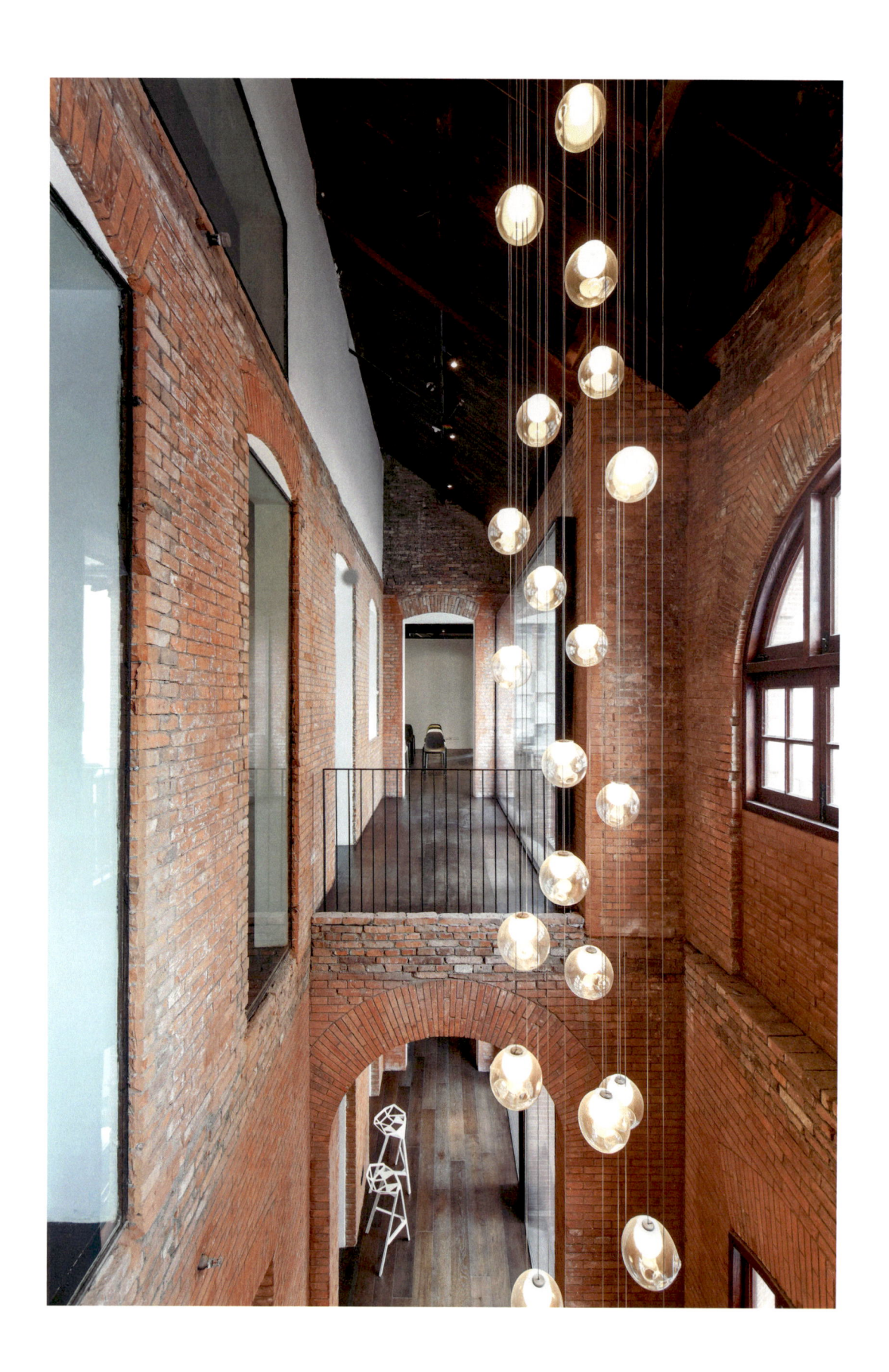

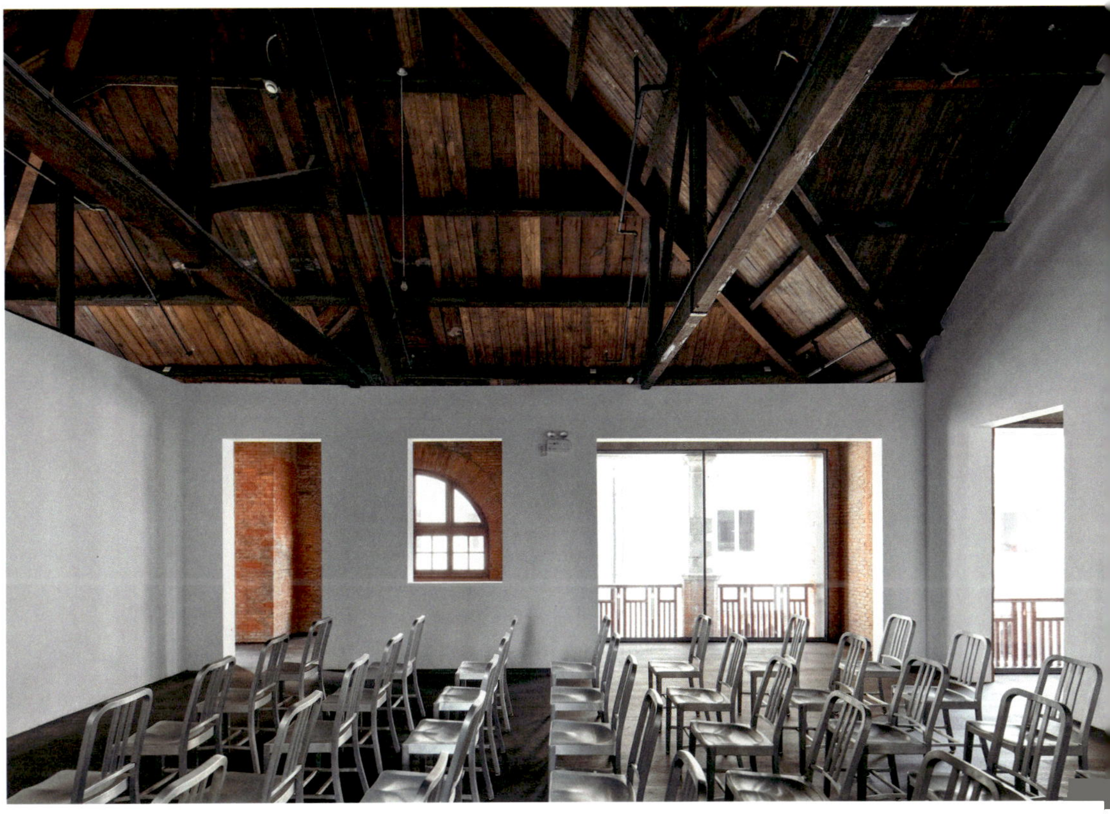

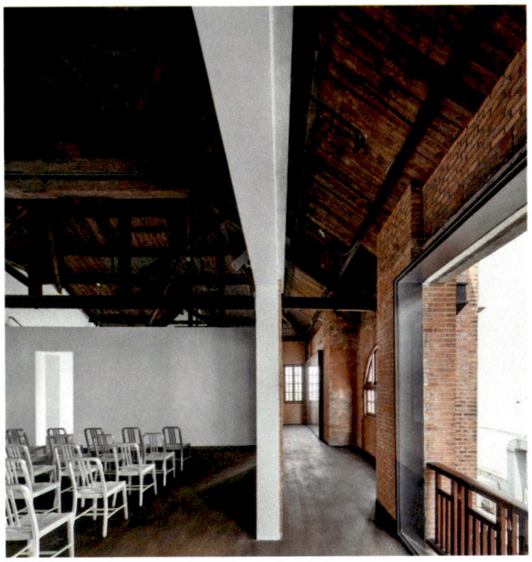

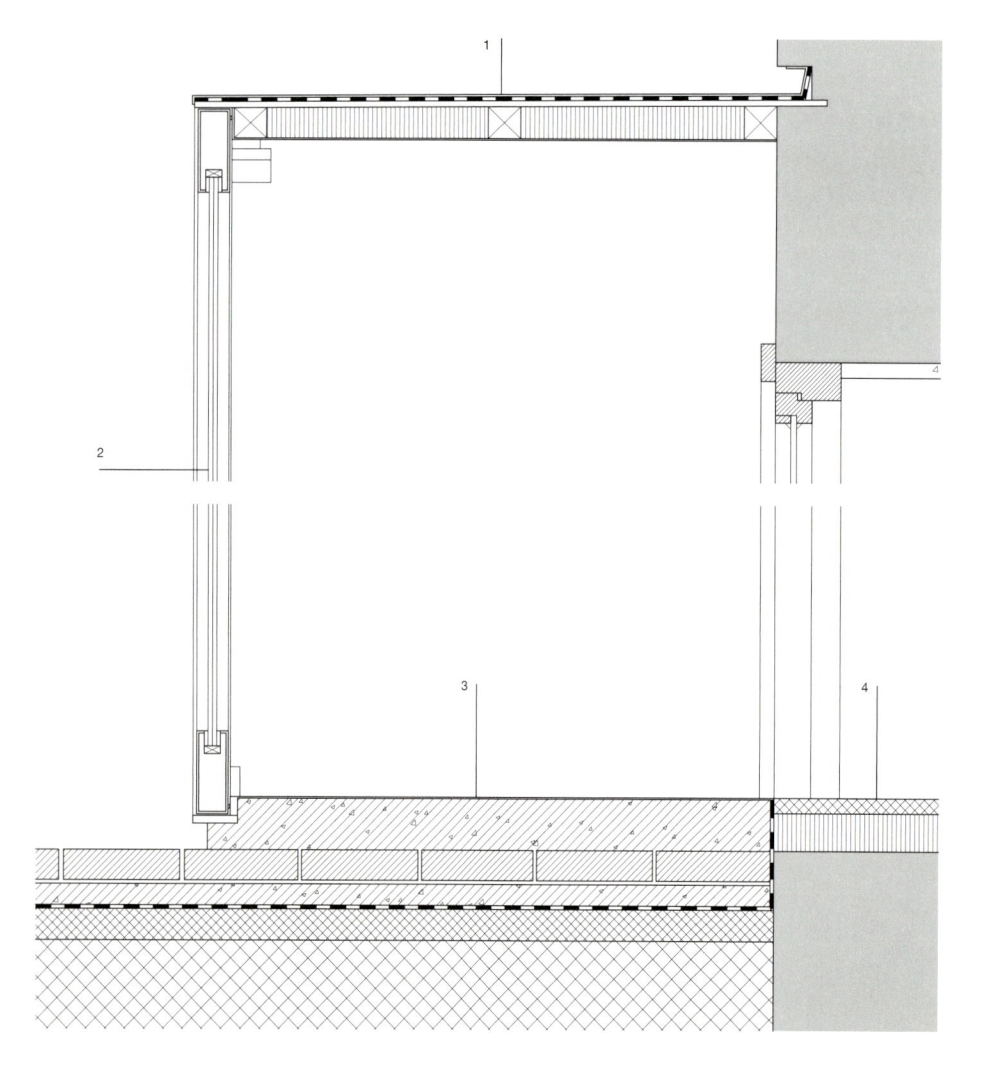

1 Roof structure
3-mm iron sheet
5-mm bitumen felt
8-mm steel board
40-mm battens set to falls, 1%, with XPS rigid insulation
2-mm powder-coated iron panel, matte black

2 Window
6+6-mm tempered low-iron laminated glass

3 Floor structure
2-mm powder-coated iron panel, matte black
70-mm screed
53-mm recycled gray brick
25-mm screed leveling
5-mm polyethylene membrane
Concrete base

4 Floor structure
20-mm polished concrete, cement and quartz top layer
50-mm XPS rigid insulation
Existing concrete base

1 Window
10+12+10-mm tempered low-iron insulated double glazing

2 Window sill
10-mm fluorocarbon-coated black steel
Screed laid to falls
5-mm bitumen felt
Existing brick wall

3 Floor structure
10-mm steel-angle substructure
20-mm wooden floorboard (tongue and groove)
30-mm battens
280-mm existing wood joist with 60-mm impact sound insulation and 20-mm plywood and 5-mm wood veneer

glass box | window detail

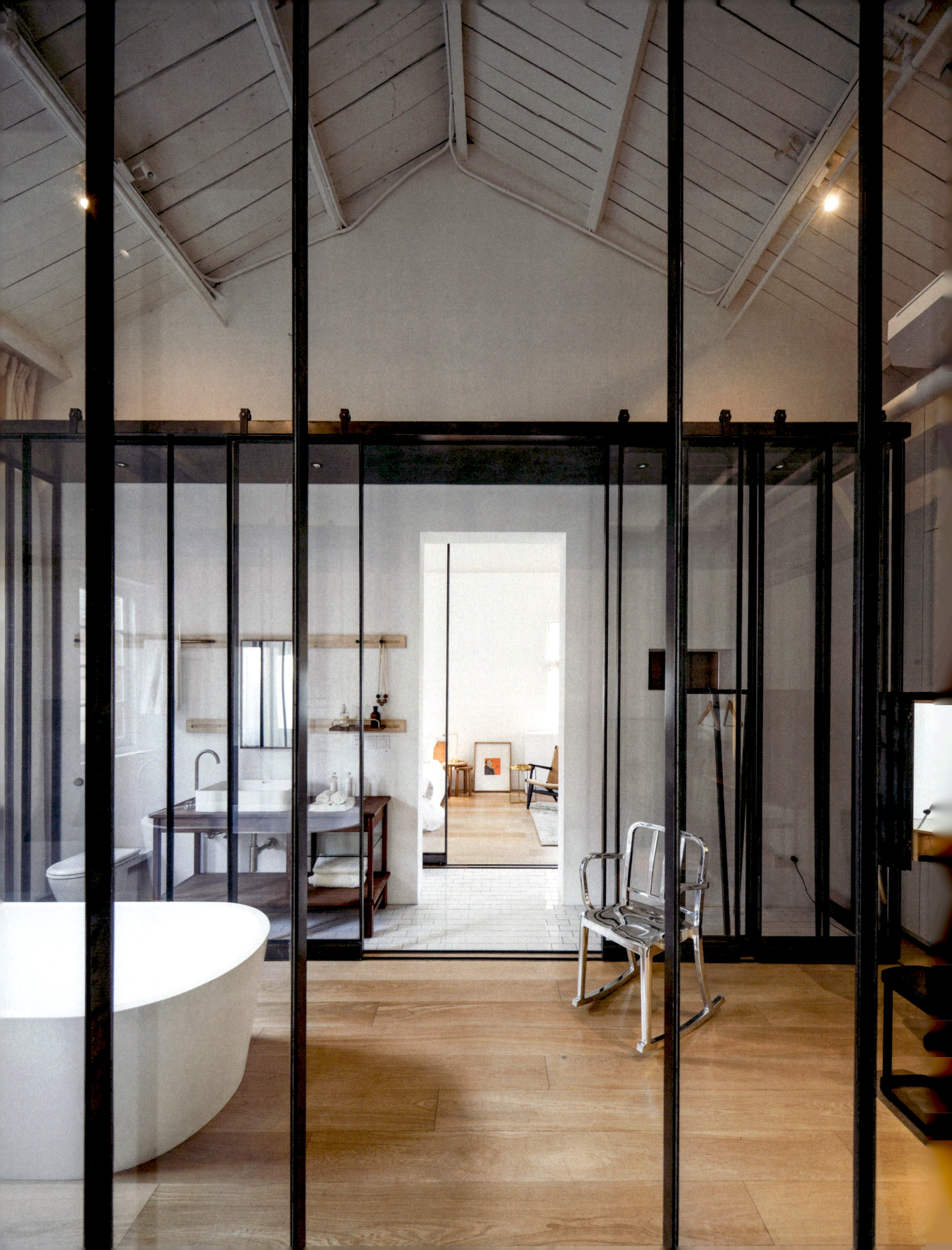

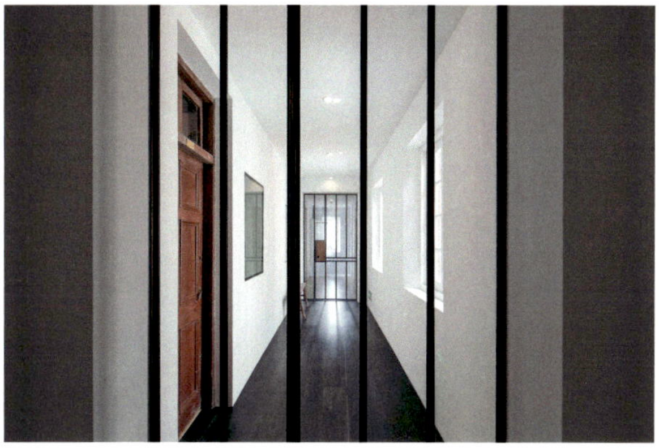

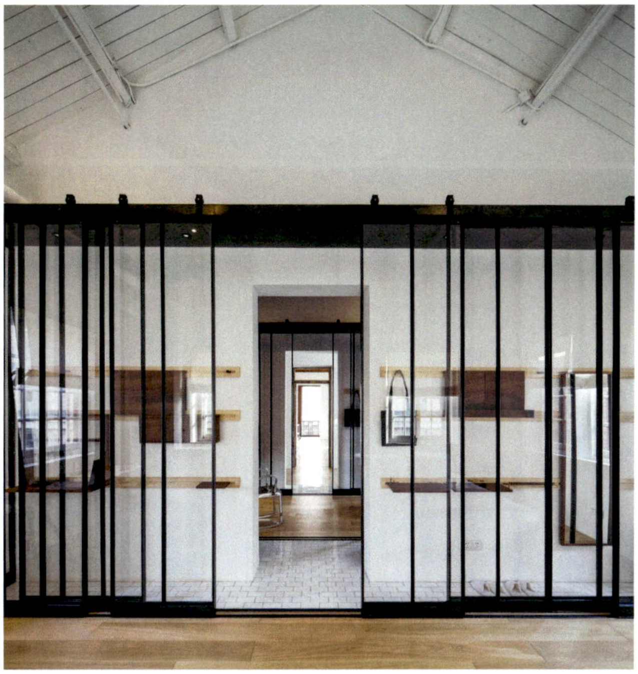

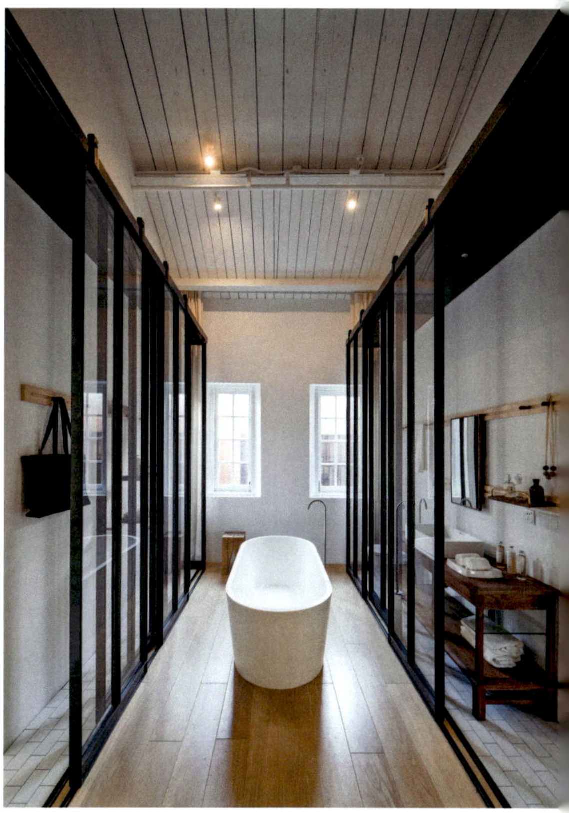

静安区 商业联合会
商业经济学会
商业企业管理协会

各地投资企业联合会

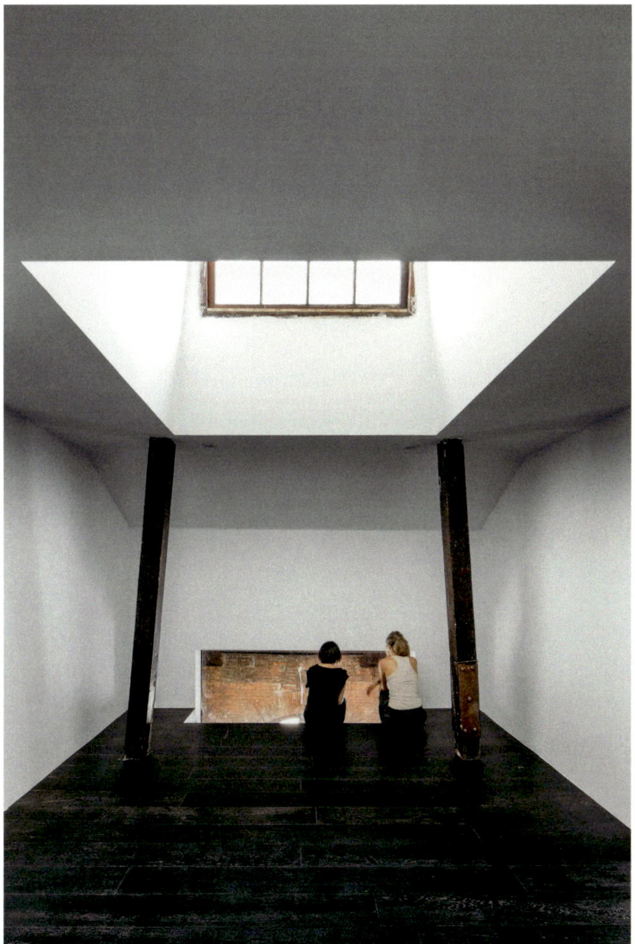

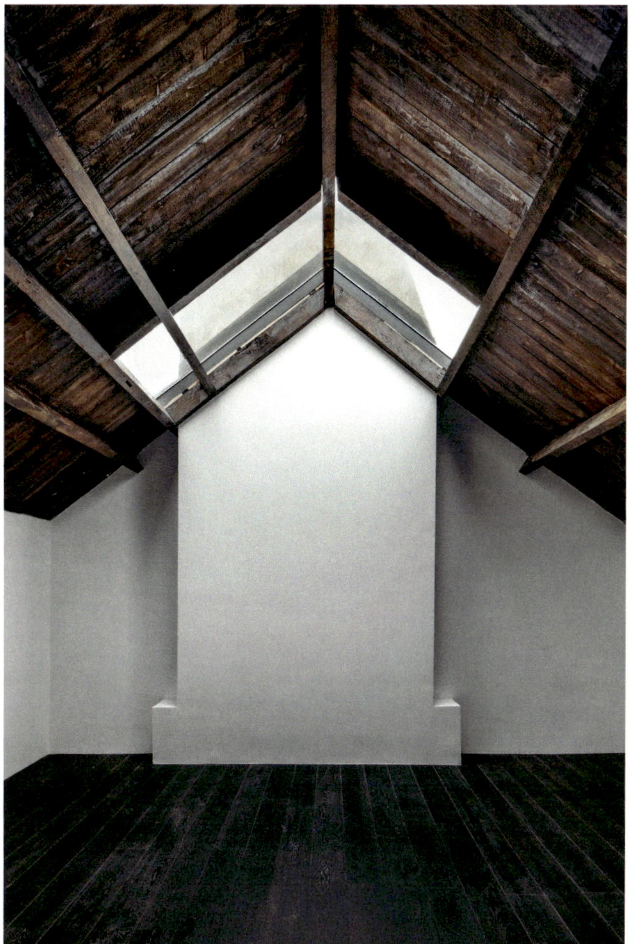

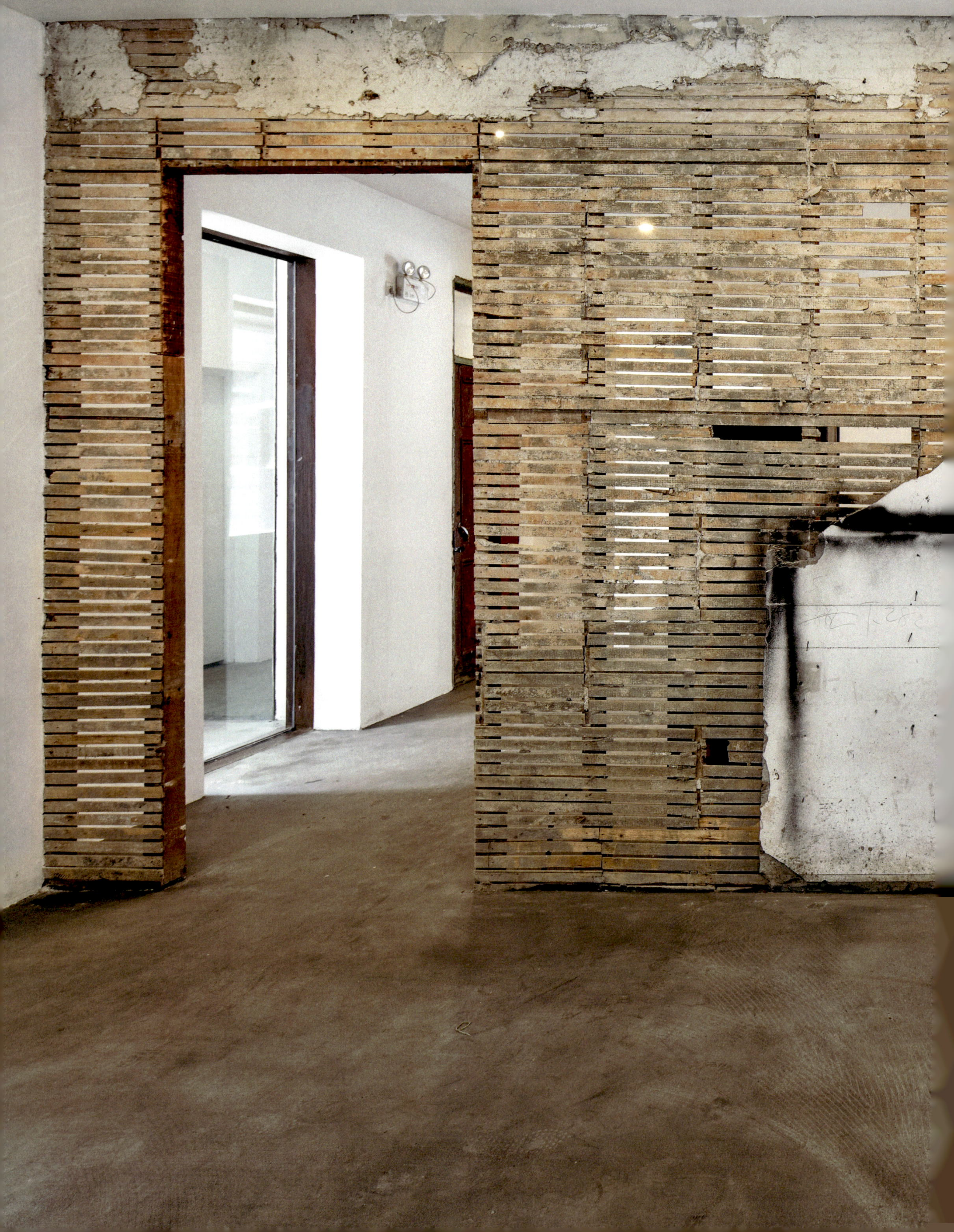

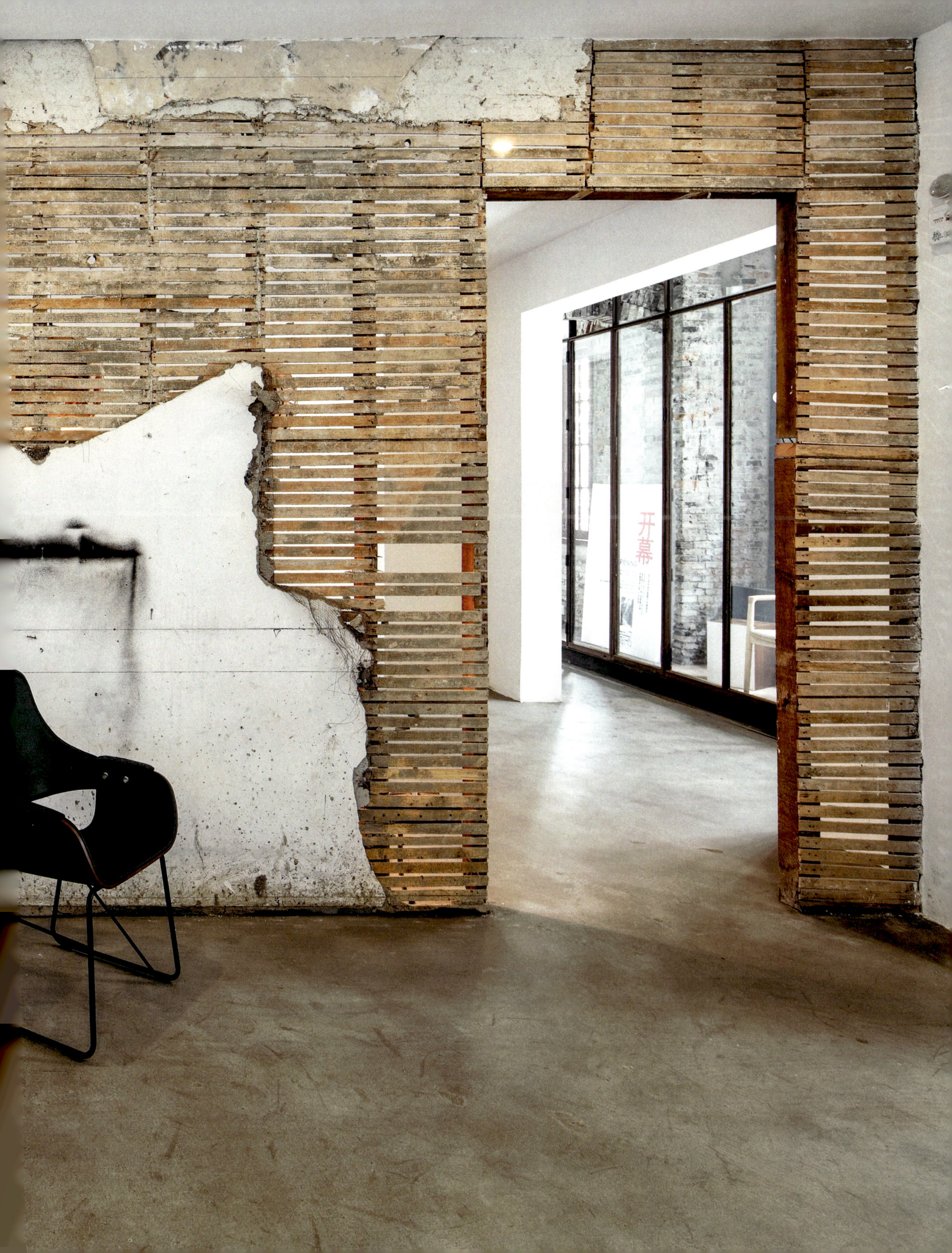
开幕

A

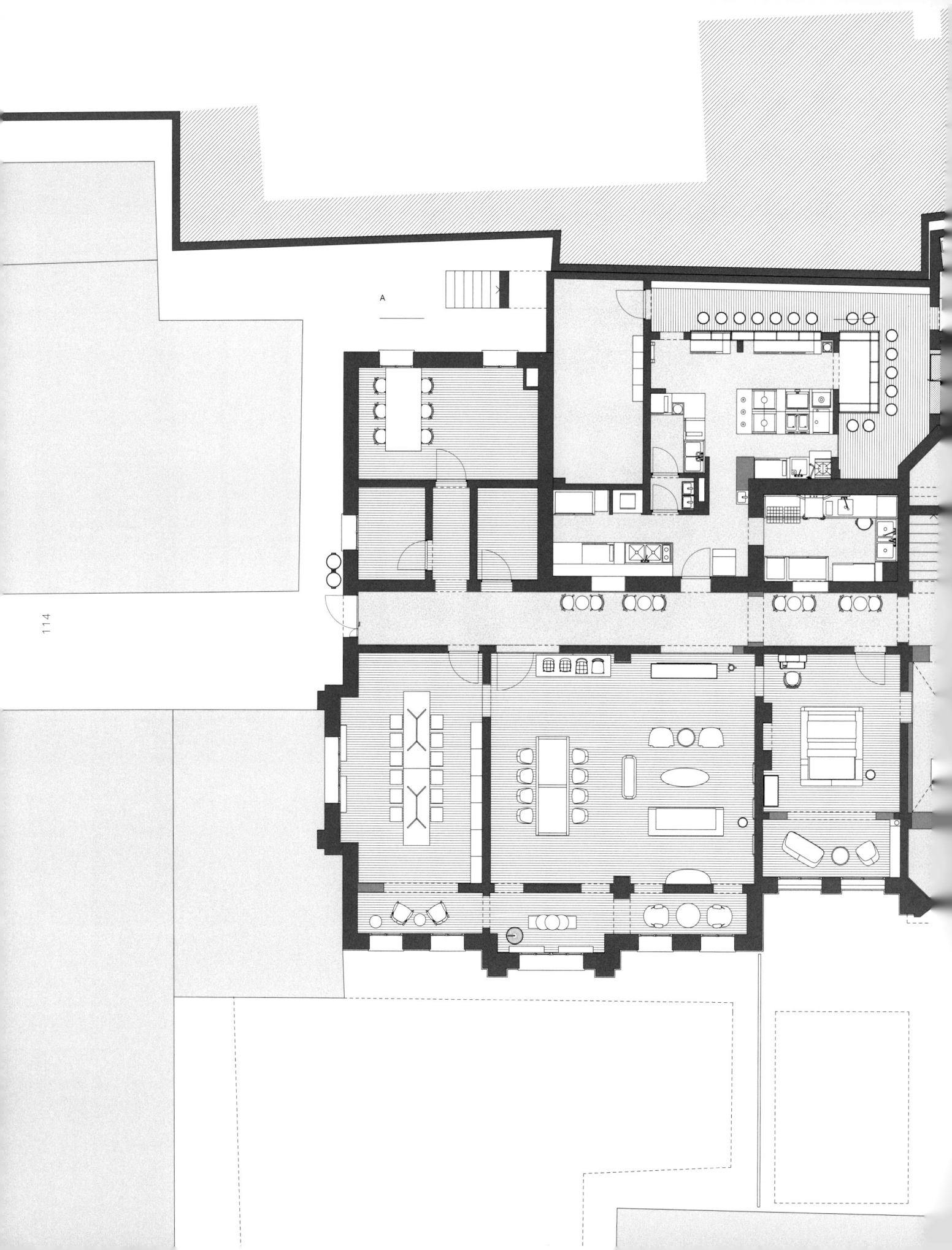

⑦ first-floor paving plan

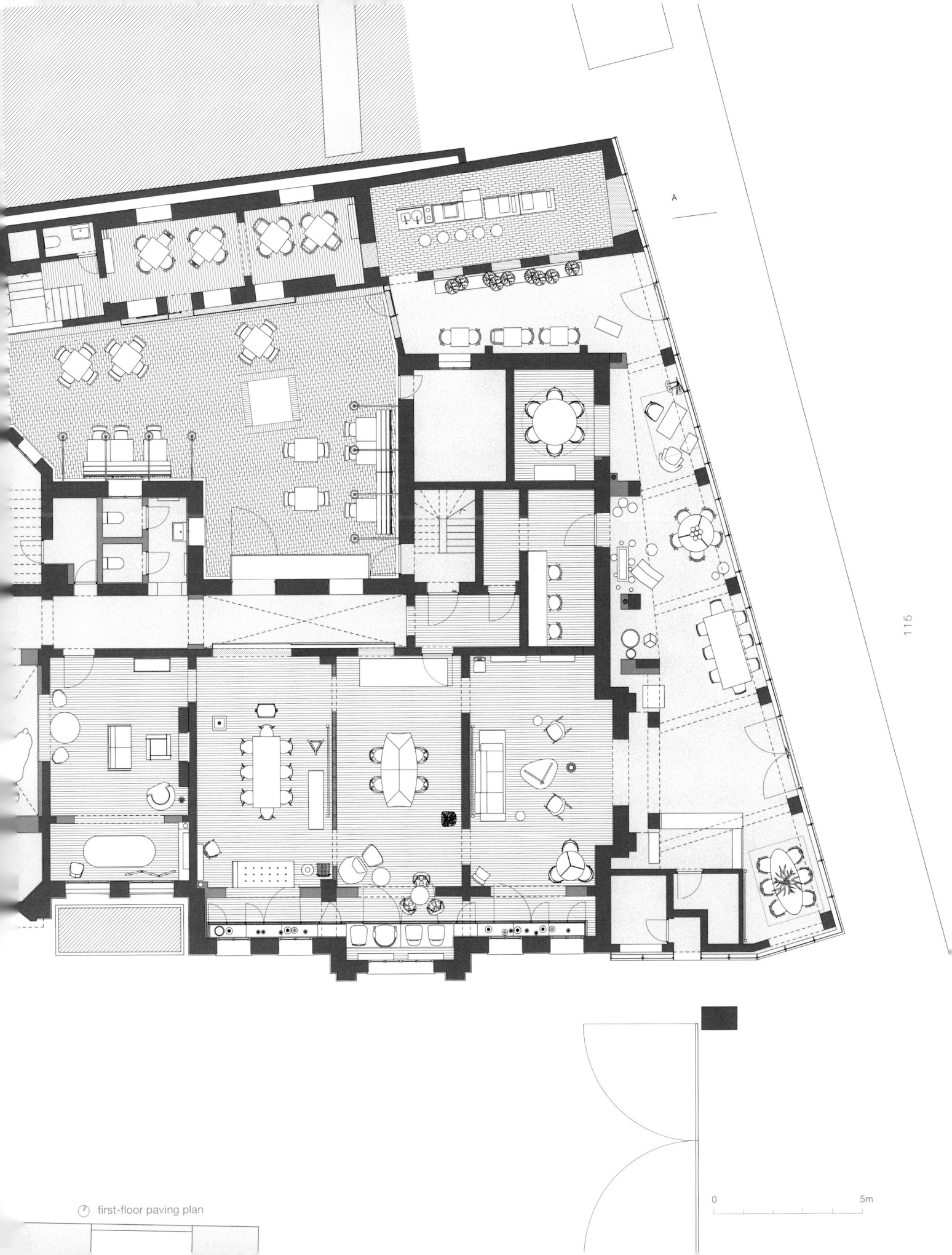

115

0 5m

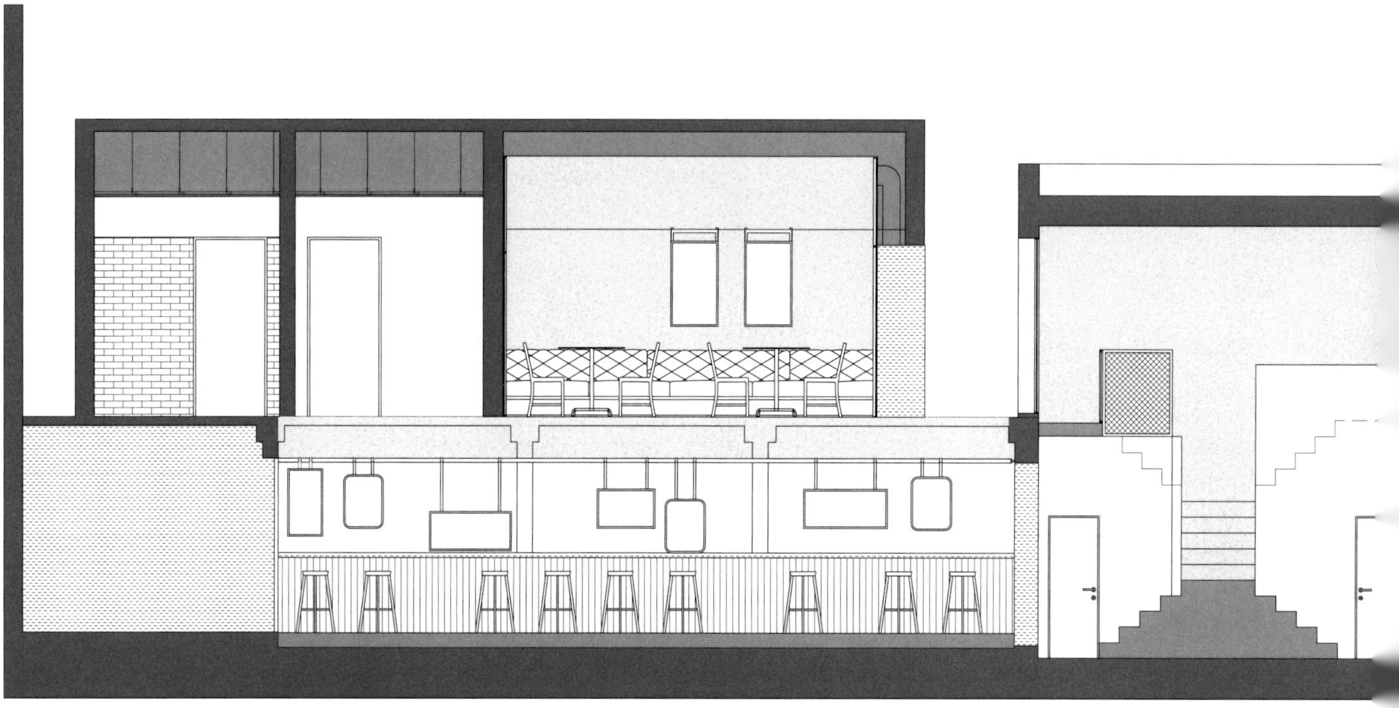

section A

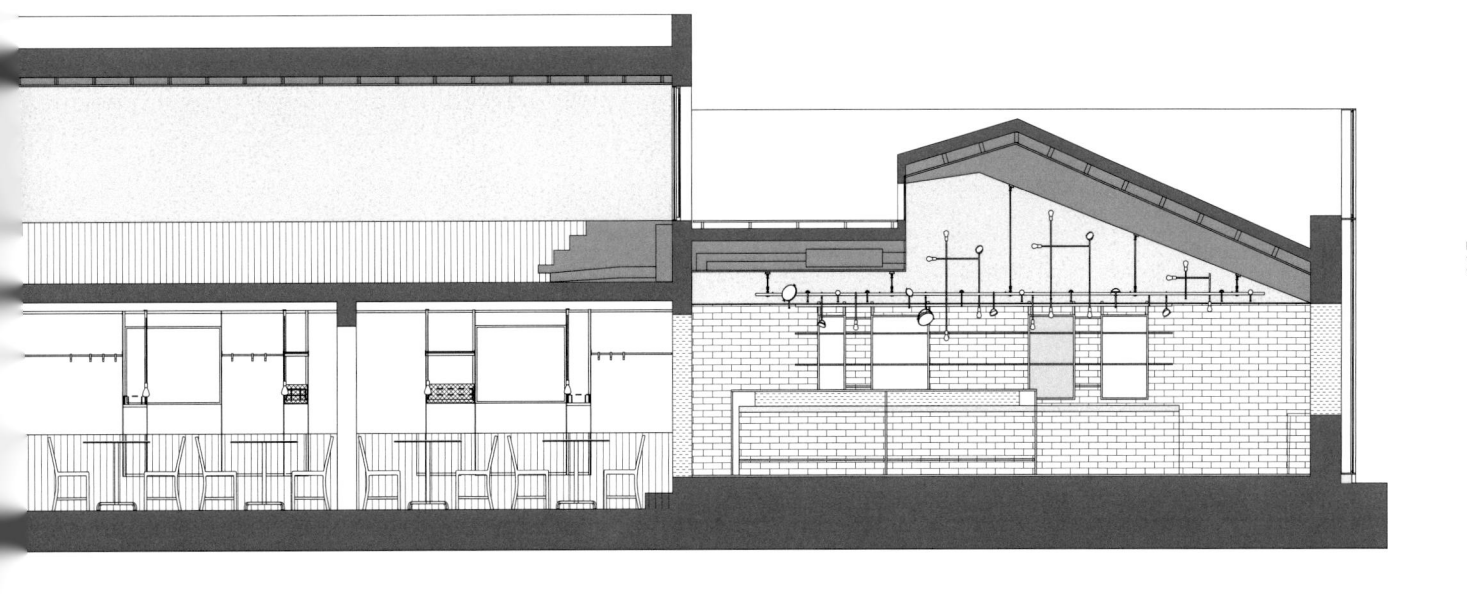

0 4m

118

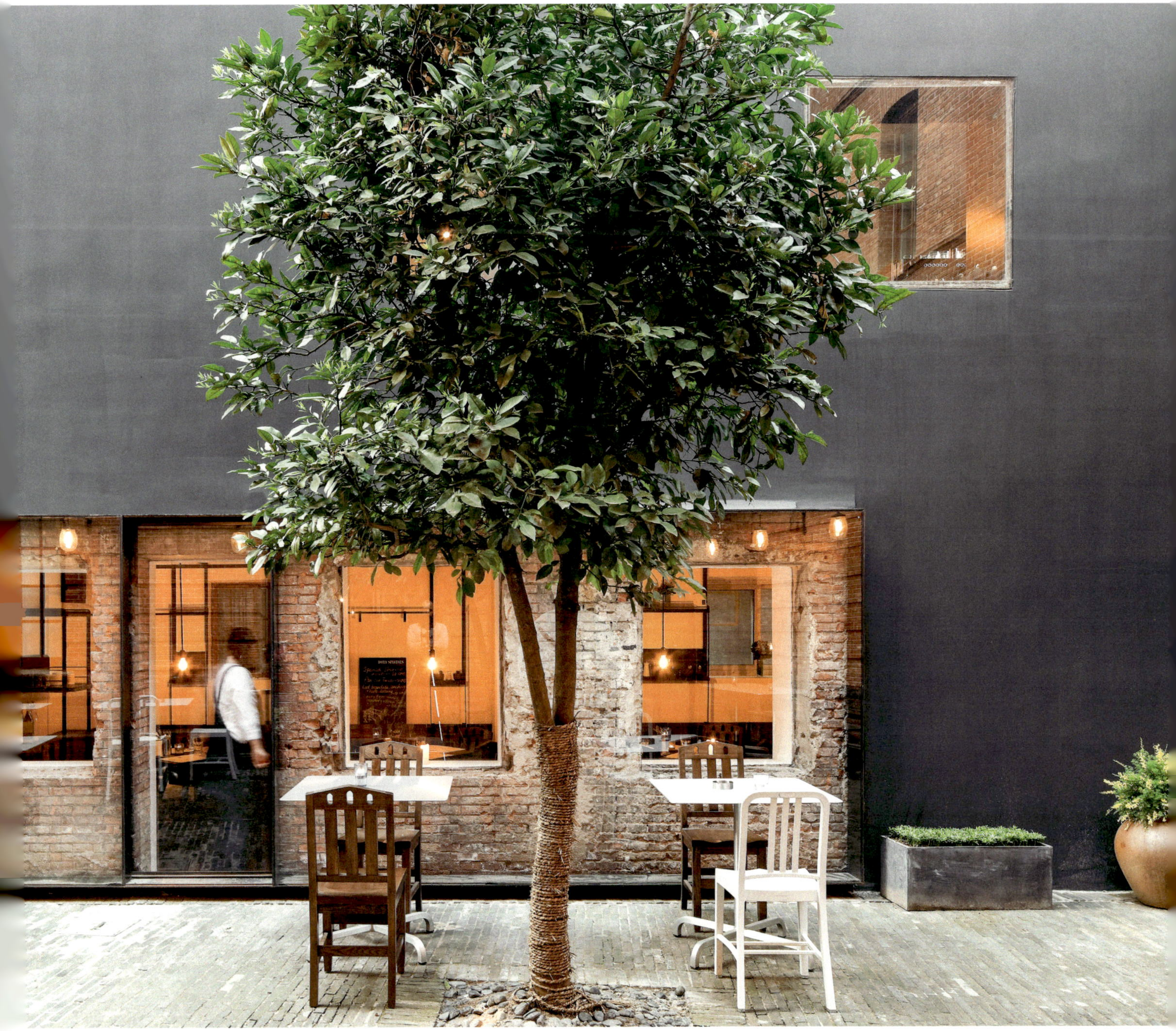

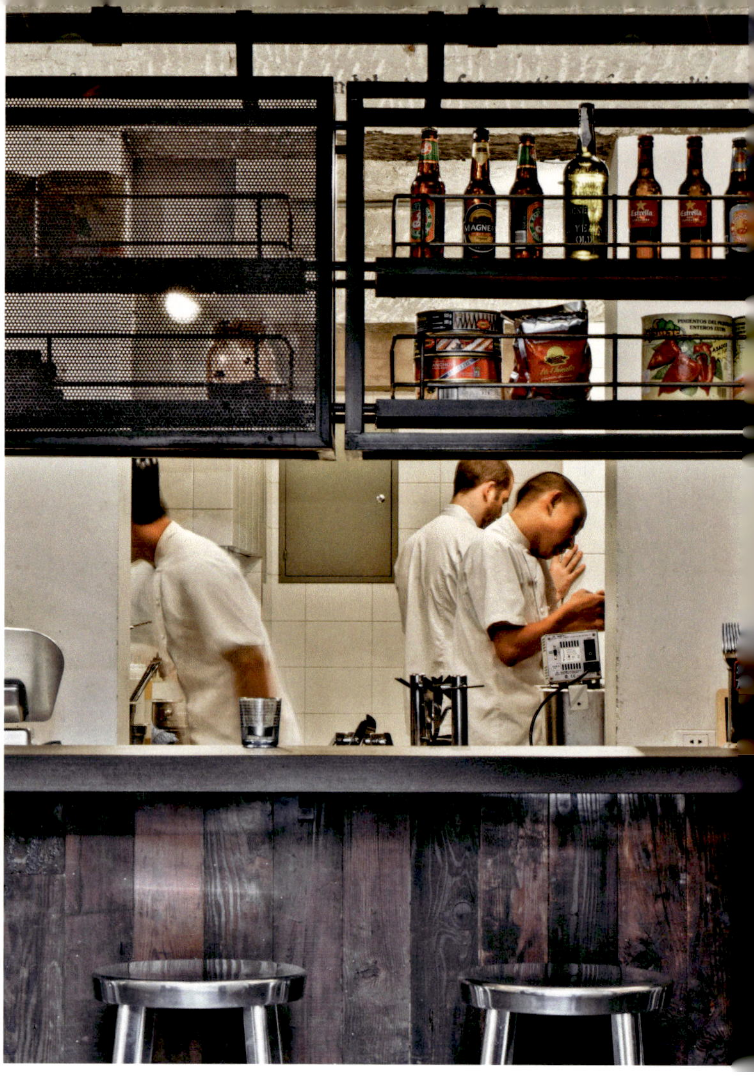

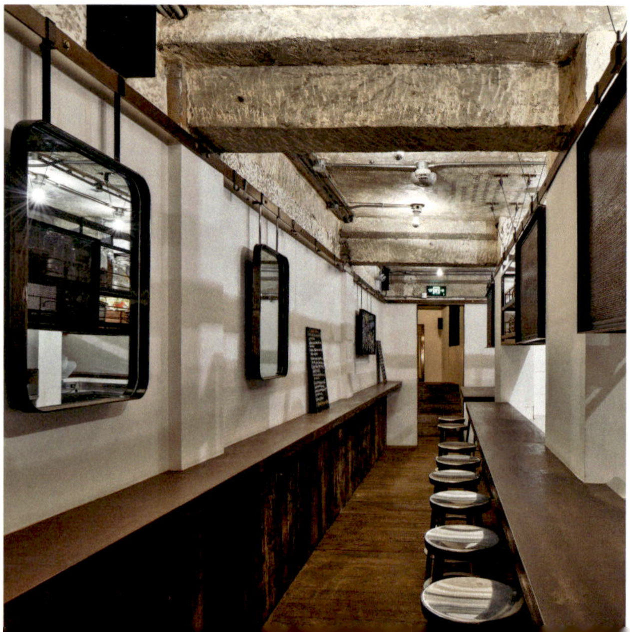

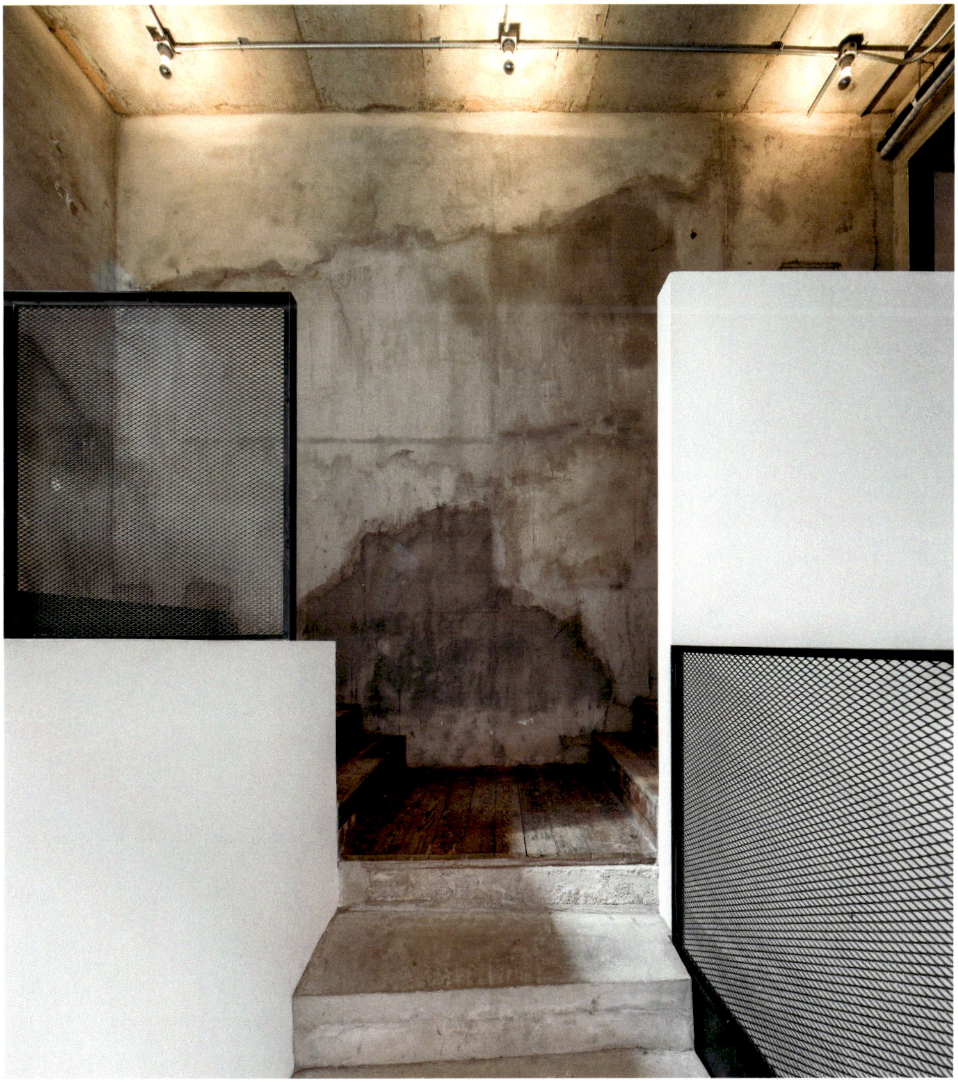

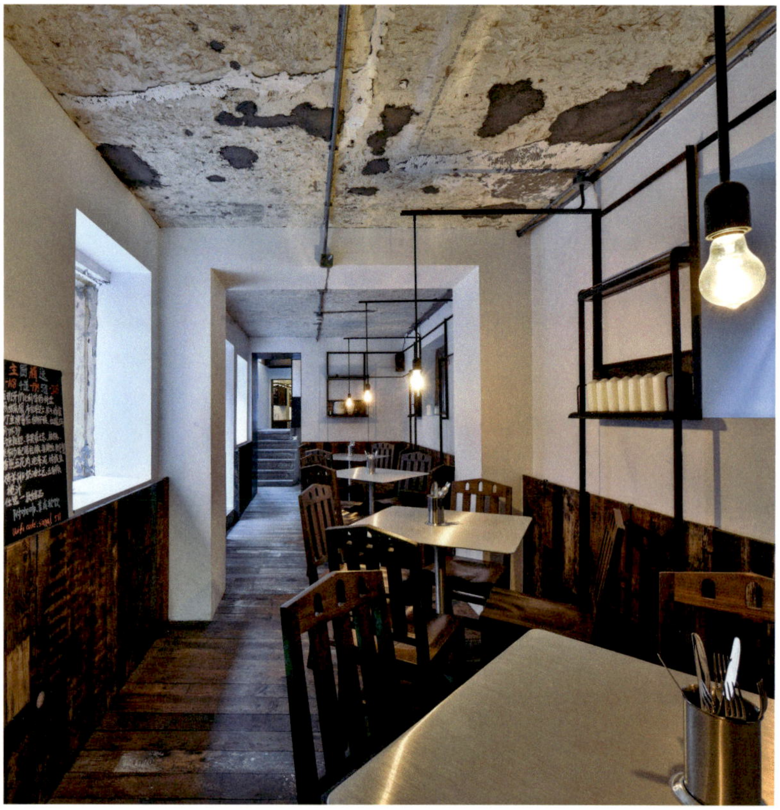

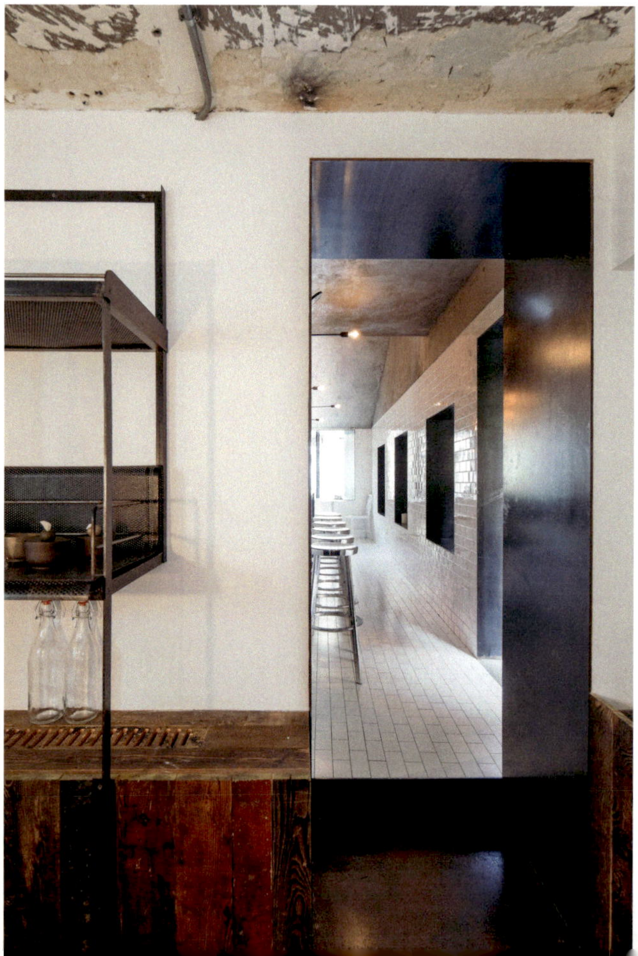

...ed and left ... James Joyce

DESSERT BAR
SPECIAL:

Creme Catalan
--- 55 RMB

Warm Chocolate
with blood oranges
--- 55 RMB

Ice Cream + Sorbet
Per Scoop ___ 15 RMB

Todays Pastry Chefs:
Kim, Tony + Damon.

DAILY SPECIALS
Spanish Iberico meats -- 68 RMB
Pan-con Tomato--38RMB
Cod brandade, anchovy + herb dressing --38 RMB
Potato fries, garlic rosemary + brava Sauce --38 RMB
Chef

I like people with depth, I like people with emotion,
I like people with the strong mind, an interesting mind,
a twisted mind, and also someone who can make me smile

... *Abbey Lee Kershaw*

THE SPLIT HOUSE
Private residence in Tianzifang, Shanghai

The unique lane houses of Shanghai, called *nong tang,* once comprised the dominant fabric that made urban Shanghai the intoxicating place that it was in the 1930s. Gradually having been demolished and replaced by high-density developments all over the city, it is now a diminishing typology. Located in the historic and artistic area of Tianzifang, the dilapidated lane house that we were commissioned to reconstruct was left with almost nothing except the existing shell. Our strategy was to rethink the typology of the lane house—keeping the split-level organization and adding spatial appeal through new insertions and cut openings—at once retaining the architectural integrity of the typology and contemporizing it for today's lifestyle.

Historically the lane houses are separated into two distinct zones: a longer and often rectangular space, with a smaller room half a level above that creates a split section connected by a winding stairway in between. These lane houses, which were previously occupied by single families, have evolved over the course of the city's economic development. They are now typically occupied by three or more parties sharing the public staircase and landings, so that neighbors living on different levels or in different rooms can interact as they move in and out of their personal spaces.

To keep the spirit of this typology alive, a new continuous metal staircase was inserted to replace the old, decaying wooden one that was no longer code compliant. It serves as both vertical access to all three levels and also a horizontal link between the front room and the room half a level above, in line with the original spatial configuration. Deviating from convention, however, all toilet facilities were inserted into the split-level stair spaces to maintain the purity of the main rooms. These bathrooms, conceivably the most intimate spaces of an apartment, are

Alfred Hitchcock. *Rear Window,* 1954
The film explores the fascination of looking and the attraction of that which is being looked at. The constructed (fictional) environment of the film shares an uncanny similarity to the living conditions we find in Shanghai. The traditional alleys, called nong tangs—*filled with secrets, desires, and memories—are authentic models of Chinese urbanity and domesticity.*

site map

0   200m

immediately adjacent to the most public stairway, separated only by a translucent glass divider. The focal staircase, which celebrates a blurring of the private and the public, is the conceptual departure point of the project, binding together the scattered spaces, while bringing vibrancy and appeal to what is normally the darkest part of the lane house.

Architecturally, the facade ornamentation built up over the last sixty years was stripped off, and large openings were created on the frontal section to bring light deep into the plan on each floor. The muted black coloring was selected to de-emphasize the exterior form, rather drawing attention to the glowing apertures. Gazing into these picture windows, as in Hitchcock's *Rear Window,* forces one to question notions of privacy, domesticity, and community within the unique environment of Shanghai's *nong tang*. By capturing the spirit of the historic past and making modern abstract insertions to meet the needs of contemporary living, we hoped to infuse new vibrancy into the lane house typology, whose original fabric seems to be dissolving too fast and too soon.

demolition plan | section

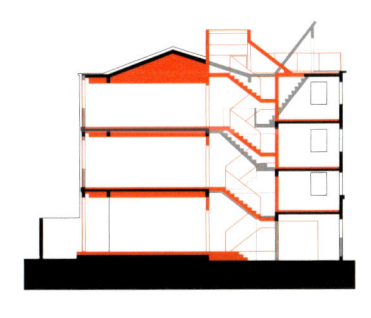

roof plan | third- to first-floor plan

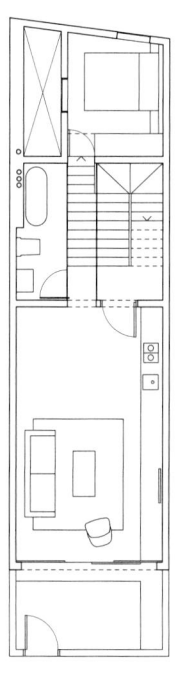

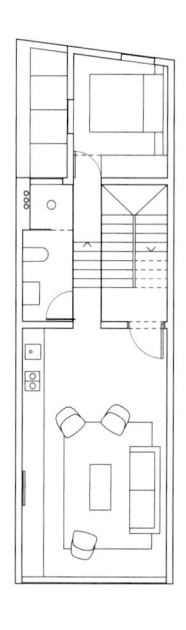

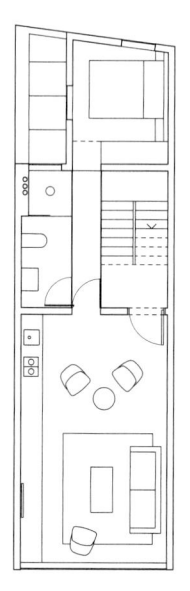

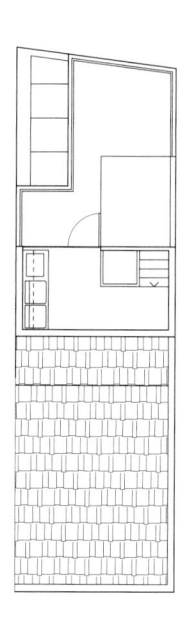

ground-floor plan   0   5m

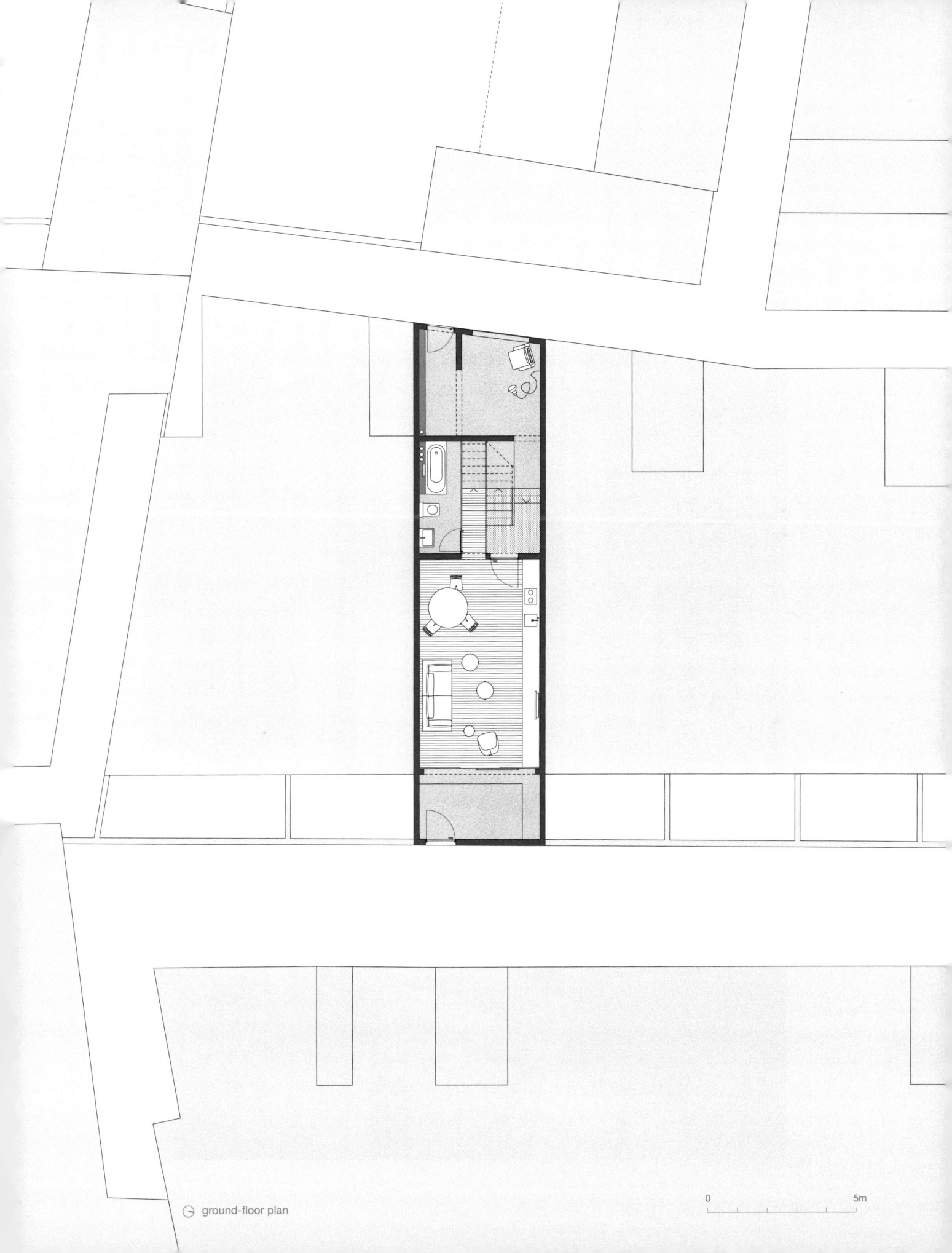

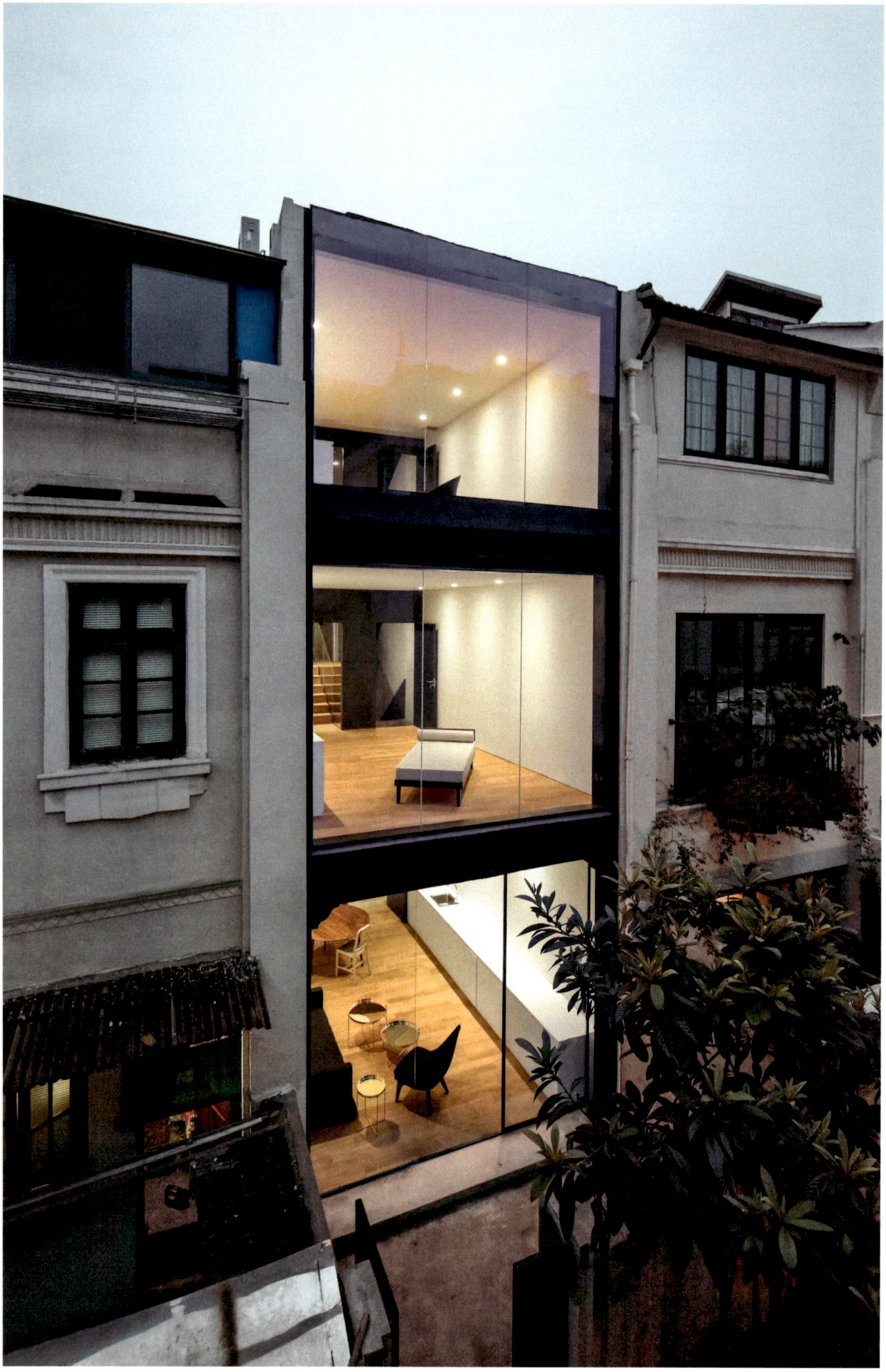

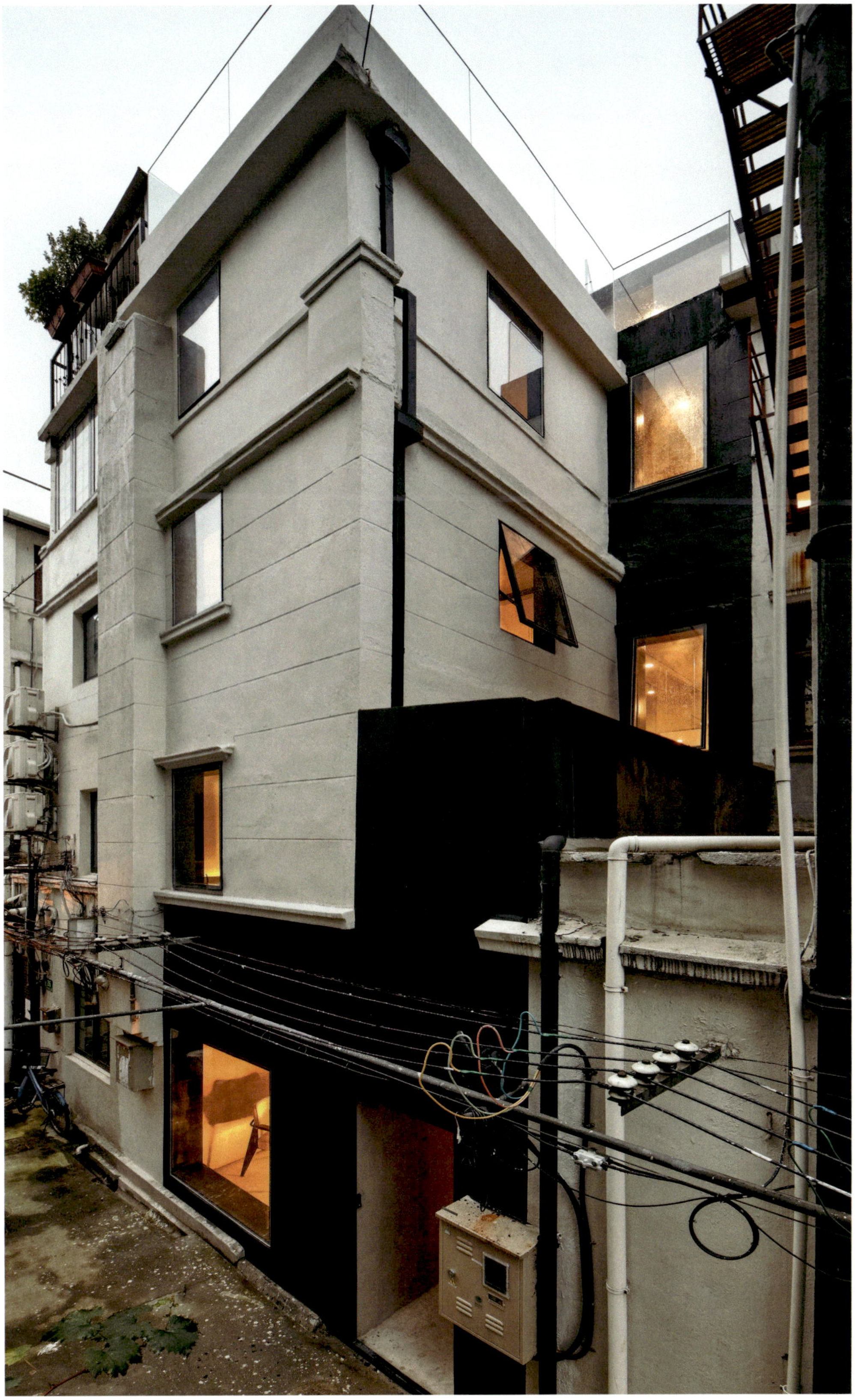

134

135

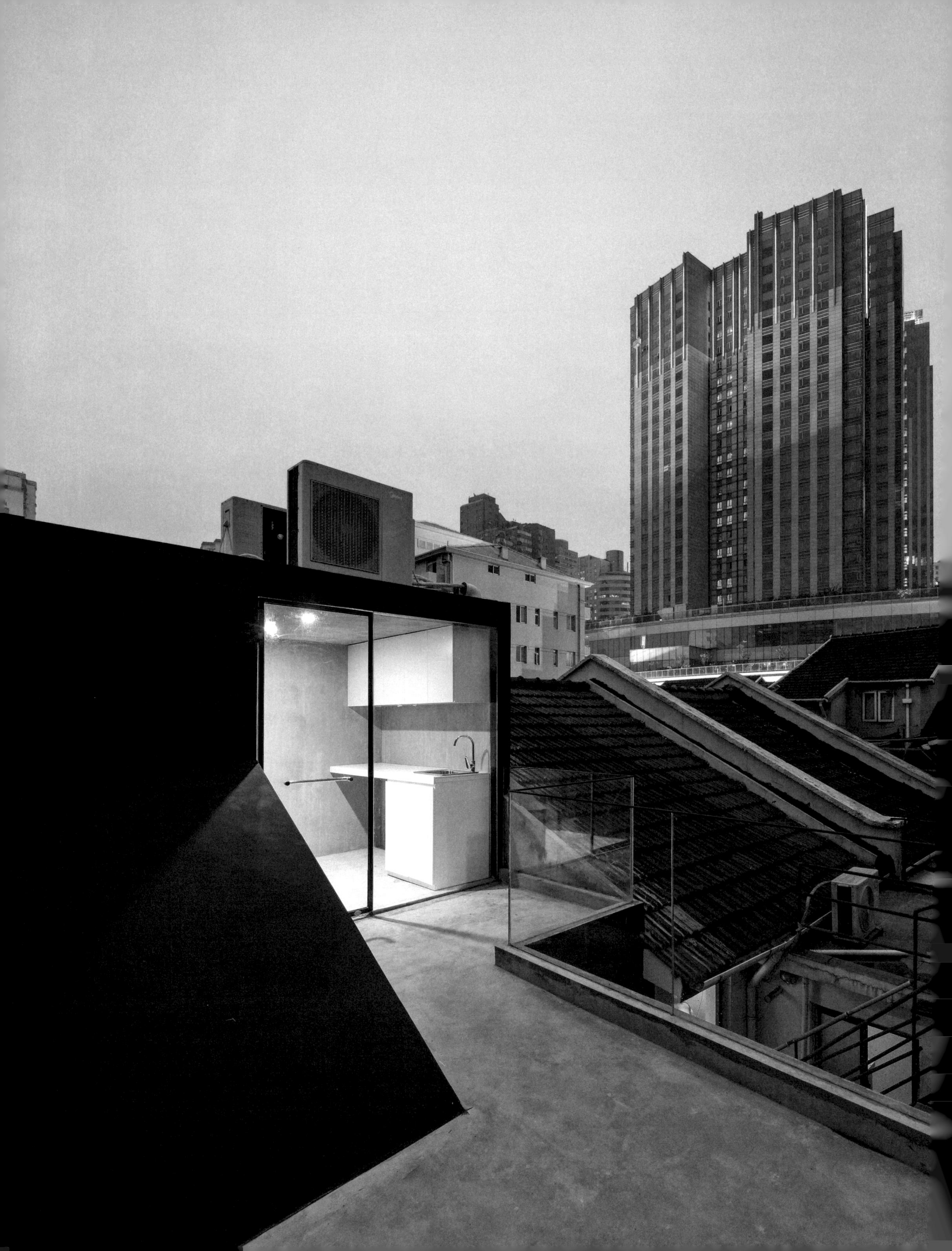

137

1 Window
5+5-mm tempered laminated glass

2 Floor structure
40-mm wood plank
20-mm wood furring strip
250-mm beam
70-mm wood blocking
20-mm wood furring strip
10-mm wood veneer

3 Staircase floor structure
8-mm corten steel
64-mm steel stud
250-mm steel beam
8-mm corten steel

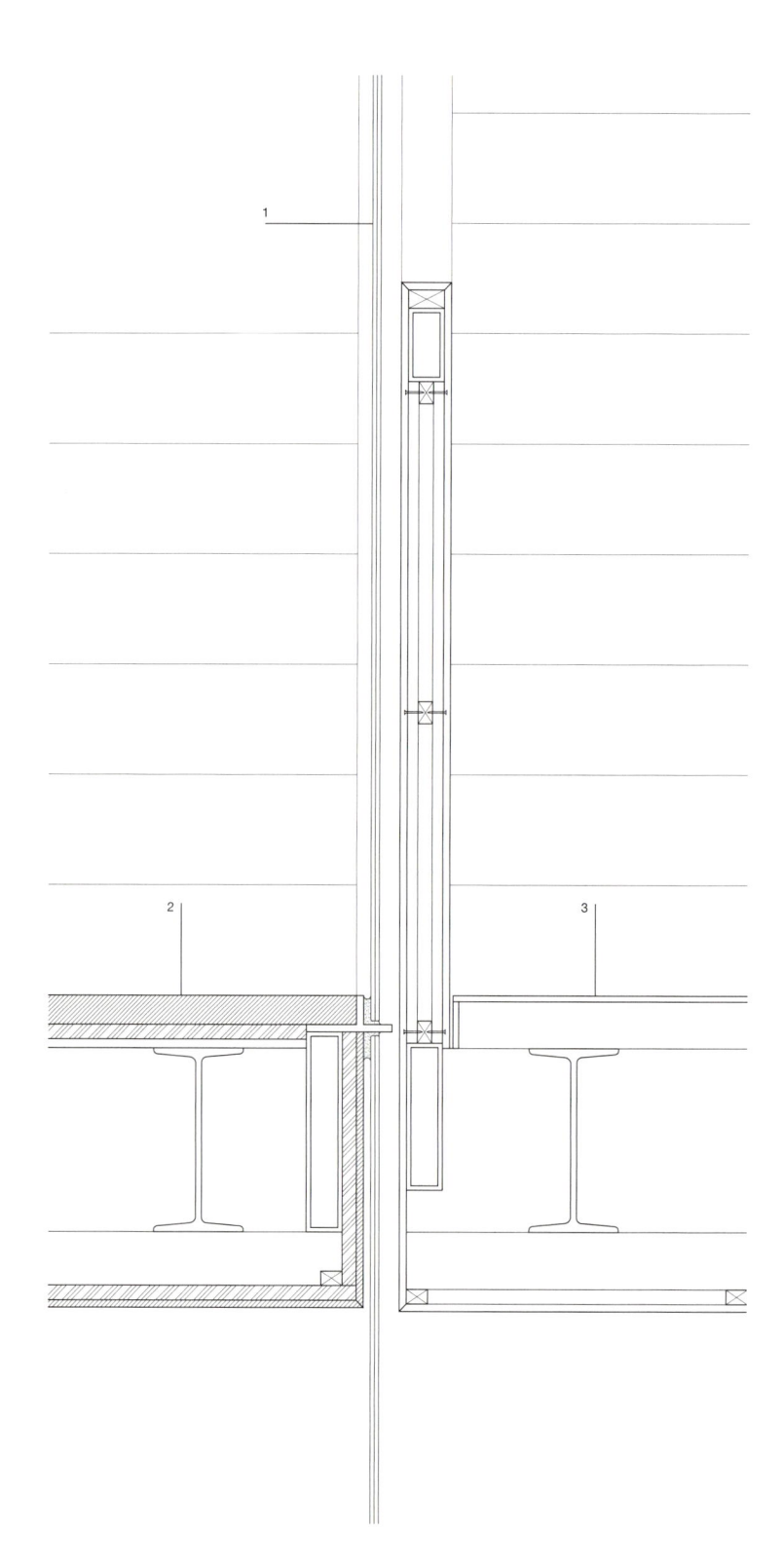

1 Window sill
3-mm fluorocarbon-coated black steel
40-mm rail with stud and cavity
3-mm polythene membrane
10-mm screed leveling
Existing concrete cornice

2 Floor structure
20-mm wood floorboard (tongue and groove)
20-mm counter-floor
45-mm battens with impact insulation
150-mm existing wood joist
230-mm cavity
50-mm V channel
15-mm paper-faced gypsum board

3 Window
6+15+6-mm insulated double glazing

4 Ground structure
80-mm cement underlayment with polished screed finish
5-mm polyethylene membrane
Reinforced concrete base

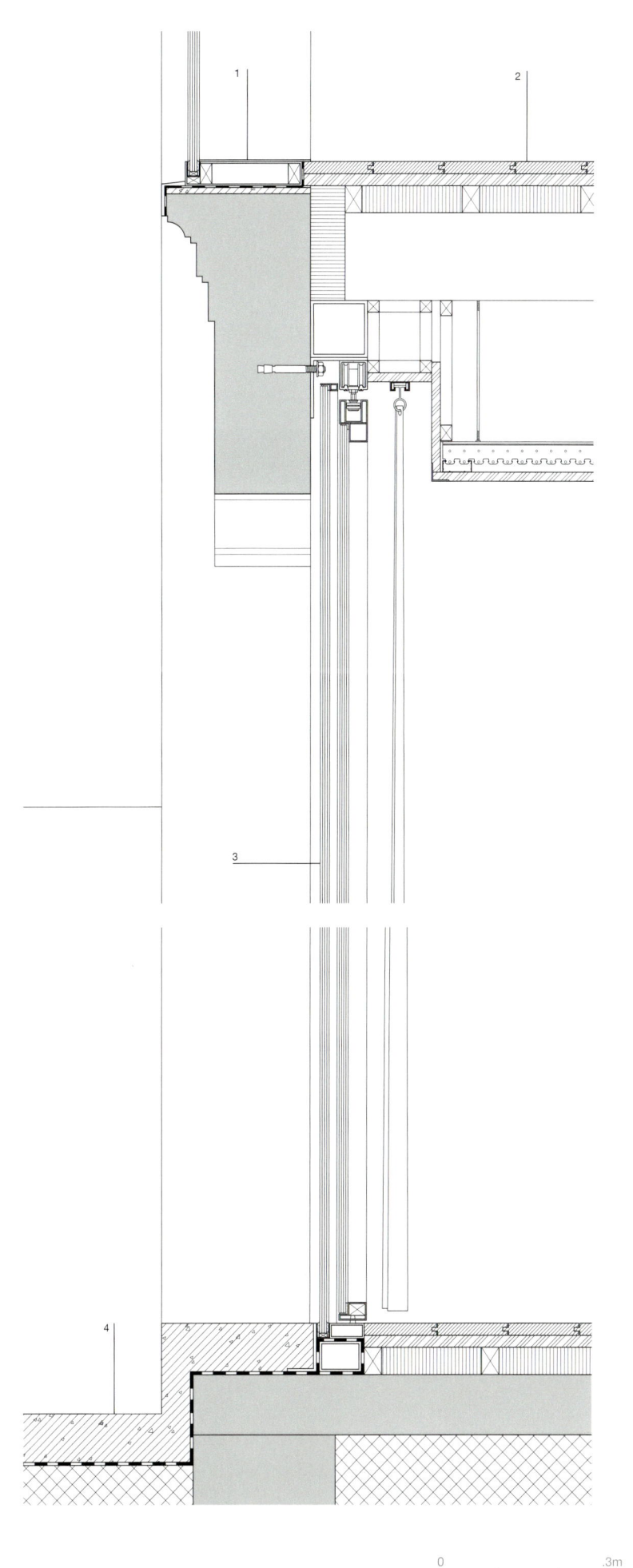

corridor and staircase detail | window detail

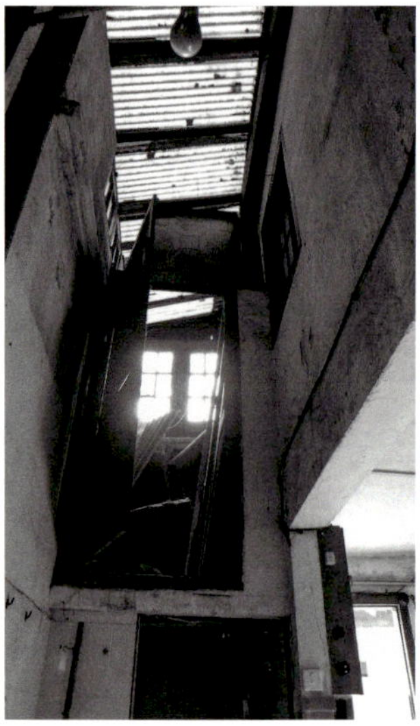

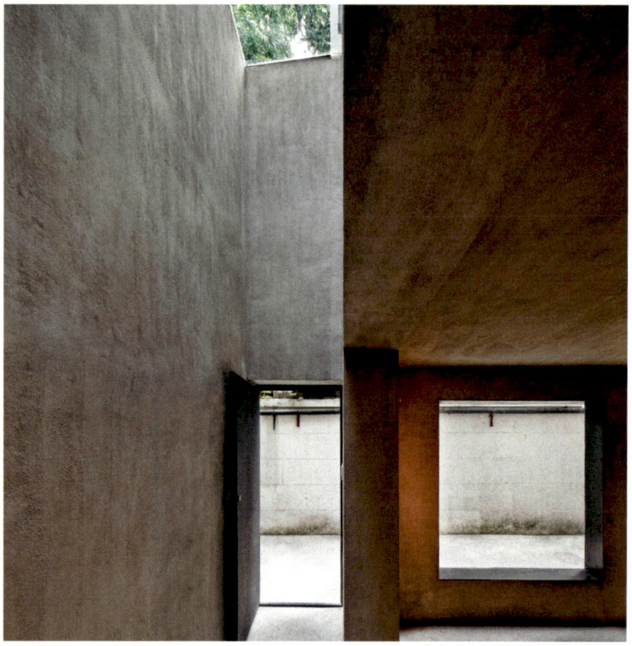

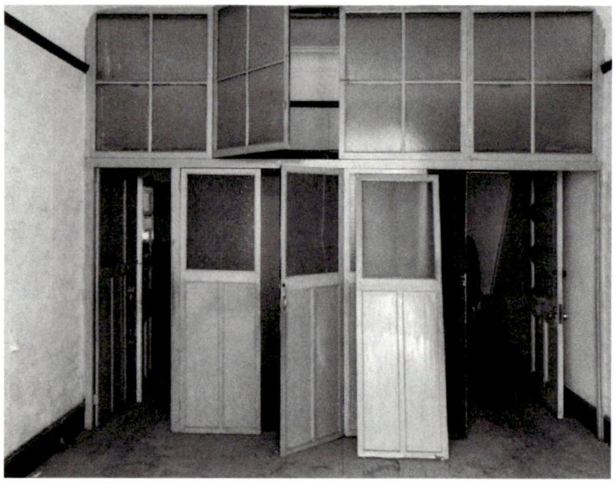

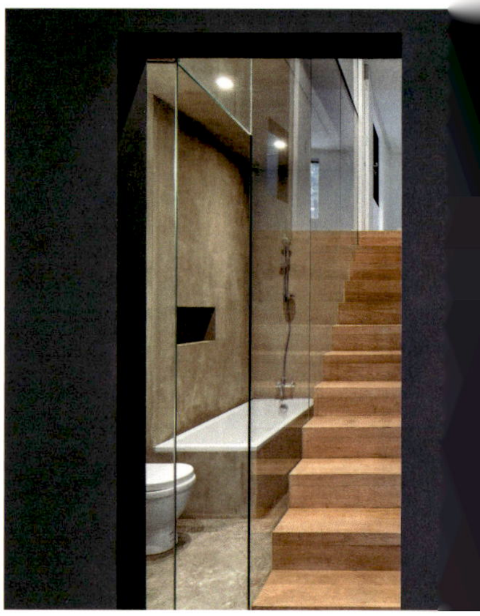

141

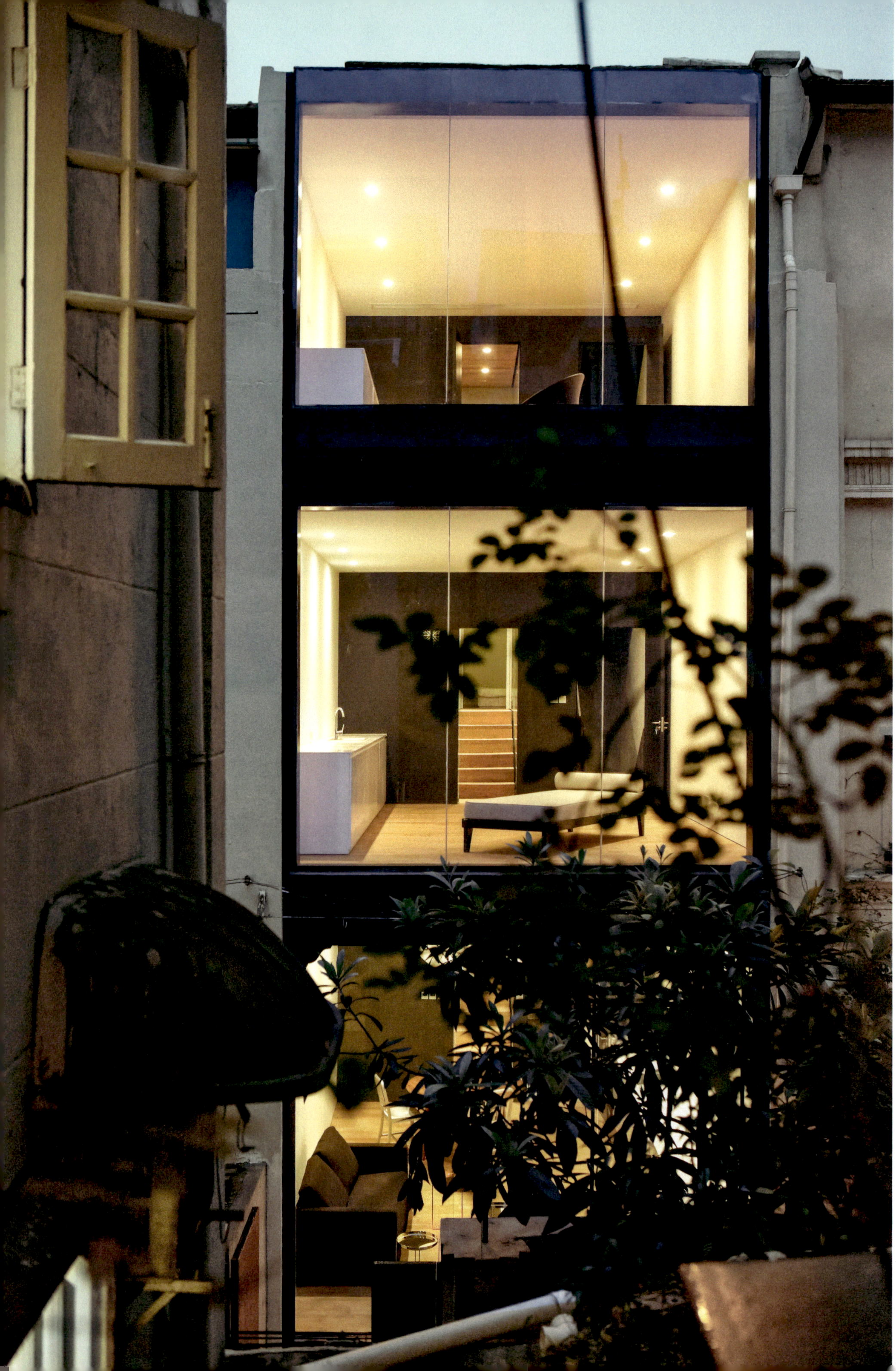

143

THE MARKETPLACE
Mercato Restaurant by Jean-Georges Vongerichten, Shanghai

Situated within the prestigious Three on the Bund, Mercato restaurant draws not only from its chef's culinary vision of a bustling Italian marketplace, but also from the rich historical context of its locale, harkening to early-1900s Shanghai, when the Bund was a burgeoning industrial hub. This project for us is a showcase of our interdisciplinary practice. It is all about storytelling and using our full arsenal as designers to convey the narrative: Space planning, materiality, detailing, furniture design, graphic identity, and even accessories all work together to enhance the concept and the space.

Stripping back the strata of finishes that have built up after years of renovations, the design celebrates the beauty of the bare structural elements. Three on the Bund was the first building in Shanghai to be built out of steel, and the decision to reveal the original steel columns pays homage to this extraordinary feat. Against the textured backdrop of the existing brickwork, concrete, and plaster moldings, new insertions are clearly demarcated. Stepping out of the lift, one notices immediately the Victorian plaster ceilings above, their gorgeous aged patina juxtaposed against raw steel insertions: a series of lockers along the wall, a sliding metal gate threshold, and the suspended rail from which a collection of eclectic glass bulbs hang—the opulence of old Shanghai coinciding with a grittier side. Constantly playing the new against the old, the design is a reflection of the complex identity of not only the historical Bund, but of Shanghai itself.

Making reference to the restaurant's name, the vibrant atmosphere inside the main dining space recalls a streetside marketplace, featuring at its center the Bar and the Pizza Bar, both encased in steel mesh and wire-glass boxes with recycled wood canopies. Above, a network of tube steel members, inspired by old-time butcher's rails, intertwine with the exposed ductwork and form a system for hanging both shelving and lighting. Like a deconstructed sofa, the banquettes along the edge of the dining area are made from wood salvaged on site and embedded into a metal frame. The attached light fixture reaches over the diners and creates a visual enclosure. The corridors and Private Dining Rooms feature in the space as

site map

0   200m

metal frames filled in with panels of varying materials: reclaimed wood, natural steel, antique mirror, metal mesh, textured glass and chalk board—inspired by old warehouse windows.

Diners seated along the edges of the room experience a different sort of ambiance. To bring lightness into the space, the perimeter represents an in-between zone: between interior and exterior, between architecture and landscape, between the domestic and the urban. Clad in white travertine, the walls here act as a temporary departure from the otherwise rich textures and palettes. Small custom mirrors at each window reflect the breathtaking views of the Bund beyond, drawing the far reaches of the city into the dining space.

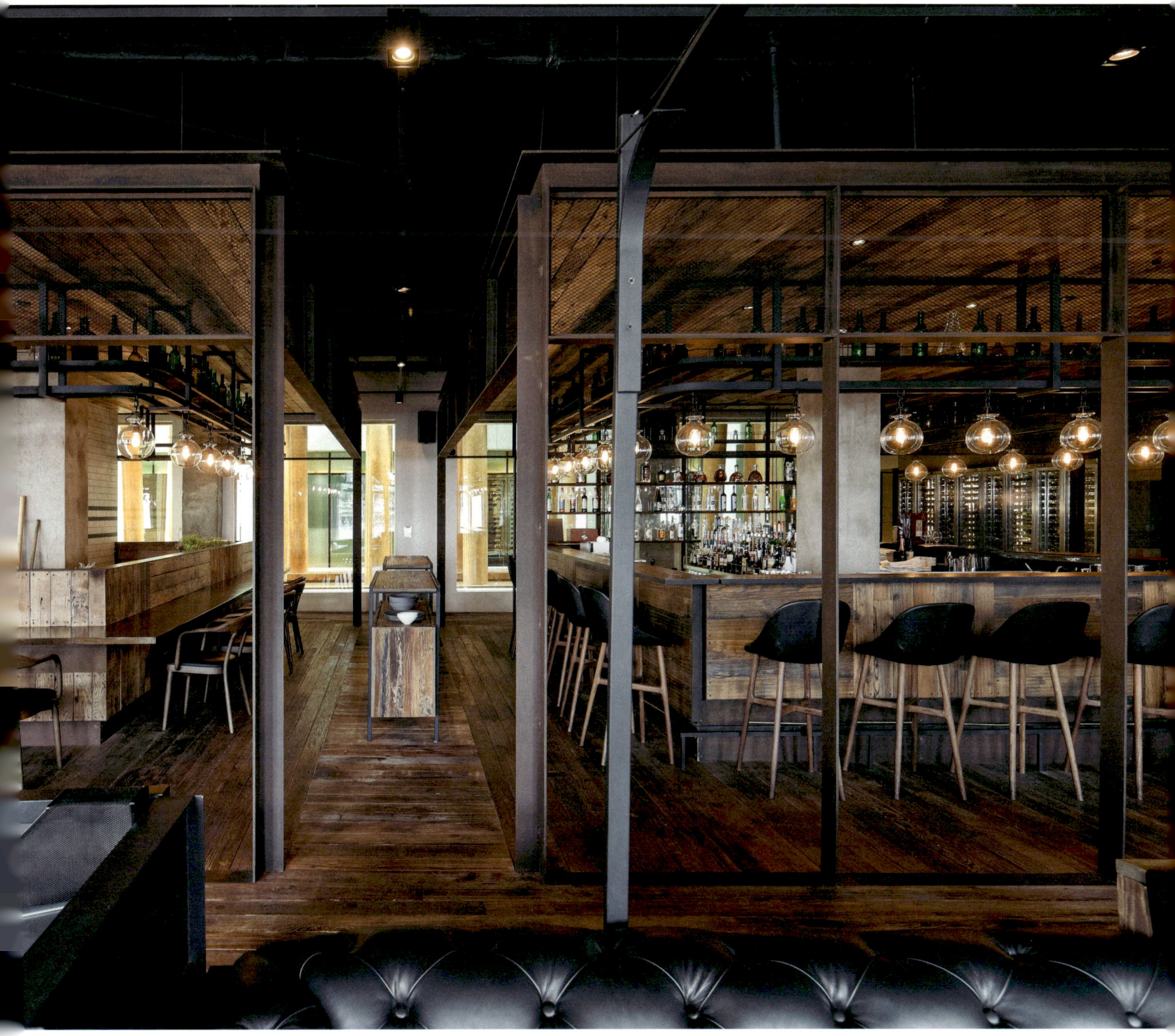

148

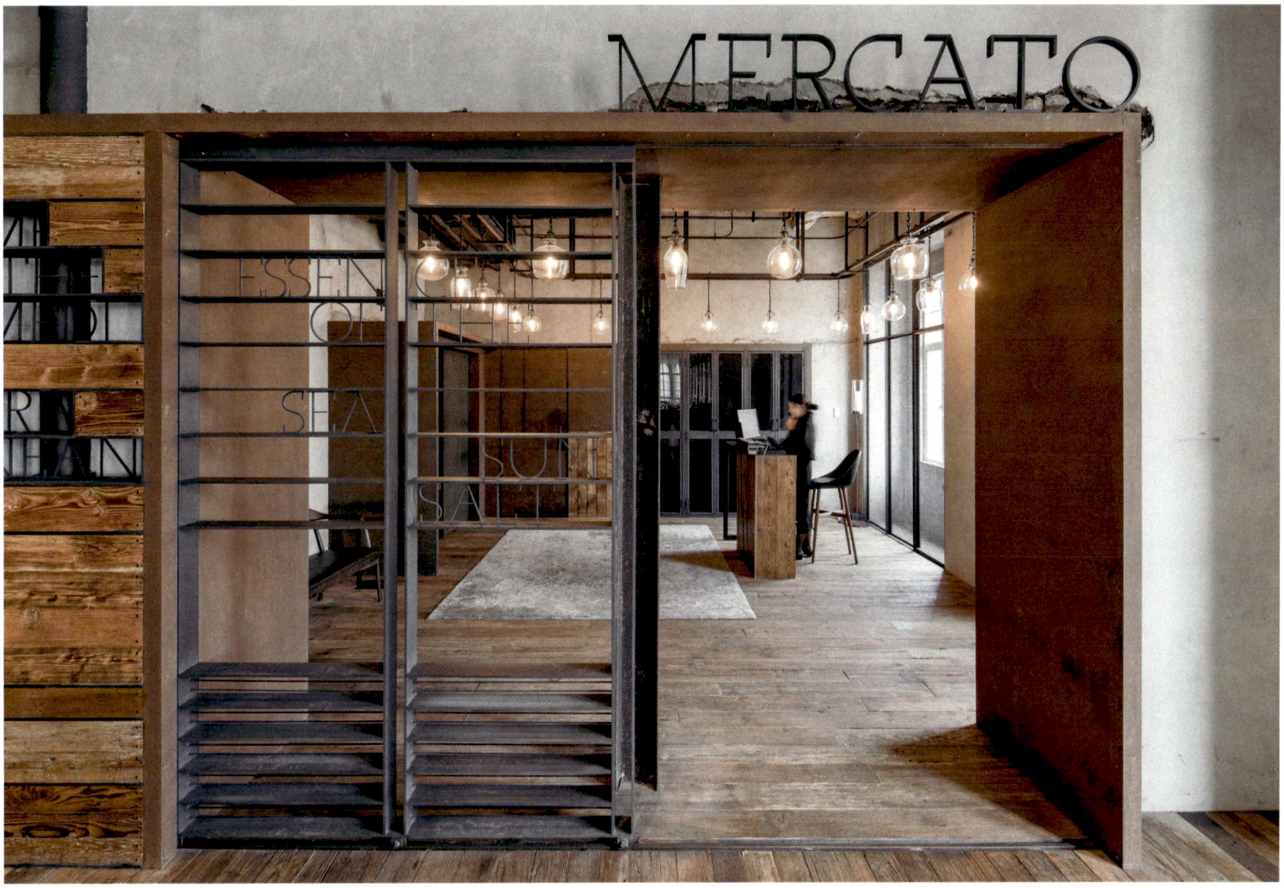
MERCATO

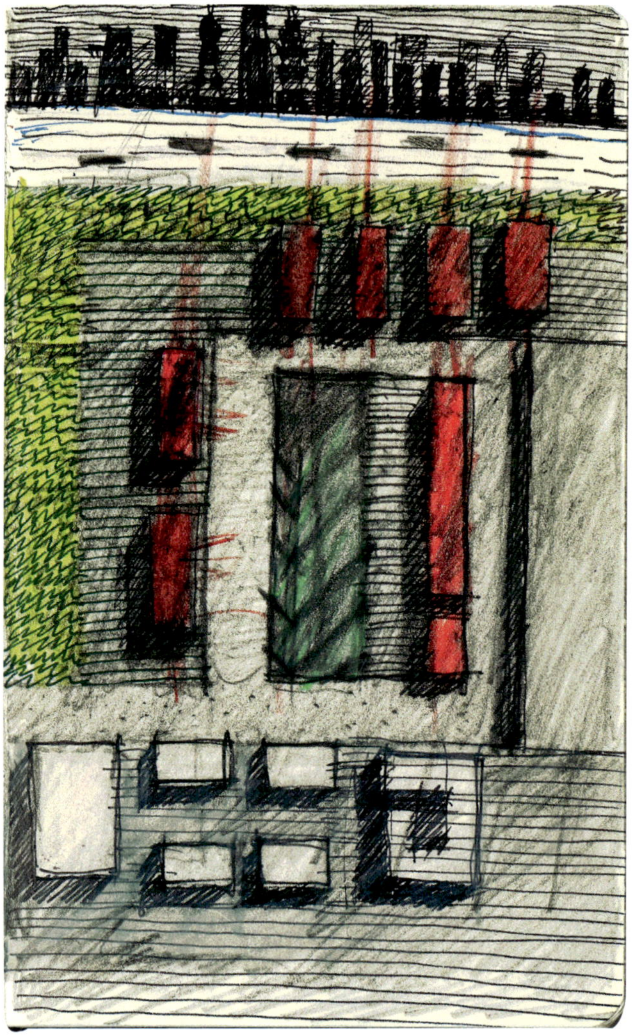

demolition plan

0 15m

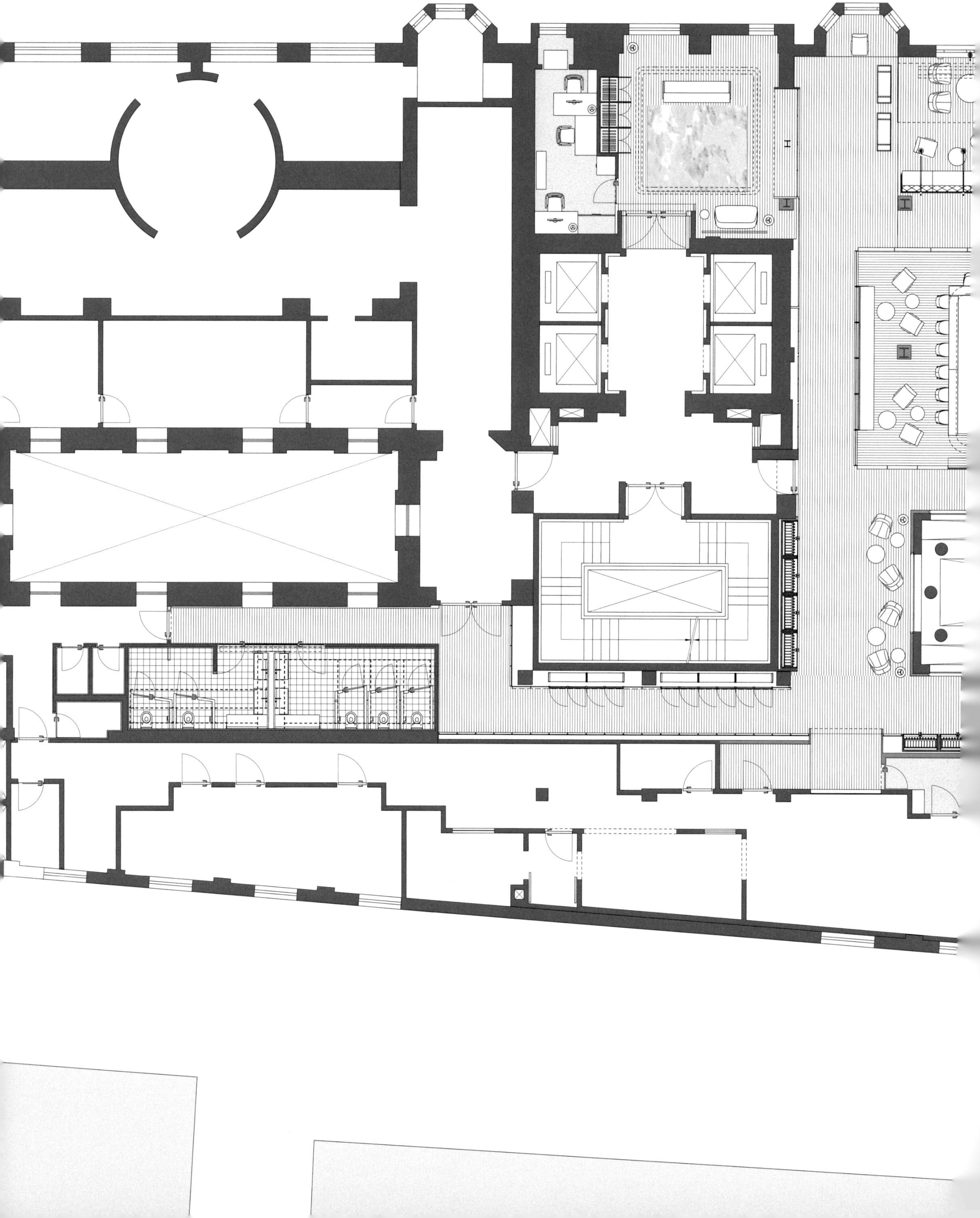

plan

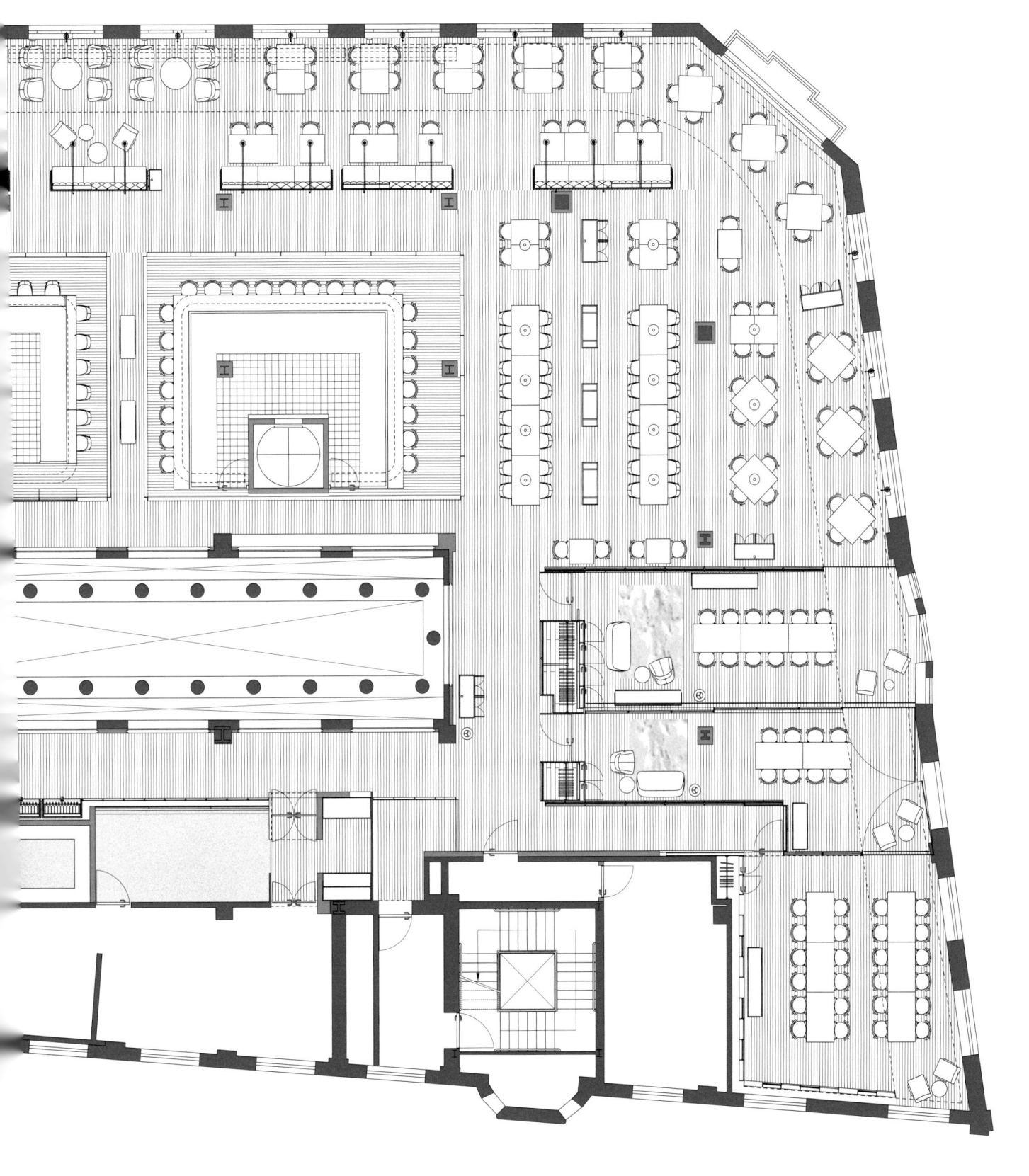

0 5m

MERCATO

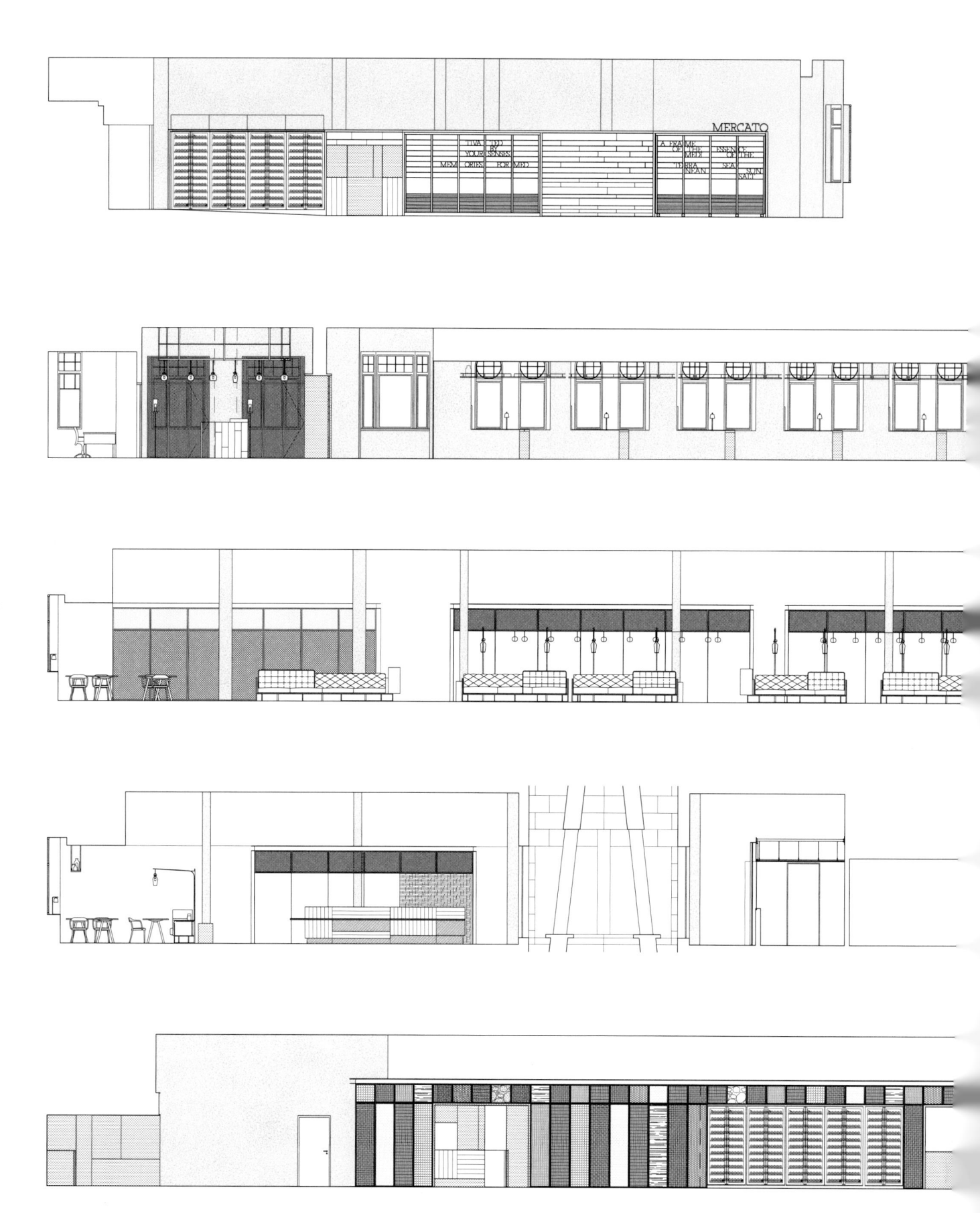

TIVA TED YOUR SENSES MEMORIES FOR MED

A FRAME OF THE MEDI TERRA NEAN

ESSENCE OF THE SEA SUN SALT

elevations

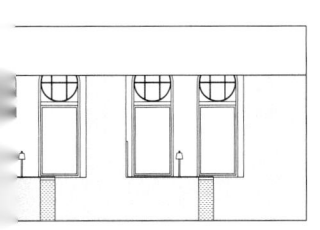

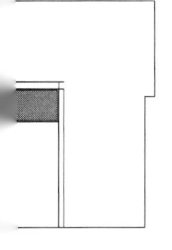

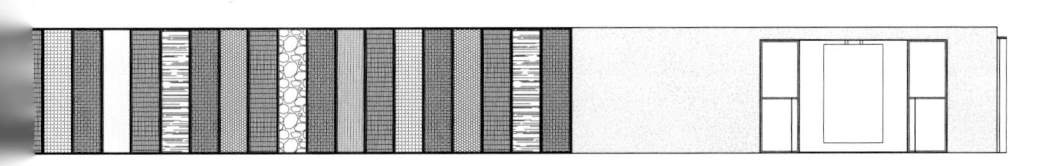

155

0   5m

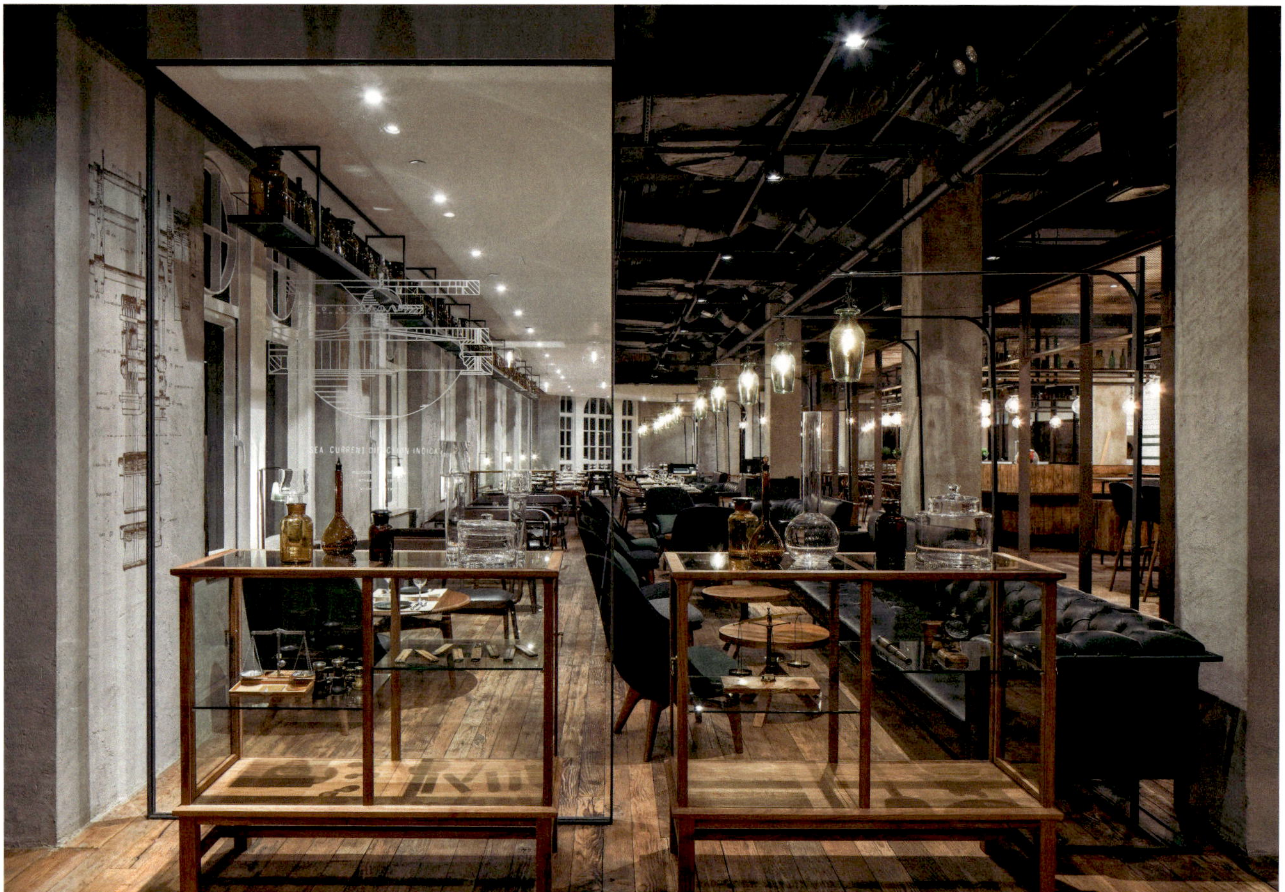

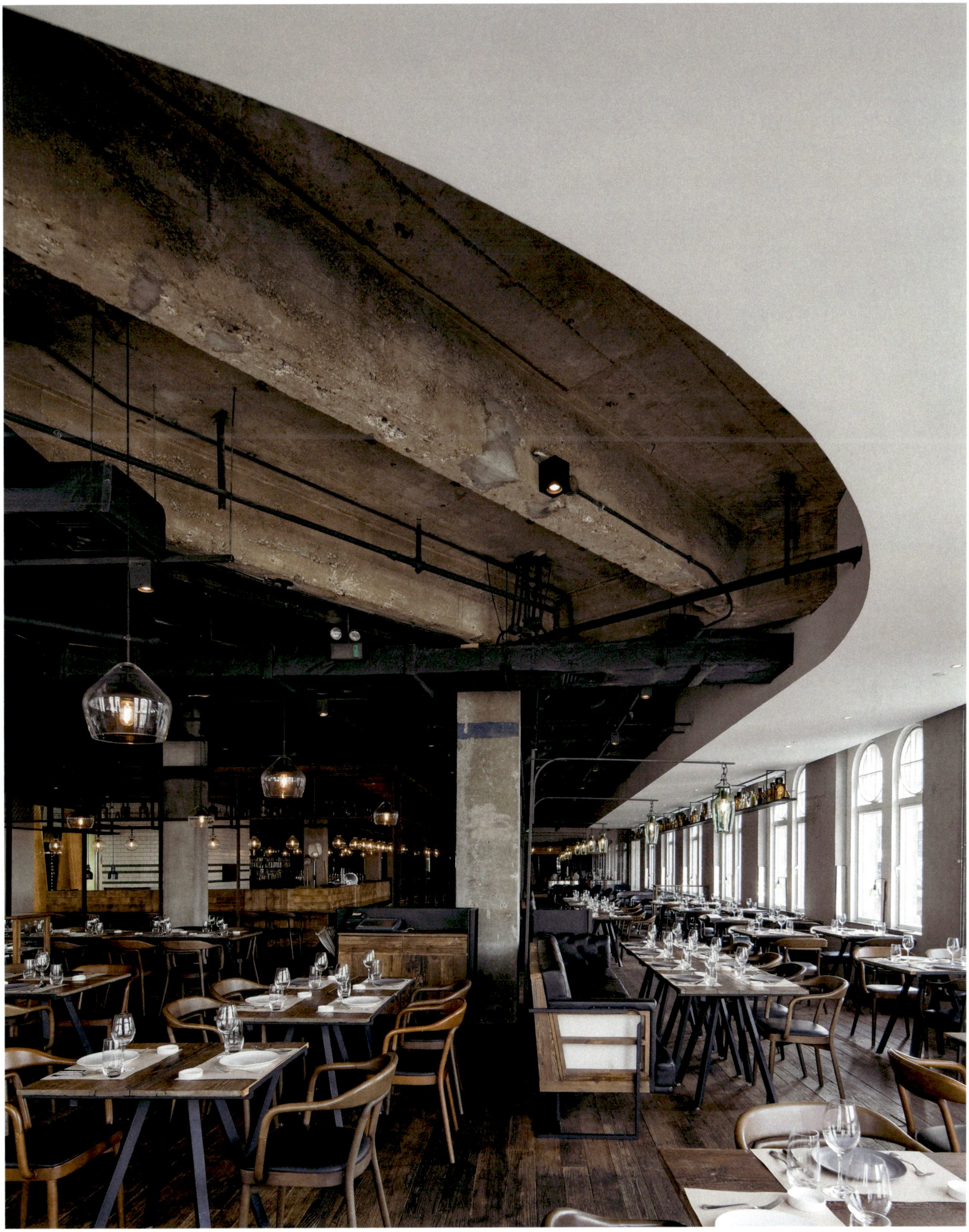

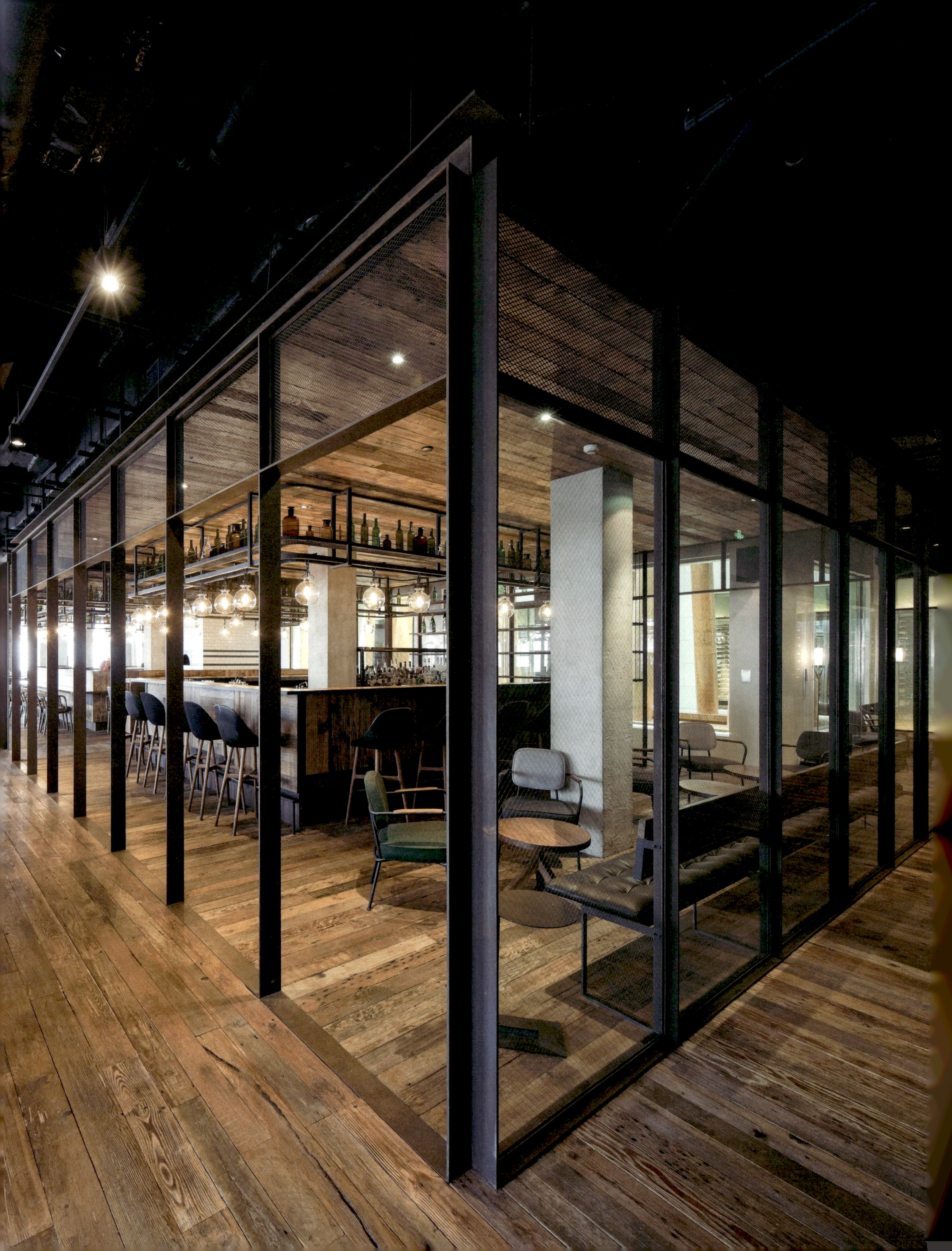

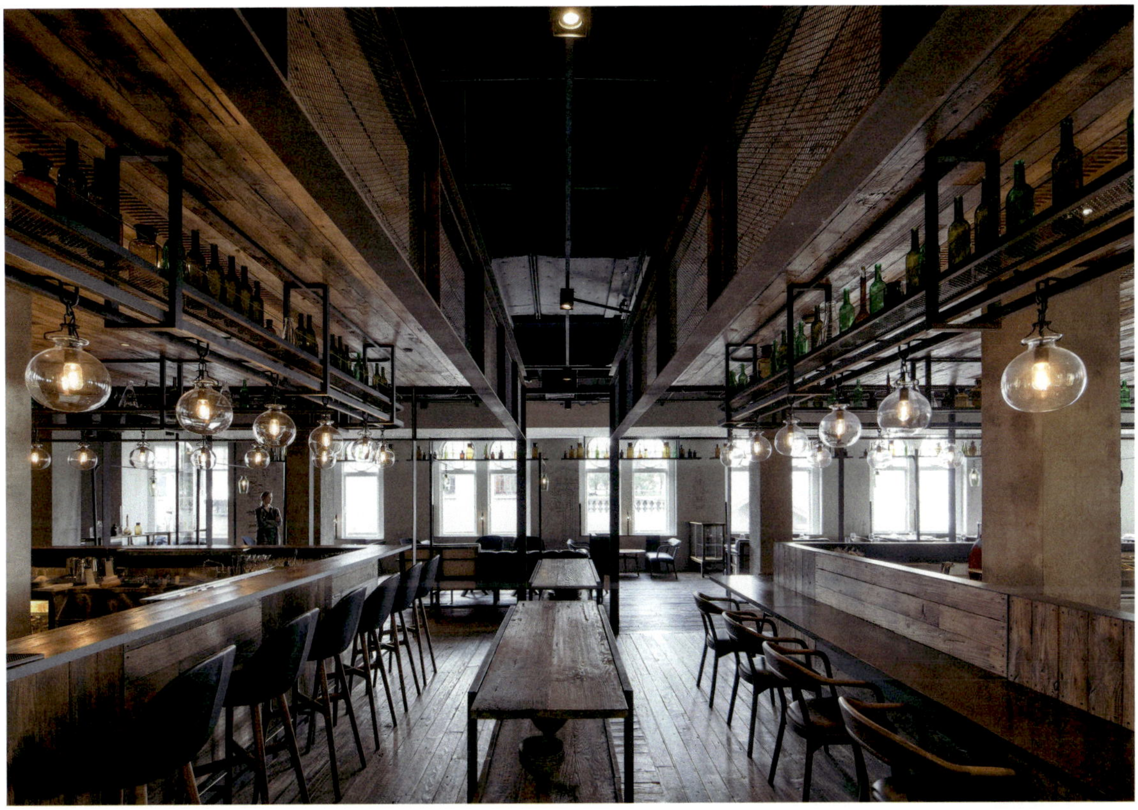

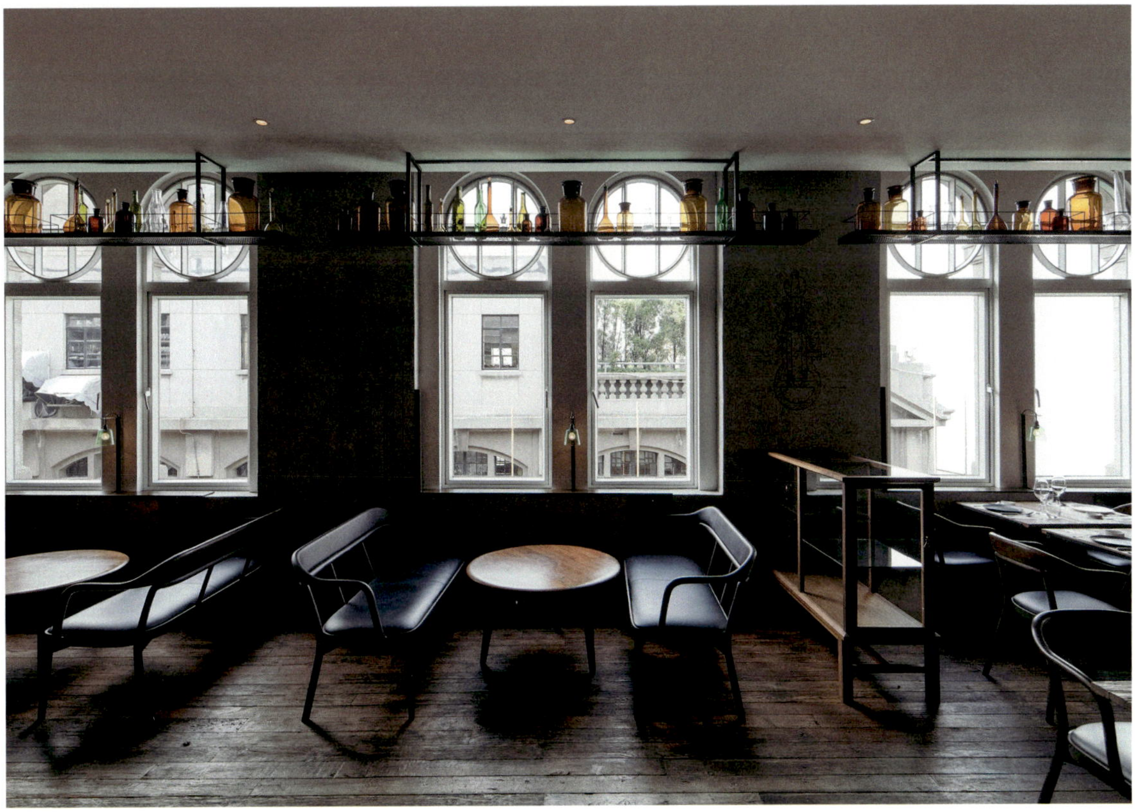

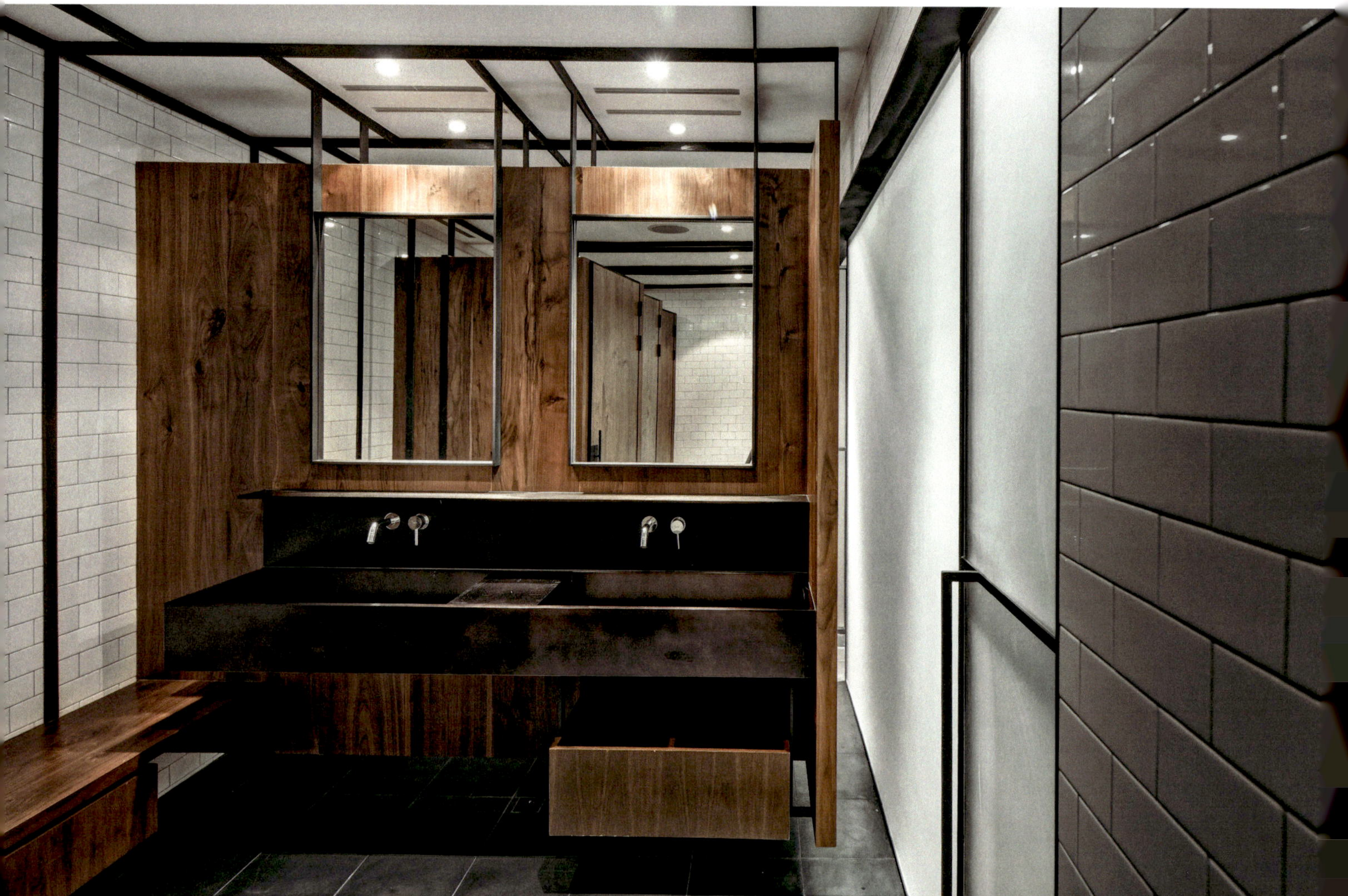

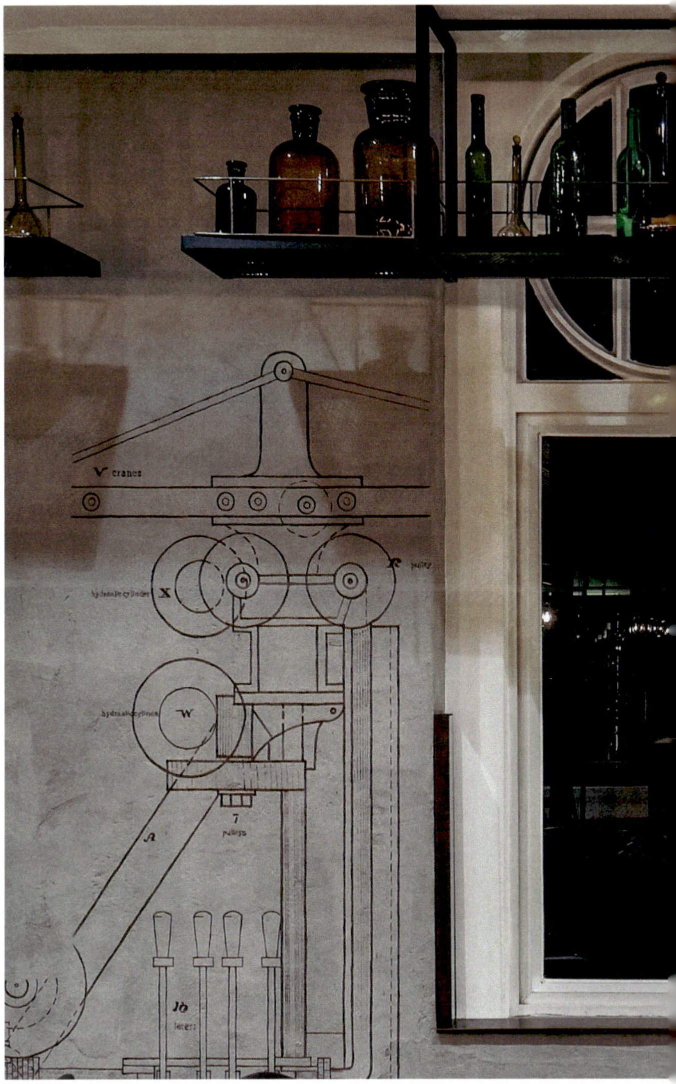
V cranes
X
W
7
levers

THE RECYCLED LANE HOUSE
Camper China Showroom, Shanghai

In many of our projects we have dealt intentionally and sensitively with the notion of old versus new. With historic building renovations, it has been a conscious effort to delineate what is an existing element and what is our new insertion. For Camper the context of the site was a bit less straightforward. The existing building is a warehouse-type structure built around the early 2000s, rather unremarkable historically and spatially. And the client's brief specified the inclusion of contextual references, so given the site's location within an alleyway, we wanted to take the notion of the Shanghai *nong tang* alley and extend it into the building. In a sense we were inverting our typical practice: Rather than injecting the new into the old, we were extending the old into the new (or new-ish).

Being Camper's first "home" in Shanghai, we placed a traditional two-story lane house into the existing structure and then literally cut out a section from it, to create the sense of the brand opening itself up to the lanes of the city. An oversized mirror faces the cut section and further extends the lane into the building. To draw a clear distinction, everything from the existing building is kept in neutral hues: white paint on the walls and structures, and gray epoxy floors. The house structure, on the other hand, consists of richly textured materials; utilizing reclaimed materials, brick and wood planks, from nearby lane houses being demolished, was a way to memorialize the gradual and tragic destruction of Shanghai's historic urban fabric.

Drawing more inspiration from the surrounding neighborhood, the project recreates a unique condition found in the *nong tang:* horizontal bars which span across narrow alleys for hanging laundry. We reinterpreted this phenomenon as a feature shoe display where Camper products dangle from steel hooks at various heights and can be viewed from different angles high and low. A new skylight addition above heightens the experience of being in an exterior alley by casting long linear shadows across the walls throughout the day. In one of the back "alleys" there is even a terrazzo wash basin which has been relocated directly from a *nong tang,* where communal sinks are quite a common occurrence.

Robert van der Hilst. *Chinese Interiors,* 1990–1993
This photo series has always resonated with us, because it captures the reality of the city that we have chosen to situate our practice in—the grittiness and rawness on the one side, and the incredible warmth and humanity on the other side. These layers and textures of inhabitation are not only what inspires us, but what we aspire to (re)create.

site map

0   200m

164

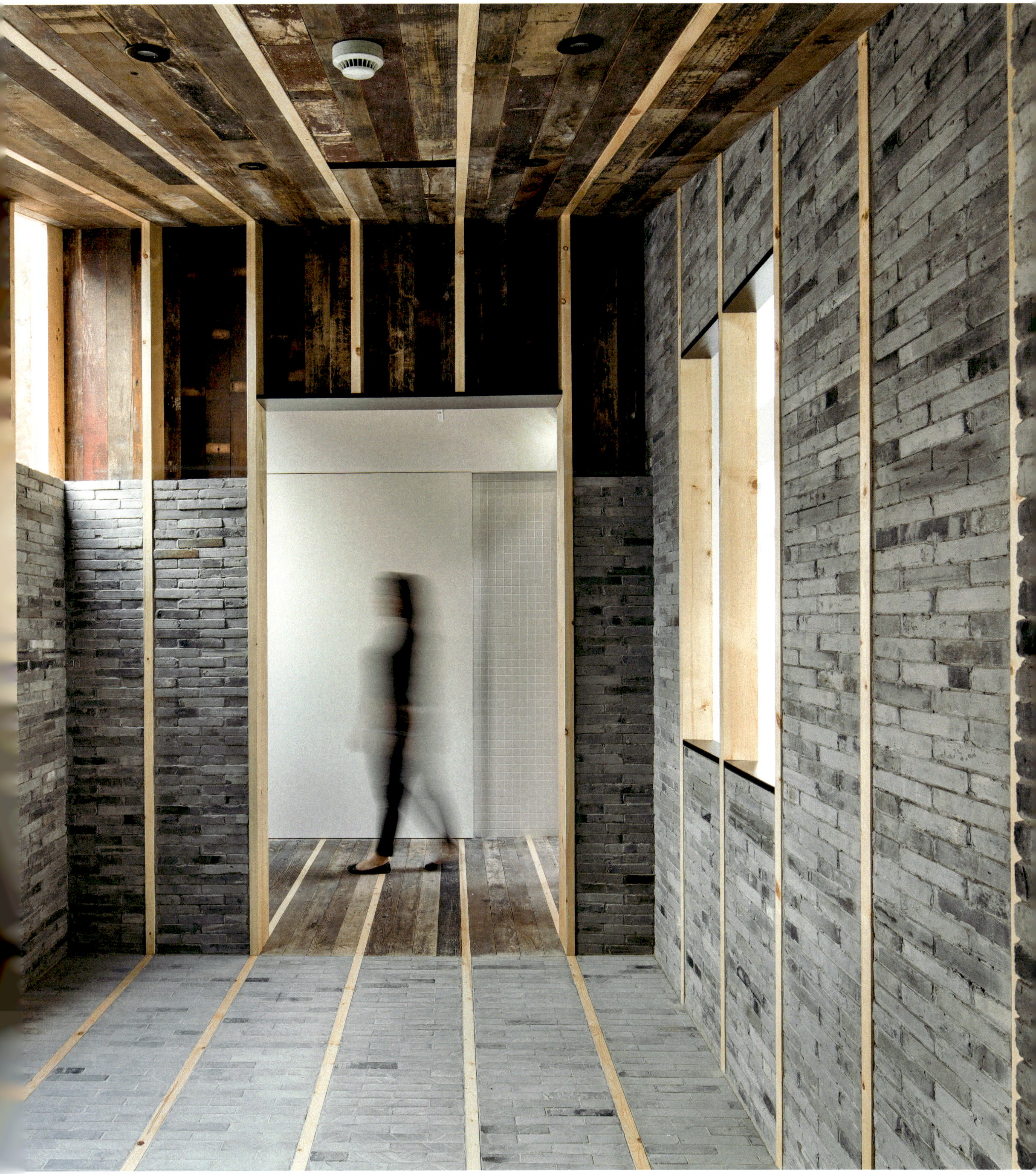

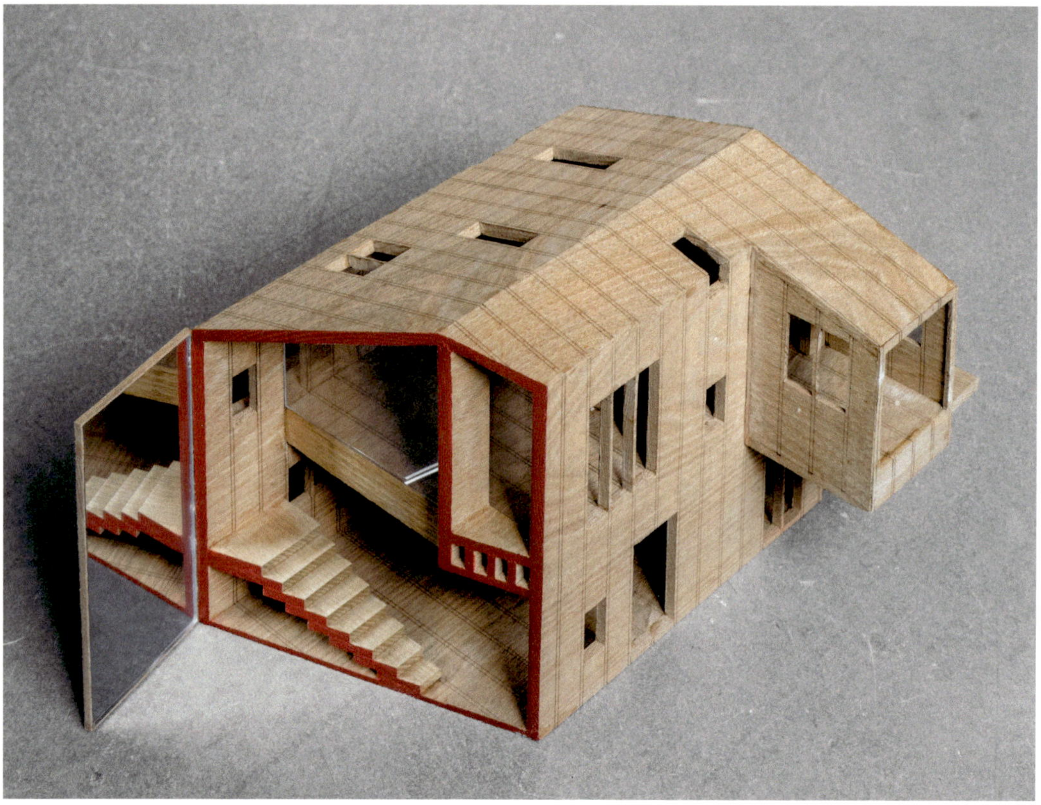

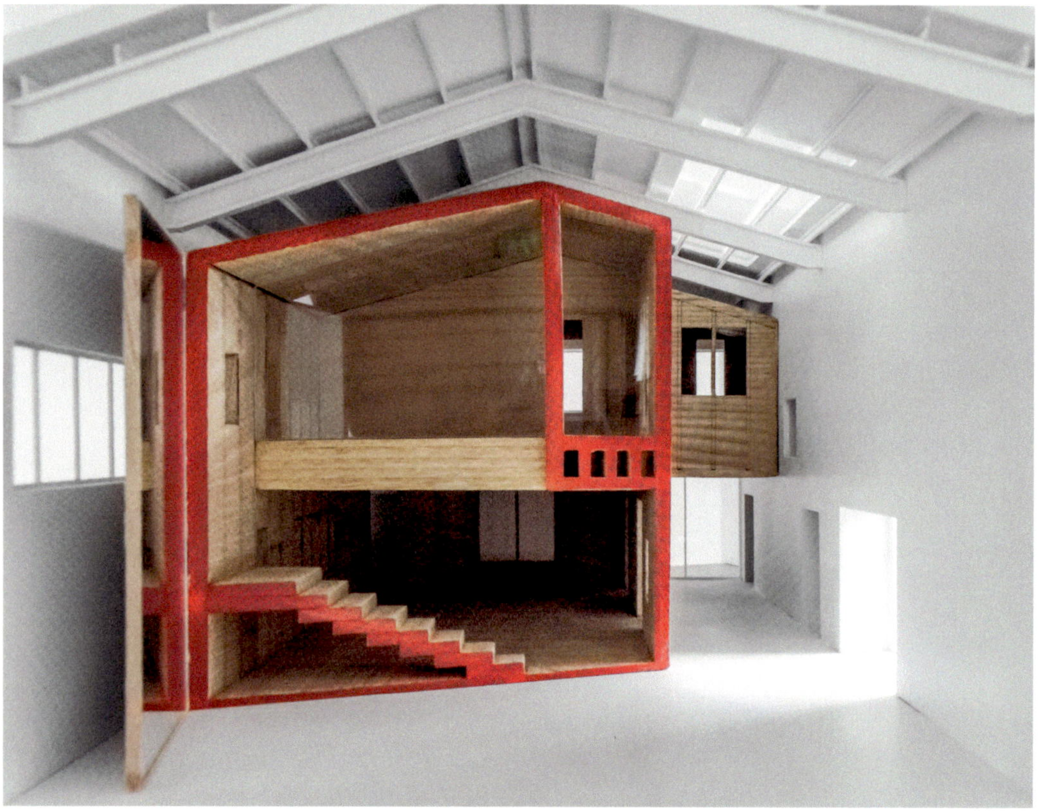

demolition plan | section

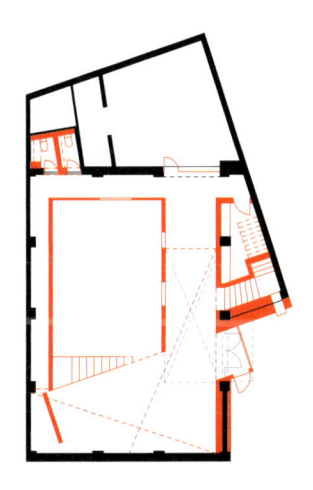

0   15m

167

168

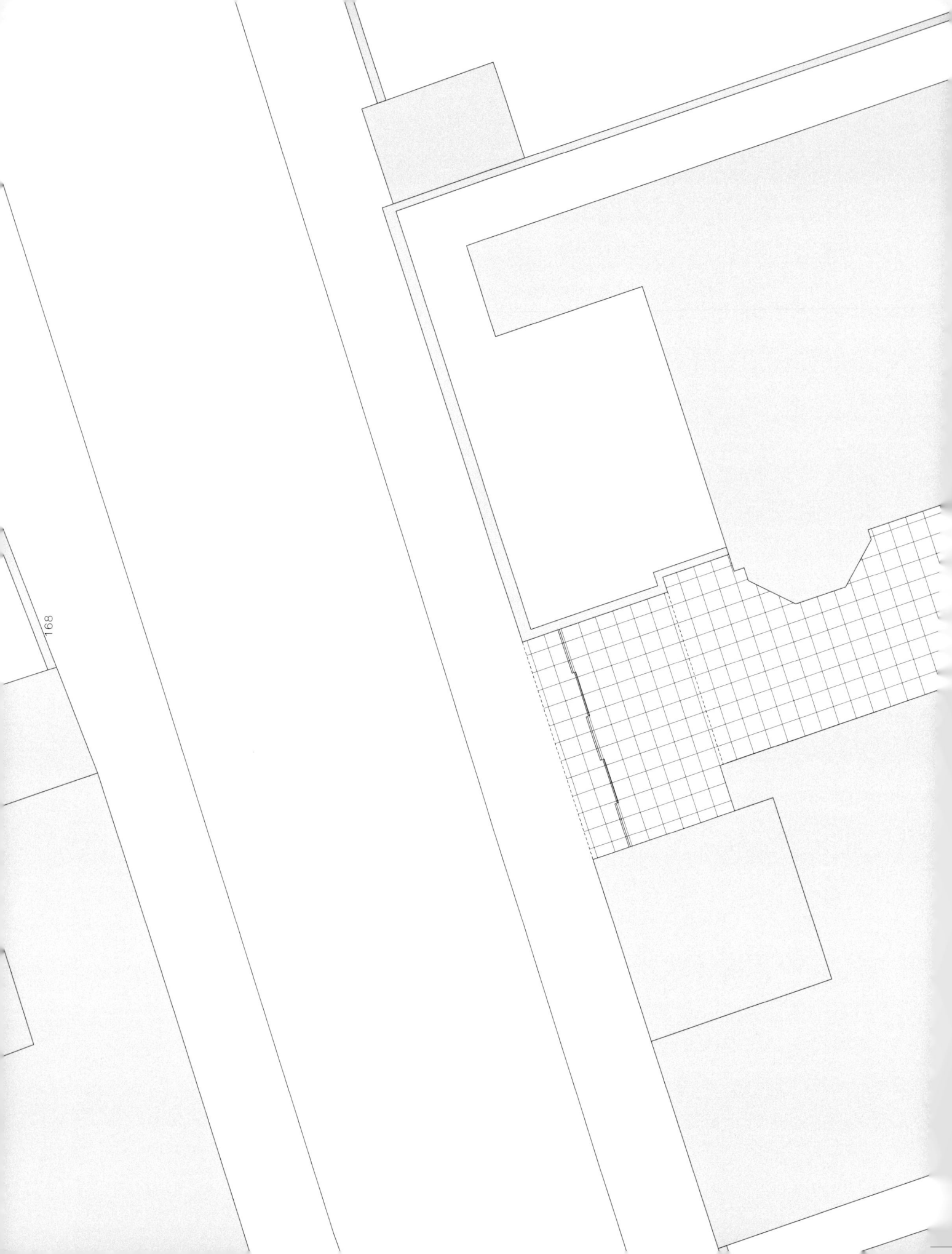

ground-floor plan

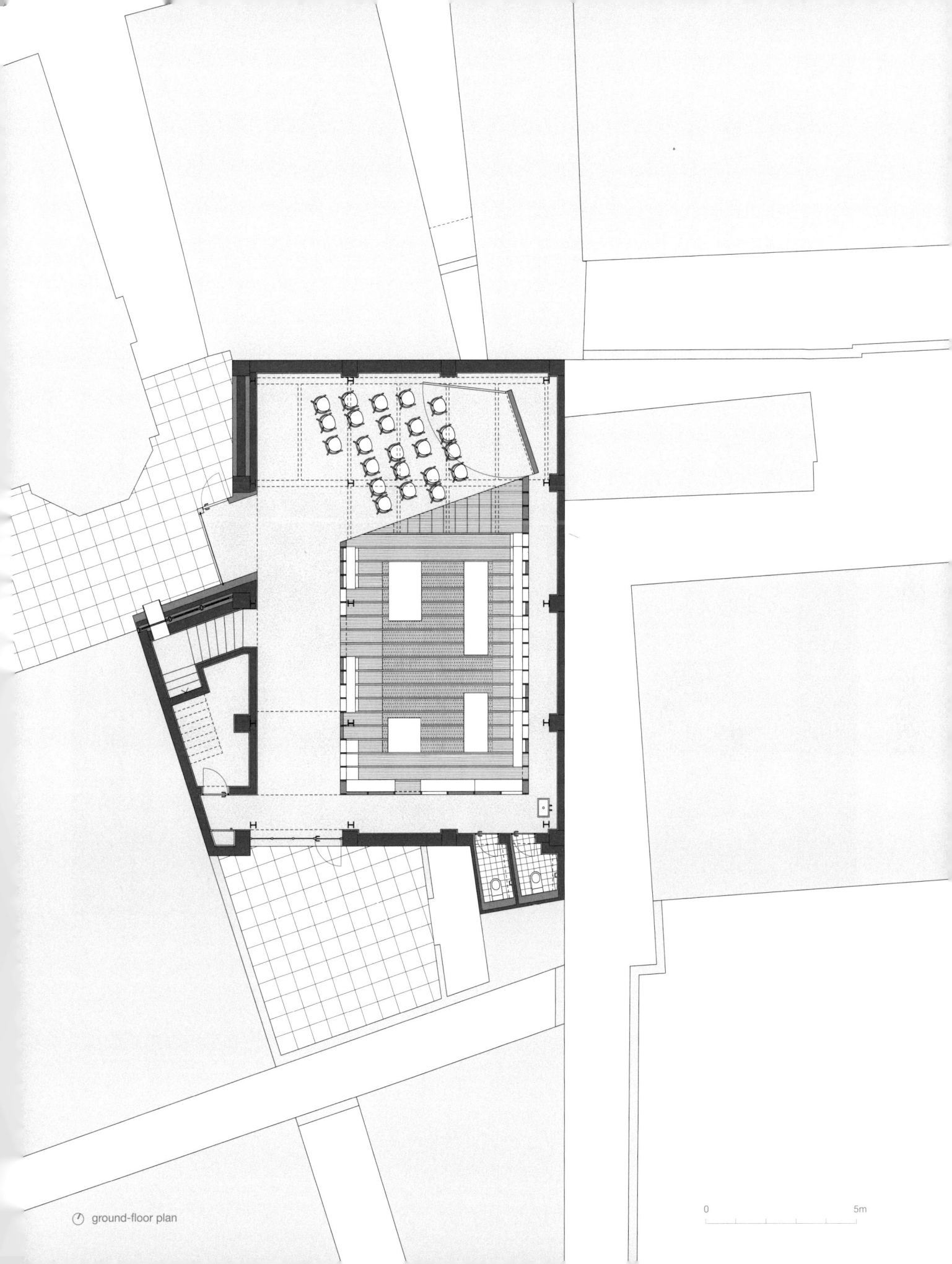

0   5m

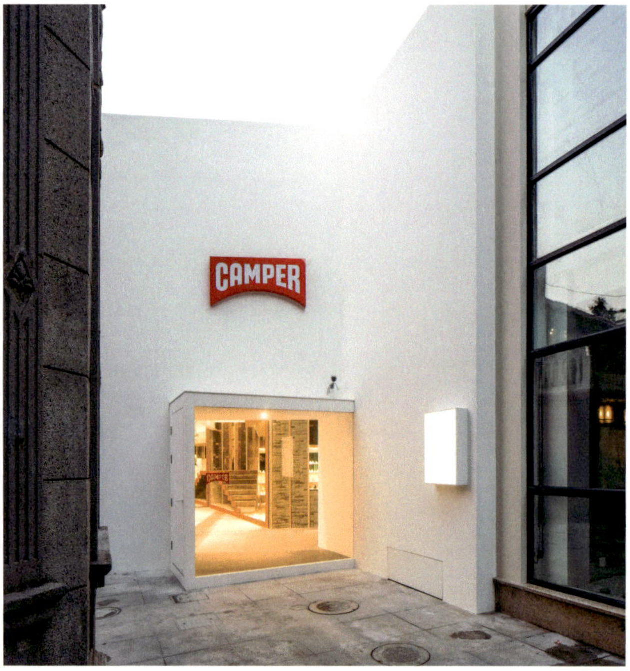
CAMPER

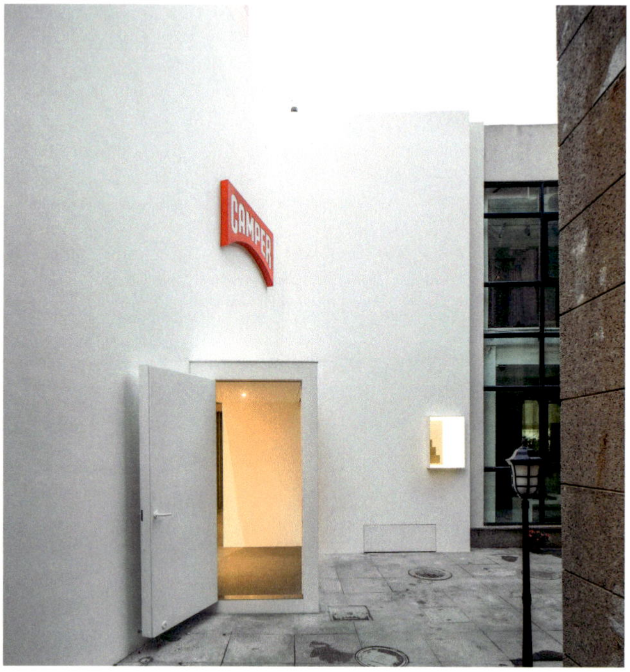
CAMPER

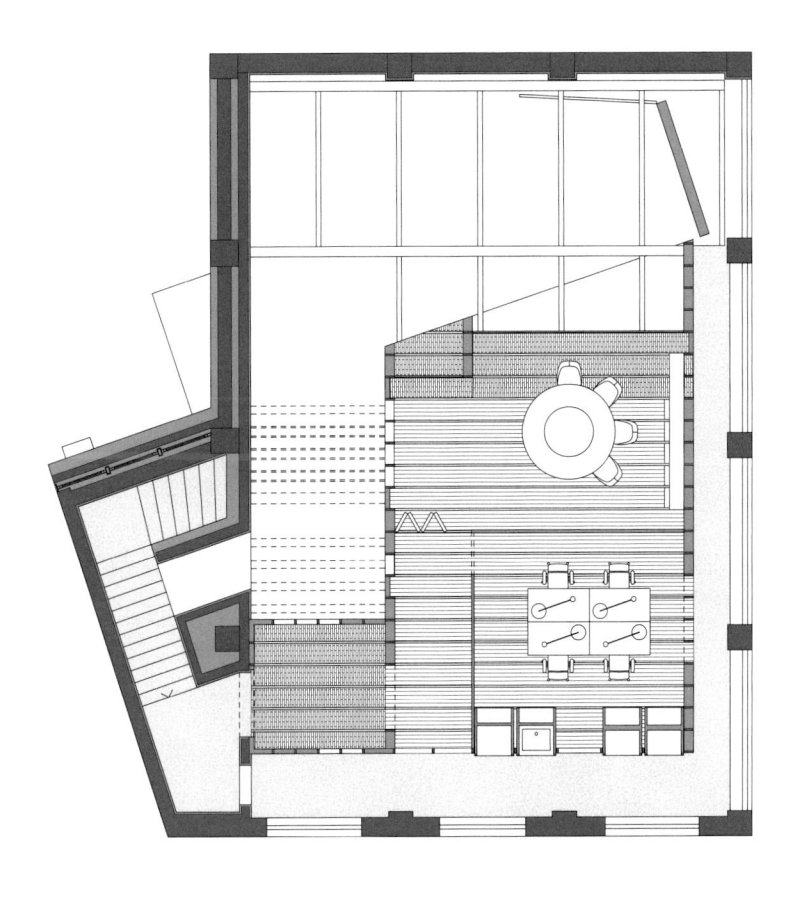

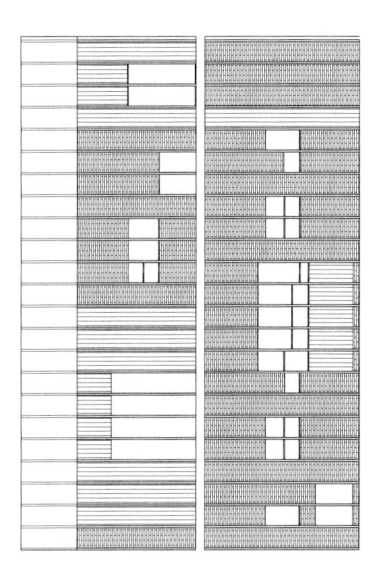

second-floor plan | section

171

0　　　　5m

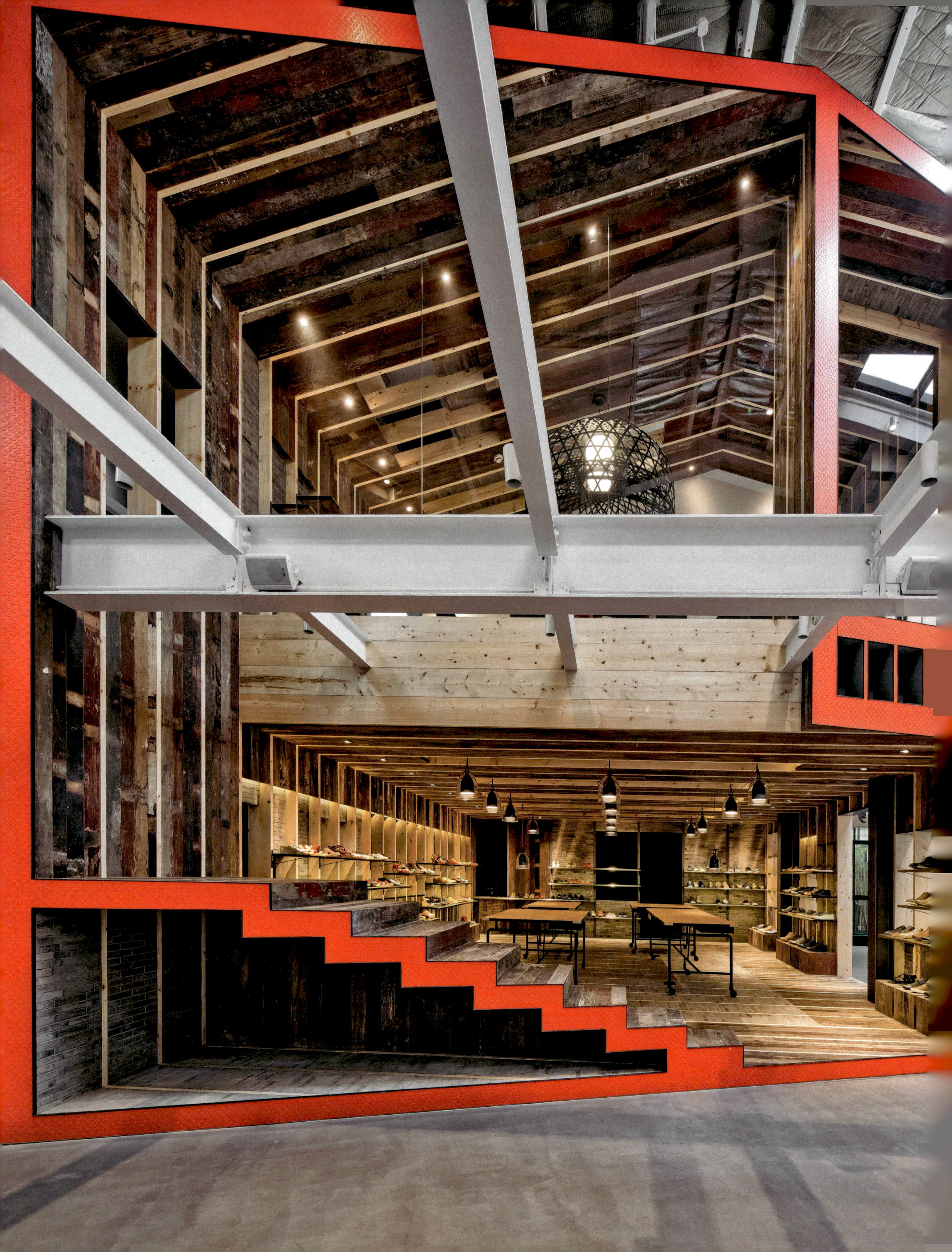

173

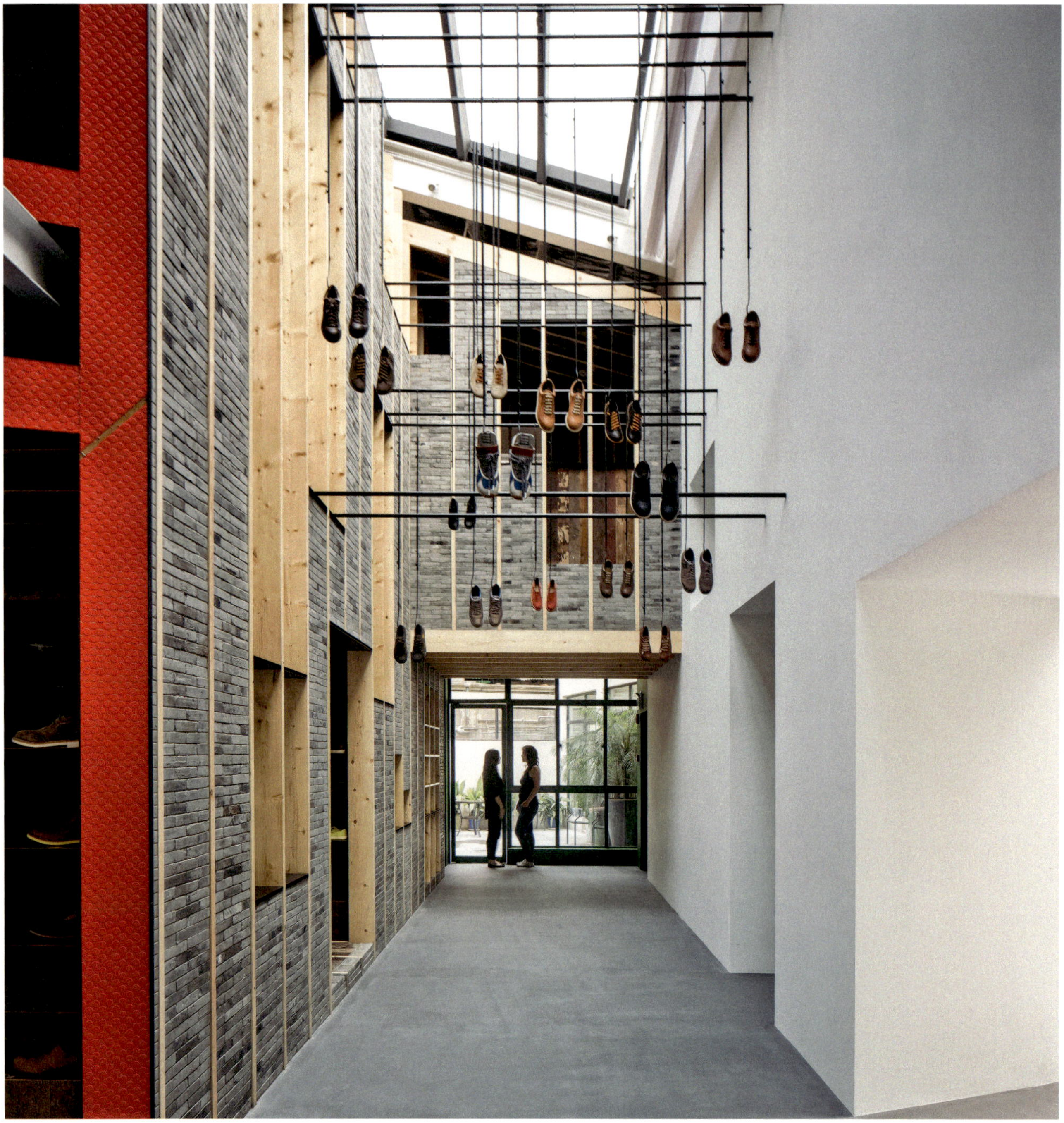

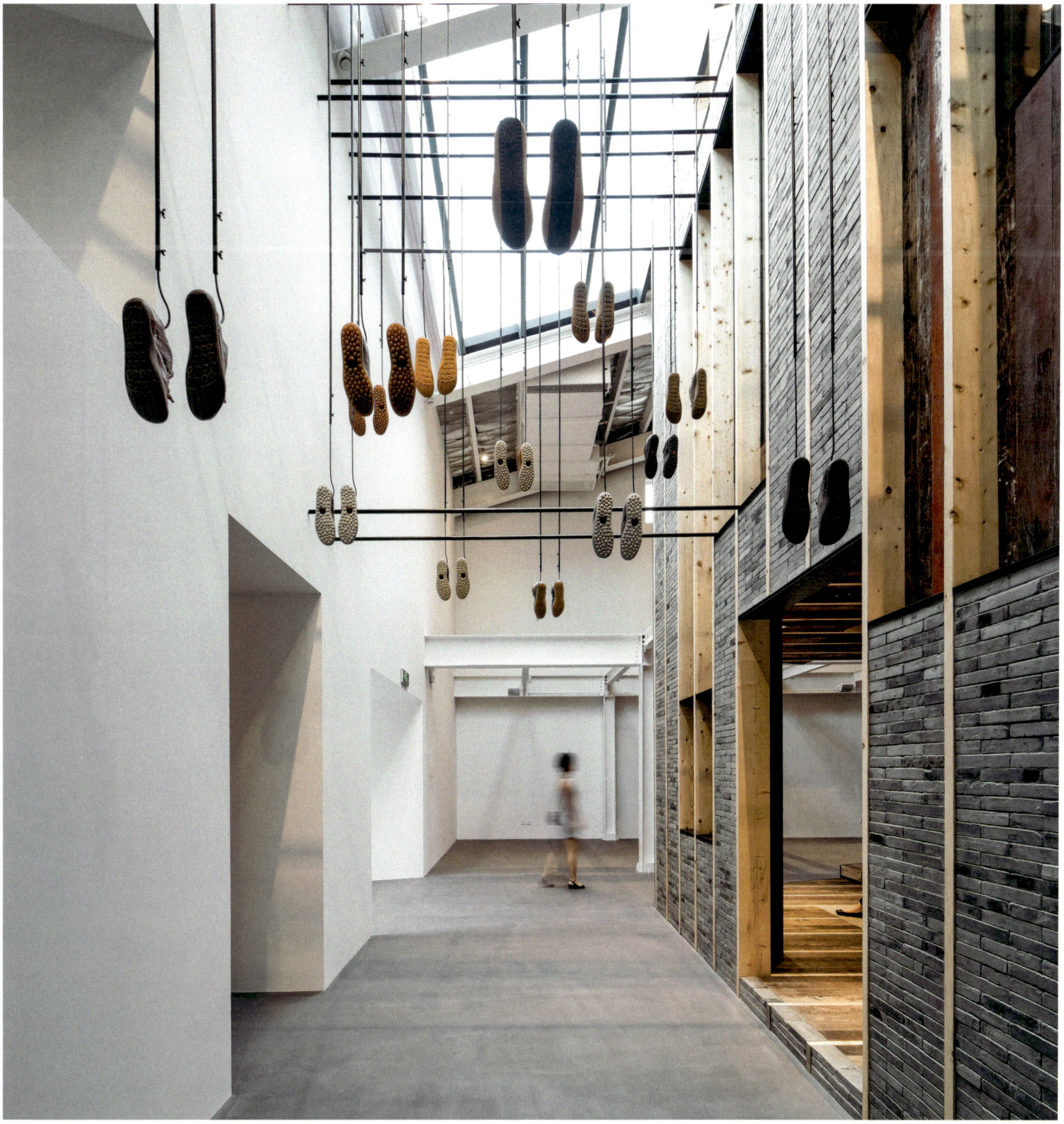

176

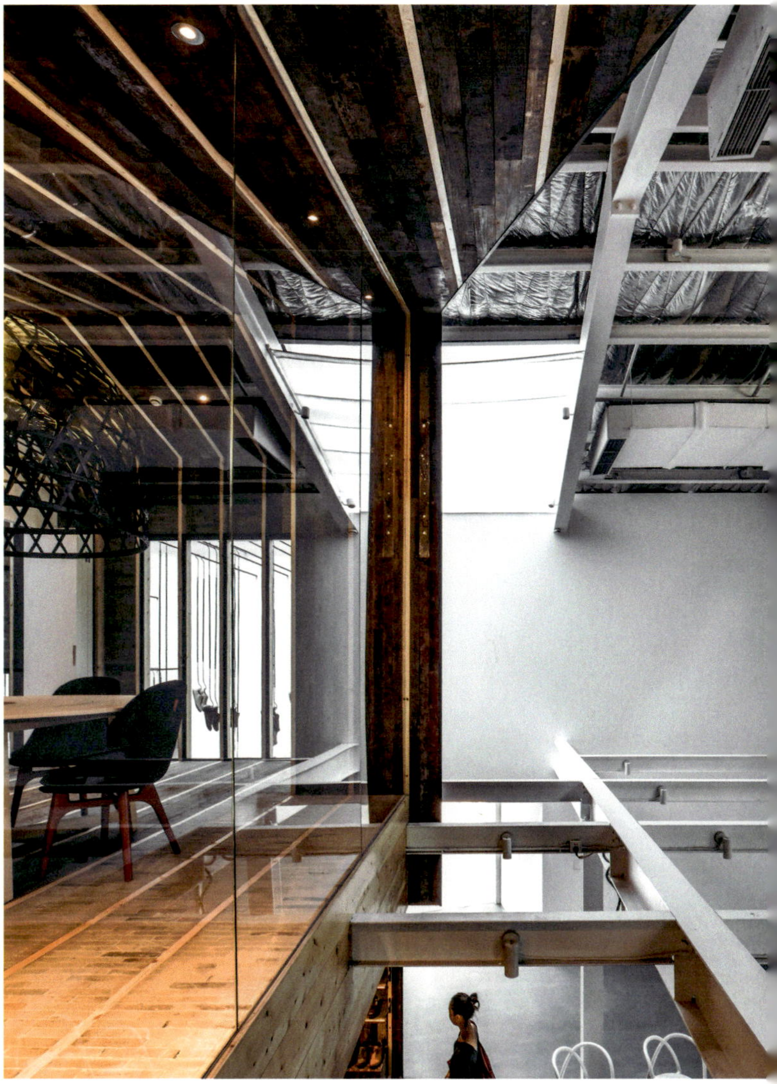

178

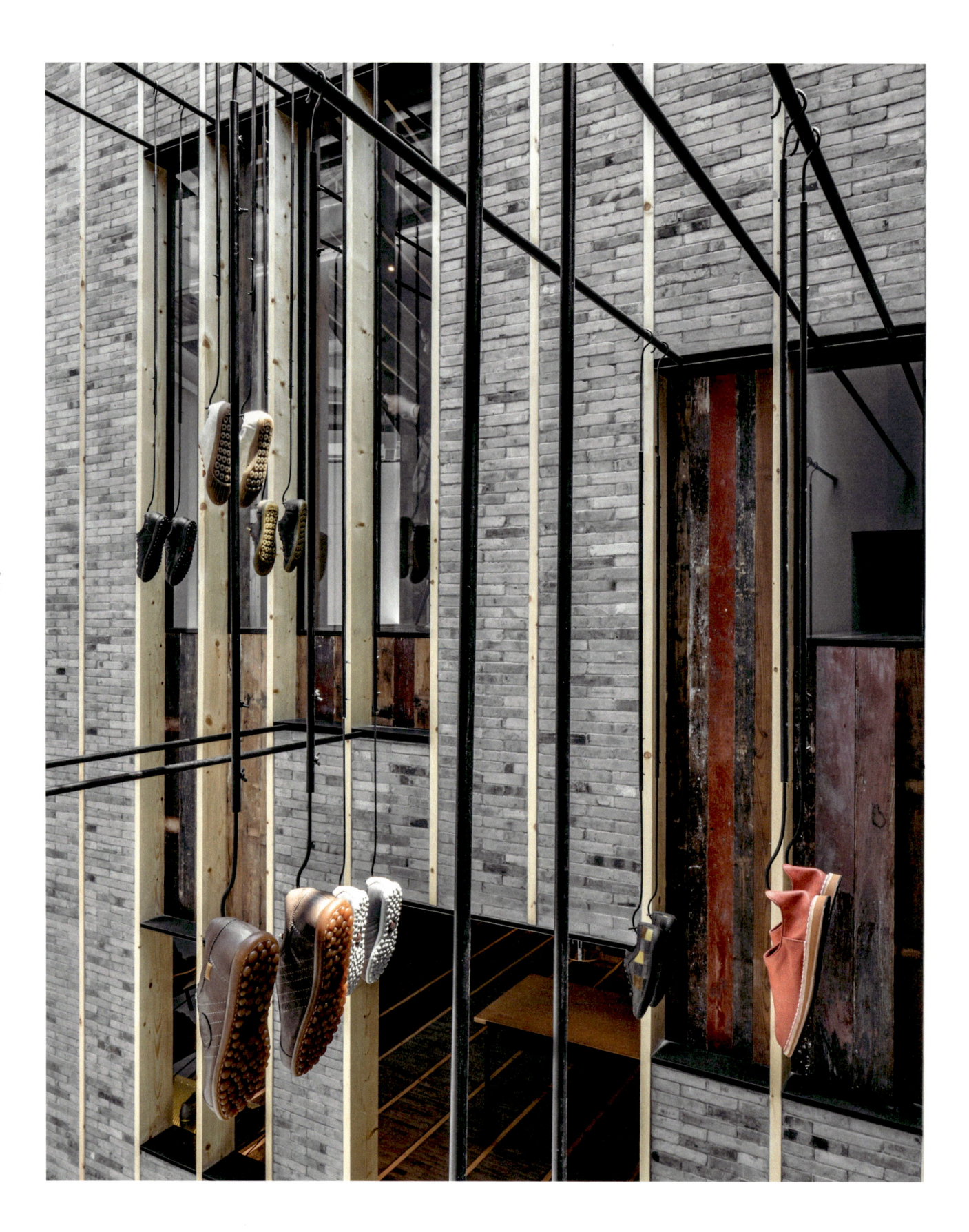

179

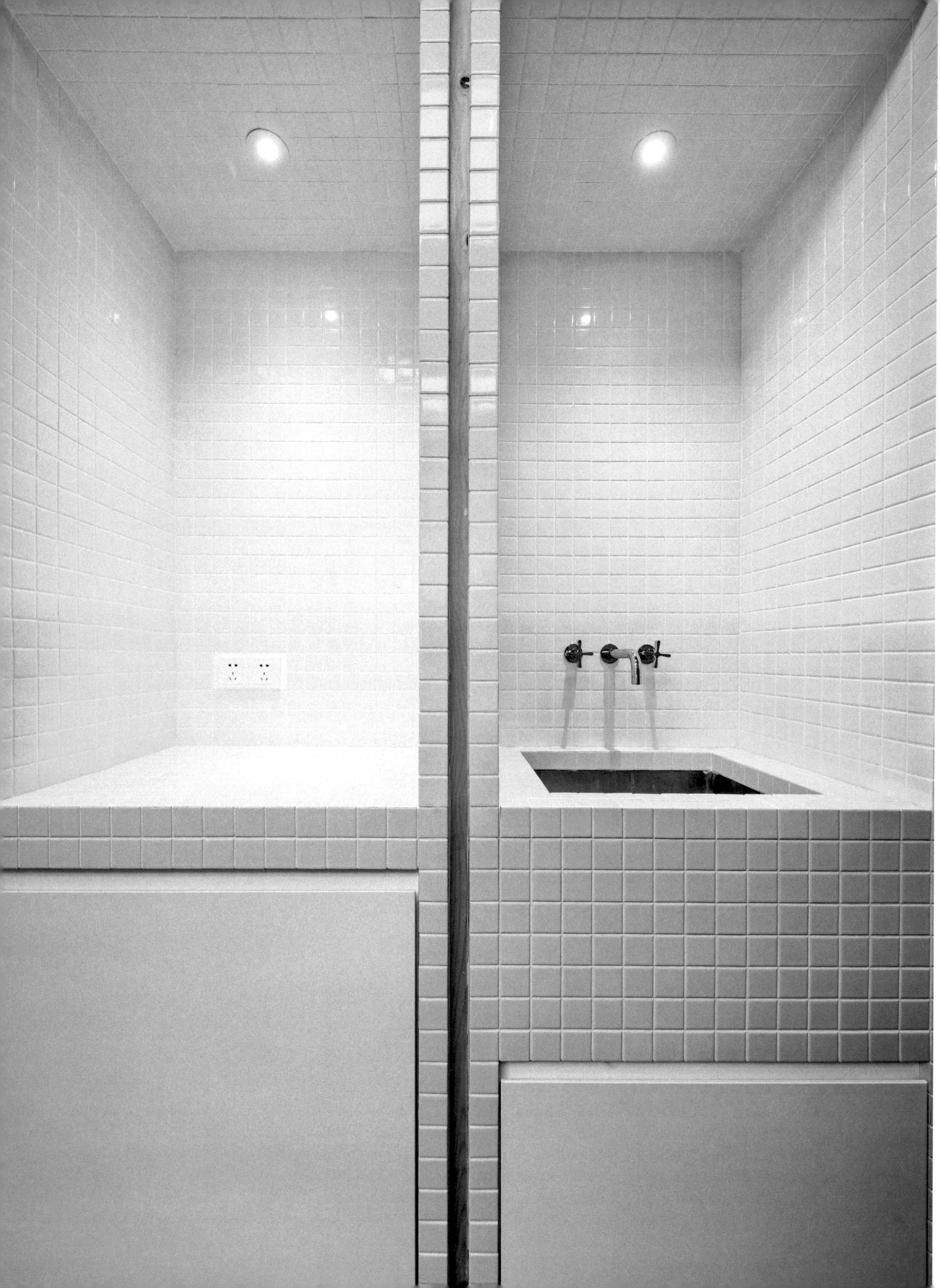

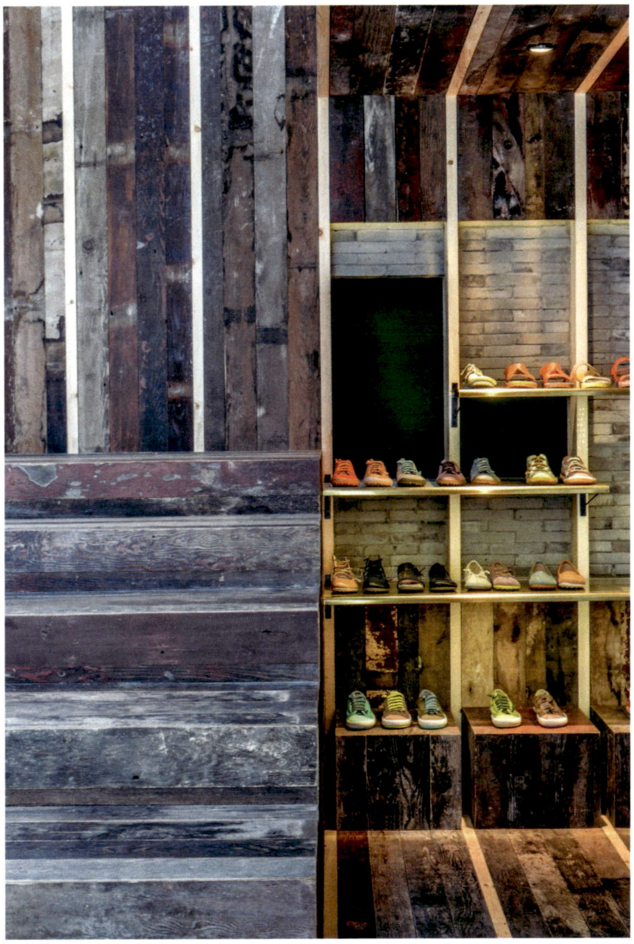

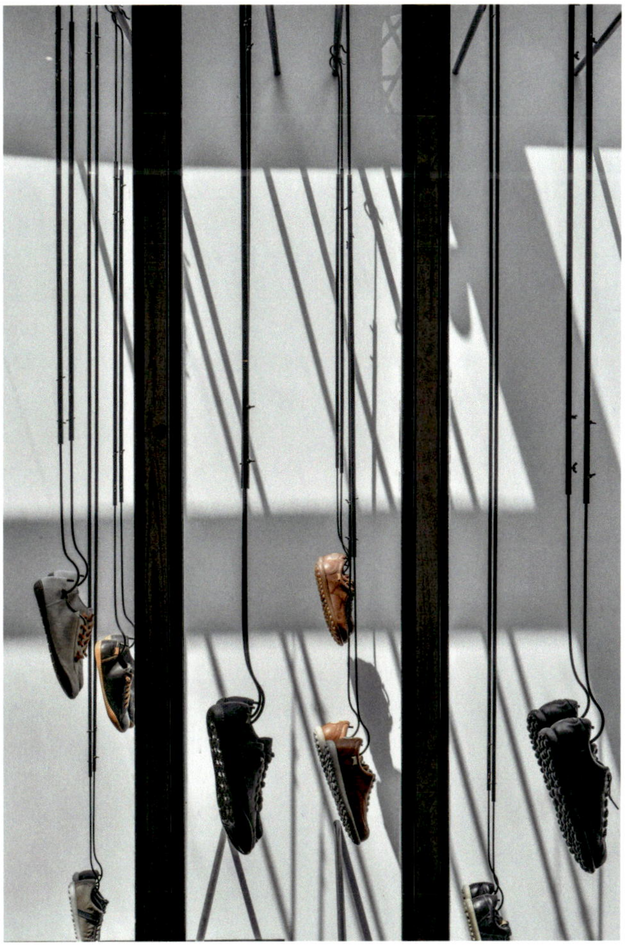

THE OVERLAPPING LAND/HOUSE
Private Residence, Singapore

For a private residence in Singapore, we wanted to pay homage to the client's Chinese roots by taking cues from the *siheyuan* courtyard house, a vernacular typology found in northern China. In essence, the courtyard house can be thought of as a spatialization of Chinese notions of domesticity. It expresses the relationship between periphery and core, celebrating the inner zone as a gathering space. It speaks to the complex relationships between the "self" and the "communal," layering the public and the private in a spatial procession. While respecting these ideologies, we also realized the need to contextualize the project, which is situated in a tropical climate and accommodates four families across three generations.

Rather than simply adopt the rudimentary formation of a courtyard house, we evolved it from a blockish mass into two elegant L-shaped volumes which open up the inner courtyard to the surrounding lush nature. Lifting the private living quarters off the ground, the ground surface across the site is expressed as a monolithic base which flows seamlessly from inside to outside. The transparent glazing of the first floor allows the landscape to penetrate into the interior, while the living spaces begin to spill out into gardens and pools. In effect, the entire stretch of land is occupied; the whole site becomes "home."

The layering and overlapping of materiality in the house is a key strategy in reinforcing the notion of continuity, from the uninterrupted stone ground plane with glass enclosed public areas to the wood-clad private spaces above. The ebonized teak louvers that envelop the exterior and the perforated oak panels on the interior are all operable, allowing inhabitants to create their own spaces—from airy and exposed to cocooned and private. Double-height spaces reveal the strata of the materially distinct layers, while at the same time encouraging interaction between the personal and communal realms. Blurring the boundaries of inside/outside, land/house, private/public, this house embodies the complex spatial conditions necessary to respond to the complex nature of inhabitation, family, and domesticity.

Aneta Grzeszykowska & Jan Smaga, *Plan #10*, 2003
When the boundaries of sites or between inside and outside spaces are blurred, this allows for a different experience of space, occupying a larger space than intended. Aneta & Jan's series of photos documents the interiors of ten apartments in Warsaw. They use a unique photography technique in which the overall picture seems "scanned" by stitching together an aggregate of aerial photographs (like Google Earth). This particular image is striking in that the image is cropped at (supposedly) the fence/property boundary so we see the house as a room in the extended field of the landscape.

site map

0   200m

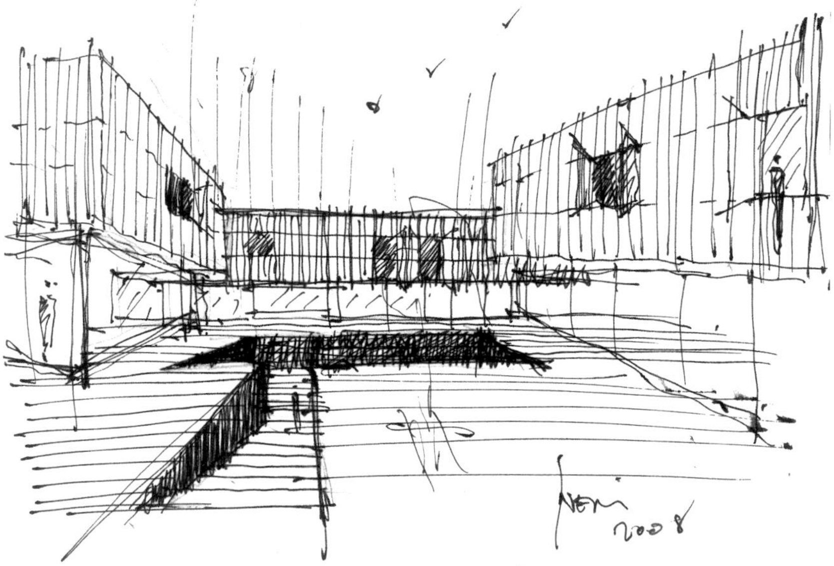
2008

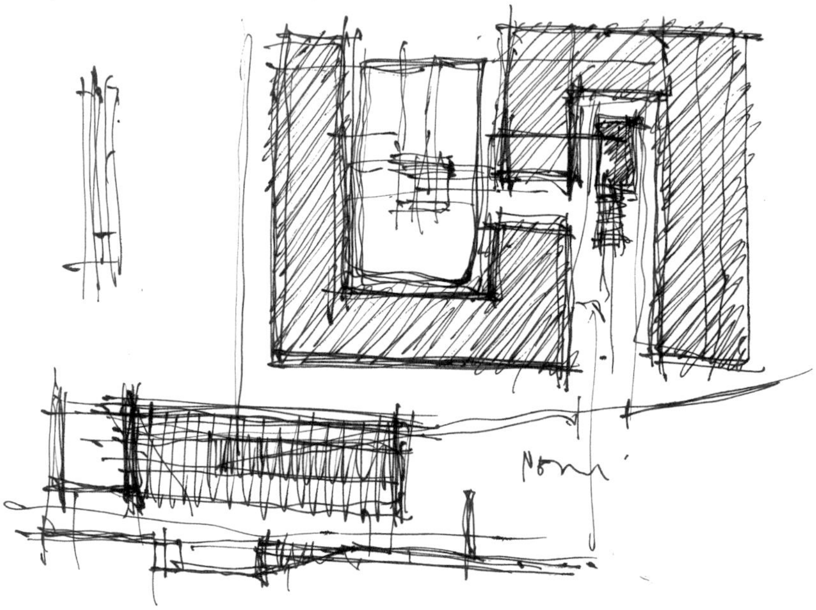

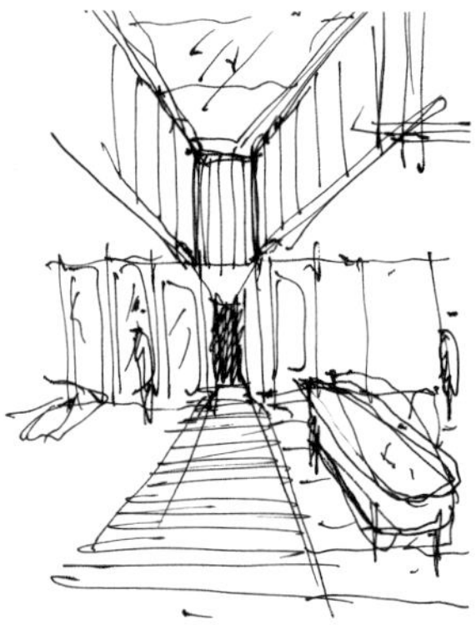

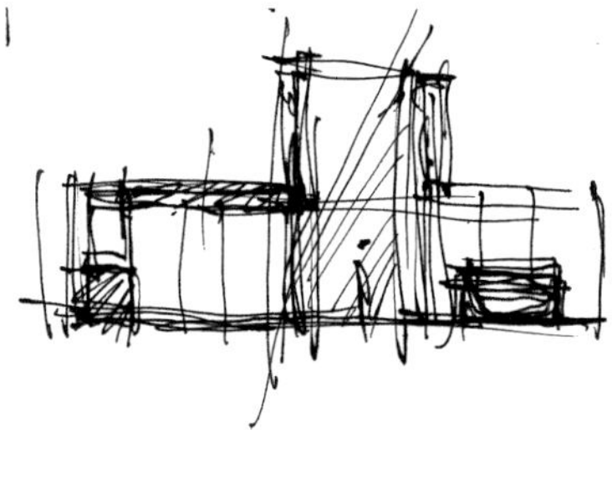

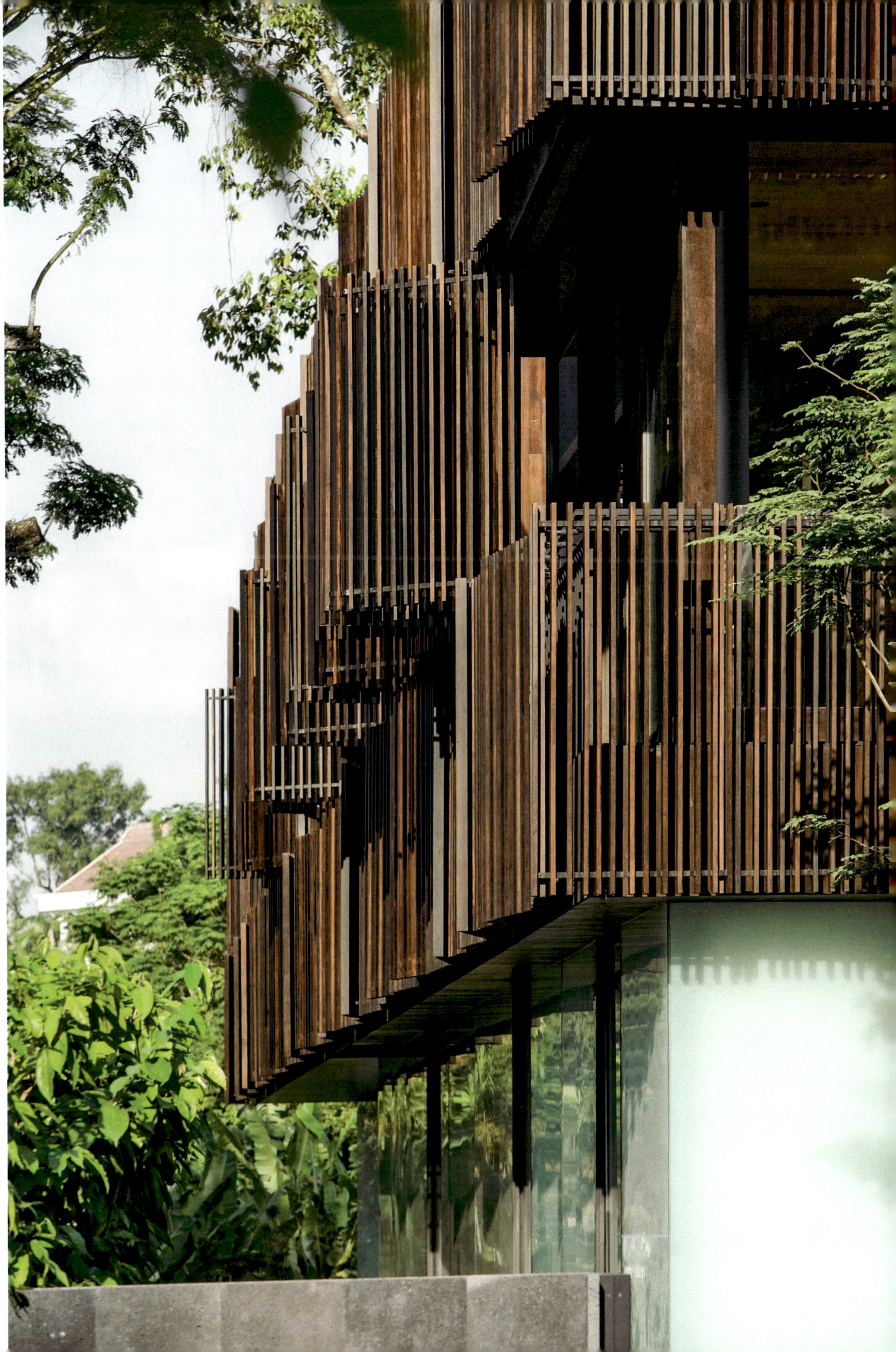

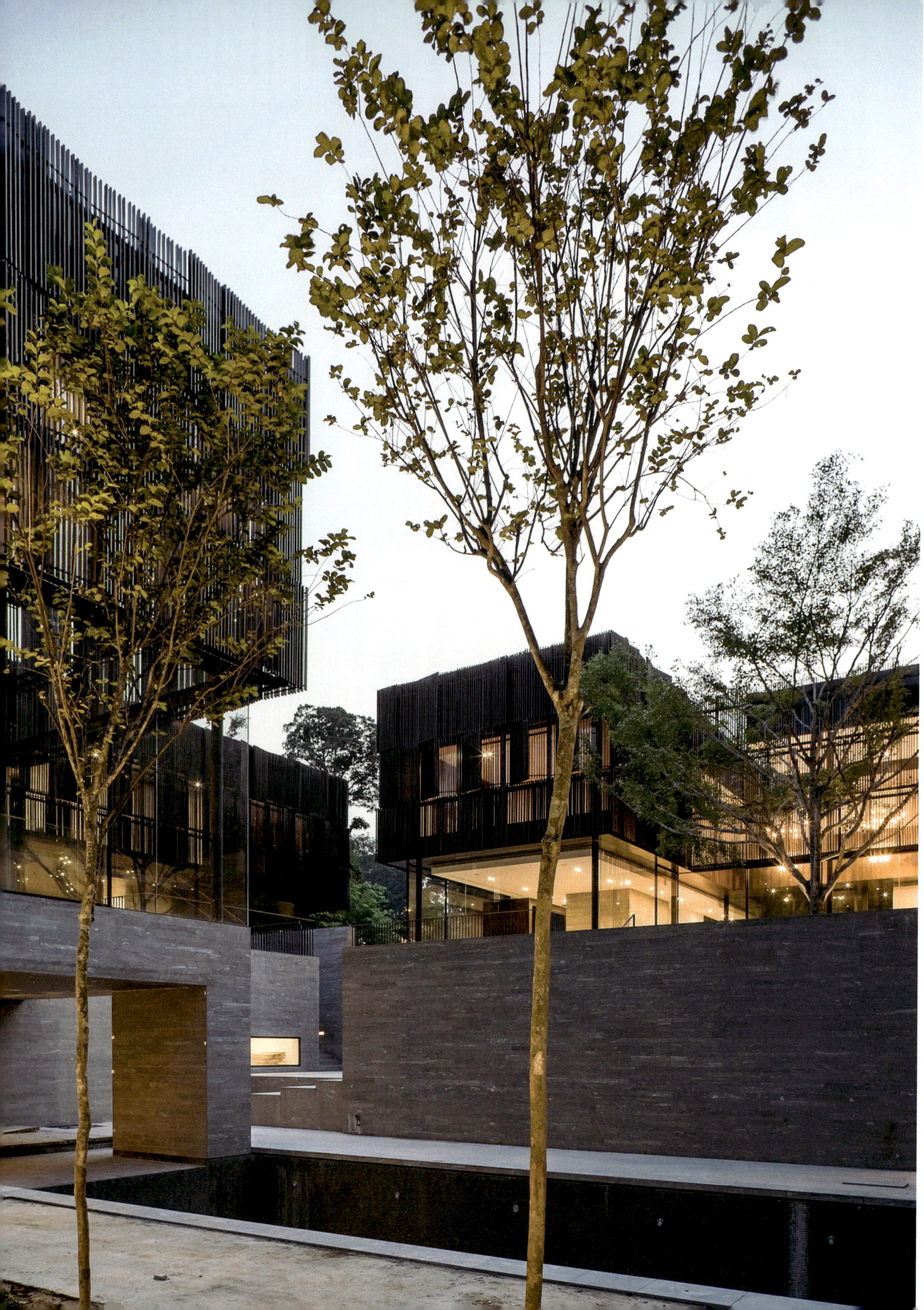

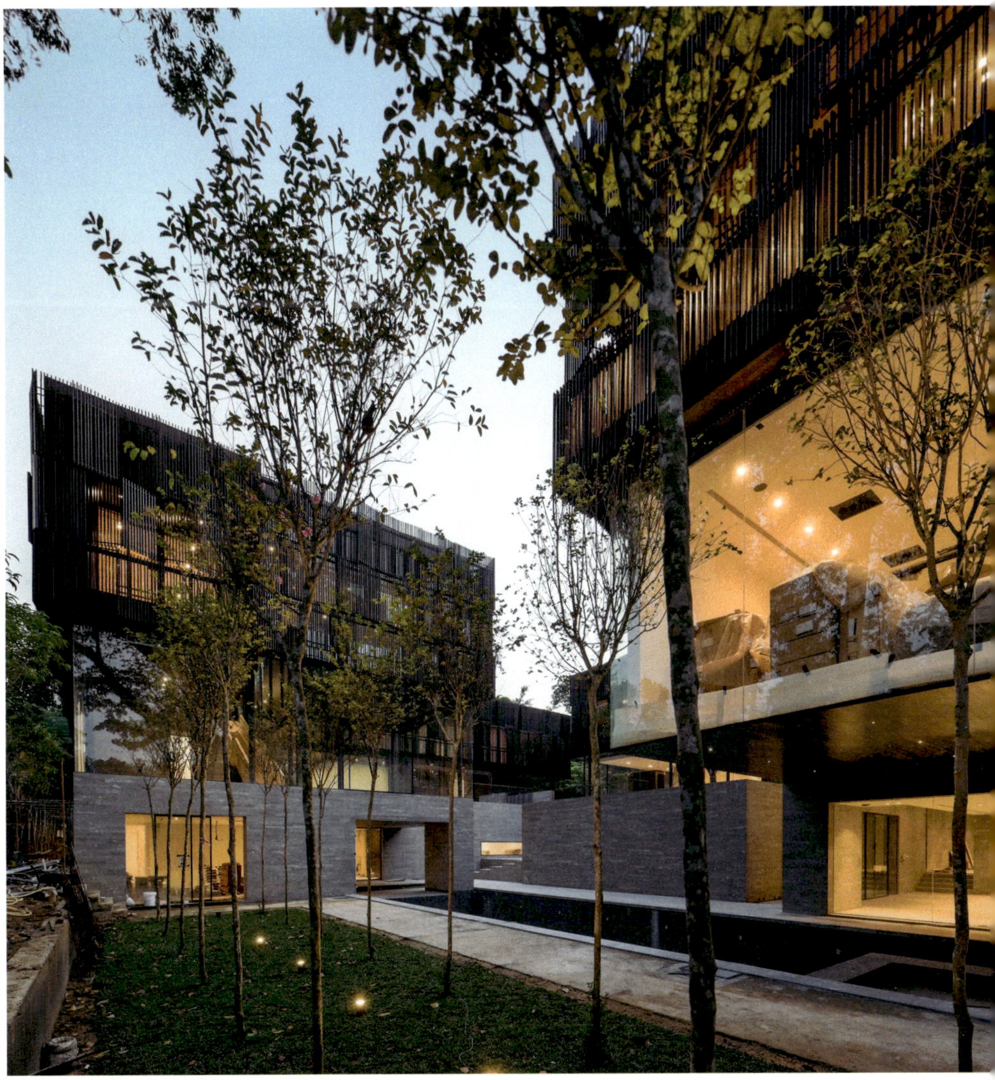

first-floor plan

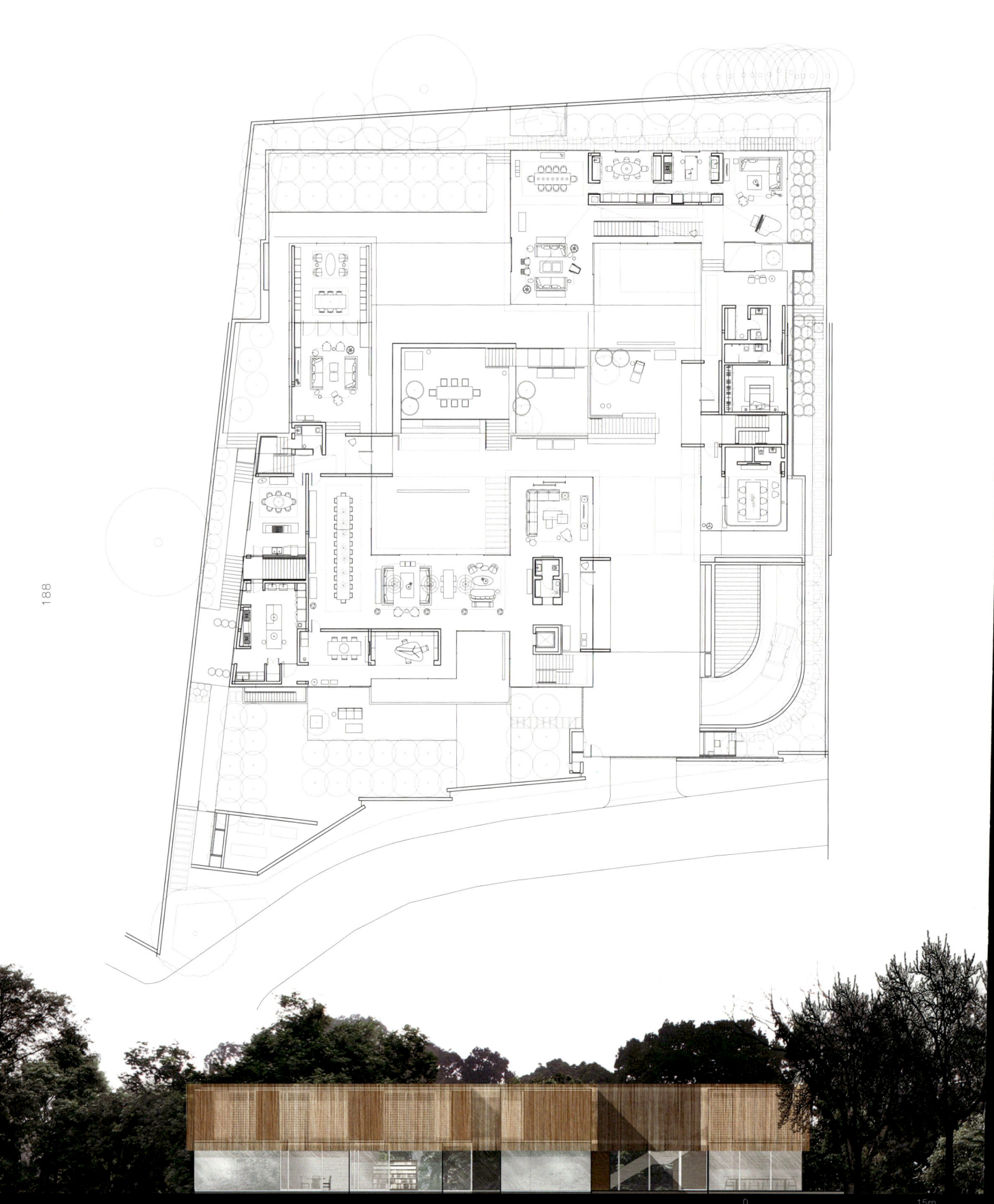

0   15m

189

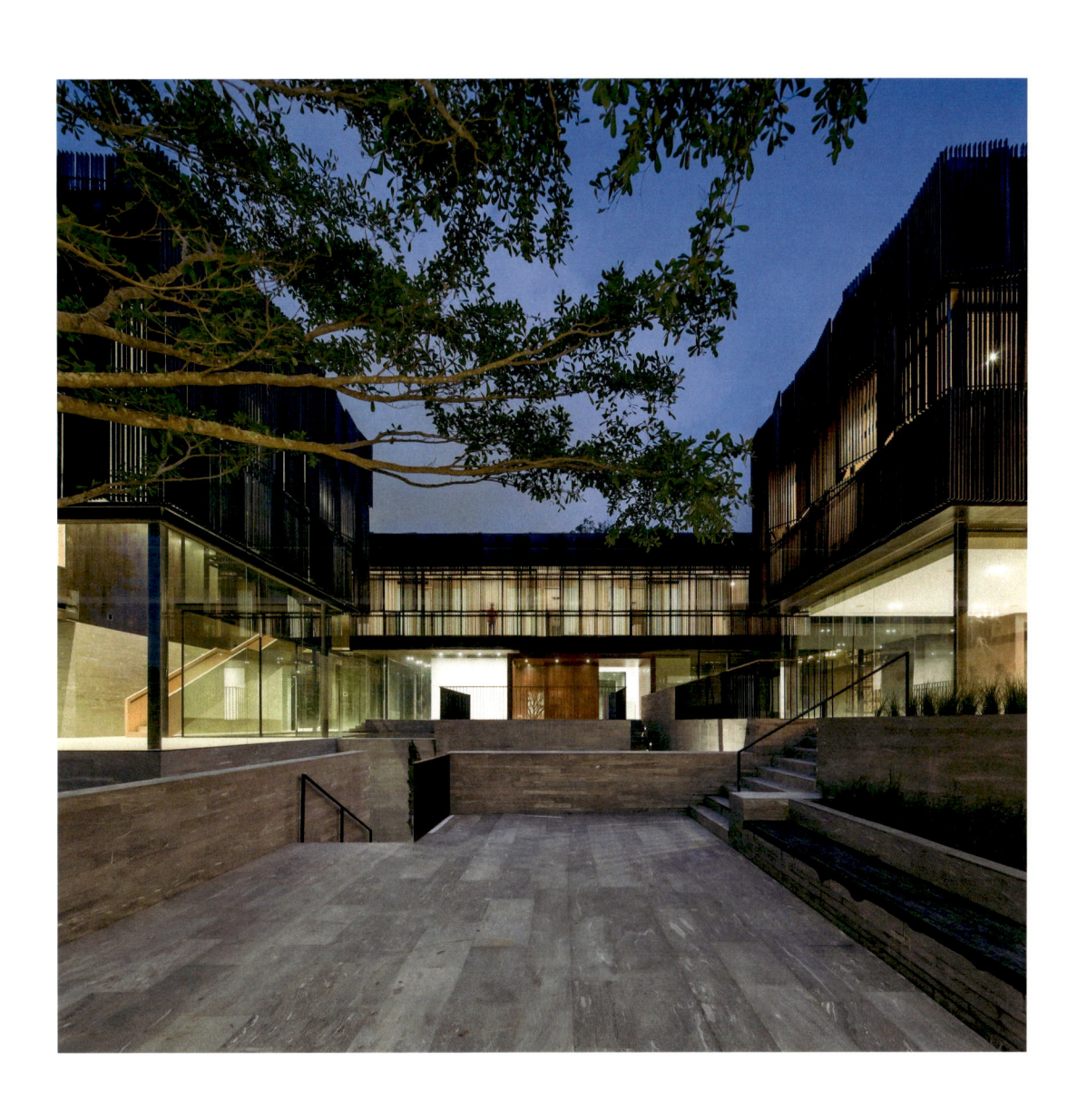

190

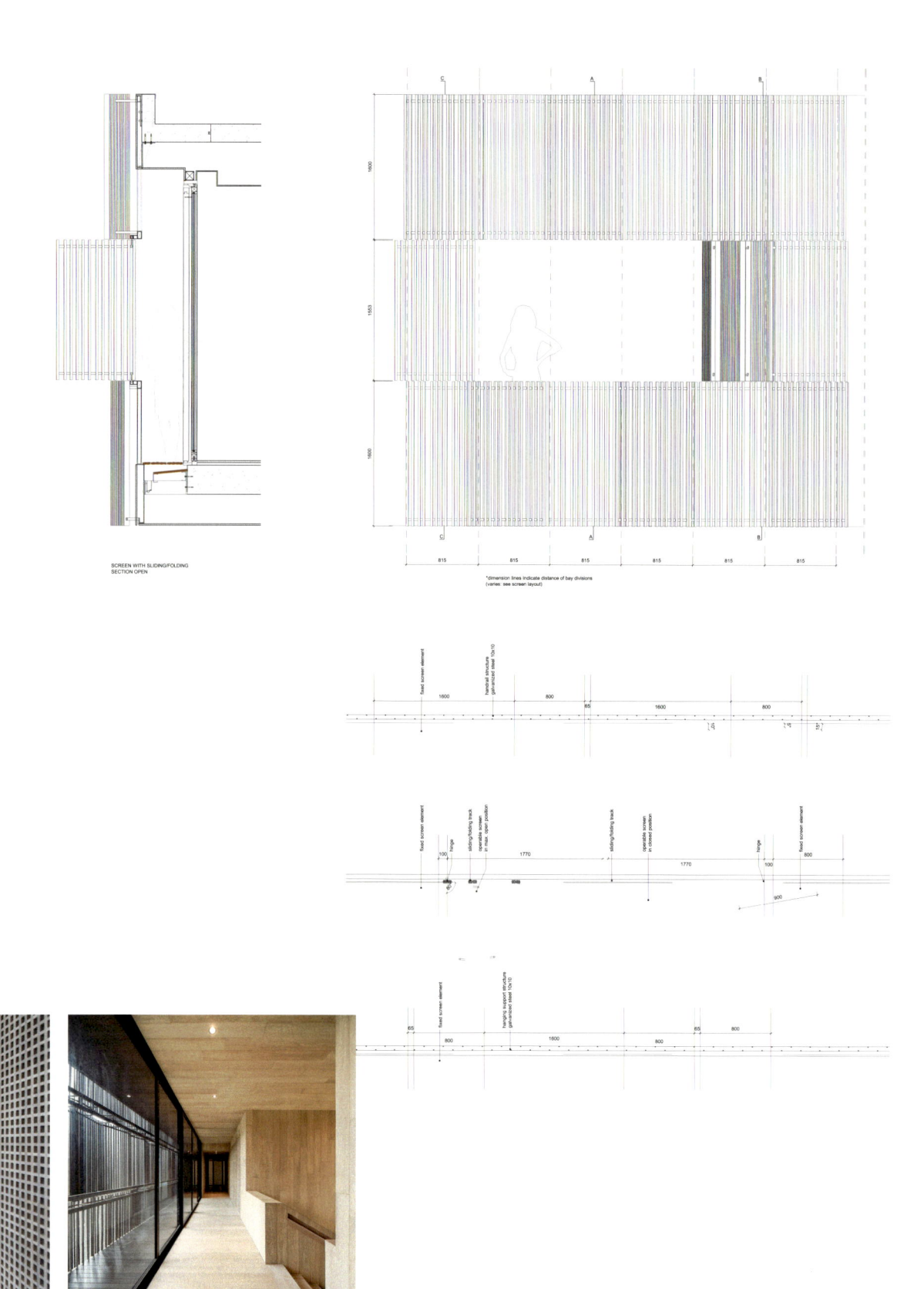

SCREEN WITH SLIDING/FOLDING
SECTION OPEN

*dimension lines indicate distance of bay divisions
(varies: see screen layout)

curtain wall detail

0   4m

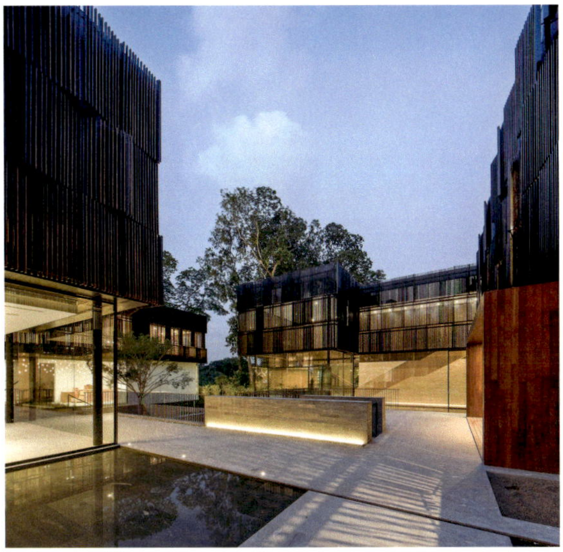

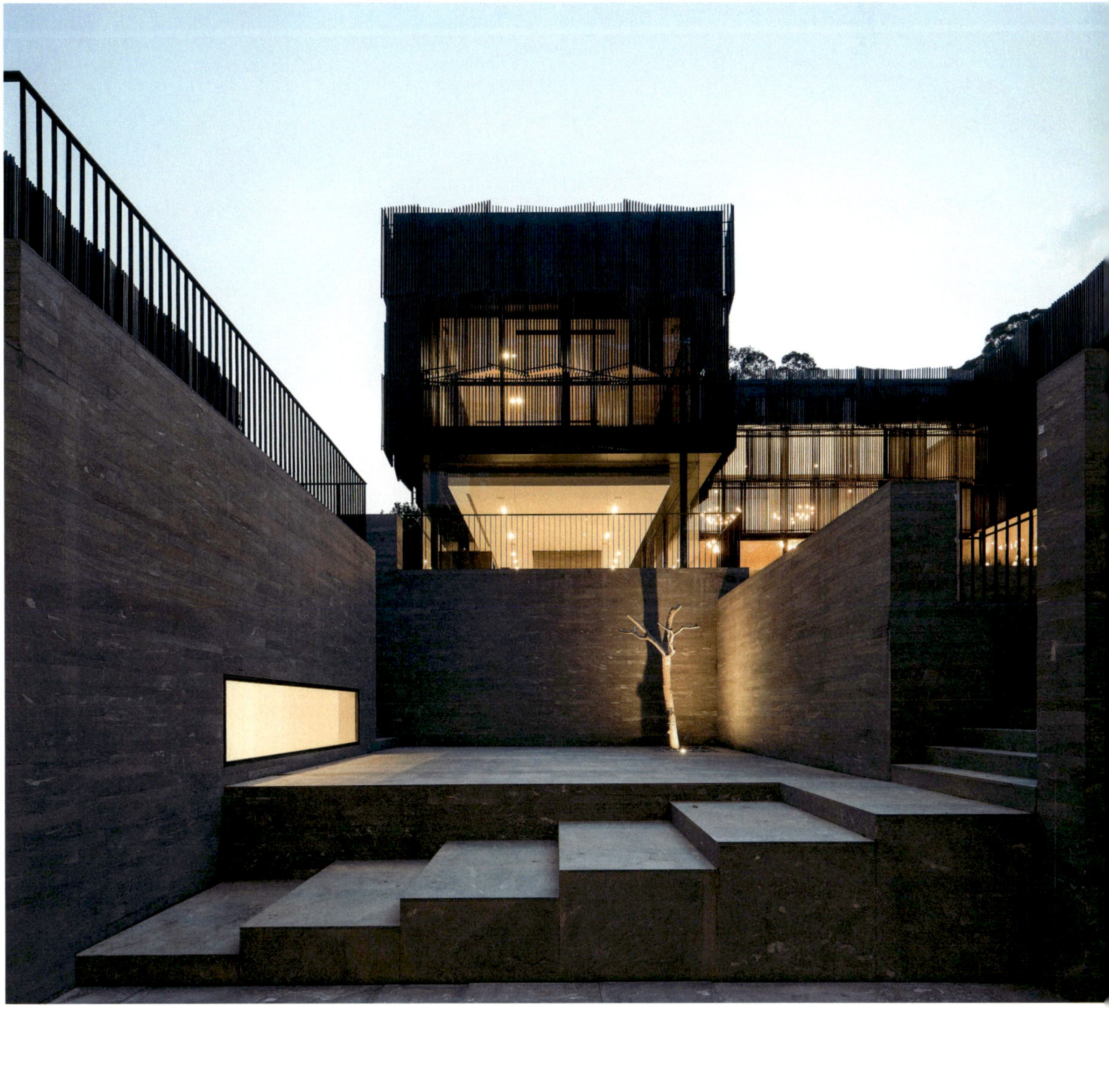

ongoing projects

THE SHUNTING HOUSE
Indian River Private House, Florida

Unlike many of our urban projects, where we are challenged to work within the constraints of a compact site, the site for this house is located in a lush natural landscape along the Indian River in Florida, USA. The client had envisioned a typical suburban house, meaning a concentrated structure in the middle of the site, and we proposed instead to take advantage of the whole site by spreading out the building, flattening it, and integrating the landscape into the building itself. The notion of "shunting," as used in relation to railroads, was the inspiration for the site planning. Splaying the building and shifting individual elements enabled us to capture specific views and fully integrate the house into the site and vice versa.

The architectural scheme is pared down to two elements—roof and room—existing in a symbiotic relationship, each supporting the other. Each box represents a unique function and the roof acts as a connecting element to tie them all together. By minimizing the box envelope to essential functions only and relegating the circulation to the interstitial spaces there is a natural blurring of interior and exterior, a model of domesticity which we have come back to again and again, inspired by the vernacular courtyard house typology found in China.

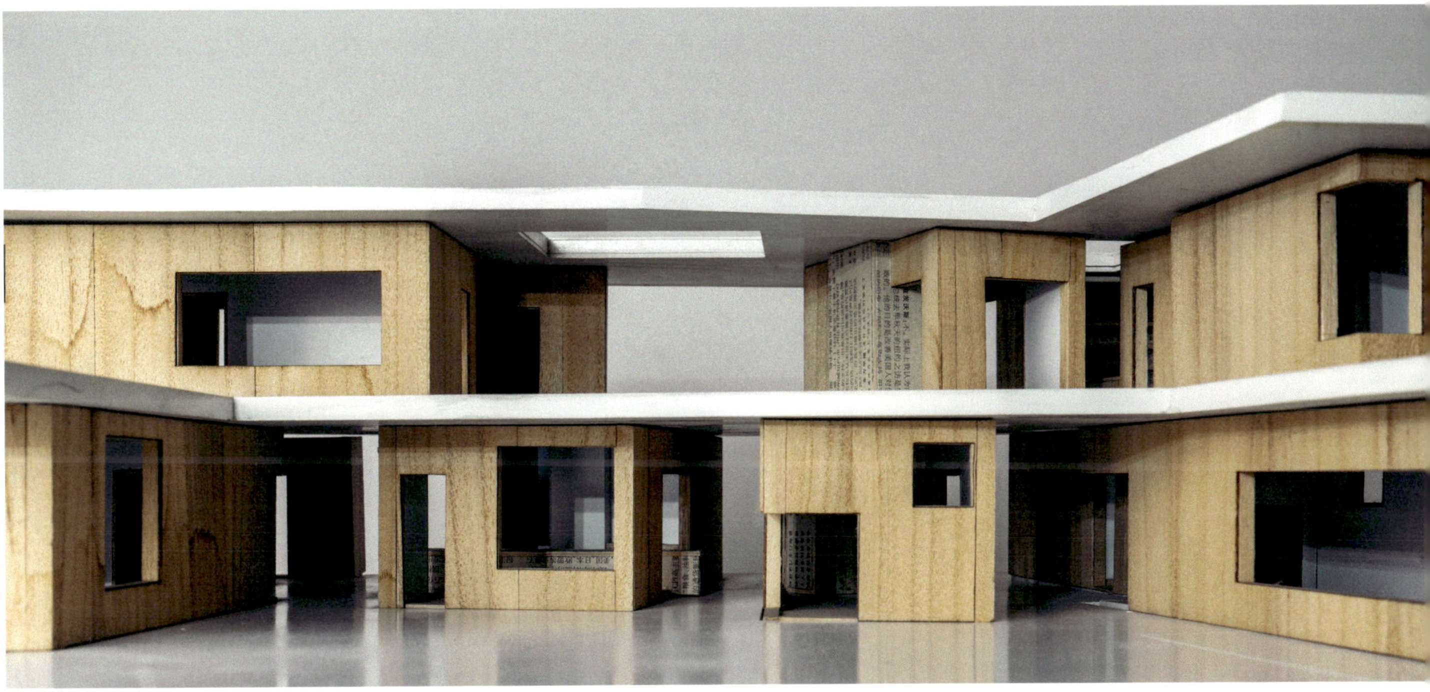

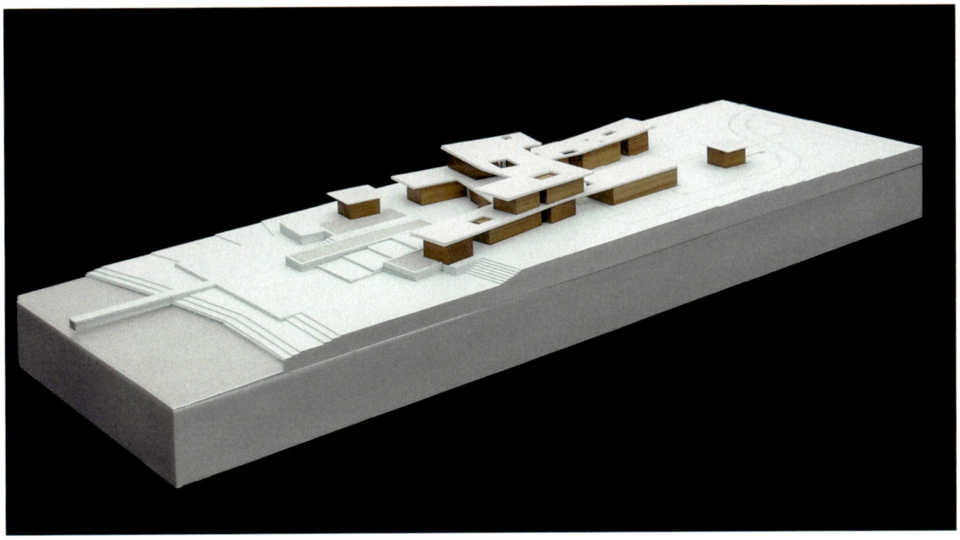

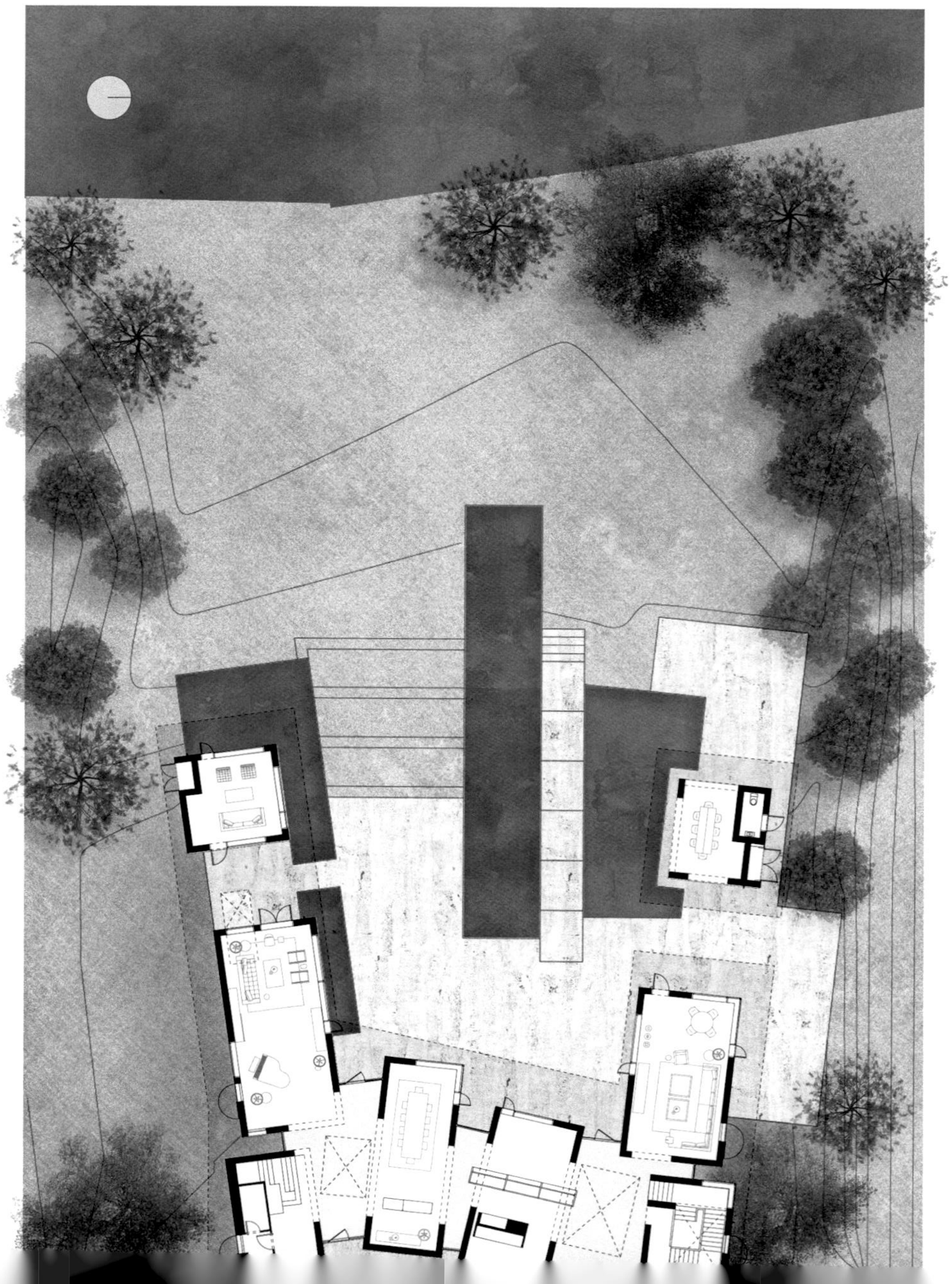

site plan

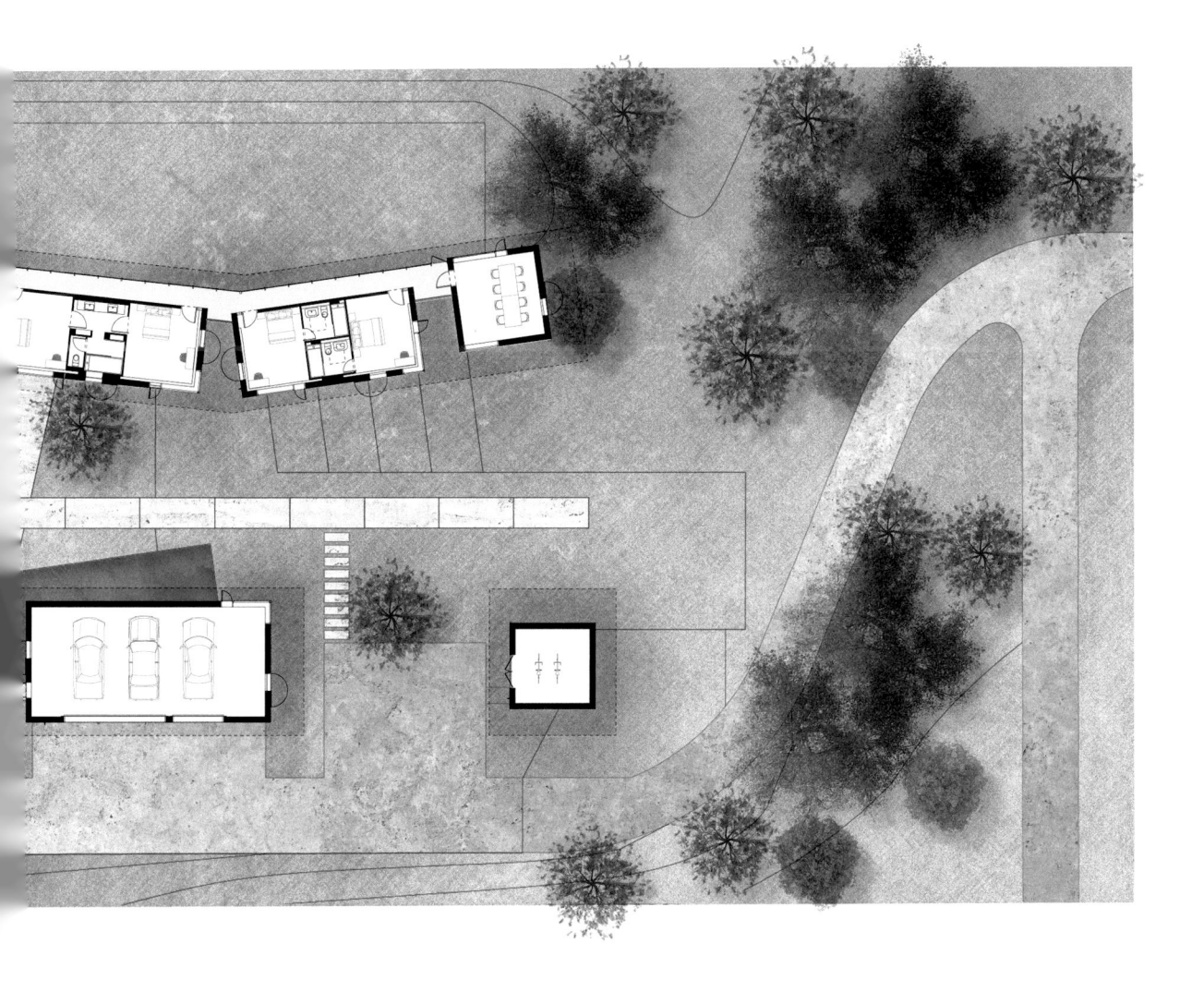

0　　15m

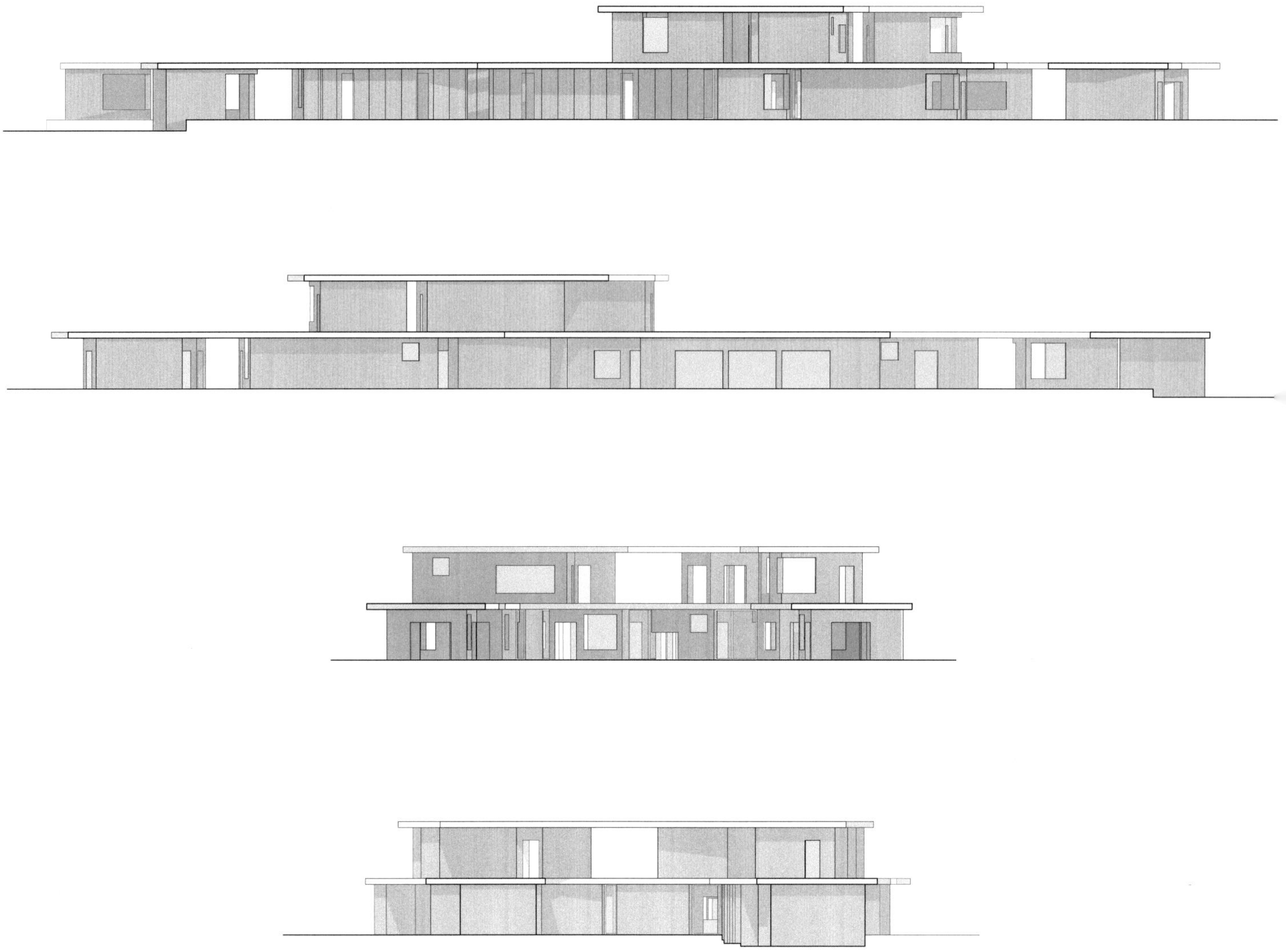

elevations

0　15m

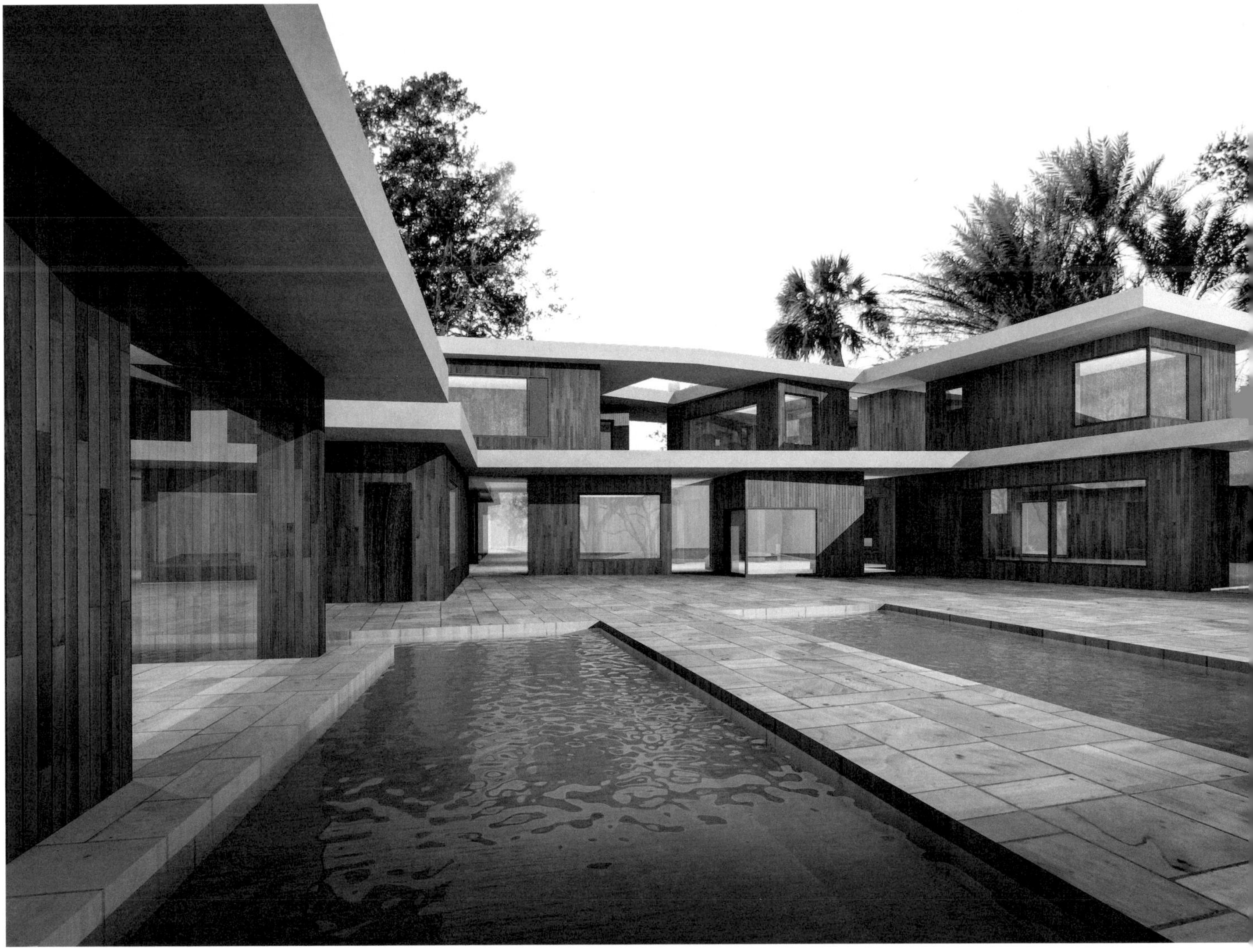

THE MAGISTRATES COURT
Bow Street Boutique Hotel, London

Researching and understanding the rich history of the site, prominently located across from the Royal Opera House in London's Covent Garden, was the starting point for this project. Originally two distinct buildings—the Bow Street Magistrates' Court and Police Station—we used a courtyard insertion in the interstitial space to stitch them back together as a coherent whole. In order to create dialogue with the immediate material context, we chose to use local red brick masonry in a lightweight screen structure to envelope the new part of the building.

Rather than simply follow the brief of a hotel with a museum component, our idea was to conceptualize the project as a museum with a hotel component, where the building itself is an artifact on display. As such, it was crucial to maintain many of the spatial and material elements of the existing structure. Not only are a lot of the original details of the building kept and restored, we reconfigured several existing rooms to accommodate new functions. Former prison cells are combined to form a unique hotel room type, where guests can experience first-hand the building's history through inhabitation. The main double-height courtroom space is transformed into the central dining area of the hotel restaurant, while retaining the original gallery configuration and seating arrangement. Experientially, the modern-day visitor's journey traces that of the building's many previous occupants. Temporarily encapsulating guests in another time and place, the hotel acts as a living museum or inhabitable installation.

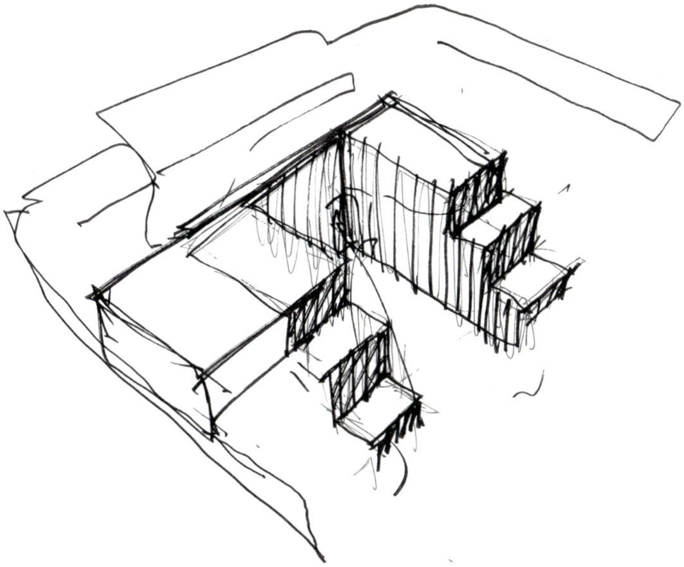

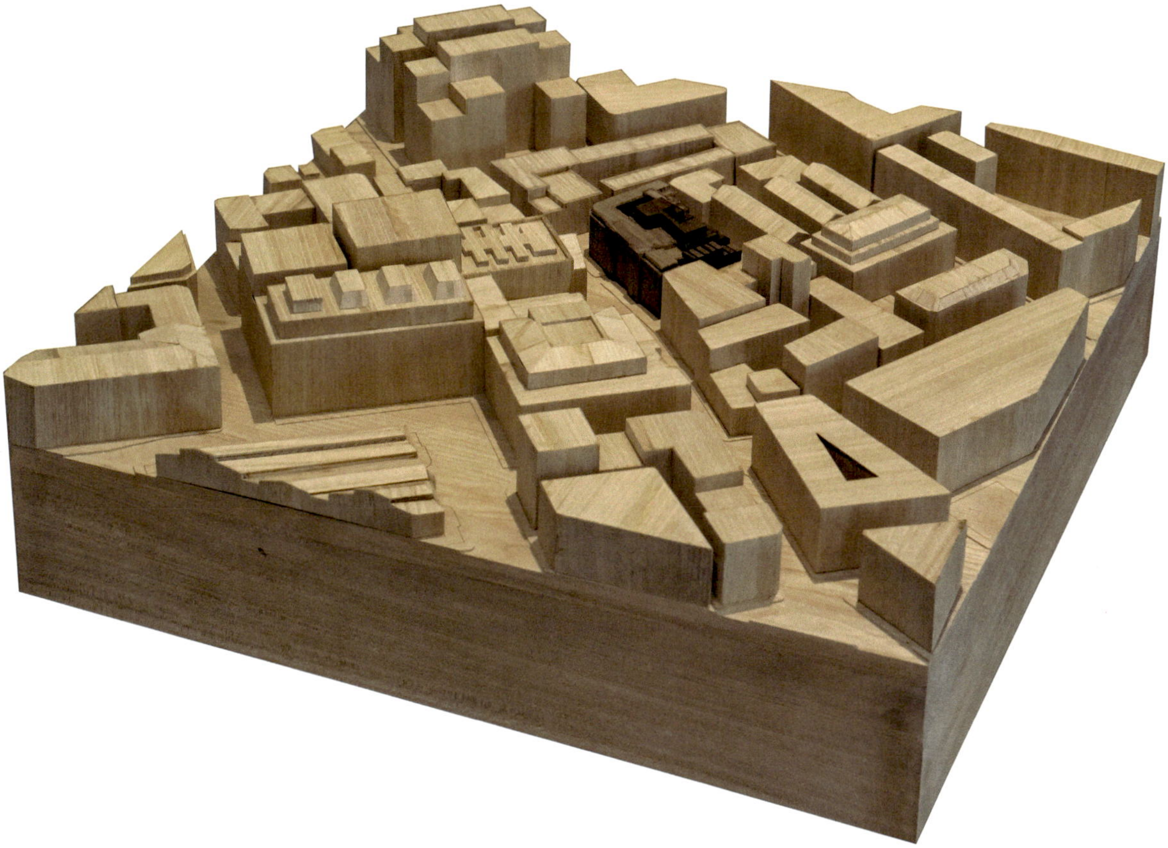

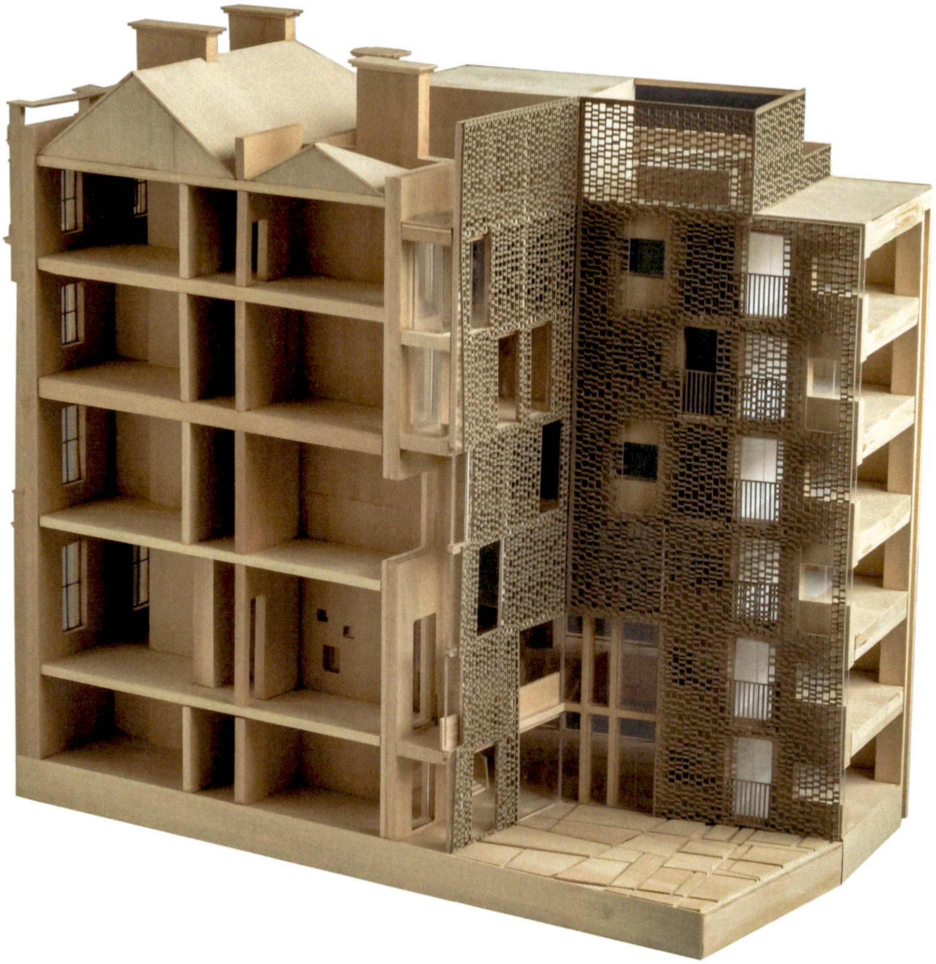

203

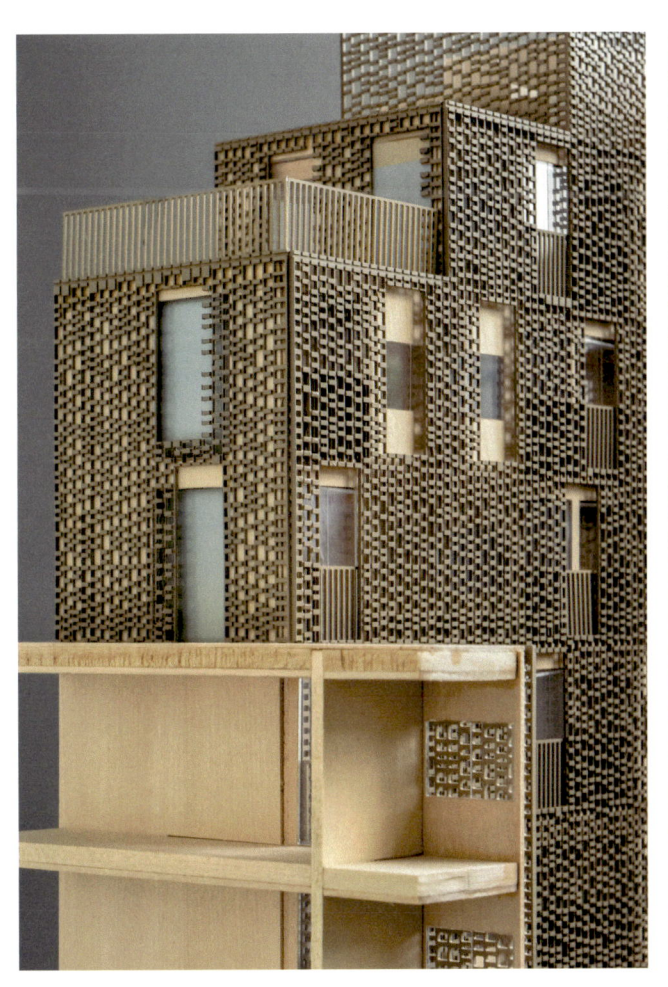

RECESSED BLACKENED METAL PARAPET
NEW RED BRICK TO MATCH EXISTING
HANDRAIL FIXED TO UPSTAND 1100 AFFL
PERFORATED BRICKWORK PARTIALLY IN FRONT OF WINDOW
HANDRAIL TO PROVIDE 1100MM GUARDING
COMPANION LADDER WITH GATE ACCESS ONTO ROOF
DARK GREY RAINSCREEN CLADDING
COMPANION LADDER WITH GATE ACCESS ONTO ROOF
SOLID BRICKWORK
NEW GLAZED OPERABLE WINDOW
BLACK METAL BALUSTRADE
CANT BRICK
GLAZING
NEW RED BRICK TO MATCH EXISTING
DARK GREY METAL SCREEN
NEW AOV PANELS WITHIN CURTAIN WALL
NEW RECESSED DORMER WINDOW WOODEN FRAME + GLASS
SOLAR PANELS
LEAD ROLL ROOF JOINTS TO MATCH EXISTING
METAL STEP-OVER LADDER
NEW HOPPER + RAINWATER PIPE TO MATCH EXISTING
RECLAIMED NATURAL GREY SLATE TO MATCH EXISTING
HANDRAIL TO PROVIDE GUARDING
TOP OF MEP PLANT
FFL NEW 4/F
FFL NEW 3/F
FFL NEW 2/F
FFL NEW 1/F
FFL NEW MEZZANINE
GROUND FL(e)
U/S OF SLAB(e)
3rd FLOOR(e)
2nd FLOOR(e)
1st FLOOR(e)
GROUND FL(e)
3500
3100
3100
3100
3100
3100
2990
3870
3730
4489
NEW RED BRICK TO MATCH EXISTING
NEW AOV PANEL WINDOW
NEW STUCCO TO MATCH EXISTING
NEW METAL BOLLARDS
NEW BLACKENED METAL AOV PANEL
NEW BLACKENED METAL DOOR
NEW WINDOWS
NEW DOOR TO MEET UKPN REQUIREMENTS

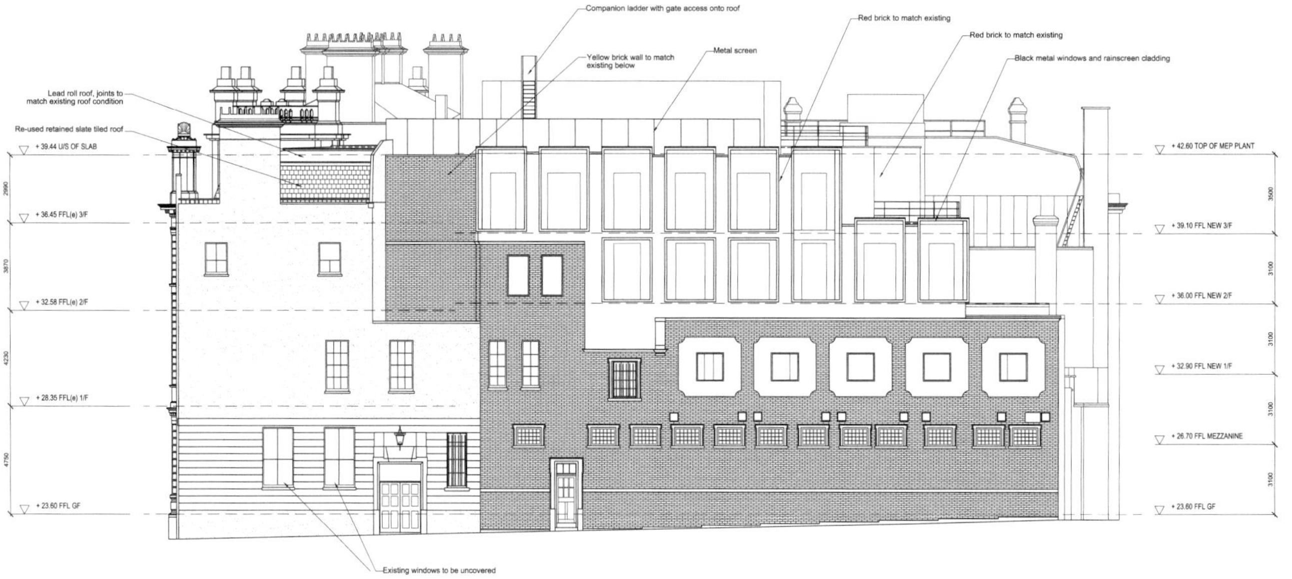
Companion ladder with gate access onto roof
Red brick to match existing
Red brick to match existing
Yellow brick wall to match existing below
Metal screen
Black metal windows and rainscreen cladding
Lead roll roof, joints to match existing roof condition
Re-used retained slate tiled roof
+ 39.44 U/S OF SLAB
+ 36.45 FFL(e) 3/F
+ 32.58 FFL(e) 2/F
+ 28.35 FFL(e) 1/F
+ 23.60 FFL GF
2990
3870
4230
4750
+ 42.60 TOP OF MEP PLANT
+ 39.10 FFL NEW 3/F
+ 36.00 FFL NEW 2/F
+ 32.90 FFL NEW 1/F
+ 26.70 FFL MEZZANINE
+ 23.60 FFL GF
3500
3100
3100
3100
3100
Existing windows to be uncovered

elevations

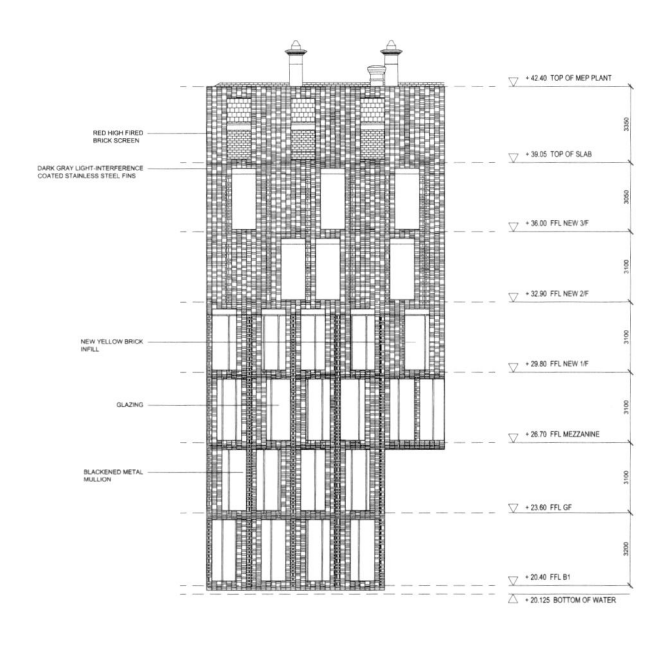

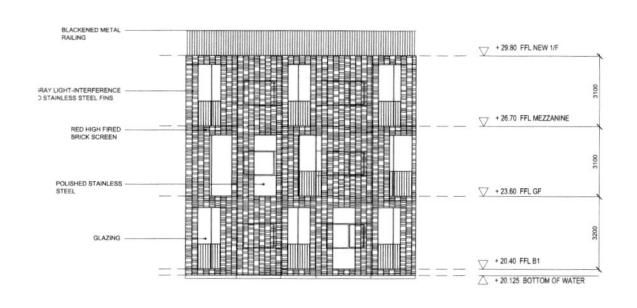

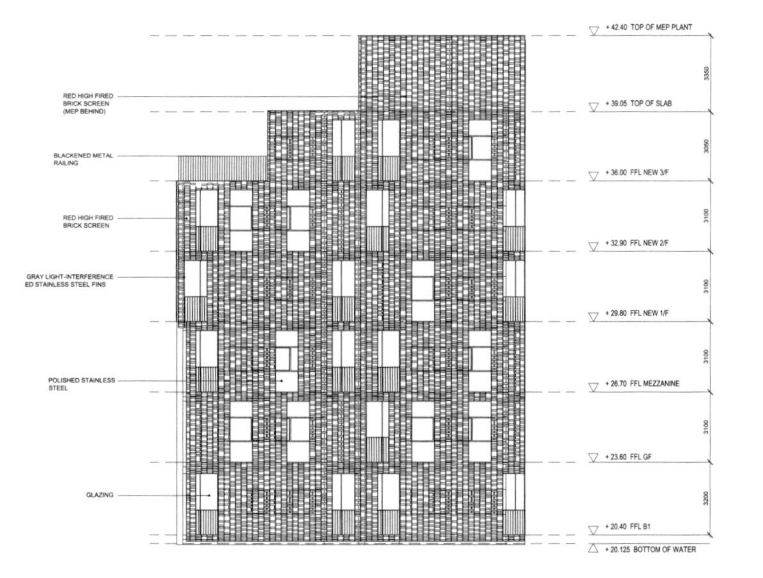

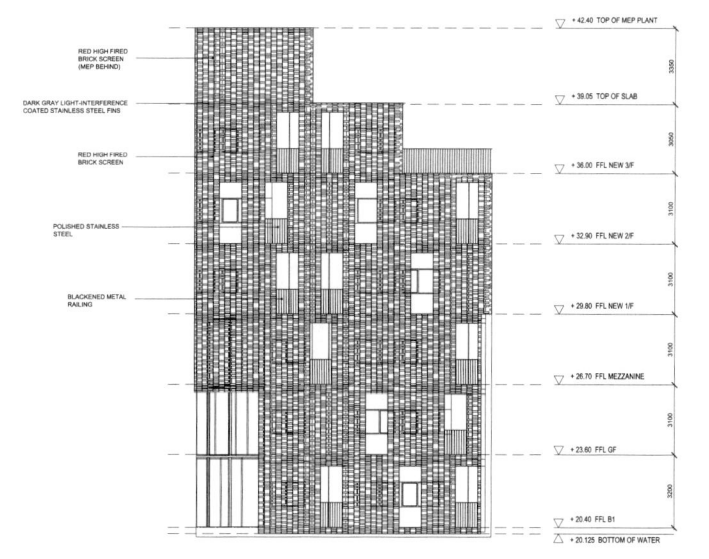

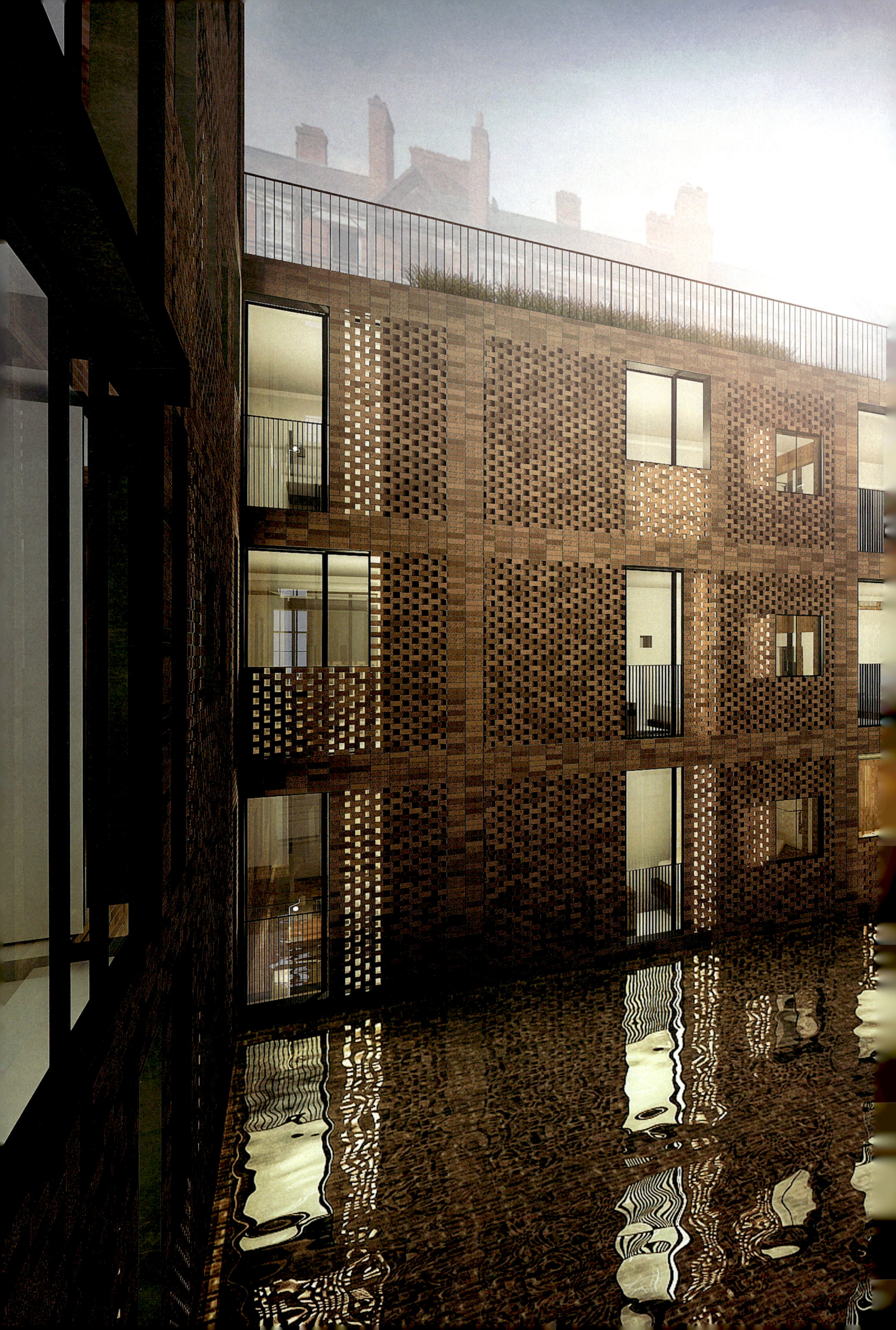

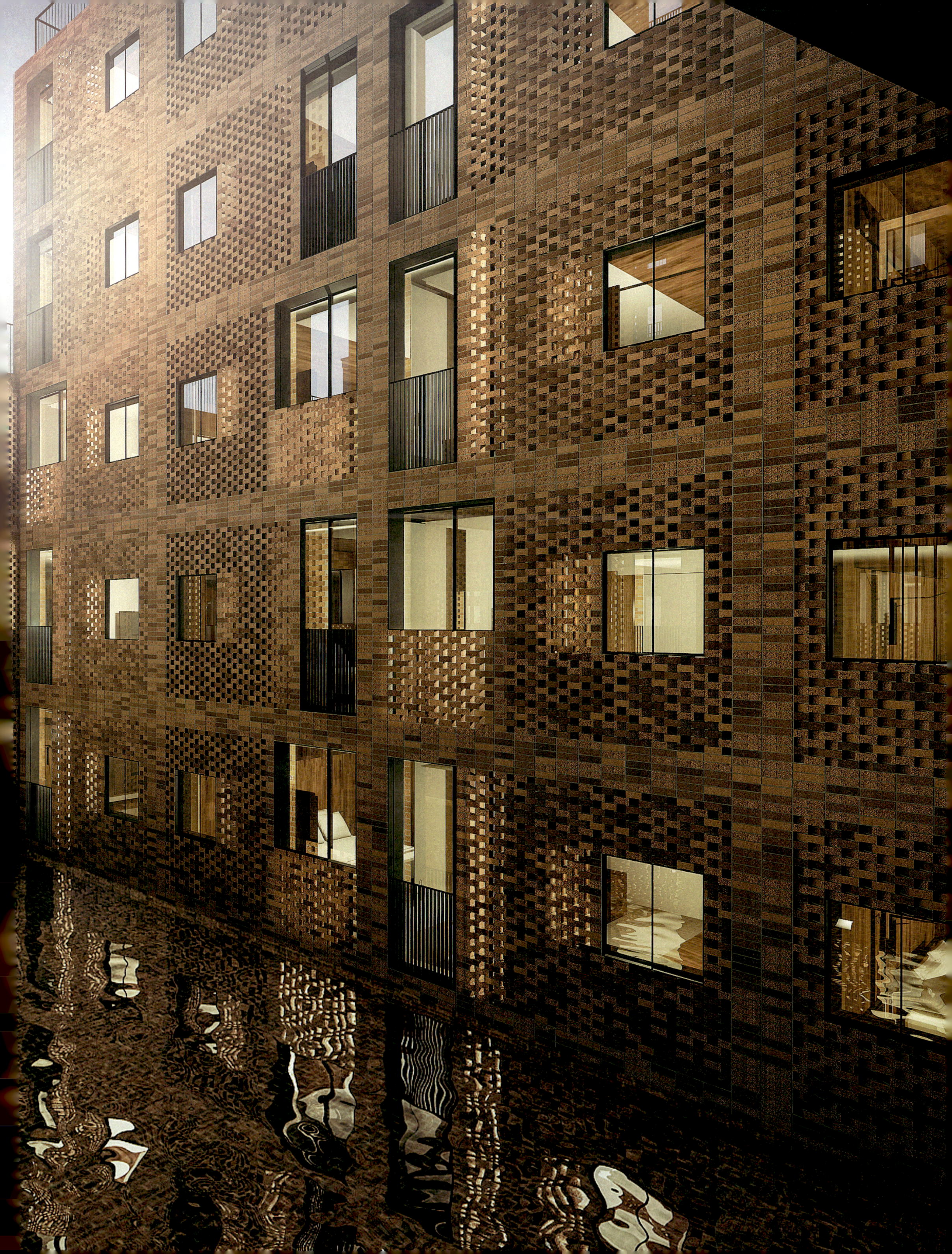

plan

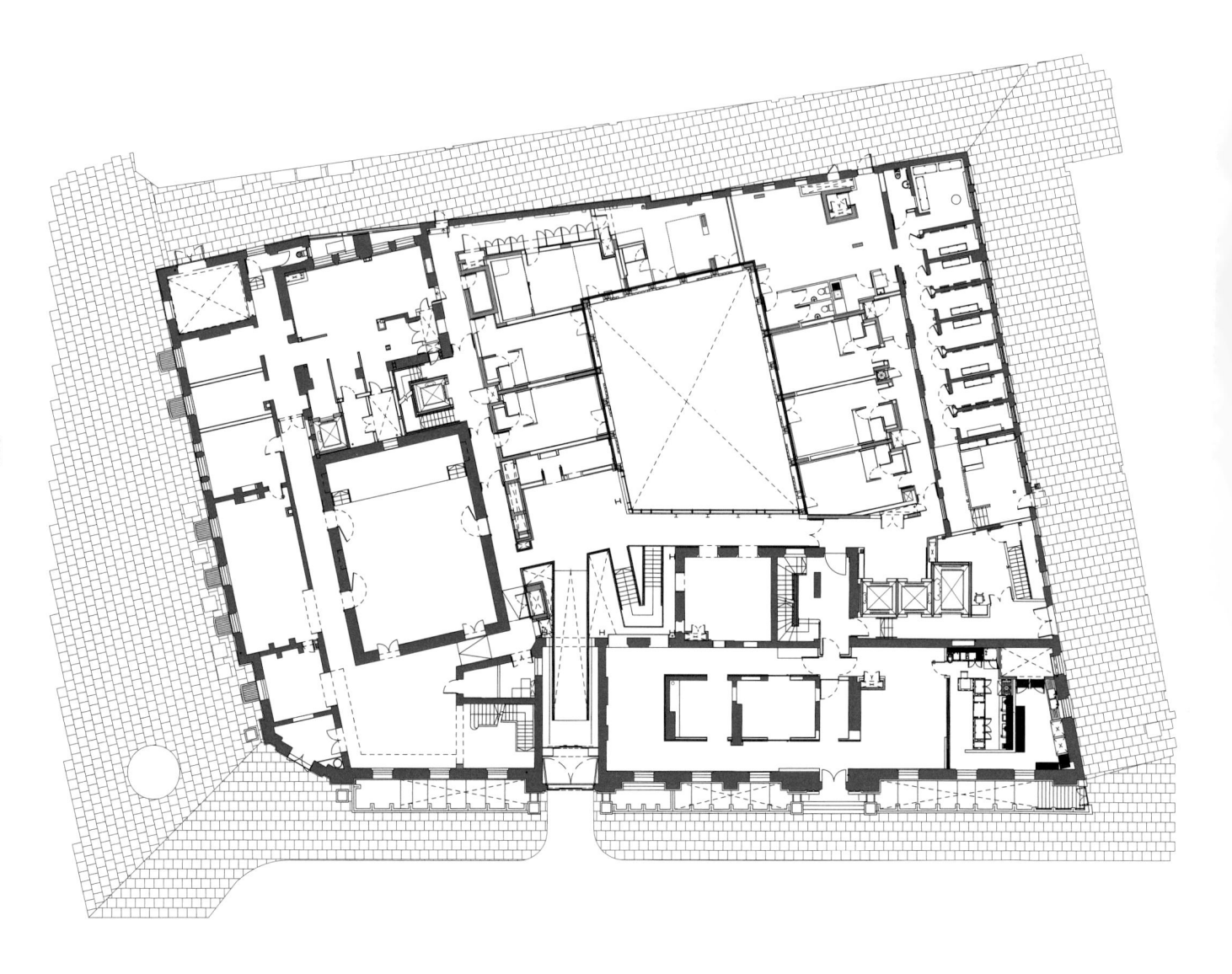

0 15m

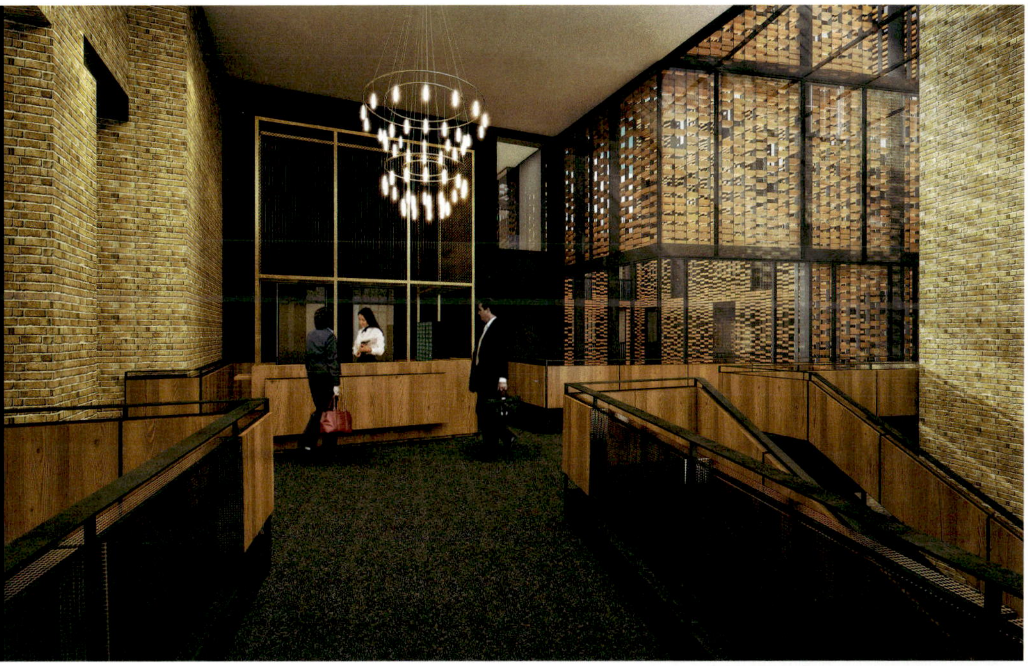

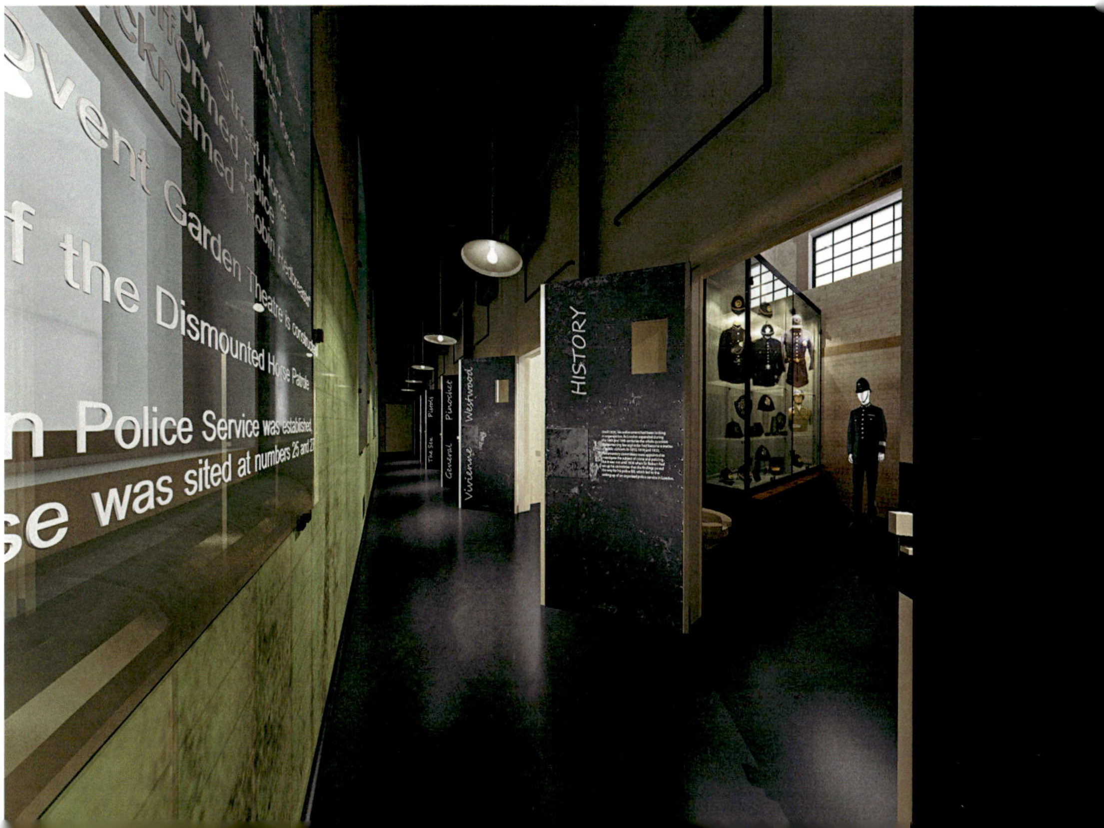

BOW STREET POLICE COURT AND STATION.

TRANSVERSE SECTION OF PRINCIPAL COURT

LONGITUDINAL SECTION OF PRINCIPAL COURT

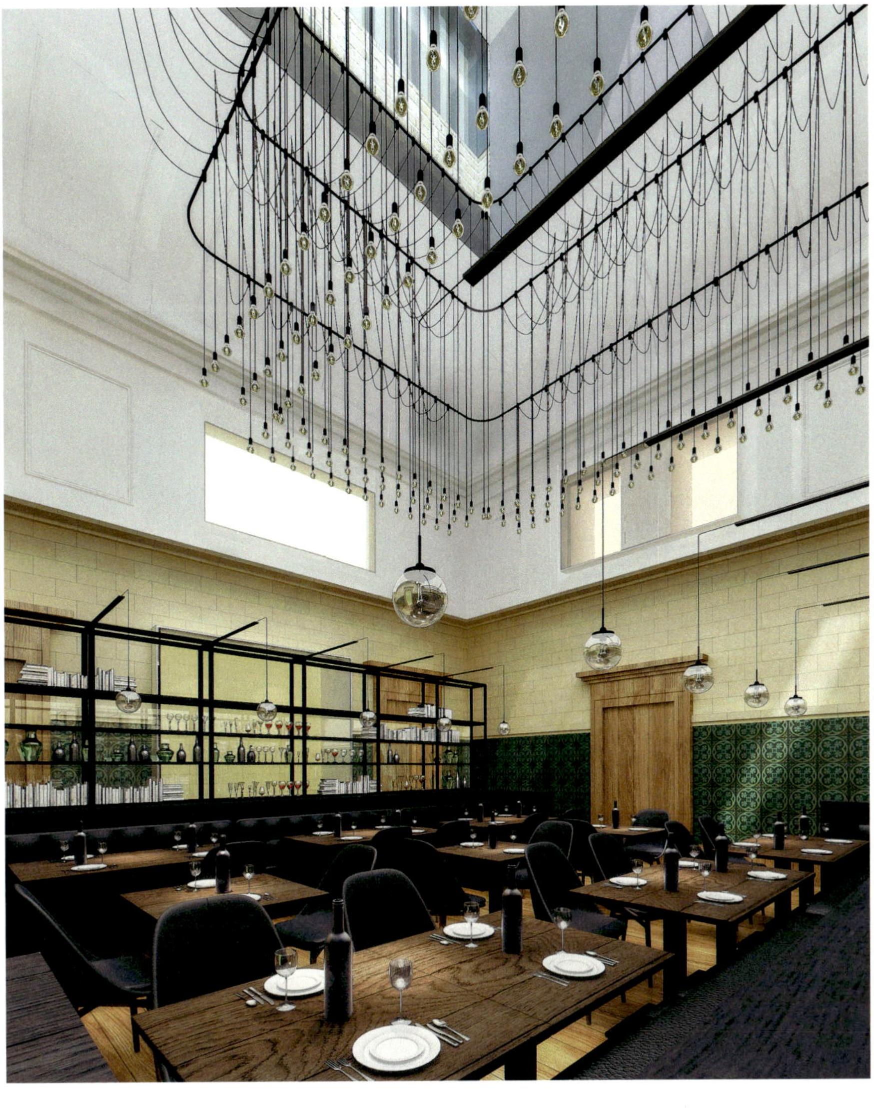

THE GARDEN UNITS
Residential Tower, Kuala Lumpur

The new-build twenty-story high-end residential tower development called for very large unit sizes, ranging in area from 800 square meters over one level to 1600 over two levels. Given the generous unit sizes, as well as the context of Kuala Lumpur's verdant tropical surroundings, we conceived of the building as a series of individual garden villas assembled together, rather than a typical residential tower. With that in mind, we designed four unique layout configurations that could be alternated, in order to break through the standard stacking of identical floor plates, which results in bleakly uniform and anonymous buildings.

In consideration of the regional climate we recognized the need for shade and chose concrete as the outer envelope of the building, in both solid and perforated varieties based on the function it encases. At the same time, we took the opportunity to integrate as much greenery and landscape into the building itself as possible, giving over close to 30 percent of floor area to exterior space: balconies, pools, and hanging gardens. This creates a highly inhabitable in-between zone—covered and shaded but open air—a spatial typology that is commonly found in tropical living environments. Wood insertions highlight private living areas and lend a warmer atmosphere to the most domestic spaces.

213

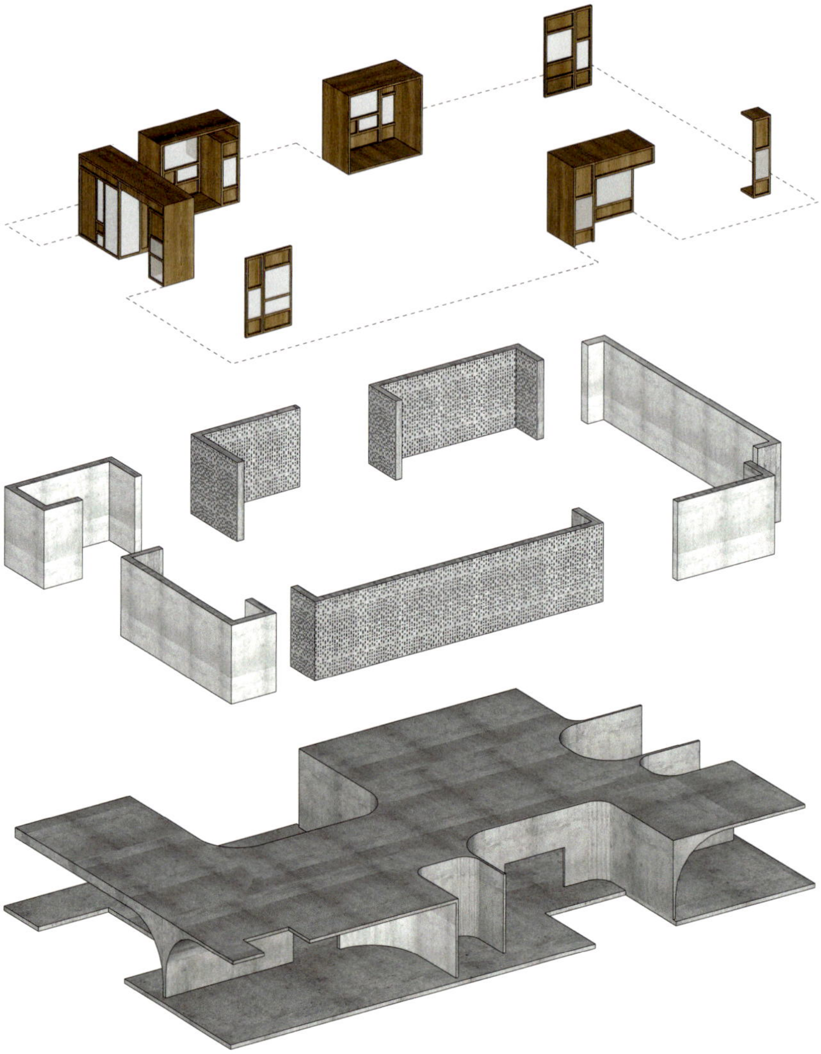

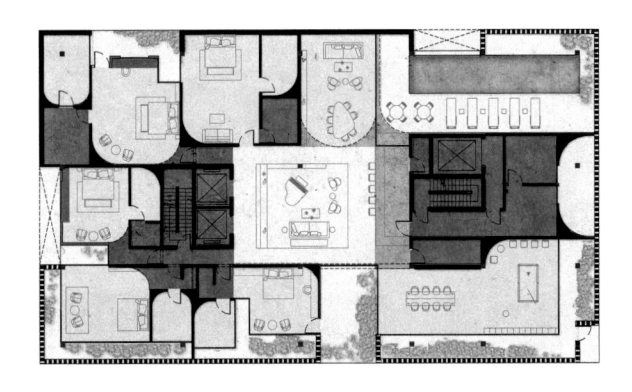

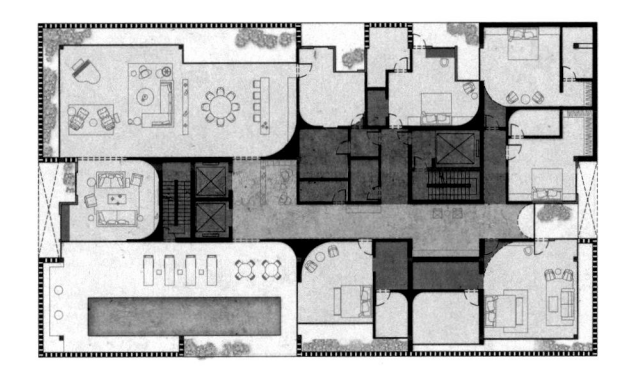

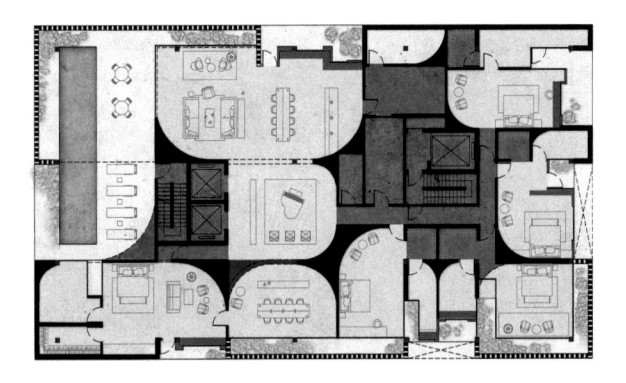

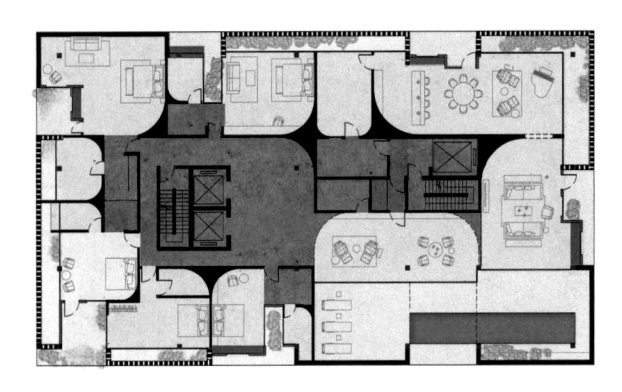

typical plans

0　　　　20m

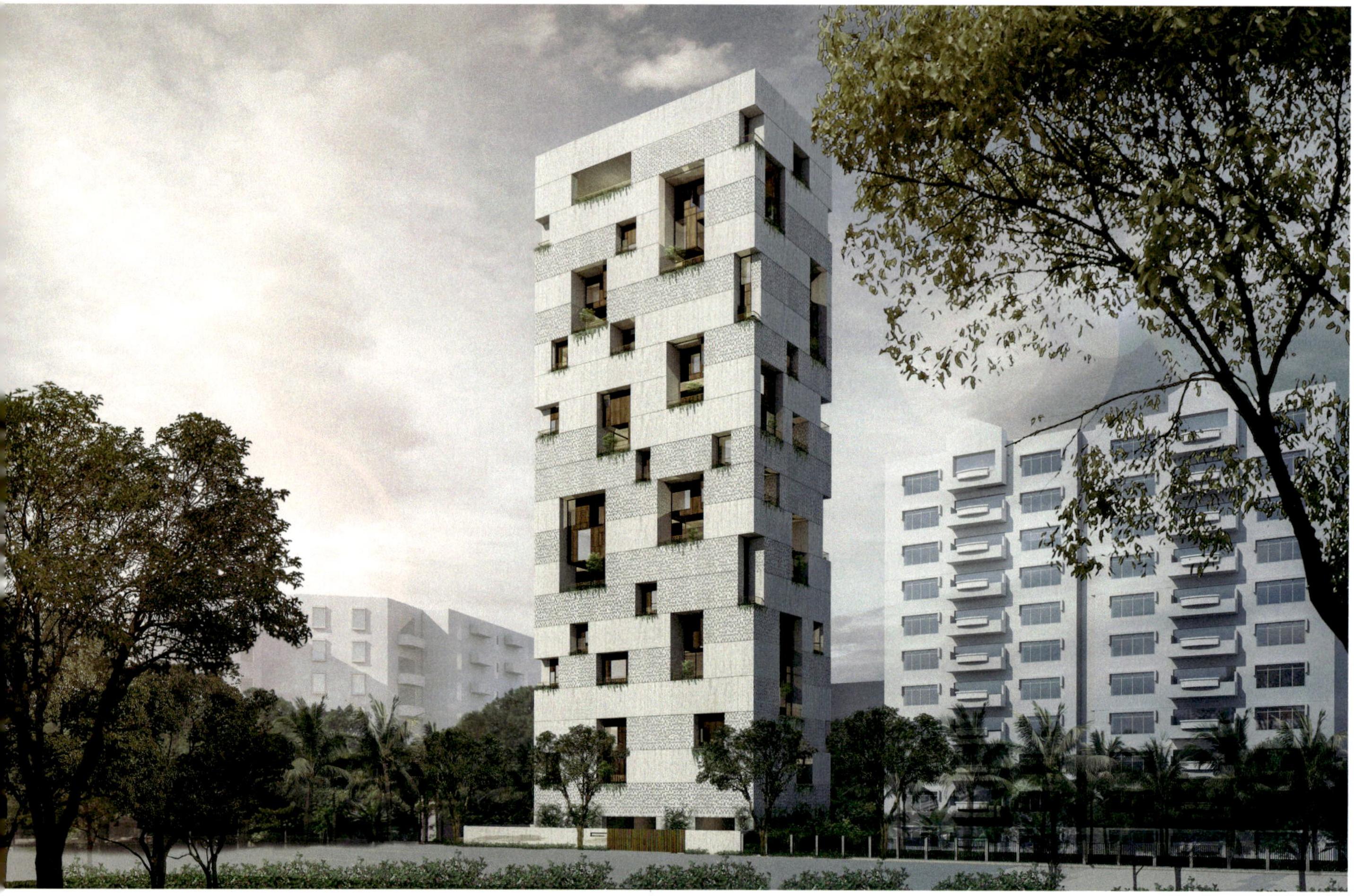

217

THE HERITAGE JOURNEY
Sentul Contemporary Art Museum, Kuala Lumpur

Occupying the former British colonial railway headquarters, the Sentul Arts Center is a contemporary art museum that is part of a larger plan for an extensive arts complex in Sentul Park, Kuala Lumpur. The placement of artworks in a lush natural context is the fundamental driver of the design. Unlike urban museums, whose locations necessitate layers of security, the Sentul Arts Center allows for a gradated discovery of the building in its context, inverting the relationship between interior and exterior. In addition to the main building, three pavilions, used for both dining and art, extend the activities into the natural surroundings with a lightweight canopy structure that floats gently across the landscape.

The design for the museum creates a voyage through the heritage building and culminates in the white-box gallery insertions. The existing brick facades are contrasted with modern interventions, allowing a full appreciation of the building's many layers. Guardrails, windows, paving, and lighting are all given a richness of material and detail that contrasts with the more abstract forms of the gallery volumes. Linear circulation through all three floors reveals the existing layers as a single sequence, curating the history written on the walls of the building itself. Carefully positioned windows and expansive terraces provide many levels of engagement with the outside, framing views of trees and surrounding nature.

219

220

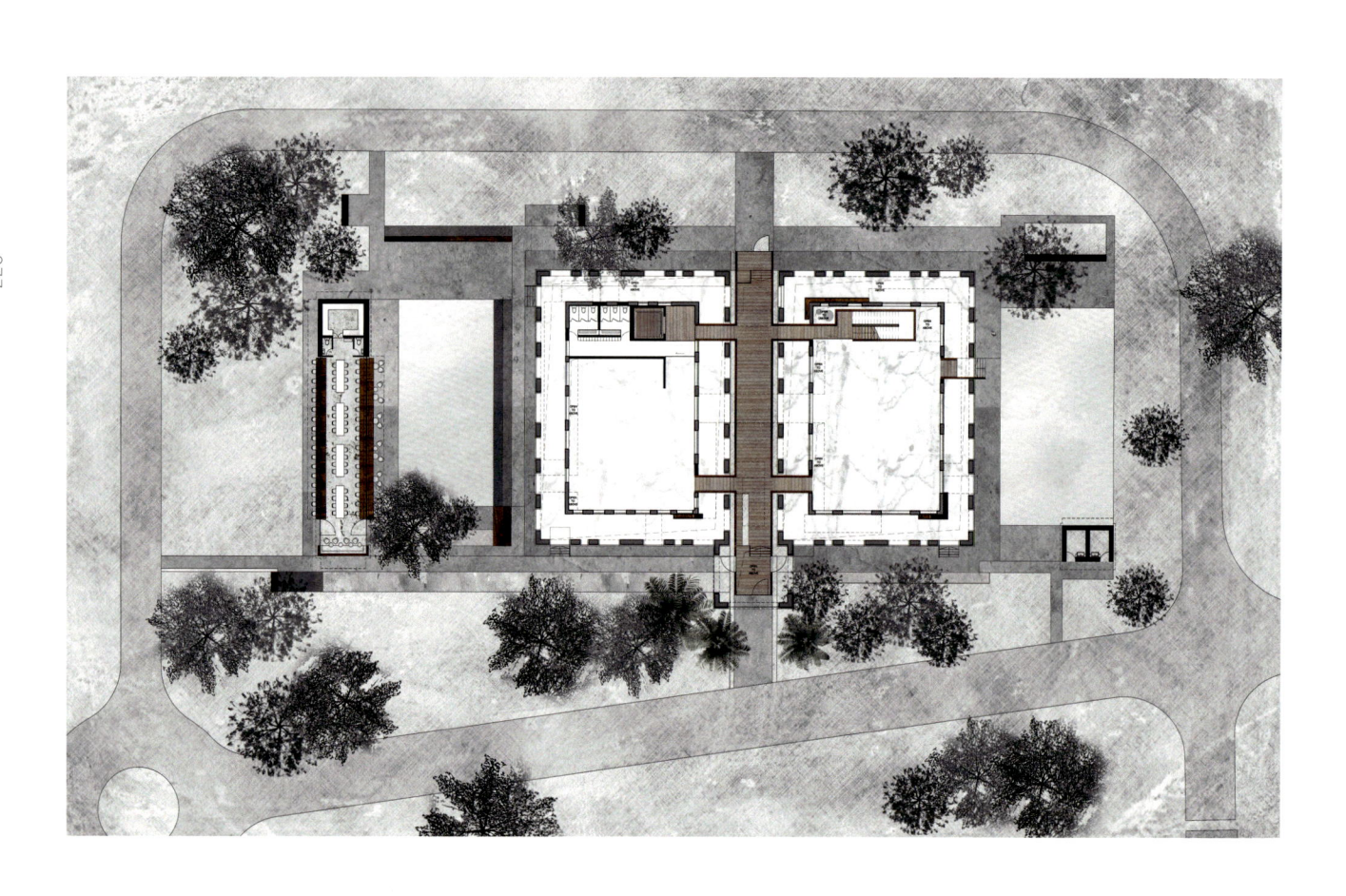

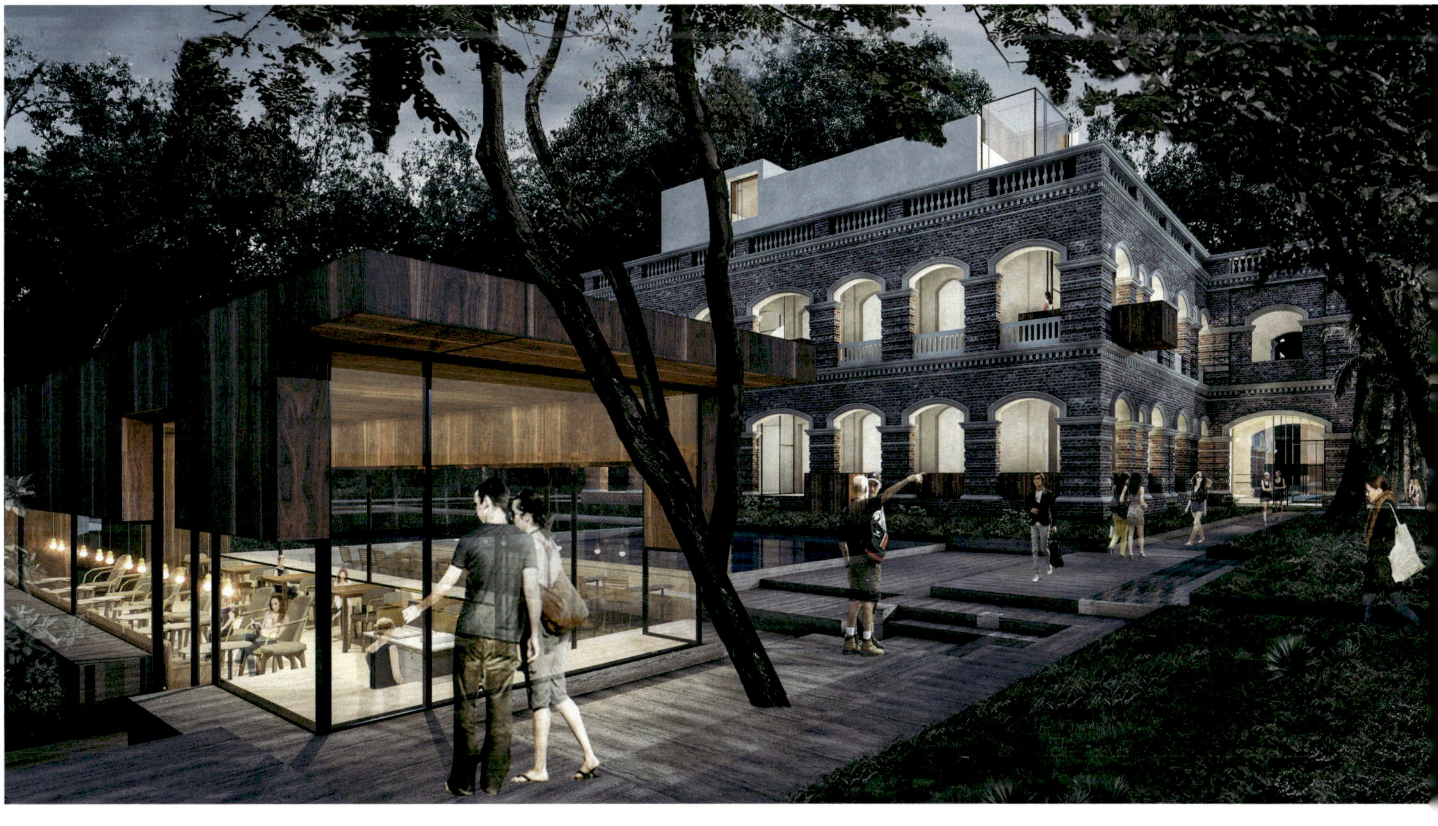

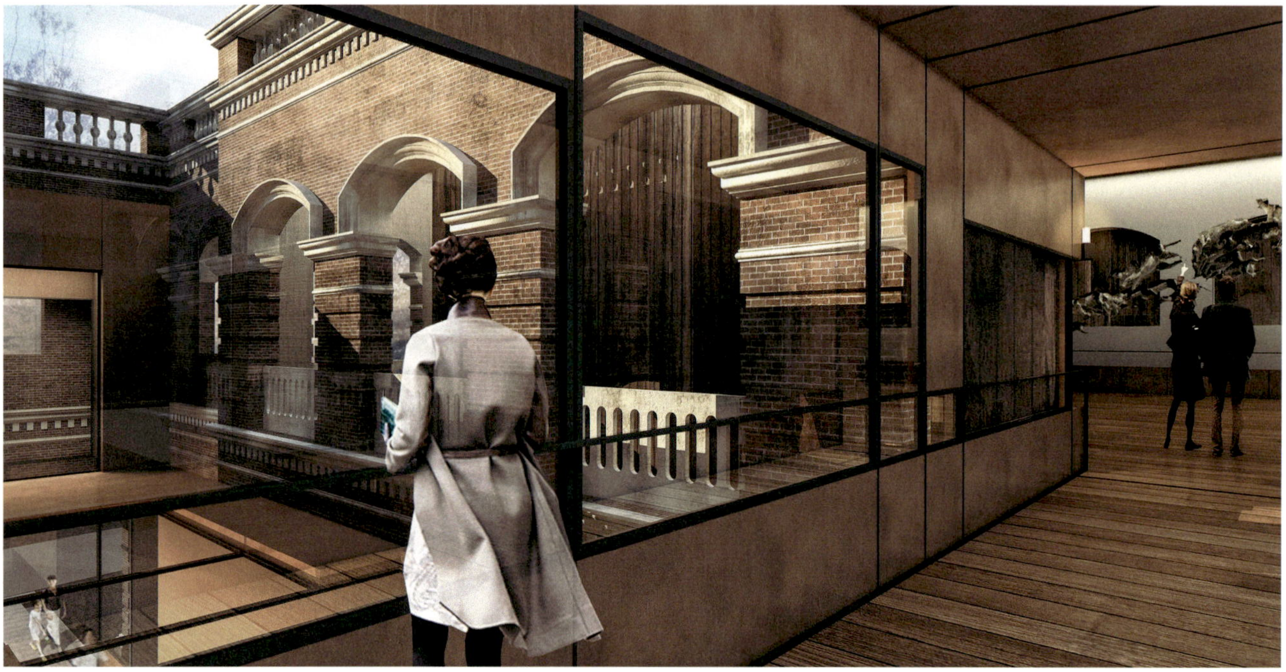

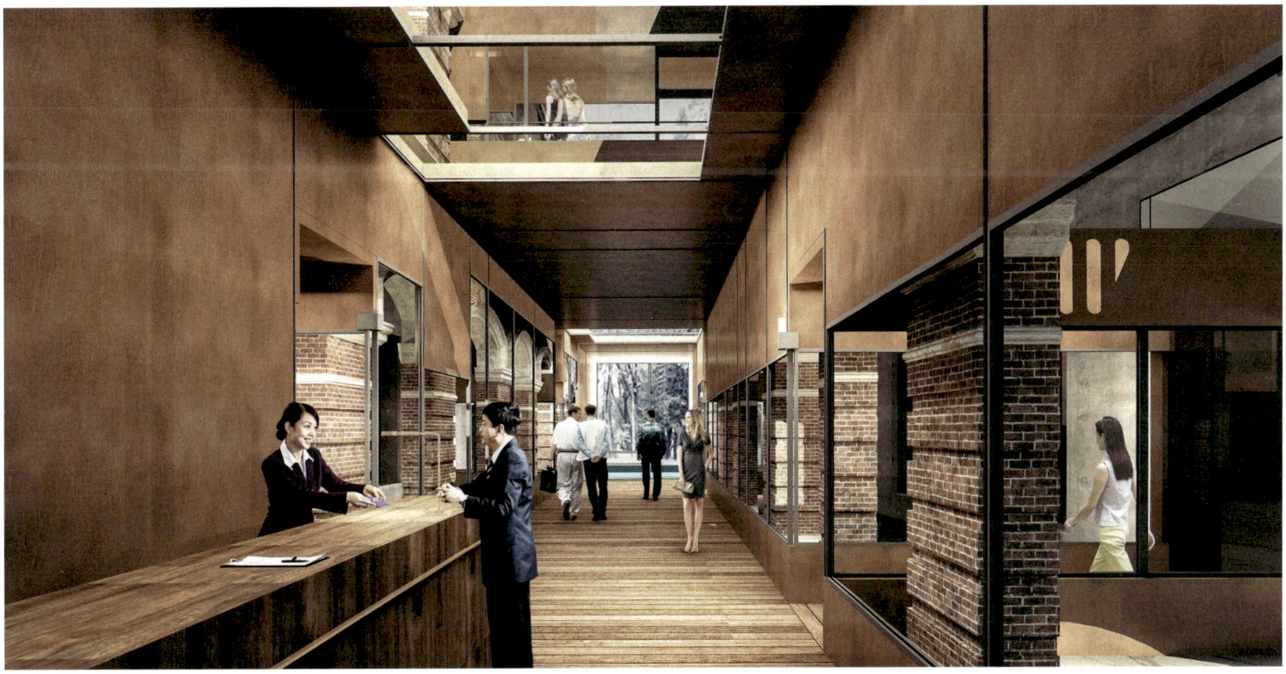

products

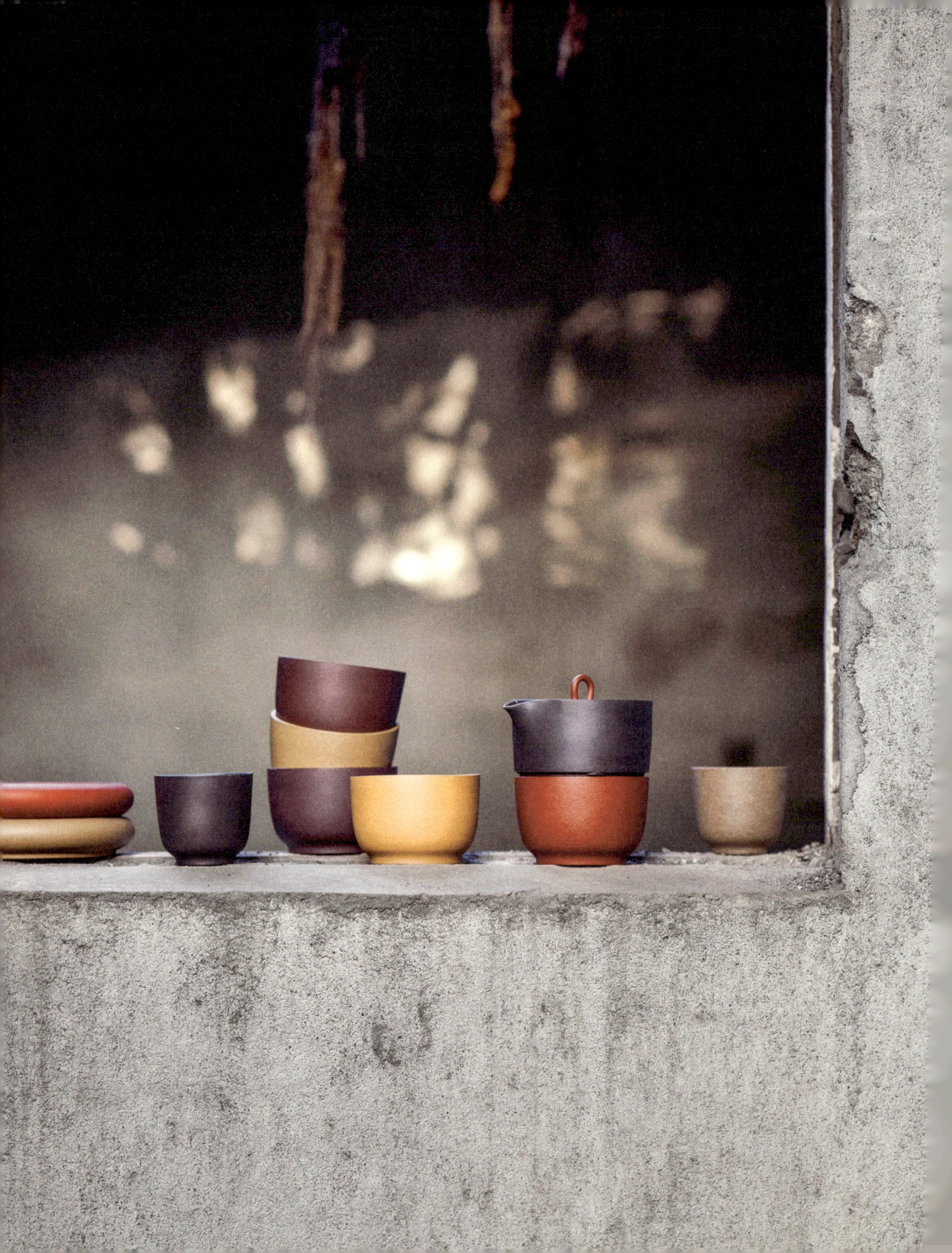

ZISHA TEA PROJECT 2004–2006
for Neri&Hu

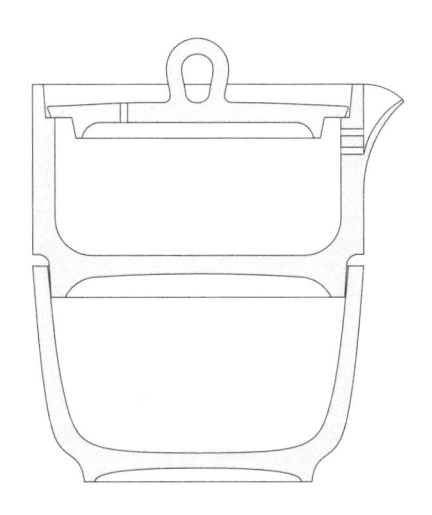

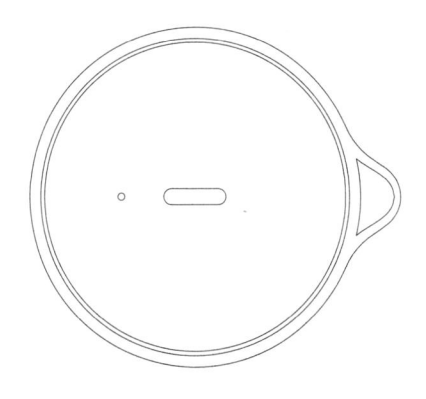

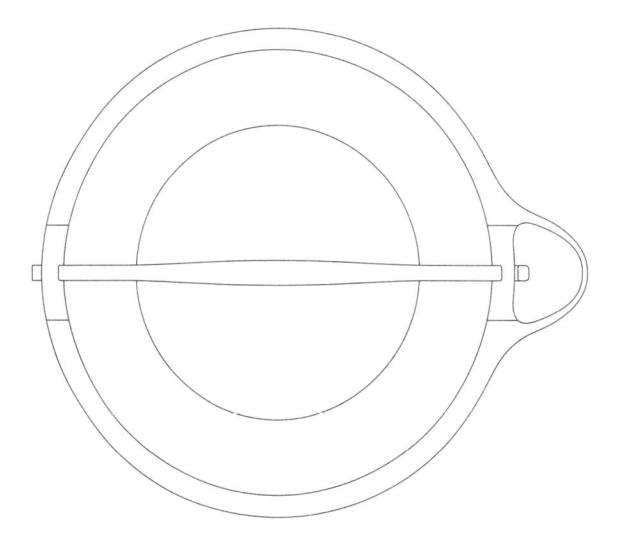

dimension teapot 130 × 140 × 160 mm | single pot with cup 90 × 100 × 120 mm
large tray 150 × 150 × 25.5 mm | small tray 80 × 80 × 13.5 mm
large cup 90 × 90 × 57 mm | small cup 64 × 64 × 57 mm
material zisha clay, bronze
used in projects the commune social
design team lyndon neri, rossana hu, brian lo, zhili liu

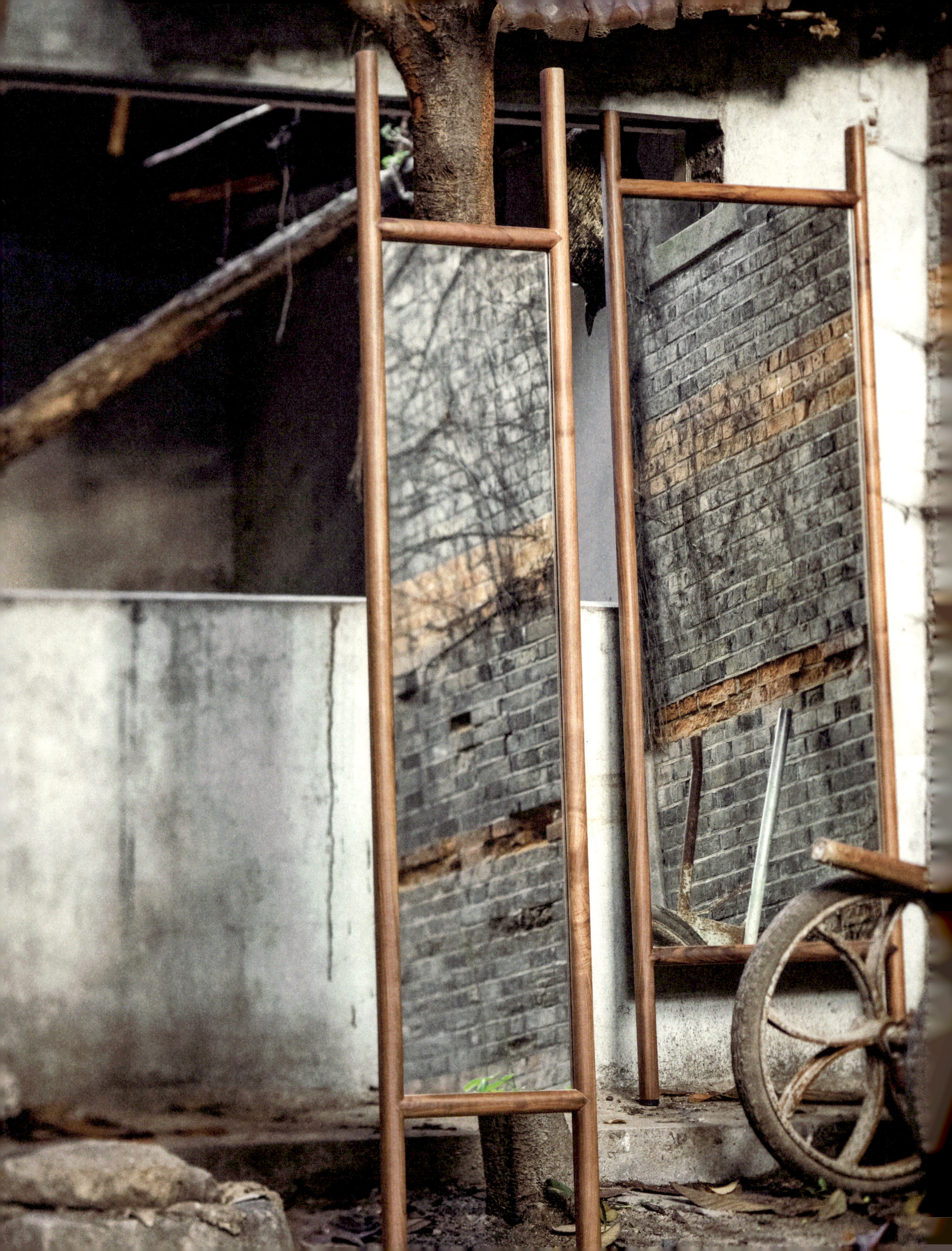

EXTEND MIRROR 2004–2006
for Neri&Hu

dimension 980 × 2200 × 50 mm | 680 × 2200 × 50 mm | 430 × 2200 × 50 mm
material mirror glass, walnut
used in projects waterhouse at south bund, rethinking the split house
design team lyndon neri, rossana hu, brian lo

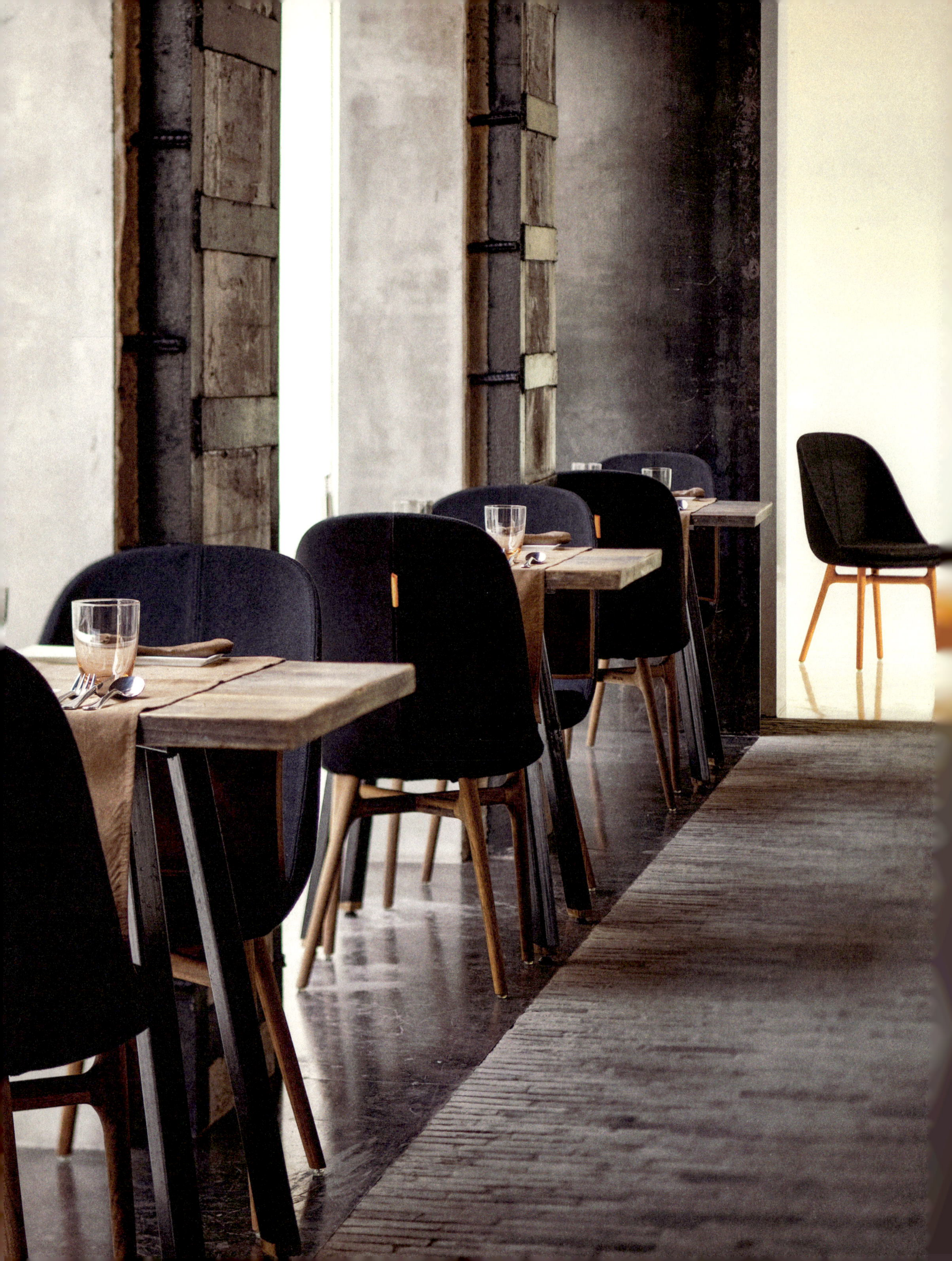

SOLO CHAIR 2006–2007
for De La Espada

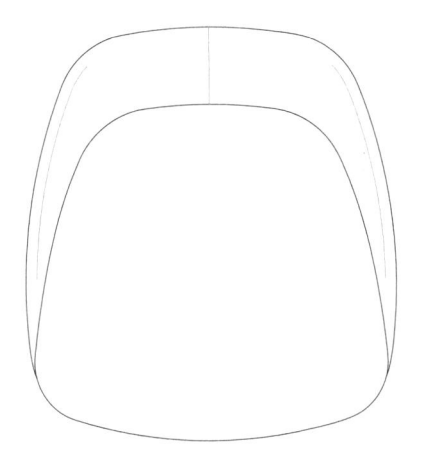

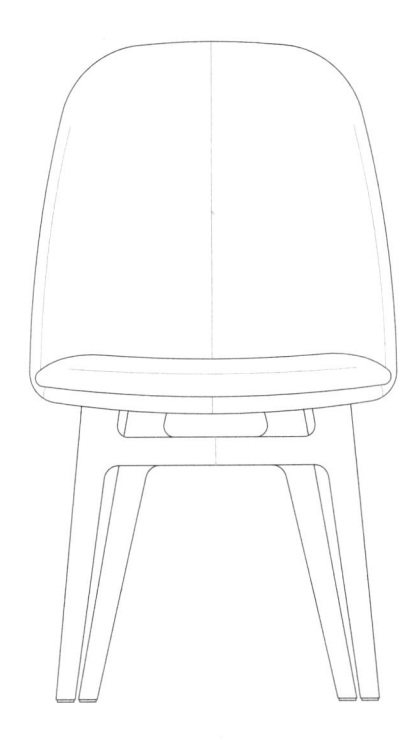

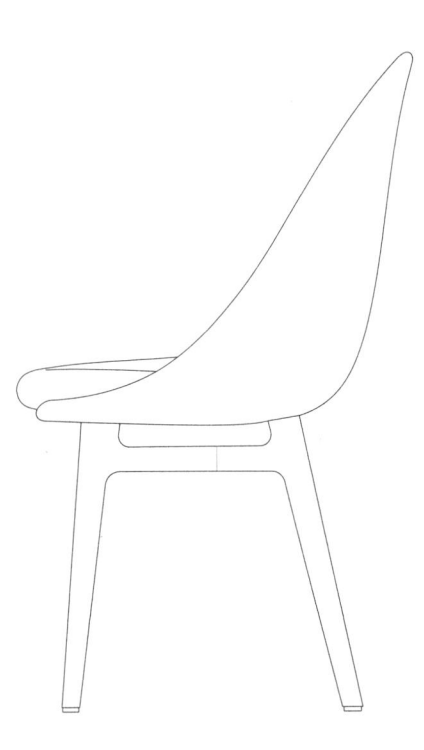

dimension 505 × 550 × 870 mm
material walnut, fiberglass shell
used in projects waterhouse at south bund, design republic design commune, rethinking the split house, mercato, camper showroom/office
design team lyndon neri, rossana hu, brian lo, zhil liu, yun zhao

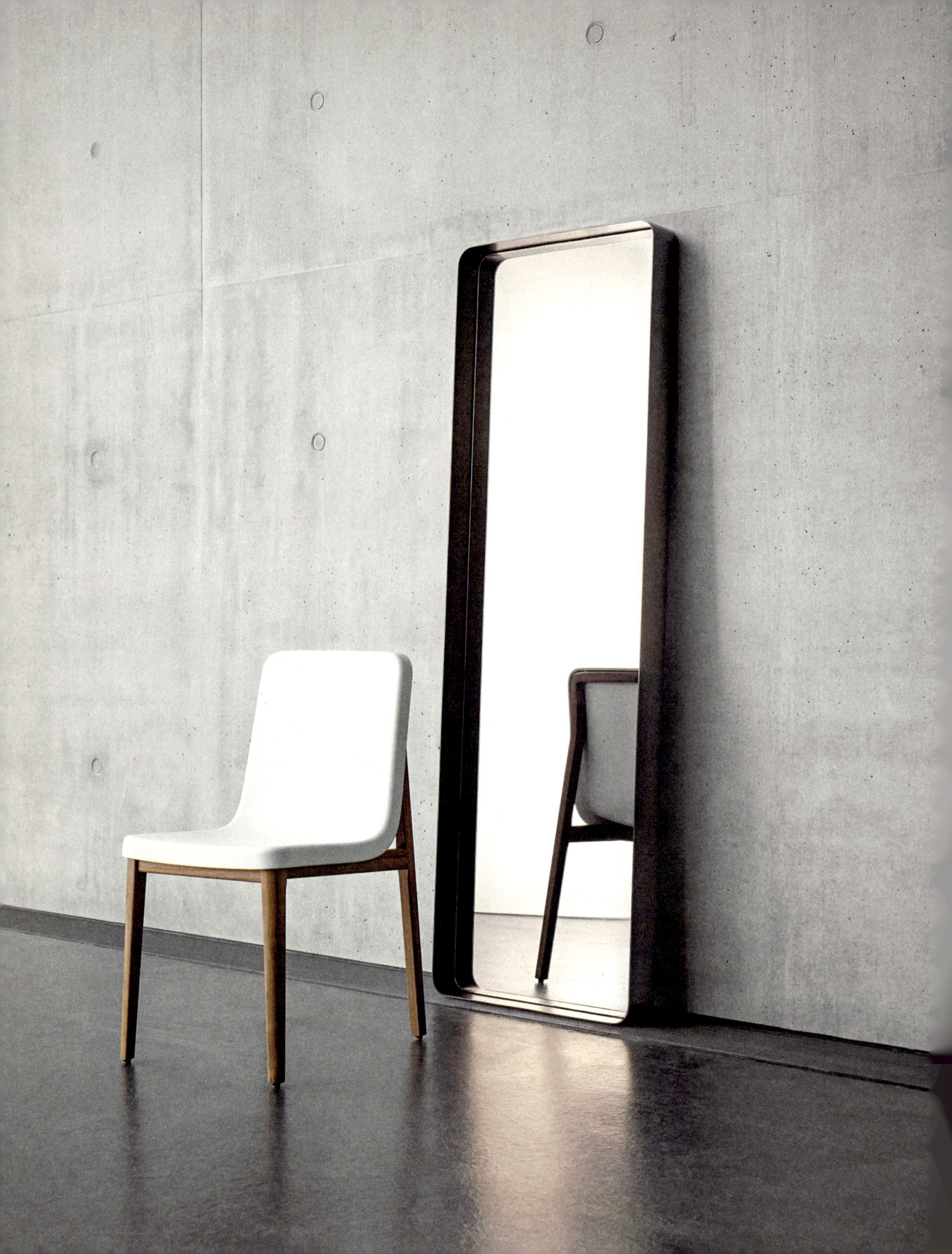

SEDAN CHAIR 2010–2014
for Classicon

dimension 450 × 540 × 840 mm | 850 × 650 × 740 mm
material abs molded seat, leather or fabric upholstery, tubular steel or walnut
used in projects bow street boutique hotel and police station, le meridian hotel
design team lyndon neri, rossana hu, brian lo, ximi li

0   40cm

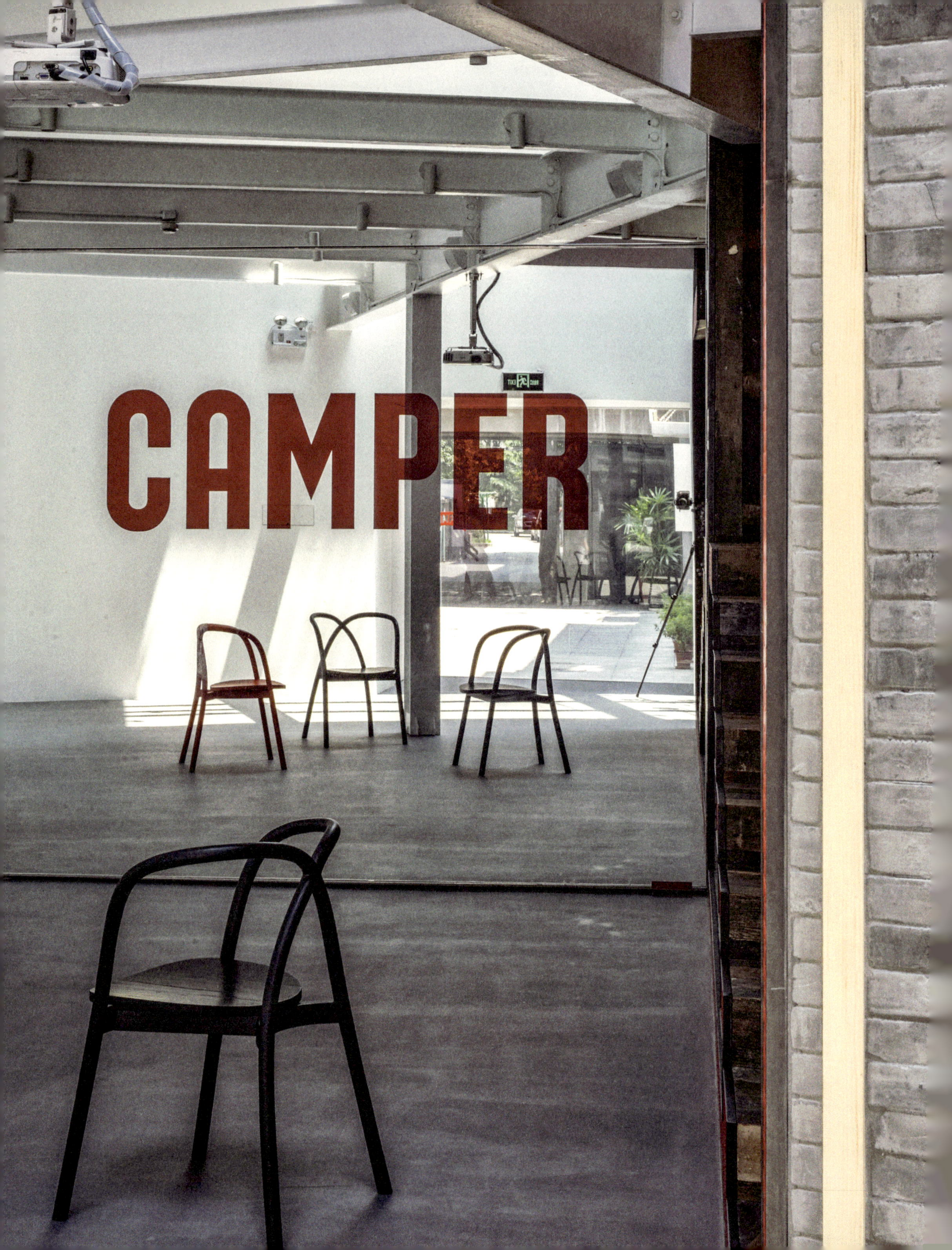
CAMPER

MING CHAIR 2012–2013
for Stellar Works

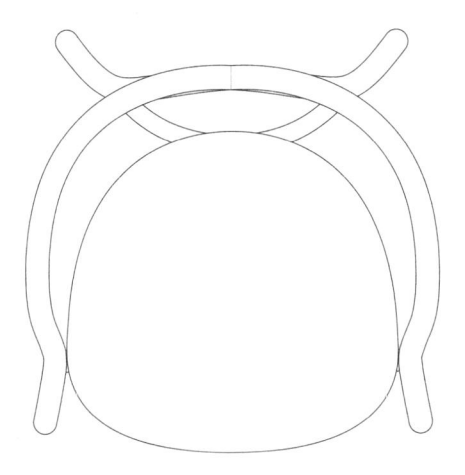

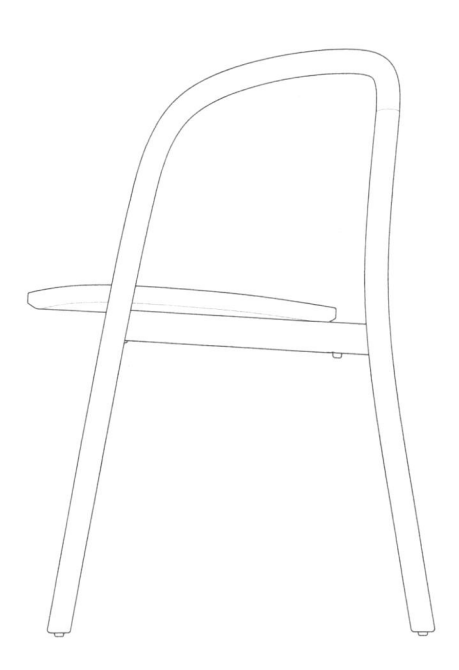

dimension 560 × 560 × 775 mm
material ash, painted in black, white and red
used in projects camper showroom/office
design team lyndon neri, rossana hu, brian lo, yun zhao, ximi li

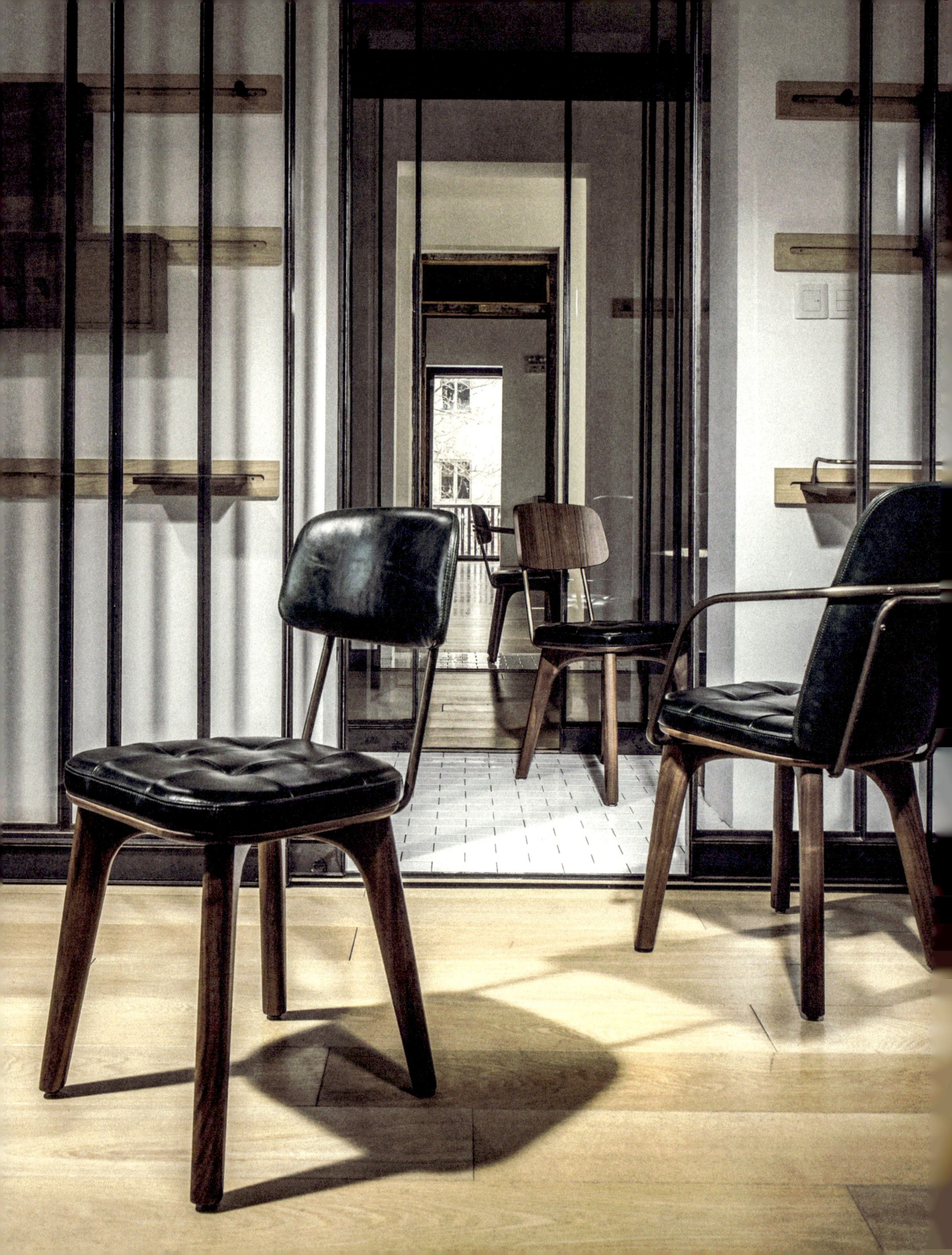

UTILITY CHAIR 2012–2013
for Stellar Works

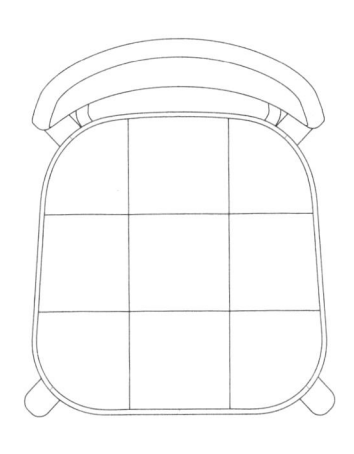

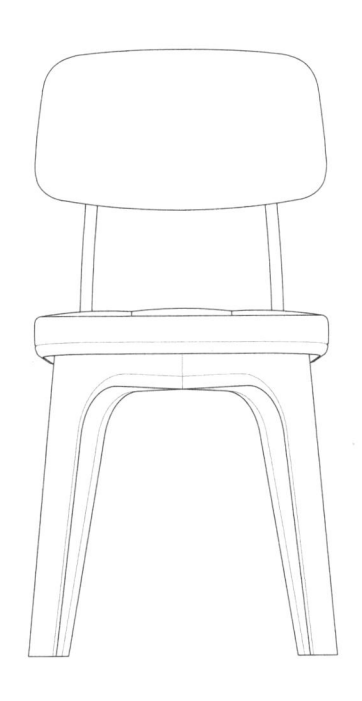

dimension 422 × 497 × 800 mm | 707 × 728 × 827 mm
material walnut, high-density foam, bent plywood
used in projects bow street boutique hotel and police station, the assemblage, le meridian hotel
design team lyndon neri, rossana hu, brian lo, ximi li

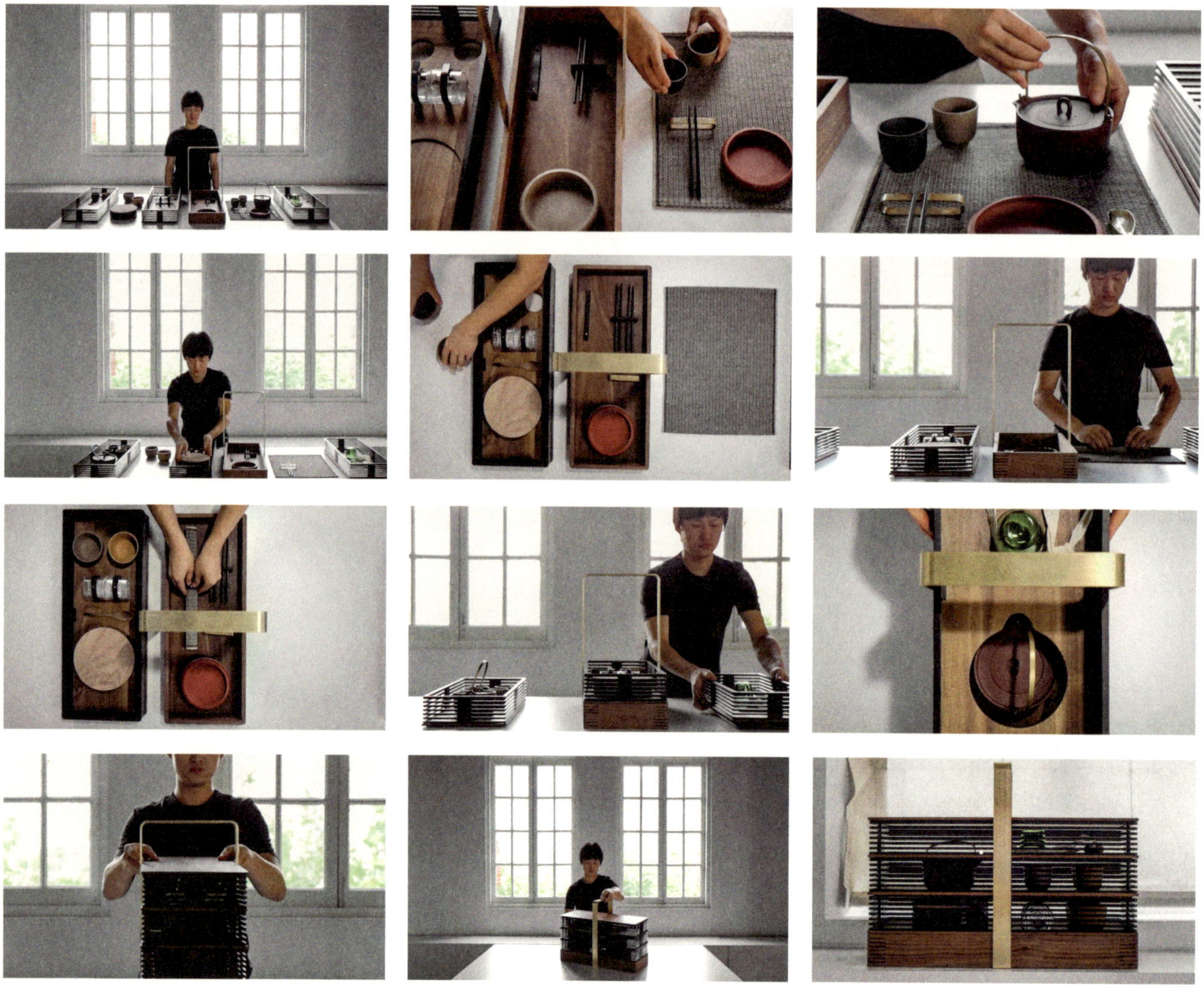

WILD FEAST PICNIC BASKET 2013–2014
Neri&Hu for Wallpaper Handmade sponsored by Jaguar

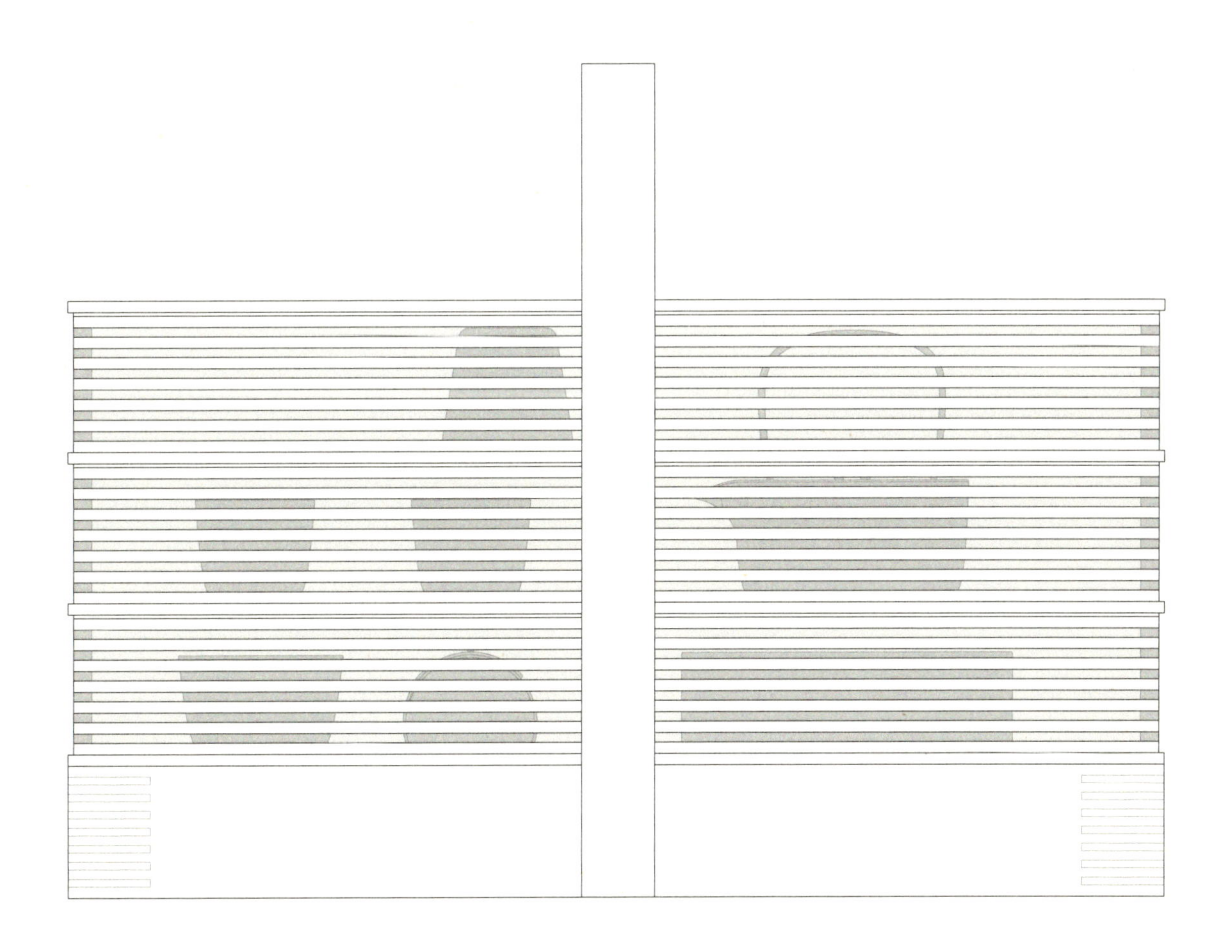

dimension 600 × 240 × 441 mm
material walnut, bronze
used in projects design republic design commune
design team lyndon neri, rossana hu, brian lo, ximi li, jingfeng fang

appendix

PROJECT DETAILS

The Reverse Courtyard
Design Republic Flagship Store
Retail
Address: 1F, No. 5 Zhongshan East No.1 Road, Huangpu District, Shanghai, China
Completion date: August 2006
Design period: November 2015–January 2006
Gross square footage: 600 sqm

Interior designer: Lyndon Neri, Rossana Hu, Erika Lanselle, Windy Zhang, Gary Leung
Graphic designer: Christine Neri
Graphic works: Signage

The Vertical Lane House
Waterhouse at South Bund
Boutique hotel and restaurant
Address: No. 1–3 Maojiayuan Road, Huangpu District, Shanghai, China
Completion date: May 2010
Design period: May 2008–April 2010
Gross square footage: 2,800 sqm

Architectural and interior designer: Lyndon Neri, Rossana Hu, Debby Haepers, Chunyan Cai, Markus Stoecklein, Jane Wang
Graphic designer: Yang Su, Christine Neri, Vivi Lau
Graphic works: Signage, nterior wall and floor graphics
Product designer: Brian Lo, Zhili Liu, Yun Zhao
Custom furniture: Restaurant tables, check-in counter, cabinet, bedroom furniture
By Neri&Hu: Solo dining chair

The Black Box
Neri&Hu + Design Republic Offices
Office, retail
Address: No. 88 Yuqing Road, Xuhui District, Shanghai, China
Completion date: July 2009
Gross square footage: 1,500 sqm

Architectural and interior design: Lyndon Neri, Rossana Hu, Jonas Hultman, Lei Xiao, Lei Zhao, Arnaud Baril, Erika Lanselle, Anita Liu, Joy Qiao
Graphic designer: Yang Su
Graphic works: Signage
Product designer: Yun Zhao
Custom furniture: Conference room shelves

The Recontextualization of History
Design Commune
Retail and one-room hotel
Address: No. 511 Jiangning Road, Jing'an District, Shanghai, China
Completion date: November 2012
Design period: September 2010–November 2012
Gross square footage: 2,400 sqm

Architectural and interior designer: Lyndon Neri, Rossana Hu, Chunyan Cai, Jane Wang, Karen Fu, Peng Guo, Peter Eland, Jonas Hultman, Markus Stoecklein, Christina Cho, Jeongyon Mimi Kim, Ye Lu, Federico Saralvo, Lei Zhao, Lei Xiao, Darcy Tang
Graphic designer: Christine Neri, Hao Zhou, Siwei Ren
Graphic works: Signage
Product designer: Brian Lo, Yun Zhao, Nicolas Fardet, Xiaowen Chen
Custom furniture: Reception desk
From Neri&Hu: Solo lounge chair, table, counter stool

The Recontextualization of History
Commune Social
Restaurant
Site Address: No.511 Jiangning Road, Shanghai, China
Completion date: March 2013
Design period: April 2012 - November 2012
Gross square footage: 295 sqm + 200 sqm (outdoor)

Architectural and interior designer: Lyndon Neri, Rossana Hu, Chunyan Cai, Yan Wang, Peng Guo, Karen Fu
Graphic designer: Christine Neri, Siwei Ren, Ivo Toplak
Graphic works: Logo & branding, graphic collaterals, signage
Product designer: Brian Lo, Nicolas Fardet, Xiaowen Chen
Custom furniture: Dining chair, dining table, bench, reception desk
From Neri&Hu: Zisha tea set, Boli Glass

The Split House
Private Residence in Tianzifang
Private residence
Address: No. 27, Lane 255, Ruijin No. 2 Road, Luwan District, Shanghai, China
Completion date: August 2012
Design period: March 2011–July 2012
Gross square footage: 193 sqm (including yard and terrace)

Architectural and interior designer: Lyndon Neri, Rossana Hu, Tony Schonhardt, Lei Xiao, Lei Zhao, Peng Guo
By Neri&Hu: Solo lounge chair and table

The Marketplace
Mercato Restaurant by Jean-Georges Vongerichten
Italian restaurant
Address: 6F, No. 3 Zhongshan East No. 1 Road, Huangpu District, Shanghai
Completion date: July 2012
Design period: October 2011–July 2012
Gross square footage: 1,000 sqm (not including kitchen area and lift lobby area)

Interior designer: Lyndon Neri, Rossana Hu, Briar Hickling, Mariarosa Doardo, Joy Qiao, Amy Hu
Graphic designer: Christine Neri, Ivo Toplak
Graphic works: Signage, gate graphics, wall graphics, glass graphics, logo, menu
Product designer: Brian Lo, Yun Zhao, Xiaowen Chen, Jean-Philippe Bonzon
Custom furniture: Pendant with glass shade, plate-style floor lamp, pendant hanging on rail system, windowsill green shade lamps, dining chair, lounge sofa, lounge chair, POS, vitrine display cabinets, display tables, side boards, low tables small wood, low tables small metal, round large low tables, reception counter
By Neri&Hu: Solo lounge chair

The Recycled Lane House
Camper China Showroom in Shanghai
Retail, showroom, office
Address: No. 101 Gao'an Road, Xuhui District, Shanghai, China
Completion date: July 2013
Design period: November 2012–July 2013
Gross square footage: 300 sqm

Architectural and interior designer: Lyndon Neri, Rossana Hu, Alex Mok, Peter Eland, Lina Hsieh, Jacqueline Min, Duan Ni
Graphic designer: Christine Neri, Siwei Ren
Graphic works: Signage, opening invitation and collaterals
Product designer: Brian Lo, Jean-Philippe Bonzon
Custom furniture: Showroom pendant with glass shade, showroom tables, pressroom Lazy Susan, office tables, special edition camper Solo chair
By Stellar Works: Ming chair

The Overlapping Land/House
Private Residence in Singapore
Private residence
Location: Singapore
Design period: November 2006–January 2012
Gross square footage: 2,888 sqm

Architectural and interior designer: Lyndon Neri, Rossana Hu, Dirk Weiblen, Tony Schonhardt, Shelley Gabriel, Alena Fabila, John Dy, Kevin Azanger
Product designers: Briao Lo, Yun Zhao, Xiaowen Chen, Ximi Li
Custom furniture: Dining table
By Neri&Hu: Solo dining chair, Solo lounge chair, Section side table

The Shunting House
Indian River Private House
Private residence
Location: Melbourne, Florida, United States
Design period: June 2006–December 2008
Gross square footage: 1,140 sqm

Architectural designer: Andrew Roman, Candice-Lee Browne, Claudius Lange, Shelley Gabriel, Alena Fabila, Erika Lanselle, Peter Eland, Jonas Hultman, Alexandra Tailer, Stephanie Chu

The Magistrates Court
Bow Street Boutique Hotel
Boutique hotel, restaurant, and museum
Address: 28 Bow Street, London, United Kingdom
Competition: January–March 2011
Design period: September 2012–Present
Gross square footage: Approximately 9,000 sqm

Architectural designer (competition): Lyndon Neri, Rossana Hu, Dirk Weiblen, Erika Lanselle, Federico Saralvo, Xiao Lei, John Dy
Architectural designer (post-competition): Lyndon Neri, Rossana Hu, Erika Lanselle, Alexiares Bayo, Anita Bergamini, Joe Hutton, Amy Caiwei Zhao, Briar Hickling, Jacqueline Min, Riku Qi, Alex Mok, Peter Eland, Aleksandra Duka, Anna Siu, Anne-Charlotte Wiklander, Abigail Whalen, Xiaoxi Chen, Helen Wu, Karen Fu, Dirk Weiblen
Graphic designer: Christine Neri, Siwei Ren
Graphic works: Signage, environmental graphics
Product designer: Nicolas Fardet, Zhao Yun, Brian Lo
Custom furniture: Public furniture and lighting, all room furniture, bed, bathroom details and lighting
By Classicon: Sedan chair
By Neri&Hu: Solo Chair
By Stellar Works: Utility chair

The Garden Units
Kuala Lumpur Residential tower
Address: Diatas Lot 40431 Jalan Kapas Wilayah Persekutuan, Kuala Lumpur, Malaysia
Design period: February 2014–January 2015
Gross square footage: 20,000 sqm

Architectural designer: Lyndon Neri, Rossana Hu, Dirk Weiblen, Tony Schonhardt, Ellen Chen, Karen Lok, Isabelle Lee, Harry Thomson, Fong Win Huang, Lei Zhao

The Heritage Journey
Seuntul Contemporary art museum
gallery, art pavilions, restaurant
Address: Sentul West, Jalan Strachan, Kuala Lumpur
Design period: May 2014–Present
Gross square footage: 2,903 sqm

Architectural designer: Lyndon Neri, Rossana Hu, Aleksandra Duka, Tait Kaplan, Sean Shen, Anna Siu, Carmen Marin, Sandra Subic

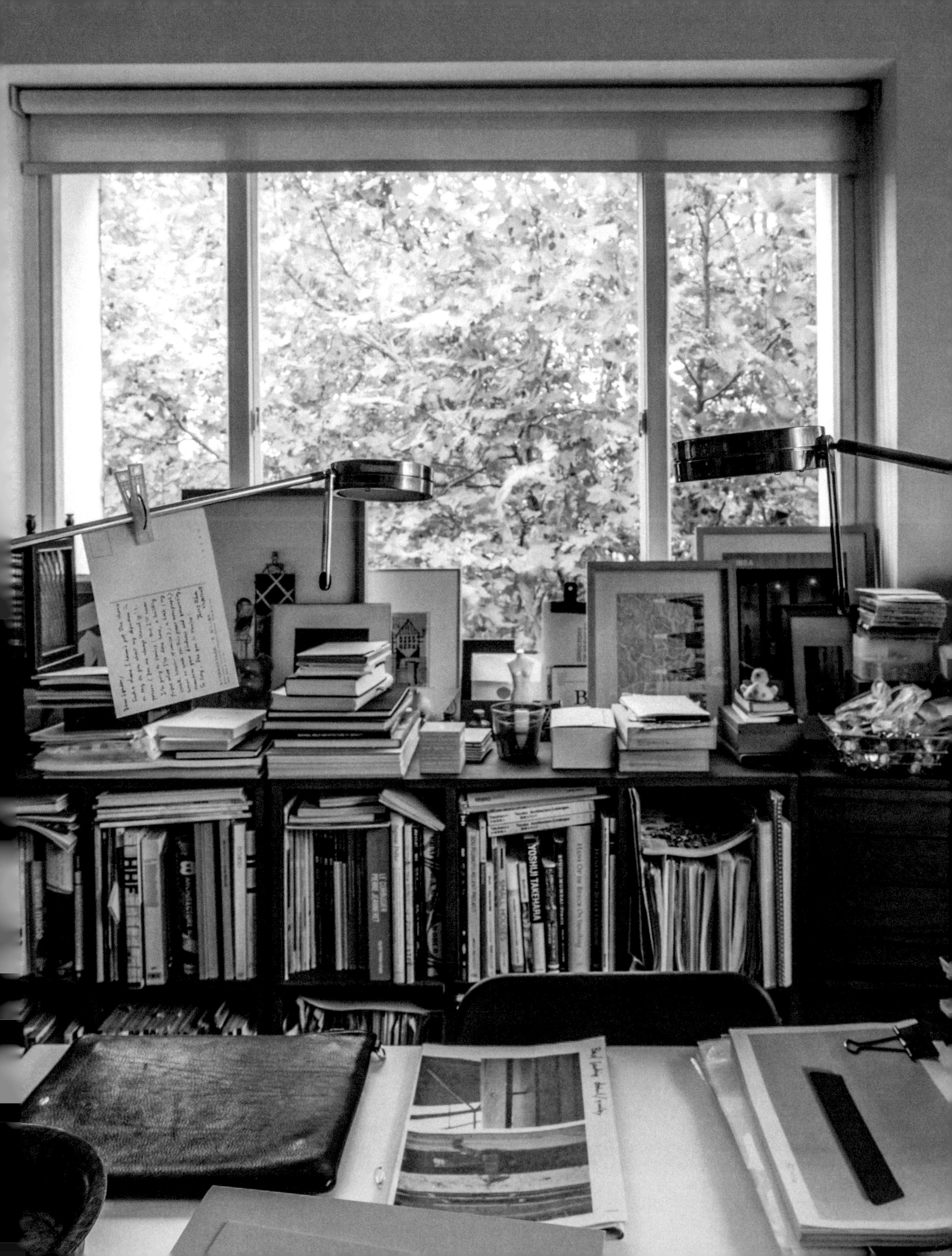
YOSHIUI TAKEHARA

BIOGRAPHIES

LYNDON NERI, ROSSANA HU

Lyndon Neri and Rossana Hu are the founding partners of Neri&Hu Design and Research Office, an interdisciplinary international architectural design practice. Lyndon Neri and Rossana Hu were named Maison & Objet Asia Designers of the Year 2015 and *Wallpaper** Designer of the Year 2014. In 2013, they were inducted into the US Interior Design Hall of Fame. Their practice has been awarded INSIDE Festival Overall Winner, AR Awards for Emerging Architecture winner by *Architectural Review,* and named one of the Design Vanguards by *Architectural Record.* In 2006, Lyndon Neri was selected by *i-D Magazine* as one of forty designers globally who deserve more attention in 2007. Rossana Hu received a Perspective Magazine Award as one of the "40 under 40" prominent designers shaping Hong Kong and Greater China.

Lyndon Neri holds a Master of Architecture from Harvard University and a Bachelor of Arts in Architecture from the University of California at Berkeley. Prior to starting his own practice, he was the Director for Projects in Asia and an Associate for Michael Graves & Associates in Princeton for over ten years and also worked in New York City for various architectural firms.
Rossana Hu holds a Master of Architecture and Urban Planning from Princeton University and a Bachelor of Arts in Architecture and Music from the University of California at Berkeley. Before establishing Neri&Hu, Rossana worked for Michael Graves & Associates, Ralph Lerner Architect, Skidmore, Owings and Merrill, and The Architects Collaborative.

Other than working as architectural professionals, Lyndon Neri and Rossana Hu have been actively involved in teaching and research. They have been invited to speak, exhibit, and judge for many prestigious events and programs all over the world.

Lyndon Neri and Rossana Hu are also founders of Design Republic, a retail concept store based in Shanghai that offers a unique collection of products created by the world's best design talents.

Besides architecture and interiors, Lyndon and Rossana have designed products for brands including Classicon, Fritz Hansen, Gandia Blasco, JIA, LEMA, MOOOI, Nanimarquina, Parachilna, Porro, Stellar Works, Wallpaper* Handmade, Meritalia, BD Barcelona Design, neri&hu, among many others. In 2015, Lyndon Neri and Rossana Hu were appointed Creative Directors of Stellar Works.

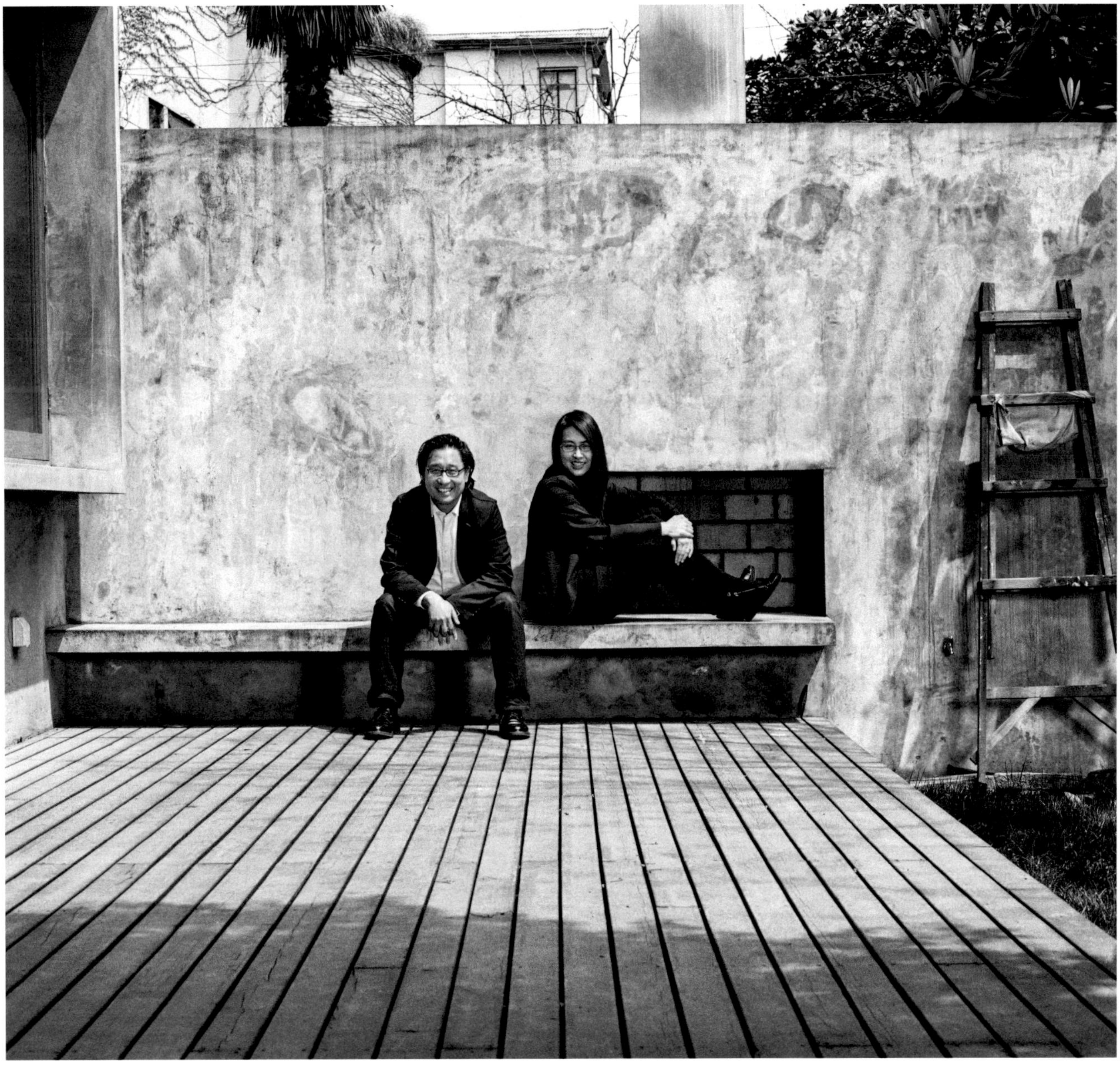

NERI&HU DESIGN AND RESEARCH OFFICE

Founded in 2004 by partners Lyndon Neri and Rossana Hu, **Neri&Hu Design and Research Office** is an interdisciplinary architectural design practice based in Shanghai, China with an additional office in London, UK. Neri&Hu works internationally providing architecture, interior, master planning, graphic, and product design services. Currently working on projects in many different countries, Neri&Hu is composed of a multicultural staff who speak over thirty different languages. The diversity of the team reinforces a core vision for the practice: to respond to a global worldview incorporating overlapping design disciplines for a new paradigm in architecture.

Neri&Hu's location is purposeful. With Shanghai considered a new global frontier, Neri&Hu is at the center of this contemporary chaos. The city's cultural, urban, and historic contexts function as a point of departure for the architectural explorations involved in every project. Because new sets of contemporary problems relating to buildings now extend beyond traditional architecture, the practice challenges traditional boundaries of architecture to include other complementary disciplines.

Neri&Hu strongly believes in research as a design tool, as each project bears its unique set of contextual issues. A critical probing into the specificities of program, site, function, and history is essential to the creation of rigorous design work. Based on research, Neri&Hu desires to anchor its work in the dynamic interaction of experience, detail, material, form, and light rather than conforming to a formulaic style. The ultimate significance behind each project comes from how the built forms create meaning through their physical representations.

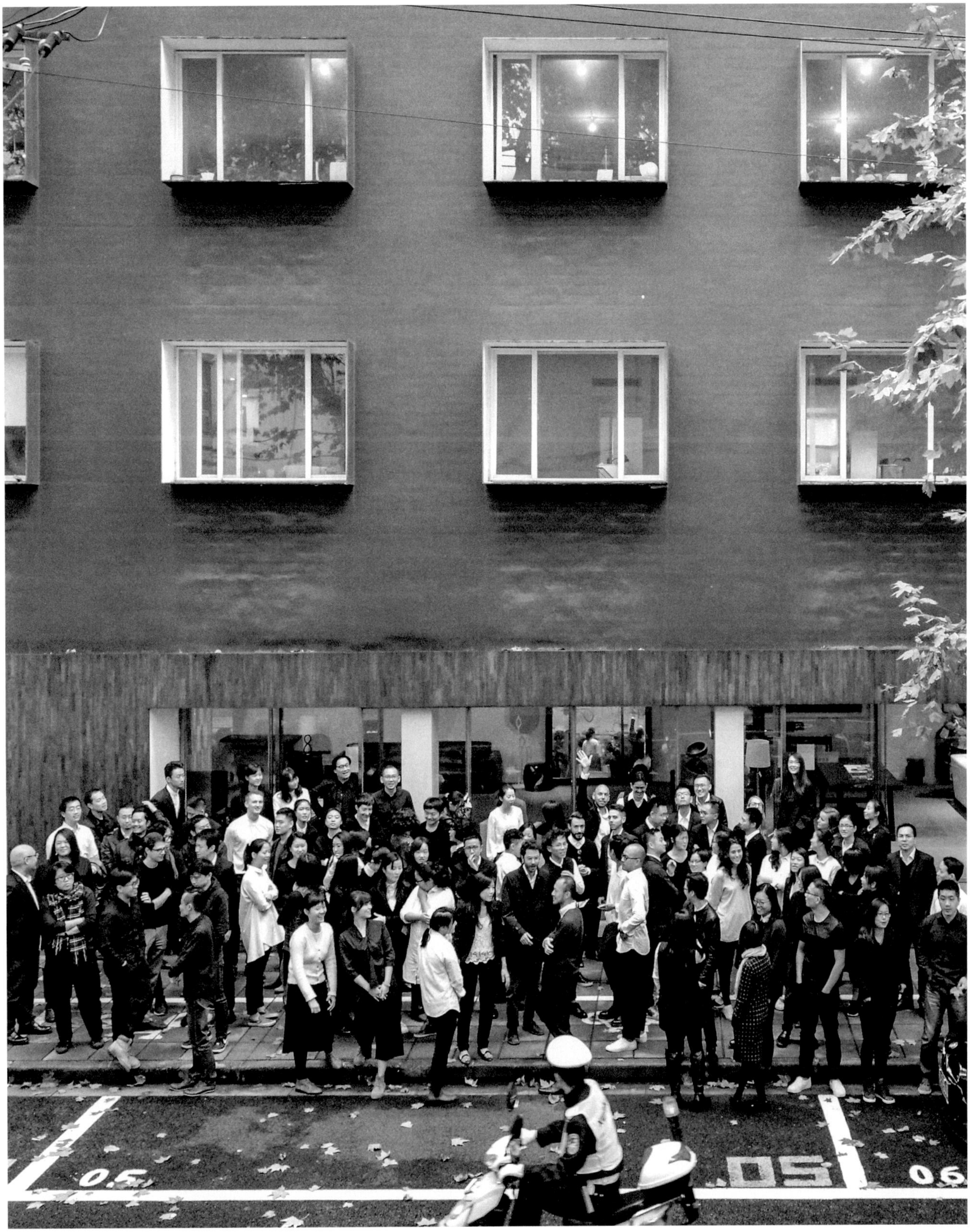
05
05
06

DAVID CHIPPERFIELD

David Chipperfield established David Chipperfield Architects in 1985. He was Professor of Architecture at the Staatliche Akademie der Bildenden Künste, Stuttgart from 1995 to 2001 and Norman R. Foster Visiting Professor of Architectural Design at Yale University in 2011, and he has taught and lectured worldwide at schools of architecture in Austria, Italy, Switzerland, the United Kingdom, and the United States. In 2012, David Chipperfield curated the 13th International Architecture Exhibition of the Venice Biennale. In 2014, he was appointed Artistic Director of the Italian furnishings firm Driade.

He is an honorary fellow of both the American Institute of Architects and the Bund Deutscher Architekten, and a past winner of the Heinrich Tessenow Gold Medal, the Wolf Foundation Prize in the Arts, and the Grand DAI (Verband Deutscher Architekten- und Ingenieurvereine e.V.) Award for Building Culture. David Chipperfield became Royal Designer for Industry in 2006 and was elected to the Royal Academy in 2008. In 2009, he was awarded the Order of Merit of the Federal Republic of Germany and in 2010 he was honored for services to architecture in the UK and Germany. In 2011, he received the RIBA Royal Gold Medal for Architecture, and in 2013, the Praemium Imperiale from the Japan Art Association, both given in recognition of his lifetime achievement.

ALEJANDRO ZAERA-POLO

Alejandro Zaera-Polo (born in Madrid, 1963) is an accomplished contemporary architect. His work has consistently merged the practice of architecture with theoretical practice, deftly integrating architecture, urban design, and landscape architecture in his projects. His practice has produced critically acclaimed and award-winning projects for the public and private sector on an international scale.

He trained at the Escuela Técnica Superior de Arquitectura de Madrid, graduating with Honors, and went on to do a Master in Architecture (MARCH II) at the Graduate School of Design, Harvard University, USA, where he graduated with Distinction. He worked at OMA in Rotterdam between 1991 and 1993, prior to establishing Foreign Office Architects in 1993 and AZPML in 2011.

Alejandro Zaera-Polo has also had an extensive involvement in education at an international level since 1993. 2012–2014, he was the Dean of Princeton SoA, and of the Berlage Institute in Rotterdam from 2000 to 2005, where he also held the Berlage Chair at the Technical University in Delft, the Netherlands. He was the inaugural recipient of the Norman Foster professorship at Yale University, School of Architecture between 2010 and 2011 and has been a Visiting Critic at Columbia GSAPP and UCLA School of Architecture. He led a Diploma Unit between 1993 and 1999 at the Architectural Association in London and is now a tenured professor at Princeton SoA.

In addition to his professional and academic roles, Alejandro Zaera-Polo is recognized as an original theorist and thinker of contemporary architecture, with a sharp capacity to identify social and political trends and translate them into the architectural discourse. His texts can be found in many professional publications such as *El Croquis, Quaderns, A+U, Arch+, Log, AD,* and *Harvard Design Magazine.*

COLLABORATORS

NERI&HU DESIGN AND RESEARCH OFFICE STAFF
CURRENT

Akrawit Yanpaisan, Aleksandra Duka, Alena Fabila, Alexiares Bayo, Alfie Huang, Amy Huang, Ana Ameyugo, Andy Zhang, Brian Lo, Cage Lu, Cao Fang, Caroline Li, Carmen Marin, Carrie Lv, Carmen Xu, Carolina Mancini, Chloe Chiu, Chris Chen, Christine Chang, Christine Neri, Cindy Sun, Claire Watson, Daisy Yuen, Daoliang Li, Davide Signorato, Delia Zhou, Dong Wu, Elan Tao, Ellen Chen, Elisa Ascari, Emily Zhang, Erika Lanselle, Esther Qian, Federico Salmaso, Federico Saralvo, Feixia Huang, Fino Fan, Fong Huang, Gianpaolo Taglietti, Gordon Tse, Haiou Xin, Hannah Davies, Helen Zhang, Hwajung Song, Jacqueline Min, Jerry Del Fierro, Jerry Guo, Jiameng Li, Jin Su, Joshua Wong, Josh Murphy, Kailun Sun, Karen Lok, Kevin Chim, Laia Martinez, Laurent Tek, Lei Zhao, Lili Cheng, Lina Hsieh, Litien Poeng, Loe Li, Leyue Chen, Lyndon Neri, Mark Zhang, Martin Chen, Mary Chiu, Megan Shen, Nellie Yang, Nicolas Dupont, Nicolas Fardet, Nika Du, Rachael Ouyang, Richard Cheng, Riku Qi, Romain Blaszyck, Rossana Hu, Sarah Xie, Sean Shen, Sela Lim, Severino Iritano, Scott Hsu, Sheng Ling, Sibyl Li, Simin Qiu, Siwei Ren, Siyu Chen, Suju Kim, Stan Yang, Suzy Hu, Tracy Fong, Valentina Brunetti, Vincent Macquart, Vivian Zhou, Wendy Tsai, Wenya Liu, William Zhang, Xiaowen Chen, Xiaoyu Huang, Ximi Li, Xin Liu, Yan Chen, Xuefei Yan, Yi Sun, Yinan Li, Yiran Wang, Yvonne Tan, Ziyi Cao, Zoé Costes, Suzy Hu, Sibyl Li, Jin Su, Zoe Wang, Helen Zhang, Lisa Zhao

NERI&HU DESIGN AND RESEARCH OFFICE STAFF
FORMER

Abigail Whalen, Aksel Coruh, Alan Song, Alex Mok, Alex Shu, Alexandra Tailer, Alexandre Zuntini, Amy Hu, Andrew Roman, Andy Li, Anita Bergamini, Anita Liu, Ann Chen, Ann Mu, Anna Siu, Annabel Monk, Annabelle Wu, Anne-Charlotte Wiklander, Annie Zheng, Anqing Zhu, Arnaud Baril, Bamboo Chen, Begona Sebastian, Ben Dennis, Bin Zhu, Brenda Xiao, Briar Hickling, Caiwei Zhao, Camile, Candice-Lee Browne, Carmen Lee, Cecilia Chan, Chao Su, Charles Ye, Chee Liu, Chen Chen Wang, Chi Chiu, Chiara Aliverti, Chloe He, Chris Ju, Chris Yuan, Christina Cho, Christina Luk, Christine Felipe, Chu Yao, Chudyk, Chunyan Cai, Cindy Jiang, Claudius Lange, Colin Dirk Weiblen, Cynthia Lai, Dagmar Niecke, Dana Wu, Darcy Tang, David Brbaklic, Debby Haepers, Derek Gou, Di Jiang, Diana Nee, Diego Caro, Diem Nguyen, Dinah Zhang, Don Chen, Dyno Du, Eary Sun, Eason Sun, Echo Cao, Echo Yue, Eero Puurinen, Effie Yu, Elaine Chau, Elaine Liu, Elaine Wang, Elena Perez, Elisa Dai, Ellen Rubel, Eva Wieland, Evelyn Chiu, Even Chen, Faan Wang, Fang Fang, Felix Fu, Gary Leung, Geng Jing, Goncalo Lopes, Gong Chenxi, Gospel Lee, Grace Li, Haibei Peng, Haiying Yan, Hao Zhou, Harry Thomson, Heather Loeffler, Helen Wu, Helena Rong, Henry Wang, Herman Mao, Hongxi Pan, Huiyi Wong, Hunter Paine, Ian Wang, Isabelle Lee, Ivo Toplak, Ivy Zhou, Jadesupa Pitsapuron, Jane Wang, Janna Yu, Javid Farazad, Jean-Philippe Bonzon, Jeong Yon Kim, Jessee Li, Jessica Lee, Jia Gu, Jia Han, Jia Lu, Jiang Yan, Jinlin Zheng, Jingfeng Fang, Joann Feng, Joe Hutton, John Dy, Johnny Lui, Jonas Hultman, Joo Tang, Josef Zhou, Joseph Lee, Josephine Chen, Joshua Perez, Joy Jiang, Joy Qiao, Joyce Xia, Justin Gong, Justus Preyer, Kathrine Chin, Katty Li, Karen Fu, Kana Wu, Kelvin Huang, Ken Lin, Kenny Zhong, Kevin Azenger, Kevin Meng, Laura Nicholls, Li Zhen, Lisa Zhao, Lisa Zhu, Lorna Santos, Louise Ma, Lynn Fang, Lynn Gu, Markus Stocklein, Martina Knotkova, Mariarosa Doardo, Mathias Krupna, Matthias Brandstetter, Megan Grehl, Meng Gong, Mengjie Cheng, Michelle Lu, Moly Gu, Nathan Deng, Ni Duan, Masaaki Uno, Patricia Joong, Patricia Segarra, Peter Eland, Priscilla Chan, Polly Deng, Rachael Sun, Rachel Hsiao, Raphael Mondato, Robin Lu, Romeo Andaya, Rui Gao, Ruth Chang, Sapphire Ming, Sandra Subic, Sara Lunneryd, Sarah Zhou , Sheila Lin, Shelley Gabriel, Shelley Zhang, Shirley Hsu, Shirley Ting, Shirley Tsui, Shoulian Yang, Shuyi Yin, Sing Yeong Pham, Siqi Zhu, Siye Chen, Siyuan Liu, Sofie Thorning, Sophia Panova, Sophia Wang, Sophie Zhou, Stanley Liu, Stephanie Chu, Sunny Chen, Talitha Liu, Tait Kaplan, Tian Tan, Tianyou Wu, Tina Feng, Ting Li, Tony Wang, Tony Schonhardt, Tuomas Uusheimo, Victor Ung, Vivi Lau, Vivianna Chai, Wang Chun, Wang Lang, Wangliang Lin, Whitney Paul, Willow Yang, Windy Zhang, Winnie Gu, Xiang Wang, Xiao Lei, Xiaoxi Chen, Xiji Liao, Xu Dan, Yang Su, Yasmin Sun, Ye Lu, Yi-Chen Chu, Yifei Lu, Yiting Kuo, Yuki Dai, Yun Zhao, Yutian Zhang, Zara Wang, Zhang Liqiao, Zhenghua Jiang, Zhili Liu, Zhiqin Liu, Zhou Bo, Zicheng Wei, Zunheng Lai, Zoe Wang

IMAGE CREDITS

All photographs, plans, and drawings by Neri&Hu Design Research Office unless otherwise stated: © Algirdas Bakas, p. 238–239; © Derryck Menere, pp. 14, 20–24, 30–33, 43, 45, 65, 72, 226, 228; © Pedro Pegenaute front and back cover, pp. ii, 4, 10, 38–42, 44, 46–47, 55 top three, 56–58, 66, 74, 75 left, 78–84, 94–97, 101–113, 118–125, 132–143, 147–149, 156, 157–159, 185–187, 189, 191; © Andrew Rowat, p. 247; © Jeremy San Tzer Ning, p. 190; © Zhonghai Shen, p. 160; © Tuomas Uusheimo, pp. 67, 75 right; © Dirk Weiblen, pp. 2, 64, 165, 170, 172, 174–181, 234, 242–245, 249.

© Andreas Gefeller, p. 88, *Untitled (Panel Building 3)*, 2004: Courtesy Thomas Rehbein Gallery Cologne; © Aneta Grzeszykowska and Jan Smaga, p. 182, *Plan 10,* 2003; © Alfred Hitchcock, p. 126 *Rear Window*, 1954; Courtesy of George Krooglik p. 88 (Jianging Road Historical Photo); © Robert Van Der Hilst, p. 162, *Chinese Interiors*, 1990–1993; © Rachel Whiteread, p. 18, *House,* 1993, concrete, commissioned by Artangel, courtesy of the artist, Luhring Augustine, New York, Lorcan O'Neill, Rome, and Gagosian Gallery. Photo credit: Sue Omerod.

Despite our best efforts, we have not been able to reach out to the holders of copyright and reproduction rights for all the illustrations in this book. Copyright holders not mentioned in the credits are asked to substantiate their claims, and recompense will be made according to standard practice.

IMPRINT

Neri&Hu Design Research Office
Works and Projects
With contributions by
David Chipperfield, Alejandro Zaera-Polo

Concept: Lyndon Neri, Rossana Hu, Josef Zhou
Text: Nellie Yang
Design: Siwei Ren, Christine Neri
Proofreading: Lisa Schons
Lithography, printing, and binding: DZA Druckerei zu Altenburg GmbH, Thuringia
Paper: FocusArt Natural 115g/m^2

© 2017 Neri&Hu Design Research Office, Shanghai/London, and Park Books AG, Zurich
© for the texts: the authors
© for the images: see image credits

Park Books
Niederdorfstrasse 54
8001 Zurich
Switzerland
www.park-books.com

www.neriandhu.com

Park Books is being supported by the Federal Office of Culture with a general subsidy for the years 2016–2020.

All rights reserved; no part of this publication may be reproduced, stored in a retrieval system or transmitted in any form or by any means, electronic, mechanical, photocopying, recording, or otherwise, without the prior written consent of the publisher.

ISBN 978-3-906027-89-0